Comparative Recognition and Enforcement

FOREIGN JUDGMENTS AND AWARDS

DROSSOS STAMBOULAKIS
Monash University, Victoria

CAMBRIDGE
UNIVERSITY PRESS

CAMBRIDGE
UNIVERSITY PRESS

Shaftesbury Road, Cambridge CB2 8EA, United Kingdom

One Liberty Plaza, 20th Floor, New York, NY 10006, USA

477 Williamstown Road, Port Melbourne, VIC 3207, Australia

314–321, 3rd Floor, Plot 3, Splendor Forum, Jasola District Centre, New Delhi – 110025, India

103 Penang Road, #05–06/07, Visioncrest Commercial, Singapore 238467

Cambridge University Press is part of Cambridge University Press & Assessment, a department of the University of Cambridge.

We share the University's mission to contribute to society through the pursuit of education, learning and research at the highest international levels of excellence.

www.cambridge.org
Information on this title: www.cambridge.org/9781009074995

DOI: 10.1017/9781009076340

First published 2023
First paperback edition 2026

A catalogue record for this publication is available from the British Library

Library of Congress Cataloging-in-Publication data
NAMES: Stamboulakis, Drossos, author.
TITLE: Comparative recognition and enforcement : foreign judgments and awards / Drossos Stamboulakis, Monash University, Victoria.
DESCRIPTION: Cambridge, United Kingdom ; New York, NY : Cambridge University Press, 2022. | Based on author's thesis (doctoral - University of Melbourne, 2019) issued under the title: Bridging the gap: transnational recognition and enforcement of judgments and awards in international commercial disputes. | Includes bibliographical references and index.
IDENTIFIERS: LCCN 2022011221 (print) | LCCN 2022011222 (ebook) | ISBN 9781316513927 (hardback) | ISBN 9781009074995 (paperback) | ISBN 9781009076340 (epub)
SUBJECTS: LCSH: Judgments, Foreign.
CLASSIFICATION: LCC K7680 .S73 2022 (print) | LCC K7680 (ebook) | DDC 347/.077–dc23/eng/20220531
LC record available at https://lccn.loc.gov/2022011221
LC ebook record available at https://lccn.loc.gov/2022011222

ISBN 978-1-316-51392-7 Hardback
ISBN 978-1-009-07499-5 Paperback

COMPARATIVE RECOGNITION AND ENFORCEMENT

This book provides the first detailed comparative analysis of recognition and enforcement of foreign judgments and awards. The transnational perspective adopted facilitates greater understanding of the present state of recognition and enforcement globally and offers insight into the establishment and operation of key modern treaties. This book represents a timely contribution, as many states have considered, or indicated an intention to sign, one or both Judgments Conventions: the 2005 Choice of Court Convention and the 2019 Judgments Convention. This book is an essential resource for policymakers, scholars, and intergovernmental organisations to understand the nature and origin of recognition and enforcement approaches, as well as their application, interpretation, and future directions.

DR DROSSOS STAMBOULAKIS is a Senior Lecturer at Monash University, and a member of the Victorian Bar. He is the Deputy Convenor of Monash's Commercial Disputes Group, and coaches the Monash Vis International Commercial Arbitration Moot team. He accepts briefs in commercial arbitration and private international law matters and is an author of a leading Australian commercial arbitration text, *International and Australian Commercial Arbitration* (2021).

Contents

Foreword

The primary focus of the book is on the various global efforts towards harmonised pro-recognition and enforcement approaches to foreign judgments. Part I explores the key regional and international recognition and enforcement approaches from a historical and functionalist comparative perspective. Part II considers the future of recognition and enforcement. The current position and the possibilities for the development of a transnational regime are informed by the experience with respect to foreign arbitral awards.

One of the most significant international legal innovations of modern times is the New York Convention on the Recognition and Enforcement of Foreign Arbitral Awards, done in 1958. Also of great significance is the United Nations Commission on International Trade Law (UNCITRAL) Model Law on International Commercial Arbitration 1985 (together with amendments as adopted in 2006), which, particularly in this context, complements and strengthens the recognition and enforcement aspects of the Convention. The New York Convention, adopted as it has been by most nations of the world, provides a regime for recognition and enforcement of arbitral awards that is well accepted globally. This has been critical in providing the foundation for the exponential growth of international arbitration, upon which world trade and investment substantially relies, as the most effective transnational dispute resolution option.

Having regard to these developments, Dr Drossos Stamboulakis comprehensively examines global and more localised regimes for the recognition and enforcement of foreign judgments together with other regimes for the recognition and enforcement of foreign arbitral awards. As is developed in detail, much insight can be gained from contrasting the experience with respect to judgments and awards. As is to be expected, with respect to judgments national sovereignty and legal cultural issues arise more centrally than they do with respect to arbitral awards. Courts are rightly concerned to administer justice according to law, according to the highest standards in the application of the law, impartially and with procedural fairness. A transnational dispute resolution regime based on national courts must, however, transcend a mind-set, identified by Lorenzen in the early twentieth century, flowing from these concerns that would stand in the way of international recognition and enforcement.[1]

As long as each country feels at heart that its own law is the best in the world, and that justice can be secured only in accordance with its rules, there is little hope of any real progress. As the solidarity of nations comes more into evidence and the justice of enforcing foreign laws under given circumstances becomes more apparent, the different systems will gradually tend towards greater uniformity (Huber, 1919, p. 400).

Issues of territorial sovereignty, the position that a foreign court decision has no extraterritorial reach unless given effect by an enforcing court on behalf of the enforcing nation and this mindset, have, as the author discusses, resulted in what may be described as an 'enforcement gap' flowing from the differential treatment that favours the recognition and enforcement of foreign arbitral awards over foreign judgments. The reasons for this 'gap' and the extent to which it is unwarranted are examined in the context of the approach and operation of various recognition and enforcement regimes, a process that highlights a variety of avenues and approaches that might close or narrow the gap. The issue of the 'gap' is certainly not a matter of mere academic interest as it may have real consequences in denying parties justice and fairness where they do not have the benefit of an arbitration agreement and hence the benefit of near universal recognition and enforcement possibilities under the New York Convention.

This is undoubtedly a definitive work on the recognition and enforcement of foreign judgments and foreign arbitral awards that will provide an invaluable guide, resource and reference for scholars and practitioners alike. It is also a very significant and important contribution in the ongoing process of development of an effective and harmonised regime for the recognition and enforcement of foreign judgments globally, and simultaneously serves to develop, enhance, and provide greater certainty with respect to the recognition and enforcement of foreign arbitral awards.

The Hon. Justice Clyde Croft AM
Supreme Court of Victoria
Melbourne, Australia

[1] Ernest Lorenzen, 'Huber's De Conflictu Legum' (1919) 13 *Illinois Law Review* 375, 400.

Preface

The recognition and enforcement of foreign decisions is at a critical juncture. Since the widespread adoption of the 1958 New York Convention, arbitral awards have benefitted from a consistent and pro-enforcement framework globally. Implementation of this Convention has been largely driven by trade-related rationales. Regional enforcement models, such as the Brussels Model within the European Union and the statutory reciprocal enforcement schemes in the Commonwealth, have also highlighted the role that harmonised approaches promoting the free circulation of judgments play in promoting trade and mutual trust and confidence between participant States.

Until recently, the same could not be said for judgments globally, despite international negotiations dating back more than a century. With the coming into force of the 2005 Choice of Court Convention in 2015 and the adoption of the 2019 Judgments Convention – collectively, the 'Judgments Conventions' – this position has radically changed. Legal architecture now exists to enable a significant narrowing, and perhaps overcoming in some respects, of the global enforcement gap between foreign judgments and awards.

This book is designed to explore key transnational recognition and enforcement architecture, namely the New York Convention, the Judgments Conventions and the regional or historical models that I refer to in this book as the Brussels Model and the Commonwealth Model (and the common law that underpins it). Even though separate and distinct instruments or approaches apply based upon whether the decision coming for enforcement is a foreign judgment or award, whether it is engendered by party autonomy as distinct from default jurisdictional rules, and whether a specific regional or historical framework applies, there can still be distilled a common core of transnational recognition and enforcement practice. This distillation involves a detailed comparison of sovereignty and legal cultural issues, including between the common and civil law. This is not to suggest, however, that the interpretation and application of each approach will have direct and immediate application to another. Instead, the historical and functional comparisons that occur in this book offer insight into the underlying – and at times differing – structures and elements that make up enforcement regimes.

This book also offers insight that may inform the future uptake, understanding and operation of judgments recognition and enforcement instruments, including the Judgments Conventions. Despite the rising tide of deglobalisation stemming from nationalist politics and the COVID-19 pandemic, the uptake of both the 2005 Convention and the 2019 Convention has received recent attention around the world, and particularly in Europe. The United Kingdom acceded to the 2005 Convention in its own right in 2020, post Brexit. Most recently, in July 2022, the Council of the European Union adopted the decision for the EU to accede to the 2019 Judgments Convention. Once a second party ratifies or accedes to it, the 2019 Judgments Convention will come into force – with immediate application across that second party and all EU member states (except Denmark, which does not automatically participate in EU freedom, security and justice measures). It is my hope that the analysis in this book will be able to be used in other jurisdictions around the world considering the same questions of implementation and, subsequently, interpretation and application of judgments recognition and enforcement regimes.

Inspiration for this book dates back more than a decade, to time spent as an intern at the Hague Conference on Private International Law, in the Hague, the Netherlands (the 'Hague Conference'). Thanks are due to the hardworking lawyers and staff, past and present, of the Hague Conference. The tremendous efforts towards the conclusion of both Judgments Conventions would not have been possible without the patient perseverance of the Permanent Bureau. Particular thanks are due to Professor Marta Pertegás, former First Secretary at the Hague Conference, and Mr Hans van Loon, former Secretary General, who oversaw much of the renewed efforts to conclude the Judgments Conventions, and contributed to making my experience at the Hague Conference such a formative one.

Working at the Hague Conference – and hence this book – would also not have been possible without the generous support of the Nygh family, who establish and continue to support a funded internship position for junior Australian law students to intern at the Hague. This bequest, in the name of the late Peter Nygh, a foremost expert in private international law, allowed me to participate in and experience the workings of private international law harmonisation. Finally, a thank you to my thesis supervisors: my primary supervisor, Professor Richard Garnett, and co-supervisor, Professor Jürgen Kurtz, for their supervision and considered comments on the thesis that spurred the creation of this book.

1

Introduction

Due to the operation of territorial sovereignty, a foreign decision has no extraterritorial reach unless and until it is given effect by an enforcing court (on behalf of the enforcing State). Although many enforcing courts regularly recognise or enforce foreign decisions, this state practice is not considered specific enough to create binding rules of customary international law mandating enforcement or recognition.[1] This is so despite recurrent arguments that giving effect to foreign decisions ought to be considered a matter of customary international law.[2] Absent treaty or supranational commitments,

[1] Ralf Michaels, 'Recognition and Enforcement of Foreign Judgments' [2009] *Max Planck Encyclopaedia of Public International Law*, para 11. Given the widespread acceptance of the New York Convention approach, most analysis has focused on foreign judgments. 'Clearly, there is no internationally acknowledged customary rule of international law that a state must recognise any judgment': Gary Born, *International Civil Litigation in United States Courts: Commentary and Materials* (Kluwer Law International 1996) 949, citing Alan Golomb, 'Recognition of Foreign Money Judgments: A Goal-Oriented Approach' (1969) 43 *St John's Law Review* 604 at 690. This position has not changed since that article was published.

[2] See, for example, Yuliya Zeynalova, 'The Law on Recognition and Enforcement of Foreign Judgments: Is It Broken and How Do We Fix It?' (2013) 31 *Berkeley Journal of International Law* 150, 154, citing the authoritative statement of Lord Blackburn in *Godard* v. *Gray* (1870) LR 6 QB 139, that it is an 'admitted principle of the law of nations that a state is bound to enforce

recognition and enforcement is then solely a matter for national law, as foreign decisions have no independent legal effect without being deferred to or incorporated by some way into the enforcing State. In the extreme, national law can insist that if disputants want to progress a matter, they must retry it within the confines of the enforcing State's jurisdiction. Such an exercise of sovereignty is not problematic in and of itself. It has value in the overall coherence of a system of entitlements premised upon municipal law, allowing for the preservation of the values and interests of the sovereign (as represented by the devolution of legal power to the enforcing court).[3] Exercise of sovereignty in this way at the enforcement stage also provides an ultimate check on what might otherwise be an unbridled or inappropriate forum or dispute resolution mechanism selection on the part of claimants.[4]

However, the fact that recognition and enforcement is solely a national law matter – subject to any treaty or supranational commitments – has led to concern about the current state of affairs favouring recognition and enforcement of foreign awards over foreign judgments.[5] This concern has colloquially been referred to as an 'enforcement gap', a 'governance gap', a 'paradox' or an 'anomaly'. It is based on the idea that it is unwarranted to give preferential recognition and enforcement treatment to awards over judgments, due simply to the original dispute mechanism chosen (arbitration versus litigation) rather than for any principled reasons.[6]

within its territories the judgment of a foreign tribunal'. For an early (and critical) exposition of this view, see, Ernest Lorenzen, 'Huber's De Conflictu Legum' (1919) 13 *Illinois Law Review* 375, 399–400. Lorenzen notes that the objections of Continental scholars to this approach arise as no uniformity can meaningfully exist where recognition and enforcement approaches derive from domestic (rather than international) legal sources. However, in practice, no norm or rule of international or customary law compelling recognition and enforcement had then (or since) evolved. Because of this, an acceptance began to be implied (however reluctant) in academic writings of State discretion in choosing whether to give effect to foreign judgments.

3 While enforcing courts exercise the power of the sovereign in this respect, they do not necessarily represent its interests. See, for example, Section 4.2, where several key drivers underpinning recognition and enforcement in the common law are explored.

4 Paul B. Stephan, 'Introduction: Recognition and Enforcement of Foreign Judgments' in Paul B. Stephan (ed), *Foreign Court Judgments and the United States Legal System* (Brill 2014) 5.

5 See, for a prominent example, early comments of the Hague Conference on Private International Law (the 'Hague Conference') – the primary intergovernmental body that has for decades attempted to facilitate a harmonised pro-recognition and enforcement approach to foreign judgments – highlighting the anomaly from a range of perspectives: Hague Conference, 'Some Reflections of the Permanent Bureau on a General Convention on Enforcement of Judgments' (Preliminary Document, May 1992), 231.

6 As Bockstiegel notes, this 'paradox' is particularly stark on a 'global' level, as, although international law is dominated and created by States, the judgments of courts that represent that State's sovereignty cannot be as readily recognised and enforced as a decision of an entirely private arbitral tribunal: Karl-Heinz Bockstiegel, 'Summary of Discussion in the Third Working Group' in Albert Jan van den Berg (ed.), *Improving the Efficiency of Arbitration*

The concern is particularly stark due to widely divergent acceptance of regimes to promote recognition and enforcement. National laws that apply to the enforcement of arbitral awards have been shaped by the New York Convention in almost every trading jurisdiction in the world. This Convention stands as a 'historical milestone' for international dispute resolution,[7] as it assists arbitration to 'escape' potentially divergent legal pluralist approaches to recognition and enforcement premised upon sovereignty. It does so by bridging what would otherwise be a completely private form of ordering – 'private law' created in and by international commercial arbitration – with a harmonised treaty-driven approach to recognition and enforcement, implemented compulsorily in domestic (municipal) law by Convention Contracting States. By contrast, the parallel judgments recognition and enforcement architecture, modelled closely on the New York Convention approach, remains embryonic in terms of global implementation. For this reason, enforcing foreign judgments remains largely a matter of national law. Given the 'suspicions' of some legal systems towards foreign judgments, there has thus been a long-held concern that the enforcement of judgments is often 'made difficult, if not impossible, by local law'.[8] Even where local law is not hostile to foreign judgments, in the words of the the preamble of the 2019 Convention, "enhanced judicial co-operation requires, in particular, an international legal regime that provides greater predictability and certainty in relation to the global circulation of foreign judgments". Without such harmonisation, the enforcement of arbitral awards remains more predictable and certain on a transnational level, impacting the overall efficacy of the international dispute resolution system.[9] Indeed, it is arguable that this differential in enforcement treatment contributes to a state of affairs where arbitration now dominates various forms of international dispute resolution, particularly in commercial matters (at the expense of litigation).[10]

Agreements and Awards: 40 Years of Application of the New York Convention (KluwerArbitration, Kluwer Law International 1999) 432.

7 See, further, Florian Rödl, 'Private Law beyond the Democratic Order? On the Legitimatory Problem of Private Law "Beyond the State"' (2008) 56 *The American Journal of Comparative Law* 743, 746–47.

8 Kurt Nadelmann, 'Jurisdictionally Improper Fora in Treaties on Recognition of Judgments: The Common Market Draft' in Kurt Nadelmann (ed), *Conflicts of Law: International And Interstate: Selected Essays* (Martinus Nijhoff Publishers 1972) 238.

9 Sundaresh Menon, 'The Transnational Protection of Private Rights: Issues, Challenges, and Possible Solutions' (2015) 5 *Asian Journal of International Law* 219, 238–39.

10 The 'pre-eminence' of arbitration has been highlighted in an arbitral context, as well as from the perspective of transnational litigation. In the context of arbitration, see: W. Laurence Craig, 'Some Trends and Developments in the Laws and Practice of International Commercial

1.1 THE ENFORCEMENT GAP AND THE IMPORTANCE OF RELATIVE ENFORCEMENT PROSPECTS

It has been posited that a large part of the exponential growth in demand for international dispute resolution services in recent decades has been met by the rise of international commercial arbitration rather than litigation. Although it is difficult to causatively attribute any one factor as underlying this 'golden age',[11] one of the key drivers supporting this growth is the relative ease of enforcement of any resulting arbitral award across borders.[12] Empirical evidence confirms this preference for arbitration,[13] and the role that enforceability plays in this choice due to its impact on commercial practice and the ability of disputants to achieve private justice.[14] This is for two key reasons.

Arbitration' (2016) 50 *Texas International Law Journal* 699, 702. From the perspective of transnational litigation, Chief Justice Menon (Supreme Court of Singapore) laments that '[c]ommentators have gone so far as to state that international arbitration has become *the* established method of determining international commercial disputes': Menon (n 9) 226 (at footnote 38).

11 Denise Huiwen Wong, 'The Rise of the International Commercial Court: What Is It and Will It Work?' (2014) 33 *Civil Justice Quarterly* 205, 205. The rise of arbitration can, at least in part, be attributed to a diverse range of factors, including the ability of parties to select a neutral forum (rather than potentially 'biased' local courts), confidentiality of proceedings and the special competence of the tribunal. This book focuses only upon the enforcement differential as a possible driver of the enforcement gap.

12 Reyes notes that, in his view (at least in the commercial context), 'the principal reason' for the growth of arbitration is the 'apparent ease' of enforcement of an arbitral award under the New York Convention: Anselmo Reyes, 'Recognition and Enforcement of Interlocutory and Final Judgments of the Singapore International Commercial Court' (2015) 2 *Journal of International and Comparative Law* 337, 340. This seems to be a view shared by a range of scholars: see, for example, Craig (n 10) 702; Gerhard Wagner, 'Dispute Resolution as a Product: Competition between Civil Justice Systems' in Horst Eidenmüller (ed), *Regulatory Competition in Contract Law and Dispute Resolution* (First edition, Hart 2013) 381.

13 See, for example, surveys undertaken by Queen Mary University London, which reflects findings that 90 per cent of practitioners and corporate counsel prefer to utilise arbitration, compared with 4 per cent preferring litigation, and that 'enforceability of awards' is seen as arbitration's most valuable characteristic: PwC & Queen Mary University of London, *International Arbitration Survey 2013: Corporate Choices in International Arbitration* (2013) <www.pwc.com/arbitrationstudy> ('2013 *Arbitration Survey*'); White & Case and Queen Mary University of London, *International Arbitration Survey 2015: Improvements and Innovations in International Arbitration* (October 2015) <www.arbitration.qmul.ac.uk/research/2015/> ('2015 *Arbitration Survey*'). Sixty-five per cent of respondents to the Queen Mary University (London) 2015 Arbitration Survey indicated that the enforceability of awards constituted, from their perspective, at least one of the 'three most valuable characteristics of arbitration': 6.

14 Beyond the impact on private parties, enforcement prospects also serve a range of public governance roles, including shaping competition between transnational dispute resolution mechanisms (and thus the quality thereof), as well as States' ability to effectively regulate transnational activity. See, for example, Tietje, who argues that international treaties – such as

First, recognition of a binding and conclusive decision in a foreign court is relied upon globally to activate preclusive legal effects, raising, in most jurisdictions, certain bars on further- or re-disputing decided issues, such as issue estoppel, claim preclusion and *res judicata*.[15] Second, enforcement is critical to securing practical justice: where recourse to foreign assets is necessary, the entire process of dispute resolution can be of limited practical utility in the face of a recalcitrant debtor or enforcing court.[16] Consequently, if it is too costly or difficult to recognise or enforce a foreign decision, this may lead to uncertainty, delays and costs in securing an effective legal outcome or remedy.[17]

The existence of an ongoing enforcement gap thus has wide consequences for disputants. First, the gap may have deleterious impacts even for disputants who are free to select between arbitration and litigation. This is because the choice of dispute resolution mechanism is generally considered to be taken based on a cost-benefit analysis, weighing up competing features and limitations. Phrased in economic terms, the enforcement landscape, to the extent to which it maintains a gap in favour of arbitration, supports an artificial monopoly in international commercial dispute resolution mechanisms. That is, the initial decision to arbitrate or litigate is influenced by the gap; a feature that extends beyond the intrinsic merits of the dispute resolution service itself. To take but one example, consider a disputant who highly values a feature (or combination of features) that national courts offer, such as the operation of *binding* precedent.[18] If the gap in enforcement treatment is wide enough in

those applicable to the recognition and enforcement of foreign judgments – form part of an emerging 'global governance architecture': Christian Tietje, 'The Changing Legal Structure of International Treaties as an Aspect of an Emerging Global Governance Architecture Focus Section: The Law of International Treaties in the 21st Century' (1999) 42 *German Yearbook of International Law* 26.

15 These bars, of course, may have significant legal and practical impacts on disputants barred from re-raising an issue but also have wider system-level efficiency and fairness motivations, premised upon finality in dispute resolution to limit socially wasteful duplication in proceedings: see, further, Kevin Clermont, 'Res Judicata as Requisite for Justice' (2016) 68 *Rutgers University Law Review* 1067, 1078 (and following), who suggests that, at a minimum, every legal system has some form of *res judicata* law.

16 HL Ho, 'Policies Underlying the Enforcement of Foreign Commercial Judgments' (1997) 46 *The International and Comparative Law Quarterly* 443, 457.

17 Hague Conference, 'Some Reflections of the Permanent Bureau on a General Convention on Enforcement of Judgments' (n 5), 231.

18 Traditionally, the development of precedent is regarded as a by-product of litigation for private parties. However, commercial parties that seek the authoritative exposition of a particular issue that arises across multiple contracts – for example, insurance companies seeking clarity on policy exclusions – may prefer to litigate, as litigation allows for the creation of binding and authoritative precedent. See, for a thorough theoretical examination of the way in which

favour of arbitration – and future enforcement prospects are important to this hypothetical disputant – it may be led to select arbitration simply to maximise its eventual recognition and enforcement prospects.

Second, where private disputants do not have the option to arbitrate – or have not exercised that option and are left to the 'default' resolution of national courts – the gap may lead to significant access to justice and fairness concerns. This may, for example, extend to disputants faced with a standard form contract with no ability to negotiate the dispute resolution mechanism,[19] or to disputants with a matter in dispute that is deemed non-arbitrable and able only to be resolved exclusively by national courts.[20] It may also extend to mandatory claims (such as tortious claims in negligence) where these fall outside any contract or where no contract is entered into between the disputants. Additionally, as arbitration is a creature of contract, it is constitutionally incapable of resolving claims that fall outside the scope of any agreement to arbitrate. Thus, certain claims that call for some form of joinder or consolidation to be effectively resolved – such as those arising from 'employer/main contractor/subcontractor' and 'insurance/reinsurance/retrocession' contracts – are not able to be achieved unless each party shares the same preferences to arbitrate.[21]

Beyond the impact on private parties, the existence of the gap over time may also lead to a reduction in effective competition between dispute resolution fora. This, according to economic theory, suggests that either prices for dispute resolution services will rise or the overall quality of the transnational dispute resolution 'marketplace' overall may falter or not improve. This process seems to be occurring, with a recent 'cacophony of voices' raising concerns with aspects of arbitral procedure (including its cost),[22] and a parallel

precedents are used, interpreted and distinguished: Neil MacCormick and Robert S. Summers (eds), *Interpreting Precedents: A Comparative Study* ([Applied legal philosophy], Aldershot 1997).

19 Carrington, for example, argues in the context of the United States that 'predatory' strategy is seen by repeat litigants restricting the choice of forum of vulnerable parties: Paul D. Carrington, 'Regulating Dispute Resolution Provisions in Adhesion Contracts Statute' (1998) 35 *Harv J on Legis* 225.

20 Including a range of consumer, employment disputes, and matters involving property rights, particularly *in rem*: see, for example, Nigel Blackaby and others, *Redfern and Hunter on International Arbitration* (6th edn, Oxford University Press 2015) para 2.124 (and following).

21 Michael Hwang, 'Commercial Courts and International Arbitration: Competitors or Partners?' (2015) 31 *Arbitration International* 193, 195.

22 These have been summarised as concerns relating to judicialisation, delay, laboriousness and rising costs; lack of ethical standards; unpredictability in enforcement due to the ad hoc nature of courts' oversight; and unpredictability in arbitral decisions due to lack of jurisprudence: see Menon (n 9) 226–27. Wong goes as far as suggesting that these are 'systemic flaws' in international commercial arbitration as a dispute resolution mechanism: Wong (n 11) 206.

drive to introduce a new dispute resolution mechanism focused on meeting transnational disputants' needs, styled as international commercial courts.[23] While this book is in no way set out or intended as a critique of arbitration, it suffices to note that to the extent that any of these criticisms have merit, they are likely to take on greater importance given that the ongoing existence of the enforcement gap, all else constant, steers disputants to arbitration.

The impact of the enforcement gap is likely to be felt more keenly over time, as the practical need for recognition and enforcement of foreign decisions continues to grow.[24] In large part, this need arises as a necessary by-product of the rise of greater cross-border and inter-(legal) system trading activity. In other words, the growth in the range and scope of activities – particularly in the commercial sphere – that take place across borders means that there is increased pressure to find effective methods to resolve international legal disputes.[25] Part of this growth can no doubt be attributed to technological progress facilitating trade (for example, the internet facilitating e-commerce), as well as a series of cultural, technological and economic factors that have made the world more interdependent in a myriad of ways.[26] Pressures are also faced in an enforcement landscape that is subject to a gap, given the continual increase in multinational activity on a transnational level, particularly in combination with multi-jurisdictional business- and asset-holding structures. Because of this, disputants often must traverse a range of jurisdictions to finally resolve matters that cross legal boundaries or to locate assets to satisfy foreign decisions. Consequently, enforcement approaches – both doctrinally and in practice – are a critical component of international dispute resolution in civil and commercial matters.

1.2 ONGOING EFFORTS TO PROMOTE RECOGNITION AND ENFORCEMENT OF JUDGMENTS

Given the practical need for recognition and enforcement, over the preceding two centuries, States have explored a diverse range of legal approaches to both

[23] These courts give rise to an increased impetus to recognise and enforce foreign judgments, as that is the product that they deliver. They can be defined based upon their genesis in and focus on attracting foreign litigants, most prominently represented by the 2015 commencement of the Singapore International Commercial Court.

[24] McLachlan, for example, charts the growth in international commercial litigation in English courts, and the impacts this has had from a private international law perspective: Campbell McLachlan, 'International Litigation and the Reworking of the Conflict of Laws' (2004) 120 *Law Quarterly Review* 580.

[25] Ho (n 16) 457–58.

[26] See, for example, Twining's critical view of economic concepts of globalisation in William Twining, 'Globalisation and Comparative Law' (Hart 2007).

boost enforcement prospects and give greater certainty to when foreign decisions will be given effect. The range of ways to do so are broad and include sector-specific rules for recognition or enforcement,[27] uniform or model laws,[28] as well as treaties across bilateral[29] and regional levels,[30] as well as the key international attempts at the multilateral level on which this book focuses. Although the range of approaches that have been pursued are diverse – often crafted for very different purposes, participants, and across a range of languages – at their core they share the same functional goal: shifting the basis for recognising and enforcing foreign decisions to standardised and defined legal rules instead of unsure and uncertain grounds based ultimately on State discretion.

The first of these approaches – bilateral negotiations – is typically pursued based on reciprocity: that is, the establishment of mutual obligations between States to give effect to foreign decisions. These bilateral approaches are often entered into between States based on shared institutional or legal history, such as between States presently or previously associated with the

[27] A range of multilateral conventions have been negotiated on substantive subject matters (across predominantly transnational industries, such as transportation and the carriage of goods), which include procedural provisions for the enforcement of foreign judgments within their subject matter: Michaels, 'Recognition and Enforcement of Foreign Judgments' (n 1) para 21.

[28] In the early 1950s the then newcomer to the Hague Conference, the United States, attempted to steer the Hague Conference towards considering 'model' (or 'uniform') legislative approaches to recognition and enforcement, based on successes in its own federated system: see, generally, Kurt Nadelmann, 'Uniform Legislation versus International Conventions as a Method of Unification of Private International Law' in Kurt Nadelmann (ed), *Conflicts of Law: International And Interstate: Selected Essays* (Martinus Nijhoff Publishers 1972) and Kurt Nadelmann, 'Uniform Legislation versus International Conventions Revisited' in Kurt Nadelmann (ed), *Conflicts of Law: International And Interstate: Selected Essays* (Martinus Nijhoff Publishers 1972). This push met resistance from other States and was ultimately abandoned. Consequently, pursuing multilateral convention remained – and to this day remains – the preferred method for pursuing transnational developments on judgments recognition and enforcement.

[29] Bilateral treaties are canvassed further in Chapter 4, where emphasis is placed on the mutual recognition scheme broadly shared by Commonwealth nations (but largely implemented on a bilateral basis), as well as the bilateral efforts of the United States as one of the major trading nations influencing the operation of the efforts of international bodies to achieve cohesion on a regional instrument.

[30] Michaels, 'Recognition and Enforcement of Foreign Judgments' (n 1), [13]; See Chapter 3 for a further discussion of regional treaties within the context of the European Union. The instruments in force between these members represent perhaps the high point that States – with a shared economic and political vision – have been able to achieve in standardising the recognition and enforcement approaches of enforcing courts.

Commonwealth,[31] but they can also arise as a process of bilateral treaty with States that do not share any such connection.[32] Despite the potential for these agreements to bridge the enforcement gap, relying on their theoretical ability to do so is 'parlous' given the dearth of these kinds of arrangements globally.[33]

Second, and more successful than bilateral arrangements, are attempts to promote the 'regional' harmonisation of recognition and enforcement practice, extending (also by reciprocity) mutual recognition and enforcement to a grouping of States all at once. Indeed, the first successful multilateral efforts towards promoting recognition and enforcement stemmed from regional instruments, primarily in Latin America, and from conventions on specific substantive subject matters:[34] the Peruvian government, as early as 1875, made the 'first attempt in the world' to codify these private international law rules.[35] This approach is most successfully demonstrated in the Brussels Model approach, originally conceived of between the six members of the then European Economic Community.[36] The Brussels Model addresses the enforcement gap between its participants, such that each participant State – at least with respect to other Brussels Model States – provides straightforward, compulsory and expeditious recognition and enforcement of the other's

[31] See, for example, Singapore's *Reciprocal Enforcement of Commonwealth Judgments Act* (Cap 264, 1985). Section 5(1) conditions a favourable recognition and enforcement approach primarily on reciprocal treatment.

[32] See, for example, Singapore's bilateral treaty with Hong Kong for giving effect to foreign judgments, enacted in Singapore in its *Reciprocal Enforcement of Foreign Judgments Act* (Cap 265, 2001), which is more directive than its approach to Commonwealth nations but is also based on reciprocity: s 3(1).

[33] Hwang notes, for example, that despite having the legislative framework, Singapore only has reciprocal arrangements with eleven of fifty-three Commonwealth States, and only with one non-Commonwealth State (Hong Kong): Hwang (n 21) 198.

[34] Michaels, 'Recognition and Enforcement of Foreign Judgments' (n 1) paras 15–24.

[35] Alejandro M. Garro, 'Unification and Harmonization of Private Law in Latin America' (1992) 40 *The American Journal of Comparative Law* 587, 589.

[36] Formally, despite beginning life in the form of the 1968 Convention (solely between the six original European Community (EC) members), the Brussels Model has since become entrenched within the EU as a directly binding Regulation, and it also extends to non-EU Lugano States via the Lugano Conventions. See, in reverse chronological order, *Regulation (EU) No 1215/2012 of 12 December 2012 on Jurisdiction and the Recognition and Enforcement of Judgments in Civil and Commercial Matters (Recast)* (2012). 'Lugano II Convention on Jurisdiction and the Enforcement of Judgments in Civil and Commercial Matters' (21/12/07). 'Regulation (EC) No 44/2001 of 22 December 2000 on Jurisdiction and the Recognition and Enforcement of Judgments in Civil and Commercial Matters' (2001) OJ L 12/1. 'Lugano Convention on Jurisdiction and the Enforcement of Judgments in Civil and Commercial Matters' (first published 1988, no date). Brussels Convention on Jurisdiction and the Enforcement of Judgments in Civil and Commercial Matters (European Economic Community) (entered into force 1 February 1973).

foreign judgments.[37] Yet, as this book explores further, it is unclear if this kind of regional approach is 'likely to be instructive' for others, given that the Brussels Model is largely premised on the basis of the European Union's (EU) extraordinary degree of mutual trust and cooperation amongst Member States.[38] In particular, the extent of harmonisation in certain regional approaches may not extend to 'sovereign relationships of a very different kind', such as those that exist on the 'global' level, and also does little to address (and indeed is not designed to address) the enforcement gap as broadly conceived.[39]

Third and finally – and the primary focus of this book – are global efforts towards harmonised pro-recognition and enforcement approaches to foreign judgments.[40] The negotiations to conventions to this effect were overseen by the Hague Conference on Private International Law (the 'Hague Conference') and its constituent Member States, and it has largely continued between States since the mid-eighteenth century. These longstanding negotiations drew liberally – and themselves contributed – on national law approaches to recognition and enforcement, the genesis of the New York Convention and other international and regional models such as the Commonwealth approach and the Brussels Model. Despite ample exemplars and experience to draw from, as well as the appearance of transnational political will – as represented by States' continued participation across successive drafting projects and rounds of negotiations – a successful broad-based instrument on recognition and enforcement was not successfully opened for signature until mid-2019.[41] The negotiating efforts nonetheless culminated in

37 Although each instrument constituting the Model achieves this task in slightly different ways. See further: Gralf-Peter Calliess, 'Value-Added Norms, Local Litigation, and Global Enforcement: Why the Brussels-Philosophy Failed in The Hague' (2004) 05 *German Law Journal* 1489, 1497.

38 Andrew Dickinson, 'What, If Anything, Can Australia Learn from the EU Experience?' in Andrew Dickinson and others (eds.), *Australian Private International Law for the 21st Century: Facing Outwards* (Hart 2014) 183.

39 ibid.

40 Ronald A. Brand, 'Jurisdictional Developments and the New Hague Judgments Project' [2013] in, 'A Commitment to Private International Law: Essays In Honor of Hans Van Loon', Intersentia, 2013 University of Pittsburgh Legal Studies Research Paper No 2013-19, 89.

41 Despite the conclusion of a 1971 instrument on precisely this topic, without States giving effect to the instrument it has been deemed to be a failure: Hague Conference, 'Convention on the Recognition and Enforcement of Foreign Judgments in Civil and Commercial Matters' (1 February 1971) ('1971 Convention') and its accompanying Hague Conference, 'Supplementary Protocol of 1 February 1971 to the Hague Convention on the Recognition and Enforcement of Foreign Judgments in Civil and Commercial Matters' (1 February 1971). The 1971 Convention is broadly considered to have been unsuccessful as a legal instrument despite representing a novel approach to judgment recognition that would have – if implemented – significantly

the 2005 Choice of Court Convention, which came into force in 2015, and the 2019 Judgments Convention, which has not yet entered into force.[42]

These many decades of experiences across recognition and enforcement instruments in both arbitration and litigation, combined with years of careful international negotiations, have led to a high degree of instrumental convergence. For example, as the comparative analysis of approaches in Part I of this book suggests, there is significant agreement upon the substantive scope and approach of recognition and enforcement instruments, including the shared adoption of established legal terminology and shared instrumental design decisions. The substance of approaches is also similarly founded upon a broad presumption in favour of recognition and enforcement, which is built upon restricting review of the merits of the original decision, pre-supposing recognition and enforcement, and strictly limiting the exceptional bases for refusing to do so. However, given the nature of international instruments, this convergence has no direct role to play in narrowing the enforcement gap until implemented in national law. As a result, the present state of recognition and enforcement of foreign judgments globally remains largely a creature of national law, influenced by bilateral and regional agreements and agreements concluded by States with similar legal systems. This, however, is likely to rapidly change if the Judgments Conventions achieve critical mass in terms of adoption. It is my desire that this book may shed some light on the merits and impact of doing so.

1.3 BOOK STRUCTURE, APPROACH AND SCOPE

In this book, I comparatively analyse the recognition and enforcement of civil and commercial decisions. In this section, I first set out why a comparative transnational frame offers the most insight before considering the approach of each part and clarifying the scope and focus of this book. Part I commences by exploring the key regional and international recognition and enforcement approaches from a historical and functionalist comparative perspective.

contributed to closing the enforcement gap: Hague Conference, 'Some Reflections of the Permanent Bureau on a General Convention on Enforcement of Judgments' (n 5), 231.

42 However, this may soon change. As of July 2022, the Council of the European Union adopted the decision for the EU to accede to the 2019 Judgments Convention. The EU acting as first mover is likely to spur further accessions or implementations of the 2019 Convention, as only one more party is needed for the Convention to come into force, with immediate application between this party and all members of the EU (excluding Denmark).

Building on this exposition, Part II of the book explores the future of recognition and enforcement.

1.3.1 *A Transnational Perspective on Recognition and Enforcement*

One of the most significant understandings arising from this book is in the complexity of exploring and comparing recognition and enforcement architecture. This is for several reasons, which can briefly be summarised as follows. First, any comparative study of private international law – including approaches to recognition and enforcement – requires consideration of an ever-changing mix of 'cultural, moral, economic, political and social contexts', which shape (and reshape) a society and legal order within it.[43] Second, while negotiated recognition and enforcement approaches are created on one level – the transnational or the international – they are fully intended to operate within a domestic context. As Stephan has noted:

> enforcement is relentlessly territorial. Even though the transformation of communications and transportation in the last century (even before the rise of the Internet) supposedly erased national borders, states continue to hold the enforcement of judgments hostage to the particular policies and values of the forum where assets are located.[44]

This means that even though most domestic recognition and enforcement regimes derive from and are influenced by an array of potentially overlapping (or competing) international and regional legal sources, analysis of their operation is inherently a domestic concern. At the same time, however, if the answer is that recognition and enforcement can only be comprehended as a series of isolated domestic practices – as a 'black box' of legal pluralism – this seems to belie what appear to be a host of historical, institutional and legal similarities in approaches to recognition and enforcement (many of which stem, ultimately, from considering and implementing international instruments and norms). Instead, it will be demonstrated that recognition and enforcement rules and norms 'flow' back and forth from domestic, regional and transnational levels. They are also subject to a process of conscious filtering at the transnational level to model developments in other approaches,

[43] Arthur von Mehren and Eckart Gottschalk, *Adjudicatory Authority in Private International Law* (The Hague Academy of International Law Monographs 5, Martinus Nijhoff Publishers 2007) 353.

[44] Extract from Paul B. Stephan (ed), *Foreign Court Judgments and the United States Legal System* (Brill 2014).

and possibly even to strive to operate according to 'internationalisms'[45] or 'global best practice'.[46]

A third reason why enforcement practice can be difficult to analyse is because transnational harmonisation efforts are designed to create legal rules that are given force at the State level, but these rules have their primary impact – unlike most treaties – on the rights and obligations of private parties. Fourth, recognition and enforcement approaches have traditionally been divided into instrumental and epistemological communities, with little substantive overlap: that of award recognition and enforcement, and foreign judgment recognition and enforcement; and two further divides exist within the judgments sphere, based upon whether the original forum was reached via an exclusive choice of court and whether any regional or historical harmonisation efforts are in place. For these reasons, capturing the intricacies and detail of the constant flow of legal rules and norms in recognition and enforcement practice is exceedingly difficult.

These concerns represent a critique of the utility of using doctrinal analysis to map recognition and enforcement practice, on the basis that doing so neglects 'real world' practice or critical aspects of 'cultural' comparison. Phrased alternatively, understanding how recognition and enforcement works in practice requires a much more detailed analysis than just the doctrinal roots of recognition and enforcement or a consideration of its functional aim. It is in this context that an increased reference to recognition and enforcement as a 'transnationalised' process or approach can assist in exploring the enforcement gap. This allows us to consider, for example, how recognition and enforcement approaches come to be applied and whether there is consistency with substance over form.

These questions reflect a key recurring criticism that assessing only doctrinal uniformity has limited explanatory capacity as to the existence of the enforcement gap.[47] As Brand notes, taking this argument to its logical

[45] A trend that was noted many decades ago in the context of English private international law but continues through today. See, for example, Otto Kahn-Freund, *The Growth of Internationalism in English Private International Law* (1960); Richard Garnett, 'Internationalism in New Zealand Conflict of Laws' (2021) 17 *Journal of Private International Law* 380.

[46] See, for a comparative overview – and critique – of the ability to model 'best practice' on a global level: Ralf Michaels, '"One Size Can Fit All": On the Mass Production of Legal Transplants' in Günter Frankenberg (ed.), *Order from Transfer: Comparative Constitutional Design and Legal Culture* (Studies in Comparative Law and Legal Culture Series, Edward Elgar Publishing 2013).

[47] See, for a clear exposition of this argument, Kevin Cope, 'Reconceptualizing Recognition Uniformity' in Paul B. Stephan (ed.), *Foreign Court Judgments and the United States Legal System* (Brill 2014).

conclusion means there is a 'total incomparability across history and culture', as any comparison that attempts to cross borders (and hence cultures) is 'labelled superficial'.[48] This is not hyperbole: a disconnect between doctrinal and cultural or functional analysis has the potential to lead to an erroneous view of the enforcement gap. For example, a focus on the doctrinal may obscure the fact that States may apply or interpret harmonised approaches in such a way as to defeat pro-recognition and enforcement aims and objectives.[49] In this sense, there is an irreducible clash of law and culture, such that a focus solely upon law – in this case as represented by a doctrinal consideration of transnational legal instruments and domestic legal instruments that implement such instruments – obscures the true position with respect to recognition and enforcement. This stands to be criticised on the basis that any legal rule or collection of legal rules represents only a 'generalization denoting a collage of legal artefacts'.[50] In Frankenberg's words, because law is both 'omnipresent' and 'ambiguous':

> to locate [law] only here or there would like trying to nail a pudding to the wall. We have to trace it everywhere: in texts, institutions, actions, ideas and fantasies – a rather disquieting but also fascinating prospect.[51]

Otherwise, comparison may be overly superficial where it is premised solely upon a comparison of doctrinal similarities and differences.[52] This reflects the perennial reminder, oft made in international commercial arbitration, that any doctrinal or instrumental analysis 'must be tempered by a trebled measure of realism' as to what actually occurs in practice.[53]

One of the key attempts to do so has been via empirical surveys of current recognition and enforcement practice. Notable efforts to capture 'worldwide' recognition and enforcement practice have been attempted.[54] Other efforts

48 Oliver Brand, 'Conceptual Comparisons: Towards a Coherent Methodology of Comparative Legal Studies' (2007) 32(2) *Brooklyn Journal of International Law* 431.

49 Discussed in Section 8.3.2.

50 Michele Graziadei, 'Comparative Law as the Study of Transplants and Receptions' in Mathias Reimann and Reinhard Zimmermann (eds.), *The Oxford Handbook of Comparative Law* (Oxford University Press 2006) 471.

51 Günter Frankenberg, 'Critical Comparisons: Re-thinking Comparative Law' (1985) 26 *Harvard International Law Journal* 411, 452.

52 This is the core thesis of Frankenberg, who has consistently criticised perceived methodological deficiencies in comparative law as a discipline: Frankenberg (n 51); Günter Frankenberg, *Comparative Law as Critique* (Elgar Studies in Legal Theory, Edward Elgar Publishing 2016).

53 Marike Paulsson, *The 1958 New York Convention in Action* (Wolters Kluwer 2016) xxii.

54 See, for example, Charles Platto, *Enforcement of Foreign Judgments Worldwide* (Graham & Trotman, 1993), which is by no means exhaustive – covering only select jurisdictions in the

have been made to empirically analyse recognition and enforcement practice on a regional basis, such as within Commonwealth Africa[55] or Asia.[56] Caffrey, for example, determines that recognition and enforcement can be comparatively analysed as forming part of one particular characterisation: such as the 'English Method', 'Indian Method', 'Japanese Method' or the 'Evidentiary Method' and the 'Appeals Method' – a designation that is partly geographical and historical, and partly based on the way jurisdictions give effect to foreign judgments.[57] Chang takes a slightly different approach, suggesting, in the context of the New York Convention, that an 'objective index' that attempts to assess the extent to which each jurisdiction complies with its recognition and enforcement obligations could be compiled.[58] In this sense, the transnational approach – and the internationally accepted way to interpret and apply it – becomes the benchmark of recognition and enforcement.

However, the key risk with empirical expositions is that they are difficult to compile, can become quickly outdated and are, by necessity, primarily descriptive in nature, offering little ability to discern a general rule or pattern across the surveyed jurisdictions. Reflecting this concern, it has been suggested that divergences in recognition and enforcement outcomes – rather than doctrinal underpinnings – should be considered empirically on a 'spectrum', according to the extent to which each transnational order obliges enforcing courts to give effect to a foreign decision.[59] That is, one way to consider this disconnect between 'practical reality' and doctrinal foundations is to express recognition and enforcement outcomes on a scale of 'outcome'

areas it reports such as the Asia-Pacific, Latin America, Europe, Canada, United States. See also Dennis Campbell (ed.), *Enforcement of Foreign Judgements* (LLP Professional Publishing 1997). Campbell's collection is expressly denoted as a 'starting point' (at p. 2) to simply point in the direction of where to go for comprehending a jurisdiction's approach. Academic surveys are also supplemented by commercial legal products – such as the Practical Law product of Thomson Reuters or the Global Arbitration Review, which provide an overview of recognition and enforcement practice in each jurisdiction covered but tend to be descriptive rather than analytical, with little general or comparative content.

55 Richard Frimpong Oppong, *Private International Law in Commonwealth Africa* (Cambridge University Press 2013).

56 Bradford Caffrey, *International Jurisdiction and the Recognition and Enforcement of Foreign Judgments in the LAWASIA Region: A Comparative Study of the Laws of Eleven Asian Countries Inter-Se and with the* E.E.C. *Countries* (CCH Australia 1985).

57 Caffrey (n 56) 65–70.

58 Teresa Chang, 'Celebrating the Fiftieth Anniversary of the New York Convention' in Albert Jan van den Berg (ed.), 50 *Years of the New York Convention: ICCA International Arbitration Conference* (ICCA Congress Series 14, Kluwer Law International 2009) 686.

59 Christopher Whytock, 'Enforcement of Foreign Judgments: Governance, Rights, and the Market for Dispute Resolution Services' in Hans-W. Micklitz and Andrea Wechsler (eds.), *The Transformation of Enforcement: European Economic Law in a Global Perspective* (Hart 2016) 53.

uniformity.[60] This measure, as distinct from doctrinal comparisons of uniformity, is an empirical measure of past disputant and enforcing court behaviour.[61] In other words, are we concerned with like foreign judgments being accorded like treatment, or are we concerned with the reasoning process utilised by the enforcing court? If the former, however, there must be sufficient bilateral recognition and enforcement practice to be able to support an empirical conclusion: such evidence is often lacking (for example, recognition and enforcement has not arisen in that bilateral relationship) and may even lead to a situation of 'recognition deadlock'.[62] Consequently, rather than focus solely on empirical or doctrinal measures, transnational experience suggests that a broader consideration of transnational ordering may assist in exploring the enforcement gap.

It is in this context of methodological and practical complexities that concepts and analyses premised upon transnational legal ordering – an investigation of the 'multifold, simultaneous, and iterative' borrowing processes inherent in transnational recognition and enforcement, implicating 'disparate actors, applications, and flows in multiple directions'[63] – come to the fore. To formalise this transnational analytical frame, it assists to adopt Halliday and Shaffer's broad socio-legal definition of a transnational legal order as a 'collection of formalized legal norms and associated organizations and actors that authoritatively order the understanding and practice of law across national jurisdictions'.[64] Such inquiry offers significant value, as despite the practical reality that recognition and enforcement is the ultimate product of State sovereignty, recognition and enforcement is increasingly understood and ordered on a transnational level. This means that comparative law State-to-State comparison (which places the State at the centre stage of analysis and legal development) is increasingly inadequate in mapping and exploring the enforcement gap. In other words, conceiving of recognition and enforcement

60 Cope (n 47) 167.

61 Yet too heavy a reliance on functionalism has itself been criticised. See, for example, early comparative law methodological criticisms in Frankenberg (n 51). Brand takes this argument further, and considers that there are 'real problems' with the use of functional method in comparative law, querying its continued prominence given the significant methodological flaws: Brand, 'Conceptual Comparisons' (n 48) 415 (and following).

62 See footnote 370.

63 Gregory Shaffer, 'Transnational Legal Ordering and State Change' in Gregory Shaffer (ed.), *Transnational Legal Ordering and State Change* (Cambridge Studies in Law and Society, Cambridge University Press 2012) 9.

64 Terence Halliday and Susan Block-Lieb, 'Settling and Concordance: Two Cases in Global Commercial Law' in Gregory Shaffer and Terence Halliday (eds.), *Transnational Legal Orders* (Cambridge Studies in Law and Society, Cambridge University Press 2015) 11.

approaches as more than their domestic doctrinal manifestations can provide greater guidance as to the extent and nature of the enforcement gap, particularly as it compels us to consider the 'blend of domestic and international legal process[es] [which] internalize norms' from the complex interplay and interaction among transnational, international and domestic lawmaking authority.[65] This calls for an analysis not just of the underlying legal instrumentation (whether domestically or transnationally) but is, instead, premised fundamentally upon incorporating socio-legal considerations of 'behaviour change' – that is, the change in 'normative orientations'[66] of actors involved or implicated in recognition and enforcement. This allows the legitimacy or authoritativeness of each recognition and enforcement approach to be assessed based upon whether it has 'contingent' and 'fragile' support or is a 'fully fledged' approach that is 'clear, coherent and accepted'.[67]

Taking a broader perspective – beyond doctrinal or empirical measures – of course, loses direct explanatory insight into the precise recognition and enforcement rules or approaches utilised in a particular legal system. However, comparison at this level of generalisation is particularly useful to assess the enforcement gap, as transnational approaches to recognition and enforcement can stand as comparators (or a 'proxy', or reference point) for this purpose. Consideration of transnational legal ordering thus offers a mechanism to assist analysis of the enforcement gap in circumstances where there are significant methodological and practical concerns about cross-cultural domestic comparison of laws. This is because a transnational analytical frame explicitly reminds us to query the existence, similarities and variation of recognition and enforcement approaches from a wider perspective. At the same time, it also reorients focus on how legal rules and norms embedded in these orders migrate or 'settle' across and between all law-making levels (and across national borders).

This book aims to contribute by exploring the (increasingly) transnational ordering of recognition and enforcement generally, rather than focusing on any singular jurisdiction's implementation of such ordering.[68] This allows a deeper understanding of the prevailing recognition and enforcement architecture, both by a consideration of the shared doctrinal underpinnings of each approach as well as an analysis of the practical experience towards harmonised

65 Harold Koh, 'Transnational Legal Process' (1996) 75 *Nebraska Law Review* 181, 183–84.
66 Halliday and Block-Lieb (n 64) 8.
67 Shaffer (n 63) 1. See also Halliday and Block-Lieb (n 64) 20.
68 See also Section 8.3, which engages in a deeper analysis of the nature of transnational ordering in recognition and enforcement.

recognition and enforcement engendered under each. Additionally, understanding the history of each recognition and enforcement approach, developed by either gradual diffusion or continuous change through law that crosses and transcends boundaries,[69] is also likely to offer insight into the future state of recognition and enforcement. This is a particularly pressing concern given that the 2005 Choice of Court Convention came into force in 2015, and the 2019 Convention may soon follow (having been signed in 2019). Notably, this book considers recognition and enforcement of foreign *decisions* overall, rather than carving out separate 'niches' for arbitration vis à vis litigation.[70] This focus on the recognition and enforcement of the product of binding international dispute resolution mechanisms overall diverges from most comparisons of recognition and enforcement, which focus heavily on solely one domain: either the recognition and enforcement of arbitral awards or, conversely, of foreign judgments. Doing so allows a richer understanding, offering insight into prevailing recognition and enforcement rules and norms; including likely evolutions or future steps of global recognition and enforcement frameworks.

1.3.2 *Part I: Past and Present*

Part I of the book analyses the key civil and commercial recognition and enforcement frameworks. These approaches are identified in Table 1.1. Part I traces the emergence of key global and regional frameworks in their historical context, analyses the differing legal instrumentation (and instrumental features) employed to achieve this task and then consolidates this analysis through a functional comparison. This comparison reveals a shared core of transnational recognition and enforcement practice that can be distilled and compared, offering insight into the present operation of recognition and enforcement instruments but also serves to ground analysis of the present state and future of recognition and enforcement (as occurs in Part II of the book).

Chapter 2 traces the emergence and approach of 'global' recognition and enforcement. As Table 1.1 suggests, these approaches are now instrumentally bifurcated, premised upon whether a decision that is to be recognised or

69 Graziadei (n 50) 443.

70 See, for an example of this practice, an otherwise comprehensive overview of regional recognition and enforcement instruments – where arbitration is explicitly excluded from the scope of review, on the basis that the New York Convention already applies to the recognition and enforcement of foreign arbitral awards: Mandi Rossouw, *The Harmonisation of Rules on the Recognition and Enforcement of Foreign Judgments in the Southern African Customs Union* (Pretoria University Law Press 2016) 41.

TABLE 1.1. *Recognition and enforcement approaches compared in Part I of this book*

	Original dispute resolution mechanism engendered by			
Recognition and enforcement 'level'		**Choice of arbitration**	**Choice of court**	**'Default' operation of a court**
	'global'[71] (treaty-based, implemented via national law)	1958 New York Convention (entered into force 1958)	2005 Choice of Court Agreements Convention (entered into force 2015)	2019 Judgments Convention (not yet in force)
	'regional' (implemented via supranational grouping or statutory enactment)		1. Brussels Model (since the late 1960s) 2. Commonwealth Model (since the 1920s)	
	domestic		Common law recognition and enforcement of foreign judgments (since the early sixteenth century)	

enforced is a product of a particular dispute resolution mechanism (arbitration or litigation) and whether an exclusive choice of court has been made (or, failing such a choice, the 'default' operation of jurisdictional rules). The reasons for doing so are explored in the context of the modern negotiations at the Hague Conference towards a harmonised private international law approach to the recognition and enforcement of judgments. The end products of these negotiations are, of course, the 2005 *Choice of Court Convention* and

71 In general, I prefer the term 'transnational', predominantly because the 'global' moniker is 'misleading': although these approaches are broadly open to international implementation, and are designed to facilitate this goal, no international legal order is truly 'global in its geographic reach': Halliday and Block-Lieb (n 64) 4. However, for the purposes of differentiating between 'regional' transnational approaches and broad-based efforts, I utilise the categorisation of 'global'.

the *2019 Judgments Convention* (collectively, the 'Judgments Conventions'). In terms of their international reach and acceptance, these conventions are in an embryonic form compared to the widely implemented 'backbone' of arbitration recognition and enforcement (in the 1958 *New York Convention*).

Given the recent emergence of the Judgments Conventions, it is useful to refer to other 'regional' or 'international' approaches to give a more detailed snapshot of the transnationalisation of recognition and enforcement practice. Chapters 3 and 4 take up this mantle. Chapter 3 analyses the broad-based and largely uniform judgments recognition and enforcement framework in place between a number of European States, referred to in this book as the 'Brussels Model'. From a recognition and enforcement perspective, the chief success of the Brussels Model is in harmonising the laws of signatory States, so that each State, at least with respect to other signatory States, provides straightforward and expeditious recognition and enforcement of judgments. Chapter 4 analyses the Commonwealth-driven approach to reciprocal recognition and enforcement, referred to in this book as the 'Commonwealth Model'. At its core, the Commonwealth Model is a statutory judgment registration system that is premised upon British dominion, seconded, only where historical ties (but not dominion) extend, by reciprocity. Because this approach substantially replicates or relies for efficacy on its common law underpinnings, Chapter 4 includes an analysis of these underlying common law foundations and approaches to recognition and enforcement.

After having analysed each approach in context, Chapter 5 sets out a functional comparative analysis. In this way, the recognition and enforcement approaches surveyed can be isolated from the context-specific domains and concerns that gave rise to them. This formalisation of comparison highlights doctrinal convergence and the increasing transnationalisation of recognition and enforcement. At first glance, the degree of convergence is somewhat surprising given that each approach is grounded in a different underlying legal instrument, separated in time by many decades, epistemologically constituted by different international actors and stakeholders, and overseen or developed by different governmental or intergovernmental organisations and, arguably, aimed at differing goals. However, read together with the historical and contextual analysis in the earlier chapters of this part, a shared core of recognition and enforcement practice can be distilled and compared. Doing so also offers an initial basis from which to analyse the future of recognition and enforcement – in terms of anticipating how existing approaches are likely to be interpreted or applied but also with respect to ways in which such approaches may develop or evolve over time.

1.3.3 Part II: The Future of Recognition and Enforcement

Building on the comparative analysis in Part I, in Part II I consider the future of recognition and enforcement. I explore this potential in two ways, in Chapter 6 and 7, respectively.

Chapter 6 commences by exploring the extent to which recognition and enforcement approaches are likely to inform each other over time. It does so by analysing the differences in legal tradition and approaches across States that have, historically, been seen as impediments to agreeing to a harmonised global framework promoting recognition and enforcement. While this argument has less resonance now that global judgments instruments have been formally adopted, it can still be generalised to suggest that these differences may inhibit the uptake of these instruments in and by national legislatures. To determine whether this is likely to be the case, I analyse the experience of the New York Convention (with respect to arbitral awards) and the Brussels Model (with respect to judgments) in overcoming perceived hurdles expressed to arise due to differences in legal tradition and approach (e.g. between civil and common law traditions).

The second factor analysed in Chapter 6 is whether divergent rationales underlying recognition and enforcement limit the extent to which experiences or lessons learnt in one approach may fruitfully extend to others. This inquiry arises given the functional and doctrinal similarities observed in Part I, in the context of recurring suggestions that experience from other transnational recognition and enforcement approaches may have either no, or limited, applicability beyond their own domains. For example, the suggestion that the New York Convention experience in relation to arbitral award recognition and enforcement is not extensible to judgment recognition and enforcement, or that regional approaches (such as the Brussels or Commonwealth Models) are not extensible to global approaches due to some unique conception of 'trust' in sovereign relationships.

Chapter 7 takes a broader perspective by considering how legal development or evolution occurs, or might occur, across each of the recognition and enforcement approaches studied in this book. To do so, I first compare and contrast the 'internal' measures that can be used to facilitate legal development. That is, features within the recognition and enforcement architecture itself that encourage or oblige autonomous interpretation or uniformity or are used to manage any divergences in interpretation and application. The desire to include such features permeates efforts to agree on harmonised recognition and enforcement, to navigate a constant and pervasive tension between specificity and flexibility: that is, fully setting out in advance the categories of foreign decisions that will be either given or refused recognition and enforcement, or allowing a degree of elasticity based upon more flexible rules. Underlying this concern is that even if consensus on achieving a high degree of specificity via strong prescriptive rules could be reached, there remains the risk of an inherent lack of uniformity presented by potentially divergent national application of international rules.

I next consider the likelihood of 'external' legal development or 'evolution'. The potential for such development turns in large part upon the underlying legal architecture utilised: in the Commonwealth Model (a reciprocal statutory regime), the Brussels Model (now predominantly the product of EU Regulations) and the 'global' instruments (treaty models requiring domestic implementation). The major focus in this section is on developments in the Brussels Model, as both the instruments in this model and the surrounding institutional frameworks surrounding European integration have undergone the most significant developments since their original formulation (compared to any other recognition and enforcement approach). At the same time, difficulties in formally 'modernising' other approaches, such as the New York Convention, stand as a counterpoint. Indeed, the legal architecture selected in global instruments – a 'minimum standards' (or 'open') approach that broadly allows implementing States to recognise and enforce decisions that fall outside of instrumental obligations – can be seen as responding to concerns with respect to legal development. This is because such recourse to domestic law can allow recognition and enforcement to evolve beyond the instrumental minimums without the need for revising the underlying treaty architecture.

The findings in each of these chapters, in addition to shared features outlined in Part I, reinforce my claim that there is an increasing 'transnationalisation' of recognition and enforcement. Understanding this allows us to draw some new insights into the way in which recognition and enforcement frameworks can be understood, interpreted and applied. This is particularly important given the incipient status of recent international instruments to promote judgments recognition and enforcement. It also assists in exploring emerging concerns about the perceived dominance of arbitration; based, in large part, upon the perception of an unwarranted 'enforcement gap' between judgments and awards in commercial disputes. The conclusion also looks to the future: considering shared experience to discern how recognition and enforcement approaches might come to be modified or develop to meet changing commercial and legal practice. The book thus offers a more fulsome comparison of recognition and enforcement approaches, cutting across a variety of discrete fields of inquiry that are traditionally isolated and constituted by divergent epistemological communities surrounding discrete legal regimes.

1.3.4 *Scope, Exclusions from Scope and Terminology Used*

Before commencing the discussion, it is necessary to clarify the precise scope of this book and some matters of terminology that arise.

The scope of this book is confined to approaches to recognition and enforcement, as developed in the respective transnational and 'international' approaches and instruments set out in Part I. It does not consider any other aspects of private international law, except to the extent to which attempts to regulate jurisdiction have been conjoined with attempts to promote recognition and enforcement internationally.[72] Additionally, this book considers the interactions between domestic and international processes, and the likely lessons from a transnational perspective; it does not, however, extend to a consideration of the direct reception of international rules into any specific enforcing State (or the context of any receiving State). Where individual State practices are highlighted, they are used as an exemplar of the way in which international approaches have been, or are likely to be, implemented or to highlight the rationales underlying such approaches, rather than as an exhaustive exposition of national law practice.[73]

A further limitation on scope is also placed as this book extends only to a consideration of 'final and conclusive' decisions between private parties in civil and commercial matters. That is, foreign decisions that have the *res judicata* effect and are no longer subject to appeal in the State of origin.[74] This means that this book does not consider, for example, issues arising due to the grant of preliminary or interim measures of protection;[75] decisions that otherwise could be primarily classified as a form of 'civil' administration or

[72] This is explored in its comparative context at Section 5.5, and it is analysed in terms of the lessons that it may offer for the 'decoupling' of jurisdiction from recognition and enforcement at Section 8.2.2.

[73] See, for example, the use of the United States as an exemplar of common law practice at Section 4.3.2.

[74] As noted by Clermont, although the precise point of finality differs across jurisdictions, 'all systems of justice deploy a core of *res judicata* that forbids routinely undoing the judgment itself': Clermont (n 15) 1069.

[75] See, further, in the context of arbitration and litigation, respectively: T. Kojovic, 'Court Enforcement of Arbitral Decisions on Provisional Relief-How Final is Provisional?' (2001) 18 *Journal of International Arbitration* 511; George A. Bermann, 'Provisional Relief in Transnational Litigation' (1997) 35 *Columbia Journal of Transnational Law* 553.

status, such as the enforcement of judgments in family law matters (including custody and matrimony);[76] the role and use of concepts such as State immunity;[77] or the use of mediated settlement agreements.[78] Additionally, for clarity, I note that although this book is written in the context of arbitral dominance as a transnational dispute resolution mechanism, it is in no way intended as an analysis of the relative merits of litigation or arbitration as a form of transnational dispute resolution.

Further, this book is confined to considering formal legal sanctions and the role that enforcing courts play in determining legal rights and obligations from a practical perspective. This is so, even though strict reference to formal legal approaches to recognition and enforcement does not represent the complete picture: many disputants comply voluntarily with foreign decisions due to a host of informal sanctions, including potential reputational costs; loss of opportunities to deal productively with other members of the 'communal network'; denial of access to knowledge of other members within this network; black listing; less favourable terms and conditions of trade; and, ultimately, exclusion.[79] In a recognition and enforcement context, it has been made clear that informal sanctions are utilised on a regular basis. For example, disputants regularly comply with arbitral awards voluntarily[80] – and it is argued the same likely holds true for international litigation.[81] At the same time, formal sanctions continue to play a role even in situations of voluntary compliance, as the degree of 'voluntary' compliance is also influenced by the enforcement prospects a judgment or award debtor faces. That is, a rational judgment or award debtor operating under the 'shadow of the law' is likely to comply if they

76 Matters such as these are usually excluded from the scope of transnational recognition and enforcement approaches, primarily as they are handled by different transnational instruments: see Section 5.3.1.

77 See, for an overview of State immunity concerns and recognition and enforcement in the context of international commercial arbitration, Hazel Fox, 'State Immunity and Enforcement of Arbitral Awards: Do We Need an UNCITRAL Model Law Mark II for Execution against State Property?' (1996) 12 *Arbitration International* 89.

78 As now covered by the United Nations Convention on International Settlement Agreements Resulting from Mediation (entered into force 12 September 2020). Note that under Art 1(3) this Convention does *not* apply to settlement agreements that have been recorded or approved and are enforceable as either a judgment or an arbitral award.

79 See, for an overview of literature discussing non-legal (or 'social' sanctions): Roger Cotterrell, 'What Is Transnational Law?' (2012) 37 *Law & Social Inquiry* 500, 520–21.

80 See, for example, Craig, who, reviewing the status of arbitration in 2015, notes that the 'vast majority' of arbitral disputes are resolved without any judicial recourse (including recourse to enforcement) whatsoever: Craig (n 10) 705.

81 Reyes (n 12) 342.

face a formal legal sanction that is likely to be adverse.[82] The corollary is that if recognition and enforcement is not readily forthcoming, voluntary compliance with a foreign decision may not occur as frequently. This may have the consequence of negatively impacting the perceived utility or attractiveness of dispute mechanisms, and, taken to its extreme, may limit the overall incidence of international trade.

Having clarified the scope of this book, it is now useful to clarify some terminology used. First, the body that renders the original decision – not the decision about whether to recognise and enforce that decision – can either be an arbitral tribunal or a court. Collectively, they are referred to as the 'rendering' or 'original' fora, and the state in which they are based is referred to as the 'rendering State' or the 'State of origin'. Where a court is involved, it is referred to in this book as the 'rendering' or 'original' court; by contrast, if the body that renders the original decision is a product of arbitration it is instead referred to as the 'tribunal'. Second, the court tasked with recognition and enforcement – of either a judgment or arbitral award – is termed the 'enforcing court'. Unless otherwise specified, 'enforcing court' refers to both recognition and enforcement, and the term 'enforcement' alone also encompasses recognition. Third, the products of both these bodies are referred to as 'decisions' in this book. Fourth, this book focuses on and utilises the term 'foreign' to refer to decisions that come for recognition and enforcement in an enforcing court in another jurisdiction: 'foreign judgments' and 'foreign awards', respectively. Importantly, this conception of 'foreign' relates only to international matters and does not include a judgment given in another province, local State or territory that fall within the same country.[83]

Finally, I turn to define the most important terms in this book: 'recognition' and 'enforcement', and the related concepts of *res judicata*, execution and *exequatur*. Modelling the language of modern instruments, throughout the book the combined term 'recognition and enforcement' is used. However, these two terms are distinct: a decision may be recognised without being

82 See generally, for the idea of bargaining in the shadow of the law, the seminal work of Robert Cooter and Others, 'Bargaining in the Shadow of the Law: A Testable Model of Strategic Behavior' [1982] *Journal of Legal Studies* 225. As Whytock suggests, transnational disputants operate in the shadow of transnational law – including with respect to recognition and enforcement: Christopher Whytock, 'Litigation, Arbitration, and the Transnational Shadow of Law' (2008) 18 *Duke Journal of Comparative & International Law* 449.

83 That is because different policy considerations are likely to apply to inter-country enforcement practices: see, for example, Ho (n 16) 443 (at footnote 2).

enforced, but to enforce a decision it must be recognised (often implicitly).[84] Recognition in this context refers to the process whereby a foreign decision is given 'the same effect that it has in the state where it was rendered with respect to the parties, the subject matter of the action and the issues involved'.[85] The kinds of decisions that are available to be recognised are those with *res judicata* effect – that is, decisions that are final and binding. This precise point differs across legal systems. As Nygh and Pocar note:[86]

> In the common law *res judicata* arises when a final judgment is given on the issues between the parties which cannot be reconsidered by the same court in ordinary proceedings, even though the decision may potentially or actually be the subject of appeal to a higher court. An English or United States court will apply this definition not only to its own judgments, but also to foreign judgments whatever the effect of that judgment may be under its own law. In contrast, many, if not most, civil law systems take the view that a judgment does not have the status of *res judicata* or '*autorité de chose jugée*' until the decision is no longer subject to ordinary forms of review.

Recognition can be useful in its own right – without enforcement – as it can serve as a defensive process through the operation of *res judicata*, allowing for some sort of claim preclusion such as issue estoppel. This ensures the finality of the foreign decision by preventing the re-ventilation of matters already dealt with in the original decision. By contrast, enforcement focuses on the procedures employed by the enforcing court to generate consequence: invoking the powers of the court to ensure compliance with the foreign decision. In many States – particularly civilian law States – enforcement requires an additional preliminary stage whereby the party seeking recognition and enforcement must first obtain *exequatur*: a declaration of enforceability from the enforcing court.[87] With this in hand, legal procedures for enforcement can occur. There is some argument about linguistic overlap between enforcement and

[84] See, for an overview of the differences from the perspective of international commercial arbitration, Blackaby and Others (n 20) [11.19]–[11.23].

[85] Peter Nygh and Fausto Pocar, 'Report by Peter Nygh & Fausto Pocar (Annexed to the 1999 Preliminary Draft Convention)' (Report, August 2000) citing the Restatement (Second) Conflict of Laws.

[86] ibid. 103. This term and others referred to in this section are explored in the context of the final 2019 Convention in Francisco Garcimartín and Geneviève Saumier, 'Explanatory Report on the HCCH 2019 Judgments Convention' [2020] 79–80.

[87] This two stage approach was, until removed in the 2012 Brussels Regulation, a necessary part of seeking enforcement under the Brussels Model: see, further, Section 3.1.5.

execution, but, briefly stated, execution can be seen as a subset of enforcement referring to the formal process by which enforcement is given effect.[88]

With these concepts defined let us commence by exploring the emergence of modern transnational or 'global' recognition and enforcement frameworks.

[88] The concept of execution being a subset of enforcement and distinct from recognition is perhaps most practically relevant in the context of sovereign immunity from *execution*. See, further, *Kingdom of Spain* v. *Infrastructure Services Luxembourg Sàrl* (2021) 387 ALR 22, where the Court concluded proceedings were only for recognition and, thus, were not protected by sovereign immunity that protects against execution.

PART I

Transnational Recognition and Enforcement

A Doctrinal and Comparative Analysis

In this Part, I set out the key transnational approaches to recognition and enforcement. Chapter 2 commences by considering the 'global' approaches with respect to both arbitral awards and foreign judgments. Chapters 3 and 4, respectively, focus on exploring 'regional' or 'international' approaches to foreign judgments: the Brussels Model, and the Commonwealth Model approach, respectively. This exercise represents an interesting counterpoint, as such an exploration requires a consideration – albeit in a limited fashion – of the primary domestic drivers underpinning each approach. Each of these approaches is considered in a thematic comparative fashion in Chapter 5 based upon the key features identified in the preceding chapters.

2

'Global' Recognition and Enforcement Approaches

This chapter analyses the key 'global' multilateral instruments that attempt to provide for and promote a harmonised and pro-recognition and enforcement approach to foreign decisions. While they are contained in a range of discrete instruments, these approaches are premised on the same idea: assisting in moving recognition and enforcement approaches towards foreign decisions to a more favourable, certain or predictable footing on an international level. This chapter first sets out the emerging transnational recognition and enforcement practice in the field of international litigation (and its product: judgments), before analysing long-standing practice in the field of international commercial arbitration (arbitral awards). First, with respect to foreign judgments, there are two key transnational recognition and enforcement instruments. However, as Section 2.1.1 explores, the legal ordering surrounding these instruments is not yet determinatively settled: the 2019 Convention has not yet entered force, and the 2005 Convention has not yet made a significant impact on recognition and enforcement given its limited scope (applying only to parties that select a rendering court exclusively) and limited practical experience (having only come into force in 2015).

Second, and by contrast, this chapter analyses the recognition and enforcement of foreign international commercial arbitral awards. This approach centres on one key instrument widely lauded for its global reach: the 1958 New York Convention.[1] Because of its wide global acceptance,[2] and over six decades of application and interpretation in and across hundreds of enforcing courts, the New York Convention approach underpins the approach of most enforcing courts around the globe towards arbitral awards. This allows it to serve as the 'backbone' of the international arbitral award recognition and enforcement regime and supports international commercial arbitration more generally by allowing for greater and more predictable recognition and enforcement outcomes.[3] The New York Convention is also supplemented by other transnational instruments, such as the UNCITRAL Model Law: which has over thirty State parties, who are also signatories to the New York Convention, that have adopted it either in part or in whole.[4] As with the recognition and enforcement experience for foreign judgments, there is also a range of bilateral agreements and regional agreements – many of which predate the New York Convention – that also serve to promote recognition and enforcement; however, it is not necessary to elaborate further on the recognition and enforcement provisions of these instruments as they by and large model the approach of the Convention and have limited reach or little 'practical relevance' given the widespread adoption of the Convention.[5] Thus, the Convention allows – at least in theory – arbitral awards to face

1 'United Nations Convention on the Recognition and Enforcement of Foreign Arbitral Awards' (7 June 1959) vol 330 ('New York Convention').

2 At present count, 157 Contracting parties: *See Status of the Convention on the Recognition and Enforcement of Foreign Arbitral Awards (New York, 1958)*, available at <www.uncitral.org/uncitral/en/uncitral_texts/arbitration/NYConvention_status.html> (accessed 20 September 2016). This degree of international acceptance makes it one of the most successful international treaties in the general field of commercial law.

3 Julian D. M. Lew and others, *Comparative International Commercial Arbitration* (Kluwer Law International 2003) [26-20].

4 This Model Law explicitly seeks to harmonise and further liberalise recognition and enforcement approaches of enforcing courts in a manner consistent with the New York Convention: Arts 35 & 36, United Nations Commission on International Trade Law, 'Model Law on International Commercial Arbitration (with Amendments as Adopted in 2006)' (1985) (the 'Model Law').

5 Karl-Heinz Bockstiegel, 'Summary of Discussion in the Third Working Group' in Albert Jan van den Berg (ed.), *Improving the Efficiency of Arbitration Agreements and Awards: 40 Years of Application of the New York Convention* (KluwerArbitration, Kluwer Law International 1999) 433.

enforcement prospects much greater than those presently available for foreign judgments globally.[6] For these reasons, rather than exploring the history of the New York Convention's approach, in this chapter I focus on the practical experience of the Convention, with a view to setting out how this approach may inform our understanding of other global approaches. I turn first to set out approaches to judgments recognition and enforcement before returning to a consideration of the approach to foreign awards.

2.1 JUDGMENTS RECOGNITION AND ENFORCEMENT

Modern efforts to harmonise judgments recognition and enforcement have been ongoing since the mid-twentieth century, under the auspices of the Hague Conference on Private International Law (the 'Hague Conference').[7] The Hague Conference's primary mandate is to harmonise rules of private international law,[8] stemming from the idea that:[9]

> the Earth is one, but the world is not: it is divided in innumerable legal systems of private law, much more than there are States ... All these problems arise because the world is still a patchwork of legal systems and, with increasing mobility and communication the number of people, families and companies that are faced with these problems is increasing exponentially.

The Hague Conference's conception of legal jurisdictions acting as a 'patchwork' reflects concerns, discussed in Chapter 1, that recognition and

6 The remainder of this chapter outlines the global efforts with respect to developing and promoting global instruments to promote the recognition and enforcement of foreign judgments.

7 The Hague Conference is a member-driven intergovernmental organisation that has no mandatory authority and is funded primarily by its Member States: Statute of the Hague Conference on Private International Law (entered into force on 15 July 1955) (US), Arts 9–11. See, for a recent exposition of the Hague Conference's approach to unifying private international law: Jan von Hein, 'The Role of the HCCH in Shaping Private International Law' in Thomas John and others (eds.), *The Elgar Companion to the Hague Conference on Private International Law* (Elgar Companions to International Organisations Series, Edward Elgar Publishing 2020).

8 This goal is now codified in the Hague Conference's formal legal structure: Statute of the Hague Conference on Private International Law (entered into force on 15 July 1955), Art 1. The concept of private international law, in a broad sense, extends beyond solely conflict of laws rules but also extends to the coordination, harmonisation and unification of laws: Alejandro M. Garro, 'Unification and Harmonization of Private Law in Latin America' (1992) 40 *The American Journal of Comparative Law* 587, 587.

9 Hans Van Loon, 'The Hague Conference on Private International Law: Current Problems and Perspectives' in *Cursos de Derecho Internacionaly Relaciones Internacionales de Vitoria–Gasteiz (Courses on International Law and International Relations at Vitoria–Gasteiz)* (Universidad del País Vasco (University of the Basque Country), 1983) vol 3, 17, 22.

enforcement problems may lead to unnecessary uncertainty and expense for private disputants. For these reasons, efforts to regulate aspects of private international law – including the recognition and enforcement of foreign judgments – continue to make up a key component of the Hague Conference's agenda. To this end, and somewhat unusually for an intergovernmental organisation, the Hague Conference pursues a 'legislative' agenda (albeit solely at the instigation of – and by the cooperation and voluntary agreement of – its members).[10] These legislative efforts in terms of recognition and enforcement were until the conclusion of the 2019 Convention commonly referred to as the 'Judgments Project'.

The Judgments Project's ultimate aim was to create a broad treaty-based recognition and enforcement framework to be readily implemented in Contracting States. This approach depends upon a starting presumption of enforceability of foreign judgments coupled with severely curtailing the enforcing court's ability to review either the jurisdiction of the rendering court or the merits of the original decision. Implicit in this approach are in-built exceptions on predominantly 'procedural fairness' ('natural justice') grounds, including a limited public policy defence. Consequently, the decision by an enforcing court to give effect to a foreign judgment suggests only that the enforcing court is satisfied with the fairness and impartiality of the adjudicative process of the original dispute heard in the rendering court. It does not represent an adoption nor represent a re-review of the merits of the original dispute. As Chapter 5 explores further, this presumption and limited exception approach is shared with many other transnational recognition and enforcement approaches. To better understand the nature of judgments recognition and enforcement, I first set out a brief history of these modern efforts before considering their final treaty form.

2.1.1 *Towards 'Global' Transnational Recognition and Enforcement*

This section sets out a brief historical overview of the Judgments Project[11] in a bid to provide context to the two key Hague Conference instruments that now

[10] Hans Van Loon, 'The Hague Conference on Private International Law' (2007) 2 *Hague Justice Journal* 3, 3. See, for an overview of the way that the 'three sisters' of private law harmonisation – the Hague Conference, UNIDROIT and UNCITRAL – operate and intersect: William Brydie-Watson, 'The Three Sisters of Private International Law: An Increasingly Co-operative Family Rather than Sibling Rivals' in Thomas John and others (eds.), *The Elgar Companion to the Hague Conference on Private International Law* (Elgar Companions to International Organisations Series, Edward Elgar Publishing 2020).

[11] For an early history (from approximately the mid-nineteenth century until the 1970s), see: Kurt Nadelmann, 'Multilateral Conventions in the Conflicts Field: An Historical Sketch' (1972) 19

attempt to promote and harmonise the recognition and enforcement of foreign judgments. Before commencing, and as will be apparent shortly, it assists to note that the Judgments Project approach was expressly modelled upon and intended to align with the approach that has been in operation for many years in the recognition and enforcement of arbitral awards (discussed further in the second half of this chapter) and the judgment enforcement architecture under the Brussels Model (discussed in Chapter 3). Additionally, the Judgments Project also sought the ambitious aims of reconciling the divides – if any – between civil and common law approaches to recognition and enforcement, for example as embodied in the common law underlying the Commonwealth Model (see Chapter 4) – which overlaps with similar legal harmonisation efforts seen in the Brussels Model (see Chapter 3).

In summary, work on the Judgments Project can be divided into four logically distinct periods. The first period, from the mid-1960s until 1992, relates to the early efforts to synthesise and consolidate recognition and enforcement norms from a range of Hague Conference Member States, to form the body of the legal rules in any legal instrument. As part of this process, a range of legal instruments were produced and opened for signature, but some never became operational and others were not widely adopted. Drawing inspiration from these unsuccessful instruments, the second period canvassed, 1992–2001, reflects the then renewed push of Hague Conference Member States to develop legal rules on recognition and enforcement, again in the form of a 'global' convention but this time in a form that aimed to regulate both direct and indirect jurisdiction. This work ultimately did not reach consensus on a suitable instrument, yet primary emphasis is placed on it in this section, as the subsequent agreement on the 2019 Convention drew heavily on the lessons learnt in these attempts. The third period, 2001–2005, saw a repurposing of this earlier unsuccessful work into a narrower convention than originally sought: the 2005 Convention.[12] This convention applies only where parties have exclusively chosen a court to hear their dispute, and has been slow to attract signatories. Between 2005 and 2010 efforts stalled, and little work was undertaken. The final time period considered, 2010–2019, saw

Netherlands International Law Review 107. For a more recent review of the background and history to the 2005 *Convention* and the 2010 'revived' judgments project see, respectively: Paul Beaumont, 'Hague Choice of Court Agreements Convention 2005 Hague: Background, Negotiations, Analysis and Current Status' (2009) *Journal of Private International Law* 125; Paul Beaumont, 'The Revived Judgments Project in The Hague' (2014) 4 *Nederlands Internationaal Privaatrecht* 532.

[12] Hague Conference, 'Convention on Choice of Court Agreements' (1 October 2015) ('Choice of Court Convention' or '2005 Convention').

the resumption and completion of the legislative mandate of the Hague Conference in the Judgments Project. I turn now to consider each stage of the Judgments Project in turn.

2.1.1.1 Pre-1992: Early Attempts to Create a Judgments Convention

Despite conflicts problems in commercial matters being given 'primary attention' in the mid-twentieth century,[13] the first tranche of multilateral conventions attempting to govern recognition and enforcement proved unsuccessful or had only limited success. For example, the Hague Conference 'Convention of 15 April 1958 on the Jurisdiction of the Selected Forum in the Case of International Sales of Goods' never received any ratifications or acceptances.[14] Despite this lack of success in terms of international instruments, Nadelmann noted that the early efforts of the Hague Conference in the mid-twentieth century – whilst not widely acceded to or ratified, and in some cases never coming in to force – can still be called 'successful' as 'ratification is not all that matters ... [i]ndirect effects must also be taken into account', including academic citations and the texts acting as a spur and prompt for discussion, as well as their role in assisting with and shaping regional and national approaches.[15]

While much of the failure in terms of promulgation of an international treaty can potentially be attributed to a diminishing global imperative over time due to developments in regional and bilateral relations between negotiating States,[16] it is also attributable to the way in which early conventions were designed. Early conventions attempted not only to regulate the recognition and enforcement of foreign judgments but, in addition, also took on the ambitious task of attempting to exclusively regulate both direct and indirect

[13] Kurt H. Nadelmann and Willis L. M. Reese, 'The American Proposal at the Hague Conference on Private International Law to Use the Method of Uniform Laws' (1958) 7 *The American Journal of Comparative Law* 239, 239.

[14] See also the Hague Conference, 'Convention on the Choice of Court' (first published 1965), which does not make detailed provision for recognition and enforcement. It never came into force and has only been signed by Israel.

[15] Kurt Nadelmann, 'The United States Join the Hague Conference on Private International Law' in Kurt Nadelmann (ed.), *Conflicts of Law: International and Interstate: Selected Essays* (Martinus Nijhoff Publishers 1972) 130.

[16] For example, the Hague Conference, 'Convention of 15 April 1958 on the Jurisdiction of the Selected Forum in the Case of International Sales of Goods' despite being signed by Austria, Belgium, Germany and Greece, has for a long time been unlikely to enter into force, given that these jurisdictions are all part of the European Union, which now has regulations that relate to the enforcement of judgments within the European Union.

jurisdiction (a 'closed double' convention).[17] Due to this, these conventions sometimes pursued only a very modest scope,[18] and modest aims,[19] and thus do not represent truly broad-based approaches to recognition and enforcement. Nonetheless, the failure of these early conventions as standalone legal instruments was a key part of negotiating States developing a nuanced understanding of what was likely to be politically and legally manageable in the recognition and enforcement realm. This understanding led in turn to the most significant early project in the bid for a broad-based global convention: the 1971 *Hague Convention on the Recognition and Enforcement of Foreign Judgments in Civil and Commercial Matters* (the '1971 Convention').[20]

The 1971 Convention is broadly considered to have been unsuccessful as a legal instrument, despite representing a novel approach to recognition and enforcement.[21] Its novelty, at the time, came from its pursuit of a broad-based approach to judgments recognition and enforcement in an 'open' or non-

[17] These terms – and the precise mix of features that have been employed across transnational recognition and enforcement instruments and approaches – are discussed further from a comparative perspective at Section 5.5.

[18] For example, regulating only limited subject matters or limited jurisdictional bases. A primary example is the Hague Conference, 'Convention of 15 April 1958 on the Jurisdiction of the Selected Forum in the Case of International Sales of Goods' (n 104), which was opened for signature but never went in to force. It applies only to the international sales of goods (Art. 1) and provides only for enforcement of judicial decisions rendered on two jurisdictional bases: pursuant to an exclusive choice of court (Art. 2) or appearance (Art. 3). This Convention was drawn up only in French, but a translation of a draft of the Convention can be found in 'Draft Convention on the Jurisdiction of the Selected Forum in the Case of International Sales of Goods' (1956) 5 *The American Journal of Comparative Law* 653.

[19] See, for example, Hague Conference, 'Convention on the Choice of Court' (first published 1965). Although broader than its predecessor in scope (not limited to the international sale of goods), it again only applies to setting the recognition and enforcement practices under the convention merely to the general enforcement rules of the enforcing State

[20] Hague Conference, 'Convention on the Recognition and Enforcement of Foreign Judgments in Civil and Commercial Matters' (1 February 1971) ('1971 Convention') and its accompanying Hague Conference, 'Supplementary Protocol of 1 February 1971 to the Hague Convention on the Recognition and Enforcement of Foreign Judgments in Civil and Commercial Matters' (1 February 1971) were formulated in 1966 but opened for signature in 1971.

[21] Hague Conference, 'Some Reflections of the Permanent Bureau on a General Convention on Enforcement of Judgments' (Preliminary Document, May 1992), 231. Despite the Convention's lack of success as an international instrument, it has been utilised in continuing efforts to develop judgments instruments. For example, the Brussels Regulation was 'greatly influenced' by work on the 1971 Convention, and adopted certain legal developments from the Convention, including the use of a list of excluded jurisdictional bases: Peter Nygh and Fausto Pocar, 'Report by Peter Nygh and Fausto Pocar (Annexed to the 1999 Preliminary Draft Convention)', 29. Consequently, the Regulation built 'to a large extent' on the 1971 Convention and was also 'negotiated in parts by the same persons': Hague Conference, 'Some Reflections of the Permanent Bureau on a General Convention on Enforcement of Judgments' (Preliminary Document, May 1992), 231.

exhaustive fashion (leaving residual recourse to national law). A second novelty was the Convention's 'single' nature, meaning that it focused solely on regulating the recognition and enforcement of foreign judgments,[22] in no way attempting to (directly) regulate the rendering court's jurisdiction. Although these instrumental design decisions – 'open' versus 'exhaustive' or 'closed'; and 'single' versus 'double' – are explored in more detail in a comparative fashion at Sections 5.4–5.6, it is useful to briefly set them out here to explore their role in negotiations towards the Judgments Project. Briefly: double, in this context, refers to the convention setting out not only rules harmonising and promoting recognition and enforcement in enforcing courts but also attempting to harmonise jurisdictional requirements in rendering courts (direct jurisdiction); single refers to a convention regulating only recognition and enforcement. A closed or exhaustive approach, as distinct from an open or inclusive approach, means that the convention aims to comprehensively map all categories of when recognition and enforcement will be granted – or denied. It leaves no residual discretion to enforcing courts.

As we will see shortly, these novelties became very important in the context of developing what eventually became the 2019 Convention. Notably, this combination of an open and single design also places the 1971 Convention closer to the more permissive open form of the 2005 Convention and the New York Convention, rather than the exhaustive Brussels Model approach (as discussed at Section 5.5). Yet, despite technically coming into force,[23] the 1971 Convention never became fully operational as no required bilateral agreements have been entered into to make the treaty operational.[24] The

[22] It does so by requiring recognition and enforcement (Art. 4) if the original judgment was rendered under certain enumerated jurisdictional bases (set out in Art. 10), subject only to certain discretionary procedural exceptions (Art. 5). The Hague Conference, '1971 Convention Supplementary Protocol' (n 41) sets out further indirect jurisdictional filters, mandatorily excluding from recognition and enforcement judgments rendered under certain jurisdictional bases (Arts. 2, 4). However, any jurisdictional base that is not expressly enumerated remains permitted, that is, not regulated by the Convention, and subject to States' discretion as to whether the enforcing court will recognise and enforce the foreign judgment.

[23] It came into force between Cyprus and the Netherlands (and, soon after, Portugal) where it is now largely displaced by the Brussels Regulations, which mandatorily apply, excluding other treaty obligations 'Regulation (EC) No 44/2001 of 22 December 2000 on Jurisdiction and the Recognition and Enforcement of Judgments in Civil and Commercial Matters' (2001) OJ L 12/1, Art 17 ('Brussels I Regulation'); *Regulation (EU) No 1215/2012 of 12 December 2012 on Jurisdiction and the Recognition and Enforcement of Judgments in Civil and Commercial Matters (Recast) (2012)* Art 15 (*'Brussels 1 Recast'*). New signatories Kuwait (in 2002) and Albania (in 2010) have also acceded to the Convention: 'Status table' of the 1971 Convention, available at <www.hcch.net/index_en.php?act=conventions.status&cid=78> (accessed 13 September 2015).

[24] That is, for the 1971 Convention to apply as between nationals of two States each contracting State must also have gone through a further implementation step of executing bilateral agreements with the other. No two States have done so.

Permanent Bureau of the Hague Conference suggests that this failure is not due to any major problems with the substance of the Convention but arises from weaknesses in the following: its complicated formal structure with a Convention and a separate Protocol;[25] its 'indecisiveness' with twenty-three *optional* items in Article 23 of the Convention; and complexity arising from the need for bilateral agreements to make the Convention (and its Protocol) operational.[26] This suggestion likely has merit, particularly as subsequent political regional developments took much of the impetus from European states acceding to or ratifying the already complex 1971 Convention.[27] This meant that within Europe (which constituted a significant part of the Hague Conference's then membership), particularly a Europe focused upon regional political and economic integration, the importance of a scheme for recognising and enforcing foreign judgments worldwide was diminished. Consequently, progress on a worldwide judgments instrument stalled for more than two decades.

As the next section explores, in 1992 efforts re-commenced to develop a new instrument, drawing in large part on the work undertaken to achieve the 1971 Convention. At that time, the Permanent Bureau indicated that it remained 'strongly convinced' that the substance of the 1971 Convention remained 'essentially valid' and could offer valuable lessons for subsequent efforts to negotiate and develop multilateral instruments.[28] This conviction was – despite a hiatus between 1992–2001 that focused on developing jurisdictional approaches – ultimately reflected in the development of the 2019 Convention's approach, which shares many similarities with the original 1971 Convention approach.

[25] Hague Conference, '1971 Convention Supplementary Protocol' (n 20). There is no sound theoretical reason for separating the two instruments – it was simply because the work on agreeing upon a list of exorbitant jurisdictional grounds was unable to be completed by one diplomatic session and was referred on to a subsequent Special Commission, which drew up the Protocol: Hague Conference, 'Some Reflections of the Permanent Bureau on a General Convention on Enforcement of Judgments' (n 21) 233.

[26] Hague Conference, 'Some Reflections of the Permanent Bureau on a General Convention on Enforcement of Judgments' (n 21), 233. C.f. Michaels, who suggests that the need for bilateral agreements is its 'biggest shortfall': Ralf Michaels, 'Recognition and Enforcement of Foreign Judgments' [2009] *Max Planck Encyclopaedia of Public International Law*, para 15.

[27] The completion in 1968 of the Brussels Convention, naturally 'commanded the allegiance' of the then European (Economic) Community States, and as the Community expanded in Europe, 'the territorial scope and legal significance of the Brussels Convention increased': Arthur von Mehren, 'Recognition and Enforcement of Foreign Judgments: A New Approach for the Hague Conference?' (1994) 57 *Law and Contemporary Problems* 271, 275. This, in combination with the entering into force of the parallel 'Lugano II Convention on Jurisdiction and the Enforcement of Judgments in Civil and Commercial Matters' (21/12/07) (which regulates the recognition and enforcement of judgments between European Member States), created a 'basically uniform' European foreign judgments regime: von Mehren 275.

[28] Hague Conference, 'Some Reflections of the Permanent Bureau on a General Convention on Enforcement of Judgments' (n 21), 233.

2.1.1.2 1992–2001: Broad-Based Judgments Efforts Resume

In 1992, after a two-decade hiatus, efforts to resume work on a new judgments instrument commenced; yet, after a decade of further negotiation, they ultimately proved unsuccessful. The driving force for commencing this work was a proposal of the United States.[29] This proposal highlighted again the 'anomaly' between the wide acceptance of the recognition and enforcement regime of the New York Convention in the arbitral field and, standing in stark contrast, the lack of a global regime for judgments.[30] This concern was singled out in particular as, in its view, the United States adopts a relatively tolerant and accepting approach towards recognising and enforcing foreign judgments,[31] as compared to the way in which judgments of these same courts from the United States are treated internationally.[32] Despite consensus between Member States at the Hague Conference on streamlining and harmonising

[29] See Ronald A. Brand and Paul Herrup, *The 2005 Hague Convention on Choice of Court Agreements: Commentary and Documents* (Cambridge University Press 2008), who date these efforts back to a letter from the United States Department of State to the Hague Conference: 'Letter to Secretary General, Hague Conference' Letter from Edwin Williamson (Legal Adviser, United States Department of State), 5 May 1992 <www.state.gov/documents/organization/65973.pdf>.

[30] This 'uneven' starting basis is particularly galling to the United States because its courts likely already exceed any potential convention requirements for recognising and enforcing foreign judgments. At the same time, however, with little change to its present recognition and enforcement regimes, a successful global instrument offers the United States the potential to realise 'a higher level of reliable expectations' that foreign countries will recognise and enforce foreign judgments of its own courts: Michael Traynor, 'An Introductory Framework for Analyzing the Proposed Hague Convention on Jurisdiction and Foreign Judgments in Civil and Commercial Matters: U.S. and European Perspectives' (2000) 6 *Annual Survey of International & Comparative Law*, 6. Traynor notes, also at 6, that in order to do so 'the United States may have to relinquish some of its present notions on jurisdiction', which are 'questionable' in the international context. This jurisdictional discussion is explored further in Chapter 4.

[31] Yuliya Zeynalova, 'The Law on Recognition and Enforcement of Foreign Judgments: Is It Broken and How Do We Fix It?' (2013) 31 *Berkeley Journal of International Law* 150, 154, describing the general approach in the United States as 'relatively generous' towards recognising and enforcing foreign judgments. Many jurisdictions impose a range of onerous restrictions on recognising and enforcing foreign judgments, including 'jurisdiction tests, requirements for reciprocity, choice of law tests, *revision au fond* [the conclusiveness of foreign judgments]': Hague Conference, 'Some Reflections of the Permanent Bureau on a General Convention on Enforcement of Judgments' (n 21), 231.

[32] Zeynalova (n 31) 151 noted that: '[e]nforcing U.S. court judgments abroad can prove especially difficult in light of divergent rules on jurisdiction, requirements for special service of process, reciprocity, and some foreign countries' public policy concerns over enforcing American jury awards carrying hefty punitive damages.' The American Bar Association also noted that the absence of a multilateral convention has 'often resulted in confusion, delay and financial hardship for holders of US judgments': American Bar Association, 'General Information Form 109A: Report' (11 December 1992) 1.

these practices, some negotiating parties were initially concerned with rules compelling enforcement of foreign judgments that they perceived to be exorbitant in some way. Consequently, years were spent negotiating around whether – and how best – to address these concerns.

Over the next decade, legal and diplomatic work continued in earnest to respond to these concerns and develop options that could lead to a suitable convention for all interested Member States at the Hague Conference.[33] Cognisant of outstanding issues with the 1971 Convention, and regional developments since then,[34] it was anticipated that any new instrument would depart from the 1971 Convention's sole focus on recognition and enforcement. To be successful, it was envisaged, it would instead aim to regulate the jurisdiction of the rendering court as well as recognition and enforcement, and it would do so in an exhaustive fashion. These two design decisions coupled with issues in the underlying doctrinal approach of the Convention led to some significant hurdles. Nygh identifies these latter doctrinal hurdles as arising in three key areas of concern:[35] exorbitant jurisdiction; the 'uneven' way judgments are treated globally absent a convention; and exorbitant damages.

Cognisant of these concerns, the initial Working Group tasked with developing the Judgments Project indicated that it would be 'overly ambitious in the context of the broad Hague Conference membership' to attempt to

[33] After receiving the proposal, and subsequent preparatory work, the Permanent Bureau indicated it saw three options for future progress (Hague Conference, 'Some Reflections of the Permanent Bureau on a General Convention on Enforcement of Judgments' (n 21) 235–36): (1) acceding to the 'Lugano II' (n 27); (2) becoming parties to the 1971 Hague Convention; or, (3) negotiating, and becoming parties to, a new judgments convention. The third option was immediately favoured, and subsequently pursued, due to issues with the 1971 Convention, and the difficulty in adapting the Lugano Convention to meet the needs of a broad-based global judgments instrument: Hague Conference, 'Some Reflections of the Permanent Bureau on a General Convention on Enforcement of Judgments' (n 21) 233 ([10]). See also Hague Conference, 'Conclusions of the Special Commission of June 1992 on General Affairs and Policy of the Conference' (Preliminary Document, August 1992) 253; Hague Conference, '17th Session: Final Act' (29 May 1993) Part B, No 2, 17.

[34] The Brussels and Lugano Conventions were, at the time, the most advanced modern instruments regulating the recognition and enforcement of foreign judgments: See Hague Conference, 'Interim Text: Summary of the Outcome of the Discussion in Commission II of the First Part of the Diplomatic Conference 6 – 20 June 2001' (Diplomatic Conference (6–20 June 2001), Commission II: Jurisdiction and Foreign Judgments in Civil and Commercial Matters, 2001) ch II–III. See also Traynor (n 30).

[35] Peter Nygh, 'Towards a Global Judgments Convention: The Proposed New Hague Convention on the Recognition and Enforcement of Judgments in Civil and Commercial Matters' (1997) 7 *Australian International Law Journal* 96, 97–101. Each of these are considered at Section 6.1.2.

pursue a convention that was both double and exhaustive.[36] This was because it foresaw difficulties in extrapolating an approach that had worked well regionally to the 'global' transnational level: namely, requiring the rendering court to assume jurisdiction on the grounds specified in the convention, and to require the enforcing court to forego examining the rendering court's exercise of jurisdiction, even if based on an 'exorbitant' ground.[37] This concern was echoed by the Permanent Bureau, which in a prescient move indicated it was 'initially sceptical'[38] about the prospects of trying to pursue a double convention (and in so doing to attempt to harmonise rules relating to jurisdiction).[39] It foresaw the very real risk that European States pursuing a double convention would attempt to 'stick as closely as possible' to legal instruments they were already familiar with rather than developing a solution that would allow or encourage broader geographical adoption.[40] Nonetheless, a majority of Member States pushed for the Hague Conference to pursue a double convention, regulating both direct and indirect jurisdiction, that also comprehensively and exhaustively set out both required and excluded grounds of jurisdiction.[41]

The push to pursue a closed double convention was based on its potentially 'great advantages' compared to a single convention like the 1971 Convention.[42] The major impetus for pursuing a double convention structure was the desire of a majority of States to avoid any convention obligations compelling them as potential signatories to navigate and follow 'confusing' jurisdictional approaches of countries such as the United States, which a single convention may have done.[43] This was because of the very real concern that a single convention, skirting over potentially controversial jurisdictional bases, would lead to a state of affairs where there would have to be mandated recognition and enforcement of foreign judgments made on 'exorbitant' grounds.[44] Thus, primarily at the behest of the up-to-then 'reluctant' European participants,

[36] The Hague Conference, 'Conclusions of the Working Group Meeting on Enforcement of Judgments' (Preliminary Document, November 1992) para 5.

[37] As the Permanent Bureau in 'Conclusions of the Working Group Meeting on Enforcement of Judgments' (n 36), noted at fn 1, this was largely the rule of the Brussels and the Lugano Conventions (see Article 28 of both Conventions).

[38] Beaumont, 'The Revived Judgments Project in The Hague' (n 11) 532.

[39] ibid.

[40] ibid.

[41] Robert E. Lutz, *A Lawyer's Handbook for Enforcing Foreign Judgments in the United States and Abroad* (Cambridge University Press 2007) 568.

[42] Nygh (n 35).

[43] Lutz (n 41) 568.

[44] ibid.

rules regulating direct jurisdiction were added to the scope of any convention that was to be negotiated.[45] However, as negotiations progressed, a compromise option of a 'mixed' convention was chosen. The advantage of pursuing a mixed convention was said to be that States could 'proceed on the lowest common denominator as regards prohibited jurisdictions and bases for recognition'.[46] As Nygh noted, at the time there was '[a] fair degree of consensus' as to both, and the mixed convention approach offered a way for countries to 'readily agree' on jurisdictional bases they had in common; and where they could not, they could be left in the 'permitted' category.[47] This was of particular importance as, unlike prior regional conventions, the global judgments approach was not designed for a 'group of contiguous States sharing similar social, economic and political objectives', making it particularly difficult to negotiate the regulation of direct jurisdiction.[48] Nonetheless, the disadvantage of pursuing this mixed convention, in the eyes of some negotiating parties, was that it did not actively restrict the recognition and enforcement of judgments rendered under what they consider to be exorbitant jurisdictional bases, instead leaving them to the discretion of the State enforcing the judgment.

2.1.1.3 1999 Draft: Finally, a Broad-Based Judgments Instrument?

Negotiations along these lines continued until a 1999 preliminary draft convention was produced, adopting what can be described as an 'open' and 'double' design (the '1999 Draft').[49] The 1999 Draft 'closely tracks' the structure and approach of the Brussels Convention[50] by setting out a scheme mandating broad recognition and enforcement of foreign judgments (with limited, mostly natural justice, exceptions), as well as rules of direct jurisdiction prohibiting the rendering court from exercising jurisdiction pursuant to certain excluded jurisdictional bases. This 1999 Draft represented a range of compromises by negotiating states, particularly around the sensitive issue of

45 Hague Conference, '17th Session: Final Act' (n 33) Part B, No 4, 17.
46 Nygh (n 35) 103.
47 ibid.
48 ibid.
49 Hague Conference, 'Preliminary Draft Convention on Jurisdiction and Foreign Judgments in Civil and Commercial Matters' (Preliminary Document, August 2000).
50 European Economic Community, 'Brussels Convention on Jurisdiction and the Enforcement of Judgments in Civil and Commercial Matters' (1 February 1973). Jeffrey Talpis and Nick Krnjevic, 'The Hague Convention on Choice of Court Agreements of June 30, 2005: The Elephant that Gave Birth to a Mouse' (2006) 13 *Southwestern Journal of Law and Trade in the Americas* 1, 3.

the jurisdiction of the rendering court. Its structure and language drew inspiration from regional instruments and the parallel recognition and enforcement framework for arbitral awards under the New York Convention[51] and their apparent and continued successes in promoting greater recognition and enforcement prospects.[52] The way it sought to regulate jurisdictional bases, as required by its 'double' form, was to deem certain jurisdictional bases as 'required' before giving effect to a foreign judgment and to deem others as 'excluded'. The compromise seen in adopting the 'open' structure is in making explicit that bases that are neither required nor excluded are treated as 'permitted', that is, not regulated by the Convention, and remain subject only to national law.[53] At the time of drafting, it was suggested that the 1999 Draft necessarily reflected a 'high degree' of compromise of all State negotiating participants, given the complexity of drafting and agreeing an extensive list of both required and excluded bases of jurisdiction.[54]

On 30 October 1999, the Special Commission of the Hague Conference adopted this Interim Draft Convention. Based on this work, it was agreed that a diplomatic conference – to finalise the adoption of the draft and transform it into an approved convention – would be held in two sessions, in June 2001 and in early 2002. By the time of the first session, most participants had consulted extensively with stakeholders within their own government. However, after the June 2001 session was held there was 'extensive criticism' of the various compromises made by both the European Union (and its Member States) and the United States.[55] While the national representatives who were negotiating the 1999 Draft were acutely aware of the compromise needed, local stakeholders were not. What followed has been described as a 'complete disaster'.[56] Based on the views of internal stakeholders who felt they were disadvantaged or not gaining enough or any advantage, the United States – and to a lesser extent the Member States of the European Union, who at least to some degree were kept in line by the European Union's

[51] 'New York Convention' (n 1).

[52] See, for example, Hague Conference, 'Some Reflections of the Permanent Bureau on a General Convention on Enforcement of Judgments' (n 21), 231.

[53] See, for direct jurisdiction: Arts. 3–13 (required), Art. 18 (excluded) and Art. 17 (permitted); for indirect jurisdiction, see: Art. 25 (required), Art. 26 (excluded) and Art. 24 (permitted) of the Hague Conference, '1999 Preliminary Draft Convention' (n 49).

[54] David Bennett, 'The Hague Convention on Recognition and Enforcement of Foreign Judgments: A Failure of Characterisation' in Talia Einhorn and Kurt Siehr (eds.), *Intercontinental Cooperation Through Private International Law: Essays in Memory of Peter E Nygh* (TMC Asser Press 2004) 20.

[55] ibid.

[56] ibid.

supranational structure – resiled from most of the compromises contained in the 1999 Draft. This result was foreshadowed by a letter from a delegate from the United States to the then Secretary of the Hague Conference, Mr Hans van Loon,[57] indicating that there was little or no prospect of the United States agreeing to a convention in the terms of the 1999 Draft terms. It has since been speculated that this was likely due to the frosty reception that the American delegation to the Hague Conference received from trial lawyers in the United States, as the 1999 Draft did not include within its ambit presumptive recognition and enforcement of jury awards.[58] The failure of negotiations on the 1999 Draft led to a new round of negotiations, resulting in a revised 2001 Draft.[59]

2.1.1.4 2001 Draft: A Regression

The 2001 Draft is widely considered to have been a regression from the 1999 Draft, which served to temporarily stall global efforts to pursue a broad-based recognition and enforcement instrument. Unlike the 1999 Draft, the 2001 Draft was not capable of being directly adopted or adapted into a legal instrument; it instead proposed alternative options, included in square brackets, which were still to be negotiated. Because of this, the 2001 Draft has been described as an 'agreement to disagree', rather than a 'true agreement'.[60] The source of these disagreements, however, is not new, harkening back to differences in opinion with respect to how far the instrument should go to allow or compel recognition and enforcement of judgements rendered under perceived exorbitant or excessive grounds, and the differences in the 'uneven' starting positions of negotiating parties.[61] Brand argues, consistently with the approach adopted in this chapter, that what proved difficult to surmount was the 'two very different sets of jurisdictional rules reflecting different legal systems' based on different 'core values'.[62] These, Brand notes, impact on fundamental legal doctrines, including the 'concept of judicial jurisdiction itself' and the way in which persons are protected through

57 Letter from Jeffrey D. Kovar (Assistant Legal Adviser for Private International Law), 'United States State Department Letter to the Hague Conference (Addressed to Hans van Loon): Dated 22 February 2000'.

58 Beaumont, 'The revived Judgments Project in The Hague' (n 11).

59 Hague Conference, '2001 Draft' (n 34).

60 Bennett (n 54) 20.

61 This is discussed further in Section 6.1.

62 Ronald A. Brand, 'Jurisdictional Developments and the New Hague Judgments Project' [2013] in, 'A Commitment To Private International Law: Essays In Honor of Hans Van Loon', Intersentia, 2013 University of Pittsburgh Legal Studies Research Paper No 2013–19, 89.

jurisdictional rules.[63] Michaels notes further that the negotiations failed due to a lack of understanding of the advantages of the Draft and the way in which the provisions operated and the lack of awareness of the 'plethora of analytically different options' open to negotiating States.[64] Both explanations are likely to have some explanative force but do not detract from the desire of States to increase the recognition and enforcement prospects of foreign judgments.

Given this ongoing desire, and conscious of not 'throwing away' work because of a diplomatic impasse, several Member States, including the United States, insisted that the Hague Conference's project be 'saved' by scaling back to a more manageable goal. This entailed leaving behind significant work efforts to reach ambitious goals such as:[65]

(1) crafting and implementing jurisdictional rules to govern a wide variety of international disputes;
(2) attempting to limit concurrent jurisdiction, parallel litigation, and unilateral forum shopping in international litigation; and
(3) requiring national courts to cooperate with one another in particularly sensitive cases – for example, in jurisdictional disputes, disputes where the substantive law to be applied differs greatly across each jurisdiction, and disputes in which the amount of damages that would be awarded in one of the countries is vastly lower or higher than what would be awarded in the other.

Based on this more restrictive mandate, attention was redirected to a less ambitious, and, for the time, more 'realistic' goal: creating a convention on jurisdiction based solely on the agreement of the parties (that is, where parties have directly chosen a judicial forum to govern their dispute).[66] This is less controversial than a convention that applies in default of choice, as it accords with the concept of party autonomy that most States allow for within the realm

63 ibid.

64 Michaels, 'Recognition and Enforcement of Foreign Judgments' (n 26).

65 Paul R. Dubinsky, 'Adventures in Treaty Interpretation (Book Review)' (2009) 57 *The American Journal of Comparative Law* 745.

66 See, for example, Jason Yackee, 'A Matter of Good Form: The (Downsized) Hague Judgments Convention and Conditions of Formal Validity for the Enforcement of Forum Selection Agreements' (2003) 53(3) *Duke Law Journal* 1179, 1178, who at the time posed the question: 'Can the Hague Judgments Convention be saved through radical downsizing?' The answer to this question is still ambiguous: the 2005 Convention is still not widely ratified or acceded to; yet, if repurposing the Convention to a radically more limited purpose counts as 'saving', perhaps that has occurred.

of private contractual obligation.[67] The end result of this scaled-back process was the 2005 Convention on Choice of Court Agreements (referred to in this book as the '2005 Convention' or the 'Choice of Court Convention'),[68] which came into force on 1 October 2015.

2.1.2 *2010–2019: The (New) Judgments Conventions*

The current transnational recognition and enforcement framework is bifurcated, due to the failure of the 2001 Draft, into two distinct instruments. The first, the 2005 Choice of Court Convention, as the Convention's title suggests, extends only to situations where disputants originally selected a particular court (or multiple courts in the same jurisdiction) to hear their dispute. The 2005 Convention extends, at present, to only six contracting parties: Denmark, the European Union, Singapore, Mexico, Montenegro and the United Kingdom (UK).[69] It perhaps goes without saying that this does not constitute widespread global adoption. However – and even though the 2005 Convention does not govern intra-European judgments recognition and enforcement (which is discussed in Chapter 3) – its coming into force is still likely to have significant impact based upon its reciprocal application between each of the EU Member States and any other Contracting States, particularly since the accession of the UK in its own right in January 2021. Additionally, it remains open for signature, and has been signed – but not yet acceded to or ratified – by China, the Republic of North Macedonia, Israel, the United States and Ukraine. The second instrument, which aims to govern jurisdictional heads other than party autonomy under which a judgment may be rendered, is the 2019 Judgments Convention. Due to its incipient status – having, at the time of writing not yet come into force – it has not had any practical impact on shaping recognition and enforcement approaches domestically.

These Judgments Conventions share a goal of promoting international trade via encouraging greater judicial co-operation. This, in turn, is expressed to 'promote access to justice and reduce costs and risks associated with cross-

67 Despite differences in implementation and approach, most States provide for, and promote, the principle of party autonomy. See, further, Alex Mills, *Party Autonomy in Private International Law* (Cambridge University Press 2018).

68 Hague Conference, 'Choice of Court Convention' (n 12).

69 'Convention of 30 June 2005 on Choice of Court Agreements: Status Table (Last Update: 1-VI-2018)' <www.hcch.net/en/instruments/conventions/status-table/?cid=98> accessed 10 August 2018.

border dealings'.[70] The way in which these goals are to be achieved is five-fold, as set out in the Explanatory Report to the 2019 Convention:[71]

> 12. Objective. This Convention seeks to promote access to justice globally through enhanced judicial cooperation, which will reduce risks and costs associated with cross-border legal relations and dispute resolution. As a result, implementation of the Convention should facilitate rule-based multilateral trade and investment, and mobility.
> 13. These goals will be advanced in a number of ways.
> 14. First and most importantly, the Convention provides a framework for the recognition and enforcement of foreign judgments in all Contracting States (States), thereby enhancing the practical effectiveness of those judgments. Access to justice is frustrated if a wronged party obtains a judgment that cannot be enforced in practice because the other party or the other party's assets are in a State where the judgment is not readily enforceable.
> 15. Second, the Convention will reduce the need for duplicative proceedings in two or more States; a judgment determining the claim in one State will be effective in other States, without the need to re-litigate the merits of the claim.
> 16. Third, the Convention will reduce the cost and timeframe of obtaining recognition and enforcement of judgments; access to practical justice will be faster and at lower cost.
> 17. Fourth, the Convention will improve the predictability of the law; individuals and businesses will be able to more readily ascertain the circumstances in which judgments will circulate among States.
> 18. Fifth, it will enable claimants to make informed choices about where to bring proceedings, taking into account the ability to enforce the resulting judgment in other States and the need to ensure fairness to defendants.

2.1.2.1 The 2005 Choice of Court Convention

The 2005 Convention was the final fruit of the then failed broad-based Judgments Project negotiations dating back to 1992, made possible by negotiators adopting a 'radically downsized' scope to the previously broad-based

[70] Francisco Garcimartín and Geneviève Saumier, 'Explanatory Report on the HCCH 2019 Judgments Convention' [2020] 48.

[71] Hague Conference, 'Judgments Convention: Revised Preliminary Explanatory Report' (Preliminary Document, May 2018) para [7]–[11].

negotiating efforts.[72] This means that the 2005 Convention only applies to international 'choice of court' agreements: that is, where parties select one or more courts of a particular legal jurisdiction to exclusively hear their dispute.[73] This is because the singular head of jurisdiction premised upon an exclusive choice of forum is, on an international level, easier to reach consensus upon; as all parties to the dispute must necessarily have expressed their desire to have their dispute resolved in that particular forum.[74] This narrowing of scope occurred as States remained eager to address the perceived anomaly in enforcement frameworks between arbitration and litigation, and were hesitant to 'throw away' work already undertaken. It should be noted at this juncture that claims have been made that the 2005 Convention is 'modelled in significant respects on the New York Convention' and 'little or no serious consideration' in drafting the 2005 Convention was given to whether this was appropriate.[75] Whether or not this is the case is discussed further at Section 8.3.2, but for present purposes it suffices to recall that any such attempt to model the 2005 Convention on the New York Convention was itself premised upon more than a century of negotiations and drafting history that preceded the 2005 Convention, and the strong influence of previous Hague Conference and Brussels Model instruments and experience.

Because of its radically reduced scope, the 2005 Convention falls far short of the ambitious goal of a broad-based multilateral convention, which was eventually realised in the 2019 Convention. Critics point out that the 2005 Convention applies only in a very small subset of international litigation disputes, which does little to narrow the variance in procedural law relating to the recognition and enforcement of foreign judgments generally across countries and does not address the skewed incentives that plaintiffs have to 'forum shop in cases not governed by forum selection agreements'.[76] The Convention's limited scope – of recognition and enforcement confined to a judgment of a Contracting State designated in an exclusive choice of court agreement – further reduces its 'utility and reach'.[77] Further criticisms of the

72 Talpis and Krnjevic (n 50) 4.
73 Article 3(1).
74 This idea of consensual agreement is 'fundamental' to arbitration: Noah Rubens, 'Group of Companies Doctrine and the New York Convention' in Emmanuel Gaillard and Domenico Di Pietro (eds.), *Enforcement of Arbitration Agreements and International Arbitral Awards: The New York Convention in Practice* (1st edition, Cameron May 2008) 449.
75 Gary Born, 'The Hague Convention on Choice of Court Agreements: A Critical Assessment' (2021) 169 University of Pennsylvania Law Review 2079, 2103.
76 Dubinsky (n 65) 745–46.
77 Richard Garnett, 'The Hague Choice of Court Convention: Magnum Opus or Much Ado About Nothing?' (2009) 5 *Journal of Private International Law* 161, 164.

2005 Convention focus on the fact that it does not cover *non-exclusive* choice of court agreements;[78] a point 'particularly lamented' by one scholar given 'their importance in commercial contract drafting'.[79] It is notable, however, that under Article 3(b) of the Convention, the choice of court or the courts of a jurisdiction (even if no specific court is selected), will be deemed to be an exclusive one, unless the parties expressly provide otherwise.[80]

The 2005 Convention provides for a double approach, in that it covers both direct jurisdiction and indirect jurisdiction (recognition and enforcement), similar to the approach adopted in the 1999 and 2001 Draft texts.[81] As with these prior instruments, it sets out the parameters for requiring and excluding grounds of direct jurisdiction that serve to privilege the choice of court agreement (Arts. 5 and 6, respectively) and then other rules for governing the recognition and enforcement of any resulting decision (Arts. 8 and 9). However, because its scope is constrained to situations where disputants have selected a court (or the courts) of a Contracting State, attempting to cover both forms of jurisdiction is a much more manageable task. For example, the general rule with respect to jurisdiction can be readily set out, as occurs in Article 5(1):

> (1) The court or courts of a Contracting State designated in an exclusive choice of court agreement shall have jurisdiction to decide a dispute to which the agreement applies, unless the agreement is null and void under the law of that State.

The logical corollary to this obligation is the general rule, provided for in Article 6, that courts of Contracting States that are 'not chosen' have an obligation to 'suspend or dismiss' proceedings in the usual course. The Convention provides a general presumption of enforceability that is subject only to limited grounds of refusal. It does so by setting a 'floor' – a minimum non-derogable standard for recognition and enforcement – but also a 'ceiling'

[78] ibid. This exclusion is to some extent mitigated by the Convention's presumption of exclusivity, *unless* the parties have expressly provided otherwise, which in many instances differs from national law: Article 3(b). Contracting States may also choose to make a declaration that they will recognise and enforce judgments given by courts of other Contracting States designated in a non-exclusive choice of court agreement: Article 22.

[79] Adrian Briggs, *Agreements on Jurisdiction and Choice of Law* (Oxford Private International Law Series 2008) cited in Garnett, 'The Hague Choice of Court Convention' (n 77), at footnote 13.

[80] Although clear from the face of the 2005 Convention, this is also set out in Trevor Hartley and Masato Dogauchi, 'Explanatory Report on the Convention of 30 June 2005 on Choice of Court Agreements' (Explanatory Report, 2007) [102]-[104].

[81] See chapters II and III of the 2005 Convention, respectively.

on these rules.[82] Article 8 establishes this approach via a general presumption that an eligible judgment 'shall be recognised and enforced', and that 'there shall be no review of the merits' of this judgment, and recognition and enforcement may only be denied 'on the grounds specified in this chapter'. Article 9 sets out the limited basis upon which recognition or enforcement *may* be refused. These grounds for refusal, as Chapter 5 explores in a comparative fashion, are broadly consistent with but not as extensive as the grounds for refusal under the New York Convention.[83]

Despite the 2005 Convention's modest acceptance internationally, its coming into force (by the accession of the EU in 2015) offers tentative steps in the direction of harmonising and promoting the global enforcement of foreign judgments. In particular, the Convention has done important work in further entrenching jurisdiction by consent as a fundamental basis of jurisdiction in private international law. It does so in a way that is sensitive to the sensitivities of international comity as between States and their judicial organs. Its recognition and enforcement framework also moves international recognition and enforcement regimes closer, based on harmonisation of international practice. By so doing, it has paved the way for a viable enforcement framework to place the enforcement prospects of international litigation – at least for disputants who consider selecting, and are able to select, a forum – on a 'more equal footing' with its arbitral counterpart, as the New York Convention.[84] Many aspects of this Convention – including its scope, reliance on reciprocity, and the precise mechanism of its presumption in favour of recognition and enforcement – are explored, in a comparative fashion, in Chapter 5. For now, I turn to consider the next, and final fruit of the Judgments Project: the development of a broad-based judgments recognition and enforcement treaty, operating in parallel with the 2005 Convention.

2.1.2.2 The 2019 Judgments Convention

In 2019, the efforts of the Judgments Project culminated in the 2019 Judgments Convention. Despite the significant diplomatic and legal hurdles negotiators

82 Brand and Herrup (n 29) 23.

83 This is primarily for the practical reason that this presumption–exception approach, as perhaps most prominently typified in the Brussels Model or the New York Convention approaches, has achieved wide success internationally, and hence has been used a model for many subsequent developments in recognition and enforcement. The comparative width of the New York Covention and 2005 Convention exceptions are explored in a critical fashion in Born (n 75) 2097–99.

84 Brand and Herrup (n 29) 25.

faced in pursuing a global judgments instrument, seldom was the Judgments Project far from the agenda at the Hague Conference over recent decades.[85] The impetus for such longstanding action was, and remains, a widely shared desire to address the 'perceived reluctance' of some States to enforce judgments originating from elsewhere.[86] Yet, most of the difficulty in reaching a mutually agreeable instrument stemmed from States' reluctance to give effect to any instrument that obliges them to recognise and enforce judgments that they may otherwise choose not to.[87] In the decades since efforts to create a multilateral broad-based judgments instrument commenced, little concrete progress was made to this end. Nonetheless, in 2010 – perhaps spurred by the fact that the 2005 Convention had at that time yet to receive the minimum of two acceptances or ratifications to come into effect – efforts to resume work along the broader lines of the original Judgments Project resumed.

At this juncture, the Council on General Affairs and Policy, the key decision-making body of the Hague Conference, left open the question of the Convention's form and content, and whether it would be single, double or mixed.[88] Despite the success of the 'mixed' form of the 2005 Convention, the hard-earned lessons of the 1992–2001 efforts proved instructive, and work reverted back to an open single convention on recognition and enforcement. This returns full circle to the approach of the 1971 Convention in terms of its single structure. Efforts to settle the text of what ultimately became the 2019 Convention were undertaken over four Special Commission meetings, from 2016 to 2018, with the final draft drawn up and refined at the 22nd Diplomatic Session of the Hague Conference (convened in mid-2019). The final Act was adopted on 2 July 2019 and opened for signature on that date. As mentioned earlier, the 2019 Convention has yet to enter into force. Note, however, that negotiating States at the Hague Conference – primarily European States – have not abandoned their desire to do what is otherwise done in a 'double' convention: to ensure that jurisdiction is regulated

85 Brand, 'Jurisdictional Developments and the New Hague Judgments Project' (n 62) 89.

86 Lutz (n 41) 568. The Permanent Bureau, in reviewing the rationale for recommencing judgments efforts, noted that it is 'unsatisfactory in itself' that no multilateral instrument had gained traction in terms of recognition and enforcement: Hague Conference, 'Some Reflections of the Permanent Bureau on a General Convention on Enforcement of Judgments' (n 21) 231.

87 At the same time, however, years of negotiation and compromise have led to a high degree of consensus in approach. For example, despite some minor debate, the substantive scope of any proposed instrument, the strong preference for recognition and enforcement with limited grounds of review and the adoption of established legal terminology are now widely shared.

88 See Hague Conference, 'Conclusions and Recommendations Adopted by the Council' (Council on General Affairs and Policy of the Conference, 20 April 2012), Council on General Affairs and Policy of the Conference.

comprehensively. Instead, they accepted a compromise to overcome this impasse, whereby the 2019 Convention on recognition and enforcement alone was to be concluded first, with an 'additional instrument' on jurisdiction to follow.[89]

Achieving consensus was a delicate balancing act, as David Goddard notes with respect to the final draft that became the 2019 Convention:[90]

> [The 2019 Convention] seeks to identify cases where recognition and enforcement of a judgment would command broad acceptance. Cases where, if one were to ask 'is it reasonable for this judgment to be recognized and enforced?', we would expect a generally positive answer across the full diversity of legal systems and approaches of Member States. The instrument seeks to walk the sometimes delicate line between maximizing the reach of the Convention, and not impairing the objective of commanding widespread acceptance. The Special Commission could have set out to produce a very narrow and uncontroversial instrument, but that would significantly reduce its practical value. If all the Judgments Convention did was restate the obvious, then that would probably add something to the international legal order because at least it would improve the accessibility of information about the law. But the 2018 Draft Convention is more ambitious than that. It seeks to go beyond stating the obvious to state the reasonable, the sensible, the things that should on reflection command broad acceptance. In doing so it seeks to restate and develop the existing law to some extent, but not to such an extent that it is asking too much of Contracting States when they come to consider whether or not to accept this instrument.

What is immediately evident is that the 2019 Convention's long drafting and negotiating history – set out earlier – has allowed the nature of these concerns to be explored in great detail. Indeed, the Convention has been agreed despite the increasingly expanded and diverse State membership of the Hague Conference. In 1992, when renewed modern efforts to craft a worldwide instrument began, the Hague Conference had thirty-seven Member States, which were predominantly developed Western European countries. In the decades since, this membership has steadily increased, and increasingly represents a much broader proportion of the global economy. At the time that the 2019 Convention was agreed, this membership included eighty-three States

89 Hague Conference, 'Report of the Fifth Meeting of the Working Group on the Judgments Project (26–31 October 2015) and Proposed Draft Text Resulting from the Meeting' (Preliminary Document, November 2015) 5. See also, on the utility of pursuing a subsequent agreement on jurisdiction, footnote 876 (and the surrounding discussion).

90 David Goddard, 'The Judgments Convention - the Current State of Play' (2019) 29 *Duke Journal of Comparative & International Law* 473, 480.

(and the EU, as a bloc).[91] The 2019 Convention's great accolade then, and is navigating the design of an instrument that is broadly accepted globally; although, the ultimate test will be in the extent to which the Convention is adopted.

The substantive approach of the 2019 Convention rests upon a broadly familiar presumption–exception model, as set out earlier (in the context of the 2005 Convention) and in Section 2.2[92] While the precise contours of this approach are comparatively analysed in more detail in Chapter 5, it assists to briefly set out this approach in the context of the Judgments Convention. Article 4 of the 2019 Convention provides:

Article 4
General provisions

1. A judgment given by a court of a Contracting State (State of origin) shall be recognised and enforced in another Contracting State (requested State) in accordance with the provisions of this Chapter. Recognition or enforcement may be refused only on the grounds specified in this Convention.
2. There shall be no review of the merits of the judgment in the requested State. There may only be such consideration as is necessary for the application of this Convention.
3. A judgment shall be recognised only if it has effect in the State of origin, and shall be enforced only if it is enforceable in the State of origin.
4. Recognition or enforcement may be postponed or refused if the judgment referred to under paragraph 3 is the subject of review in the State of origin or if the time limit for seeking ordinary review has not expired. A refusal does not prevent a subsequent application for recognition or enforcement of the judgment.

Thus, the general starting rule set out in Art 4(1) is that a judgment of a Contracting State must be recognised and enforced in another. Consistent with what is expressly set out in the 2005 Convention, and implicit in the New York Convention's approach, there is to be 'no review of the merits' of the original decision (beyond what is necessary to apply the Convention), and recognition and enforcement may only be refused in limited and enumerated grounds set out within the 2019 Convention.

[91] Since that time, this has grown to eighty-nine States (and the EU): 'Hague Conference Website: Hague Conference Members' (no date) <www.hcch.net/en/states/hcch-members> accessed 1 October 2021.

[92] These approaches are compared and analysed in Part II of this book.

The primary challenge in reaching agreement on the text of the 2019 Convention was perhaps achieving consensus on the jurisdictional bases for recognition and enforcement. According to Article 5 of the Convention, an acceptable base must be found before a judgment is eligible for recognition and enforcement under the 2019 Convention. These jurisdictional bases broadly relate to the place of operation (either the 'habitual residence' or 'place of business') of disputants, are based upon presumed disputant consent or submission to the jurisdiction of the rendering court or, alternatively, are based upon whether there is a sufficient connection between the parties or matter with the jurisdiction of the rendering court.[93] The need to find such a base is not necessary under either the 2005 Convention or New York Convention, as the base of jurisdiction underlying these instruments – party selection of a court or arbitral tribunal – already occurs before obligations to recognise and enforce in those instruments activates. Once at least one jurisdictional base is satisfied, there are some further controls placed, including the following: in Article 5(2), to protect consumers and employees (in matters relating to their consumer/employment contract) from recognition and enforcement of judgments against them; and, in Article 6, additional limitations arising out of certain property rights in immovable property that are only enforceable in the State of origin.

Article 7 of the Judgments Convention sets out what could be termed 'standard' exceptions to recognition and enforcement, which are substantially identical to those in the New York Convention and other instruments. These include, for example, a failure to notify the defendant appropriately (Art 7(1)(a)), circumstances where the judgment was obtained by fraud (Art 7(1)(b)) or where recognition and enforcement is 'manifestly incompatible' with the public policy of the enforcing court.[94] Provision is also made for recognition and enforcement to be refused in certain circumstances where multiple proceedings are contemplated or completed – for example, where proceedings are contrary to a choice of court agreement (Art 7(1)(d)), the judgment is 'inconsistent' with judgment given by a court in the enforcing State in a dispute between the same parties (Art 7(1)(e)) or it is 'inconsistent' with an earlier judgment between the same parties on the same subject matter (Art 7(1)(f)).

93 These bases and their genesis are analysed in detail in Abubakri Yekini, *The Hague Judgments Convention and Commonwealth Model Law: A Pragmatic Perspective* (Hart Publishing 2021) 195–221.

94 Note that the addition of the word 'manifestly' here represents an innovation in the 2019 Convention, building on observed and perceived issues with the New York Convention approach. This is discussed further at Section 5.2.2.

As is perhaps apparent, even at this early juncture, both this presumption–exception approach and the nature of the individual grounds for refusal and the restrictive manner of applying these grounds are largely consistent across global recognition and enforcement instruments surveyed in this book.[95] With this in mind, I turn now to consider the New York Convention's approach to recognition and enforcement of foreign arbitral awards.

2.2 ARBITRAL AWARD RECOGNITION AND ENFORCEMENT

The New York Convention is widely lauded as a resounding success as an international instrument.[96] Due to the simplicity and efficacy of its harmonised pro-recognition and enforcement approach, the Convention has largely replaced other international instruments that also relate to the recognition and enforcement of arbitral awards, including previous global conventions[97] and a range of bilateral agreements and regional conventions.[98] Its global reach is now so broad that States that are not signatory to it are marked with 'prominent "red flags"' by practitioners, and States that are signatory to it but have not implemented it fully or correctly are watched carefully.[99] Because of this, award creditors holding properly rendered international arbitral awards are likely to face predictable support in most enforcing courts. Thus, the Convention provides a 'preventative' effect to any award debtor considering resisting enforcement: given the fact that an award is likely to be enforced in most jurisdictions, a rational award debtor is likely to comply with it voluntarily.[100] This means that the 'vast majority' of awards are willingly complied with

[95] These are explored in a comparative fashion in Chapter 5.

[96] Claims that the Convention is the 'most effective instance of international legislation in the history of commercial law' and forms 'bedrock', 'fundament' or 'pillar' upon which international arbitration is built abound in the arbitral literature: see, for a summary exposition of these views, Nigel Blackaby and others, *Redfern and Hunter on International Arbitration* (6th edn, Oxford University Press 2015) 617 [11.40]; Lew and others (n 3) [26.21].

[97] The most prominent of these, which is now largely superseded by the New York Convention, is the 1923 United Nations, 'Convention on the Execution of Foreign Arbitral Awards' (25 July 1929). For this reason, I do not set out an instrumental history of this (or any other) preceding instrument.

[98] Arthur von Mehren and Eckart Gottschalk, *Adjudicatory Authority in Private International Law* (The Hague Academy of International Law Monographs 5, Martinus Nijhoff Publishers 2007) 376.

[99] Lucy Reed, 'Experience of Practical Problems of Enforcement' in Albert Jan van den Berg (ed.), *Improving the Efficiency of Arbitration Agreements and Awards: 40 Years of Application of the New York Convention* (KluwerArbitration, Kluwer Law International 2011) 562.

[100] See, further, Section 1.3.4 (n 82).

by award debtors.[101] Even in the few cases they are not complied with, these awards are usually recognised and enforced by enforcing courts applying the Convention. The strength of the enforcement prospects available for arbitral awards – largely due to the widespread dissemination and concordance with the operative provisions of the Convention – has thus become 'central' to the popularity of arbitration as an international commercial dispute resolution mechanism.[102] Indeed, this preference is strong in practice; so much so that it is now trite to describe or chart the widespread appeal and subsequent adoption of arbitration as an international dispute resolution mechanism.[103]

By design, the New York Convention offers a simple, flexible 'avowedly pro-enforcement' and strikingly international approach to the recognition and enforcement of foreign arbitral awards.[104] As the formal title of the Convention suggests – a 'Convention on the Recognition and Enforcement of Foreign Arbitral Awards' – it has the key purpose of facilitating recognition and enforcement of awards by providing international standards that presumptively assume the validity of such awards at enforcement and severely restrict the grounds for denying recognition and enforcement.[105] Additionally, the New York Convention – similar to the 2005 Convention – can be categorised as a minimal form of 'double' Convention. This is because it places an onus on Contracting States to 'recognize an agreement in writing' where a submission to arbitration has occurred.[106] This recognition requires a rendering court when it is faced with such an agreement to 'refer the parties to arbitration'.[107]

[101] Gary Born, *International Commercial Arbitration* (KluwerArbitration, Third edition, Kluwer Law International BV 2020) §26.03. Albeit another factor motivating compliance is likely to be the preservation of reputation and business relationships, as disputants interested in future business dealing do not want to be perceived as unreliable, so they may comply with properly rendered awards – even where they may be difficult to enforce – to be seen as a 'fair' disputant: Bockstiegel (n 5) 436.

[102] Simon Greenberg and others, *International Commercial Arbitration: An Asia-Pacific Perspective* (Cambridge University Press 2011) 428 [9.60].

[103] See, for example, the repeated findings in surveys undertaken by Queen Mary University London that approximately 90 per cent of practitioners and corporate counsel surveyed prefer to utilise arbitration, as most recently recorded in: White & Case and Queen Mary University of London, *International Arbitration Survey 2021: Adapting Arbitration to a Changing World* <www.arbitration.qmul.ac.uk/research/2021-international-arbitration-survey/>.

[104] Born, *International Commercial Arbitration* (n 101) §26.03; Blackaby and others (n 96) 618 [11.42].

[105] Although not explicitly mentioned in the text of the Convention itself, as Born (reviewing a range of cases and commentaries on the Convention) notes, enforcing courts have uniformly recognised these purposes: Born, *International Commercial Arbitration* (n 101) §26.03(B)(1).

[106] Article II(1).

[107] Article II(3), with the proviso that it is excused from doing so if it 'finds that the [arbitration] agreement is null and void, inoperative or incapable of being performed'.

Notably, this provision of the New York Convention is open rather than exhaustive: no constraints are placed on circumstances when courts of Contracting States can choose to give effect to an arbitration agreement that falls outside or does not satisfy the requirements in Article II.[108]

The Convention provides for a broad sphere of applicability. First, it obliges enforcing courts of State parties to give effect to any arbitral award that is not considered to be 'domestic' by the laws of the enforcing court. That is, rather than defining what a foreign award is or relying on the enforcing court's determination of what is 'foreign' to it, the Convention relies on an expansive negative definition, providing that the Convention applies to 'awards made in the territory of a State other than the State where the recognition and enforcement of such awards are sought', as well as to 'awards not considered as domestic awards in the State where there recognition and enforcement are sought'.[109] As a result, the default position that potential Contracting States to the Convention face is a recognition and enforcement framework that promotes broad acceptance of all manner of non-domestic arbitral awards. Second, subject to a potential State reservation, the Convention applies even in circumstances where the award was made in the territory of a State that is not party to the Convention.[110] Provision is made for States, however, to employ a reciprocity reservation that limits their Convention obligations to extend only to other Contracting States. If so, arbitral awards made in the territory of a foreign State that come before an enforcing court of a Contracting State will not benefit from the pro-recognition and enforcement measures in the Convention, unless that foreign State is also a signatory to the Convention. Even though half of the Contracting States have made this reciprocity reservation,[111] the sheer number of Contracting States means that any insistence upon reciprocity is now of limited practical significance.[112]

[108] This allows for domestic legal developments to improve and update New York Convention practice – so long as the minimum standard set out in the Convention is met. See, for an example, discussion of attempts to 'modernise' the requirement that an agreement be 'in writing': Section 7.2.2.1.

[109] Article I(1).

[110] Article I(3).

[111] These States are marked with (a) in the Notes section on the UNCITRAL website: 'UNCITRAL: Status of the Convention on the Recognition and Enforcement of Foreign Arbitral Awards (New York, 1958)' (no date) <www.uncitral.org/uncitral/en/uncitral_texts/arbitration/NYConvention_status.html> accessed 12 January 2017.

[112] See, for an example of the operation of the reciprocity reservation, '*Texaco Panama Inc* v. *Duke Petroleum Transport Corporation (Liberia)*' [1996] 95 Civ 37/61, where the enforcing court (located in a Contracting State) determined the New York Convention did not apply to a non-domestic arbitration award, as the reciprocity reservation was part of the law applied by the

Third, and finally, the Convention has a broad sphere of operation as it generally applies to all 'differences between persons, whether physical or legal'.[113] States are able to limit this, again via a further reservation in Article I(3), by declaring that Convention obligations apply only to arbitral agreements and awards arising out of relationships 'considered as commercial' under their own national law. A substantial minority of States employ this reservation.[114] Because each State is to determine for itself which relationships are commercial, this has led to interpretive divergence between Contracting States but also 'even *within* the same state'.[115] This potential divergence is a very real practical issue; in the extreme, it may result in States breaching their New York Convention obligations.[116] In the context of the commercial reservation, however, the clearly discernible objects of the Convention – to facilitate international trade and provide for expedited settlements of disputes arising through arbitration – still act to limit unduly narrow national definitions of the term 'commercial', and hence the range of awards that must be recognised or given effect to under the scope of the Convention.[117] Consequently, it can be surmised that the New York Convention retains a broad sphere of applicability with respect to arbitral agreements and arbitral awards, and undoubtably so with respect to commercial matters.

2.2.1 *The Convention Approach to Recognition and Enforcement*

Consistent with the Judgments Conventions, the New York Convention creates an unambiguous presumption, in Arts III and IV, that enforcing courts of Contracting States will 'recognize arbitral awards as binding and enforce

enforcing court, and the arbitral award originated from Liberia, which was not, at the time, a signatory of the Convention. Liberia subsequently acceded to the Convention in 2005.

113 Article I(1).

114 These States are marked with (c) in the Notes section on the UNCITRAL website: 'UNCITRAL: Status of the Convention on the Recognition and Enforcement of Foreign Arbitral Awards (New York, 1958)' (n 111).

115 Albeit, in the context of applications to stay court proceedings in India, as excerpted in Blackaby and others (n 96) 619 [11.47] (emphasis added).

116 See further, Section 7.1.1.

117 See, for example, the Indian Supreme Court case of *RM Investments & Trading Co* v. *Boeing Co* Supreme Court, cited in Blackaby and others (n 96) 620 [11.49], where the Court referred to these objectives as made explicit in the then applicable arbitration legislation – which among other things was designed to implement India's New York Convention obligations. As a result, the Court held that the term 'commercial' should 'be construed broadly having regard to the manifold activities which are an integral part of international trade today': *RM Investments & Trading Co* v. *Boeing Co* para 12.

them'.[118] All that is needed to activate this presumption in favour of recognition and enforcement is sufficient evidence or certification of the veracity of the award.[119] Where this can be satisfactorily proved, Contracting States undertake to recognise and give effect to foreign arbitral awards, subject only to certain enumerated – and exhaustive[120] – grounds of refusal. Importantly, these grounds for refusing recognition and enforcement do not include any ability for the enforcing court to review the merits of an award.[121] Instead, the grounds under which a party can resist recognition and enforcement are primarily procedural and generally relate to circumstances where there are fundamental defects in the arbitral tribunal's jurisdiction or the procedure under which the award was rendered.[122] In addition, the enforcing court (on its own motion) may invoke grounds for non-recognition and enforcement in certain matters that may offend vital State interests: namely, in circumstances where the subject matter of the award is not considered arbitrable or where recognising or enforcing the award would conflict with the public policy of the enforcing State.[123]

This approach – based on the initial application of a presumption in favour of recognition and enforcement, and then a consideration of potential grounds for refusal – aides award creditors seeking recognition or enforcement. This is because the burden of proof is discharged by the creditor simply meeting basic evidentiary requirements. If an award debtor wishes to resist recognition and enforcement, it faces the burden of demonstrating why and

[118] The Convention does not stipulate a recognition or enforcement procedure that enforcing courts must adopt, but instead, in Art III, it allows the enforcing court procedural latitude: any procedure is acceptable, as long as it does not conflict with any other provisions of the Convention and is not 'substantially more onerous' than the procedure applicable to domestic awards.

[119] Article IV.

[120] Despite some initial missteps in judicial interpretation of domestic equivalents of Article V of the New York Convention – most notably in the now infamous Supreme Court of Queensland case of *Resort Condominiums* v. *Bolwell* (1993) 188 ALR 655 – arbitral practitioners and the academy are largely united in the view that these defences, at least as expressed in the New York Convention, are intended to be fully exhaustive: Richard Garnett and Michael Pryles, 'Recognition and Enforcement of Foreign Awards under the New York Convention in Australia and New Zealand' (2008) 25 *Journal of International Arbitration* 899, 903–6.

[121] As Article V makes clear, the enforcing court may only refuse to recognise and enforce a judgment if one of the enumerated grounds is proven: none of these allow for a review of the merits of the dispute.

[122] Article V(a)–(e).

[123] Article V(2).

how a ground for refusal applies. Read in the context of repeated findings of enforcing courts that these grounds for refusal must be constructed 'narrowly', 'restrictively' or 'strictly applied', it is a 'heavy', 'onerous' or 'weighty' burden to discharge,[124] tending, in line with the purpose of the Convention, strongly in favour of recognition and enforcement of arbitral awards. In other words, and again consistent with the transnational approaches analysed earlier, the enforcing courts of Contracting States regularly recognise and interpret New York Convention obligations in light of the Convention's goals of being an 'effective', 'expeditious' and 'effective' framework facilitating recognition and enforcement of awards created via a 'single, uniform set of rules that apply [almost] worldwide'.[125]

The existence of clear limitations on grounds of refusal has continually been reaffirmed in case law of most Contracting States over the many years of the Convention's operation. This turns on a shared understanding that these grounds should be read narrowly by enforcing courts and not used to overcome the general pro-recognition and enforcement approach of the Convention.[126] In a 2008 Commentary on the New York Convention, van den Berg notes – based on a review of thousands of court decisions from a range of jurisdictions interpreting the Convention over decades – that the preference of most enforcing courts is to construe these grounds for refusal narrowly and only refuse to give effect to a foreign award in 'serious cases'.[127] Consistent with the view, the global 'trend' is towards acceptance of arbitral awards, whether they are 'good or bad' in terms of their decision-making process, unless one of the enumerated grounds for refusal can be made out.[128] This further suggests that, over time, the presumption–exception approach (which avoids any review of the merits of the decision) has become

[124] Quotes extracted from a selection of case law in Contracting States, cited in Born, *International Commercial Arbitration* (n 101) §26.03(B)(3).

[125] Quotes extracted from a selection of case law in Contracting States, cited in ibid [26.03(B)].

[126] See, for example, the seminal United States Court of Appeals case *Parsons & Whittemore Overseas Co Inc* v. *Société Générale de l'Industrie du Papier RAKTA* 508 F 2d 969 (2nd Circuit 1974), at 974, where the Court notes: '*[t]o read the public policy defence as a parochial device protective of national political interests would seriously undermine the Convention's utility. This provision was not meant to enshrine the vagaries of international politics under the rubric of "public policy*"'. This narrow interpretation has been consistently adopted across the public policy ground in other jurisdictions. See, for example, the Singaporean case of *Re An Arbitration between Hainan Machinery Import & Export Corporation and Donald & McArthy* [1996] 1 SLR 34.

[127] Albert Jan van den Berg, *The New York Convention of 1958: An Overview* (2008, Brussels), p 13.

[128] Blackaby and others (n 96) para 11.04.

increasingly accepted by international disputants, and it has been cemented as a cornerstone of the transnational dispute resolution landscape. I turn now to consider, in turn, the two key transnational recognition and enforcement frameworks outside of the 'global' level: the 'Brussels Model' approach (Chapter 3) and the 'Commonwealth Model' and its common law underpinnings (Chapter 4).

3

Uniform Recognition and Enforcement in Europe

The Brussels Model

This chapter analyses the broad-based and largely uniform judgments recognition and enforcement frameworks in place between most European States, referred to in this book as the 'Brussels Model'. From a recognition and enforcement perspective, the chief success of the Brussels Model is in harmonising the laws of signatory States, so that each State, at least with respect to other signatory States, provides straightforward and expeditious recognition and enforcement of judgments.[1] The Brussels Model, however, is not monolithic; instead, the term refers to a range of international instruments that share a significant degree of commonality in their groundbreaking pro-enforcement approach to foreign judgments. To the extent that either the operation of the Model overall – or discrete elements of its approach – can be isolated and reviewed, they may offer lessons for other recognition and enforcement approaches. This is because the Brussels Model, despite its regional focus, is fundamentally aimed at harmonising divergent national recognition and enforcement approaches (between participants, at least).[2] Consequently, the

[1] Although each instrument constituting the Model achieves this task in slightly different ways. See, for example, Gralf-Peter Calliess 'Value-Added Norms, Local Litigation, and Global Enforcement: Why the Brussels-Philosophy Failed in The Hague' (2004) 5, 12 *German Law Journal* 1489, 1497.

[2] This is discussed further at Section 6.1. For present purposes it suffices to note that at the time that the Brussels Convention was negotiated (between the six original EEC States), there were

Brussels Model approach, representing the first widely accepted international broad-based recognition and enforcement instrument, brings to prominence a novel approach transnationally in a number of key respects. These are considered in the comparative context in Chapter 5, but it assists to note these features before considering the Model more closely in this chapter. They relevantly include: the Brussels Model's closed, mandatory, character; its double approach, regulating both the rendering court's exercise of jurisdiction and the recognition and enforcement of any resulting judgment; its explicit mechanisms to assist with reaching autonomous or unified interpretation; and, at least in the case of EU States, its direct and immediate supremacy over non-conforming national law.[3]

While the instruments constituting the Brussels Model are indeed international, the Brussels Model diverges from bilateral and global approaches taken in the first half of the twentieth century,[4] as it is largely designed around, and operates on, a regional basis. Consequently, the Brussels Model is constituted by an overlapping lattice of legal instruments, ranging from international treaties to European Regulations, that serve to streamline and harmonise recognition and enforcement approaches between participants.[5] For clarity, these instruments, in chronological order, are the:[6]

- 1968 Brussels Convention ('1968 Convention');[7]
- 1988 Lugano Convention ('Lugano Convention');[8]

no States with a common law legal system represented, and thus it is likely that the Model reflects leading civilian law practice at the time.

3 These factors are adapted from Arthur von Mehren and Eckart Gottschalk, *Adjudicatory Authority in Private International Law* (The Hague Academy of International Law Monographs 5, Martinus Nijhoff Publishers 2007) 69.

4 Up until this point, most harmonisation efforts proceeded on the basis that this bilateral harmonisation was compatible with efforts to achieve global harmonisation: ibid. 376.

5 Although these instruments differ in their territorial application and precise implementation, the approach taken in each is broadly consistent, enabling their characterisation under the singular heading of the Brussels Model.

6 As the substance of the Brussels Model approach to recognition and enforcement is little changed from the original 1968 Convention, pinpoint references to Articles and provisions of the Brussels Model, unless otherwise indicated or obvious from the context, are made to the 2012 Recast. To determine the corresponding Article number in the other Brussels Model instruments, see: Marie-Elodie Ancel and others, 'From Brussels to Lugano – A Panoramic Table' (June 2014) <www.lynxlex.com/sites/default/files/files/From%20Brussels%20to%20Lugano%20-%20A%20panoramic%20table_0.pdf> accessed 31 January 2016.

7 European Economic Community, 'Brussels Convention on Jurisdiction and the Enforcement of Judgments in Civil and Commercial Matters' (1 February 1973).

8 'Lugano Convention' (Chapter 1, n 36).

- 44/2001 Brussels Regulation ('Brussels I' or '2001 Regulation');[9]
- 2007 Lugano Convention ('Lugano II' or '2007 Lugano Convention');[10] and the
- 1215/2012 Brussels Regulation ('Brussels Recast', '2012 Recast' or '2012 Regulation').[11]

Despite beginning life in the form of the 1968 Convention (solely between the six original European Community (EC) members), the Brussels Model has since become entrenched within the EU as a directly binding regulation, and it also extends to non-EU States via the Lugano Conventions. The expansion of the EU[12] has further cemented the Brussels Model internationally, as all Member States must adopt the Brussels Model when joining the Union. Due ultimately to the EU's economic and political momentum, the Brussels Model approach to recognition and enforcement has proved to be 'unbreakable' since its debut in the 1968 Convention.[13] In particular, legal developments in recognition and enforcement deriving from, and building upon, the Model suggest that participant States increasingly treat foreign judgments with a greater degree of automatism, as if they were from 'practically one unified territory'.[14]

Even so, States adopting the Model do not give uncritical and unconditional effect to foreign judgments. Much like the other recognition and enforcement approaches analysed in this book, national courts under the Brussels Model remain empowered to refuse recognition and enforcement if a matter is excluded from the Model or an enumerated ground for refusal (based usually on a breach of fundamental procedural fairness notions) is found. At the same time, despite the long-standing success of the Brussels Model and the EU's active participation and support for global negotiations on a broad-based judgments recognition and enforcement instrument, global negotiations (ongoing since the late nineteenth century) have yet to achieve practical success on an instrument pursuing a similar approach.

9 'Brussels I Regulation' (Chapter 1, n 36).

10 'Lugano II' (Chapter 1, n 36).

11 *Brussels I Recast* (Chapter 1, n 36).

12 From the six original European Community Members to the now twenty-eight members of the European Union. See: 'European Neighbourhood Policy and Enlargement Negotiations - From 6 to 28 Members - European Commission' (13 May 2015) <http://ec.europa.eu/enlargement/policy/from-6-to-28-members/index_en.htm> accessed 13 July 2016.

13 von Mehren and Gottschalk (n 3) 357.

14 Horatia Muir Watt, 'New Perspectives for Jurisdiction and Judgments Within Europe: A Critical View' in John Barcelo and Kevin M Clermont (eds.), *A Global Law of Jurisdiction and Judgement: Lessons from Hague* (1st ed., Kluwer Law International 2002) 255.

Consequently, the Brussels Model is of particular interest for this book, as it demonstrates that approaches to recognition and enforcement of judgments are not necessarily inherent to any type of legal system or tradition, and that harmonised rules relating to recognition and enforcement depend on a finely crafted balance to be applied widely and successfully (at least on a regional basis) between States with vast differences in legal tradition.[15]

I begin by providing an overview of the Brussels Model approach to recognition and enforcement before analysing how the Brussels Model ideal of a harmonious strong pro-recognition and enforcement approach has practically been implemented in each of the Brussels Model instruments. This part is not intended as an exhaustive article-by-article comparison of the instruments constituting the Model[16] but, rather, traces and assesses the major developments across each instrument with respect to their approach to recognition and enforcement. Doing so helps to set the scene for the comparative task, undertaken in Part II of this book, to consider the potential lessons the Brussels Model – as the high point of international cooperation on recognition and enforcement – may offer for recognition and enforcement of foreign decisions generally.

3.1 DEVELOPMENT OF BRUSSELS MODEL INSTRUMENTS

The Brussels Model, despite being implemented in five different international instruments – each with different territorial application and participants, amended many times and spanning almost half a century – presents a largely coherent and consistent approach to recognition and enforcement in civil and commercial matters. This consistency is aided by the fact that the Lugano Convention instruments are substantially the same as the Brussels instruments, as they are 'exported' to Lugano States by the same States who negotiated the Brussels instruments. Of the Brussels instruments, the 1968 Convention is a stand-alone international treaty (although regionally

[15] Because the rules underpinning the Brussels Model were drafted to be a 'fresh start', rather than amending existing laws and practice, they represent a principled and logical approach to recognition and enforcement of foreign judgments: Adrian Briggs, *Civil Jurisdiction and Judgments* (6th ed., Informa Law from Routledge 2015) 3.

[16] This has been done elsewhere in a comprehensive fashion. A comparison table readily highlights the similarities, and implementation differences, between the instruments: see Marie-Elodie Ancel and others (n 6). Briggs extensively reviews, from an English perspective, rules relating to both jurisdiction and the recognition and enforcement of foreign judgments under the Brussels Model: see generally Briggs (n 15). See also Andrew Dickinson and Eva Lein (eds.), *The Brussels I Regulation Recast* (Oxford University Press 2015).

bound), whereas Regulation 44/2001 and the 2012 Recast form part of an expanding body of interrelated legal rules given direct effect in the EU. Given developments in the law-making ability of the EU, these Brussels Regulations largely supplant what was originally considered to be a treaty matter in the 1968 Convention. The Regulations in the Brussels Model do this directly, as by design they take precedence over all non-conforming law and are immediately binding; unlike the original Brussels Convention, they do not require implementation into national laws.[17] Despite this change in legal form, each subsequent Brussels instrument represents only a minor chronological 'evolution' in the approach of the Brussels Model from the original 1968 Convention.[18] These evolutions have been relatively minor in nature, representing either a 'problem fixing' response to identified legal issues or incremental amendments to further streamline and improve recognition and enforcement procedures. As a result, the 1968 Convention is now largely relevant only as a 'stepping stone' to the rules contained in the more recent Regulations.[19]

3.1.1 *The 1968 Brussels Convention*[20]

The 1968 Brussels Convention is the founding instrument in the Brussels Model. It sets out the original comprehensive and harmonised rules on recognition and enforcement, as well as rules on direct jurisdiction.[21] Although entered into between only the original six EC Member States, it has been amended at various points to accommodate new entrants and minor

[17] von Mehren and Gottschalk (n 3) 69.

[18] Dickinson and Lein (n 16) para 1.02. The lack of any need for major changes, after almost half a century, itself supports the idea that the Brussels Model has been a success.

[19] Briggs (n 15) 5.

[20] A reference to the Brussels Convention can refer to any of the versions below, namely the: original 1968 Brussels Convention (between the six original European Community), signed 27 September 1968: [1978] OJ L304/36; the amended Brussels Convention, to which Denmark, Ireland and the UK became contracting states: [1978] OJ L304/77; the re-amended Brussels Convention, when Greece became party: [1982] OJ L388/1; the re-re-amended Brussels Convention, when Portugal and Spain became party (and also incorporating some minor textual changes): [1989] OJ L285/1; and the re-re-re amended Brussels Convention, when Australia, Finland, Sweden became party: [1997] OJ C15/1. Unless otherwise indicated, or apparent from the context, all references are to the fourth version ([1989] OJ L285/1). Each of these versions are available at: 'Texts: Brussels Convention and Protocols' (no date) <http://curia.europa.eu/common/recdoc/convention/en/c-textes/_brux-textes.htm> accessed 24 May 2016.

[21] To be recognised (and enforced) a judgment must be civil and commercial – and not be specifically excluded from the scope of the Convention (Art 1). The same holds true for every instrument in the Brussels Model (see, for example, Art 1 of the 2012 Recast).

revisions.[22] While it is a stand-alone legal instrument, the 1968 Convention draws heavily from previous global judgments developments. For example, despite the Hague Conference's 1971 Convention's lack of success, it still 'greatly influenced' the Brussels Regulation.[23] The 1968 Convention, for example, builds on the drafting work of the 1971 Convention by adopting the then novel use of a list of excluded jurisdictional bases.[24] At a high level, the 1968 Convention is the first of a series of instruments that share a strong pro-recognition and pro-enforcement emphasis and enshrine the enforcing court as the 'guardian' of the limited exceptions to this (largely premised upon important jurisdictional and procedural fairness guarantees).[25] Despite these exceptions, the scope of the Brussels Model is particularly broad: as long as a judgment on a matter is civil or commercial, and not specifically excluded, it should be recognised and enforced by enforcing courts.

As the remainder of this part will demonstrate, the practical operation of the Brussels Convention has now largely been superseded by developments in the 2001 Brussels Regulation and its 2012 Recast. The Convention does, however, retain some very limited practical application, to the extent that it applies to certain non-EU territories of Member States (to which neither of the Regulations extends). In addition, the body of case law that has developed around interpretation of provisions in the Brussels Convention is a useful reference, as later texts by and large use similar provisions to those set out in the 1968 Convention. This is particularly the case as the most recent formulation of the Brussels Model – in the 2012 Recast Regulation – represents a gradual evolution in approach, 'founded on the same core principles' as the Convention.[26]

3.1.2 *The 1988 Lugano Convention*

The Lugano Convention originally served to extend the recognition and enforcement regime of the Brussels Convention internationally to European

[22] The procedural history of the Brussels Convention amendments is outlined in detail in Briggs (n 15) 5–6. Note also that various instruments for States to opt-in – Denmark, in particular – are canvassed in this text but have been omitted here.

[23] Peter Nygh and Fausto Pocar, 'Report by Peter Nygh & Fausto Pocar (Annexed to the 1999 Preliminary Draft Convention)' (Report, August 2000) 29.

[24] This is likely due to the fact that both Conventions were 'negotiated in parts by the same persons': Hague Conference, 'Some Reflections of the Permanent Bureau on a General Convention on Enforcement of Judgments' (Preliminary Document, May 1992), 231.

[25] Muir Watt (n 14) 256.

[26] Dickinson and Lein (n 16) para 1.02.

Free Trade Association (EFTA) States outside of the then European Community. The Lugano Contracting States – preferring to maintain political independence by not sharing in the goal of 'ever closer union' of the then EC – nonetheless entered into the Convention to facilitate trade between European signatories. To do so, the Lugano Convention adopts an almost identical structure, format and approach to that of the Brussels Convention. The key operational difference is that there is no provision made for a supranational court to oversee uniform interpretation of the instrument.[27] Nonetheless, the original Lugano Convention now has little practical use given that the 2007 Lugano Convention largely supersedes it, and many of its original signatories are now members of the EU and party to the various Brussels Regulations.[28]

Relevantly, from a global perspective, the Lugano Convention indicates that the Brussels Model is not necessarily a unique legal product for tightly woven politically connected EC (now EU) States – and in a select few instances can, and does, have broader applicability internationally. This is because the Convention extends the Brussels Model outside of the EU's narrow remit, and also because it provides a process and a precedent for third States (outside of the original Contracting States) to accede to the Convention.[29] However, the limited number of Lugano Convention signatories are all European nations, and the procedure for accession of the Convention is best described as both complex and difficult to achieve politically. This is for two reasons: first, the accession of the third State requires the unanimous agreement of existing Contracting Parties; and, second, even after a third State has acceded to the Convention, Contracting Parties can still object and prevent the Convention from coming into force in relation to themselves. Nonetheless, as Chapter 7, explores in greater detail, although the Lugano Convention suggests the Brussels Model *can* have broader applicability, it has received no direct State-sponsored support outside of Europe, and thus the fundamental question remains: to what extent is the Brussels Model approach likely to be acceptable or instructive globally?

[27] The role of the CJEU in the context of Lugano States and interpretive questions is discussed further at Section 7.1.2.

[28] In addition, Liechtenstein, the only State to accede to the EFTA after 1988, has neither signed the 1988 Convention nor its successor the 2007 Lugano Convention (outlined in this section).

[29] 'Lugano Convention' (Chapter 1, n 36) Art 62. Poland is the only State to have done so (but subsequently joined the EU, so is now bound by the Brussels Regulations, which supersede Lugano Convention obligations).

3.1.3 *The 2001 Brussels Regulation*

In the 1990s, as the primarily economic motives of the European integration project were increasingly supplemented by broader shared principles of freedom, security and justice[30] – and an expanding cohort of Member States – the need for reform of the Model's approach in the 1968 Convention arose. The push for reform was also premised on the need for greater efficiency, considering that recognition and enforcement took too long, was too costly and created obstacles and disincentives to the free movement of judgments.[31] As legislative competence in private international law matters was vested in the EC in 1999,[32] reform efforts moved from amending the 1968 Convention to the creation of a legislative instrument in the form of a regulation.[33] The EC at the time noted that the use of a regulation would assist with the free movement of judgments, as it is directly binding on and applicable to Member States on promulgation.[34] In terms of recognition and enforcement, the Commission expressed that the 'mutual trust in the administration of justice in the Community' justifies automatic recognition, and 'efficient and rapid' enforcement.[35] This assists with transparency, allowing potential disputants to know how judgments will be recognised and enforced, without any need for recourse to provisions of national law.[36] Out of this desire, the 2001 Brussels Regulation was born,[37] substantially based on the text and approach of the

[30] For an overview of this process, see the European Communities, 'Treaty on European Union' (no date) vol NO C 191/1 (92/C) and the discussion in the legislative summary on 'The Gradual Establishment of an Area of Freedom, Security and Justice' (Summary of EU Legislation (available on EUR-Lex), no date).

[31] European Commission, 'Towards Greater Efficiency in Obtaining and Enforcing Judgments in the European Union' (COM(1997) 609 Final; OJ [1998] C33/3, no date).

[32] 'Treaty of Amsterdam Amending the Treaty on European Union, the Treaties Establishing the European Communities and Certain Related Acts' (Official Journal C 340 1 May 1999). See also von Mehren and Gottschalk (n 3) 73, who query whether the language in this treaty was intended to provide such a broad legislative basis to the Community; in any event, the Commission (and the EU's Member States) have now largely adopted that view.

[33] Although these reform efforts came after the 1988 Lugano Convention, because the Lugano Convention mirrors the Brussels Convention and the Convention only applies to European Union members the Regulation has no direct impact on the Lugano Convention.

[34] European Commission, 'Proposal for a Council Regulation (EC) on Jurisdiction and the Recognition and Enforcement of Judgments in Civil and Commercial Matters' (COM(1999) 348 final, 14 July 1999) Recital 6.

[35] ibid. Recitals 17-9.

[36] Dickinson and Lein (n 16) para 1.16.

[37] It has subsequently been amended at various stages, to reflect the ascension of new Member States to the European Union (in 2004, 2007 and 2013).

1968 Convention. The Regulation came into force on 1 March 2002[38] and was the primary piece of legislation in the Brussels framework from 2002 until January 2015 when the 2012 Recast Regulation came into force.[39]

The 2001 Regulation operates on a similar basis to the Brussels Convention in terms of recognition and enforcement,[40] and in 'practical effect' supersedes the 1968 Convention (although it is itself now superseded by the 2012 Recast).[41] The primary change is simplification in the recognition of judgments and the procedure for enforcing them. Yet, the differences with respect to recognition provisions are relatively minor and simply represent an incremental evolution of approach.[42] To wit: the grounds for non-recognition of judgments are reduced (removing a requirement for conformity with conflicts rules); the grounds for refusing to recognise based on public policy are narrowed (by adding the word '*manifestly*' to the requirement that the judgment be 'contrary to public policy'); and lack of service no longer hinders recognition of a default judgment if the defendant did not challenge the judgment in the rendering court. The impact of the changes on enforcement procedure is also similarly minimal: the 2001 Regulation simply removes the need for the enforcing court to consider any grounds of non-enforcement in the initial declaration of enforceability (exequatur) stage.[43] Nonetheless, as in the 1968 Convention, the 2001 Regulation still provides for a uniform exequatur procedure in two stages: first, a largely formal step of obtaining an *ex parte* declaration of enforceability; and second, an eventual challenge procedure,

[38] Or 1 July 2007 for Denmark. This is because Regulation 44/2001 originally excluded Denmark, which did not agree to be bound by the Regulation until 1 July 2007. This 'opt-out' was allowed for in Art. 1(3) of the Regulation. See [2006] OJ L120/22 for Denmark's subsequent opting in to the operation of the Regulation.

[39] Briggs traces the complex accession history of the Brussels Regulation, representing the continual expansion of the European Communities and eventual progression into the European Union in 2007: Briggs (n 15) 5–10.

[40] Recognition and enforcement procedures are substantially the same as under the Convention. Article 33 mandates recognition, subject to compulsory refusal of recognition on the same grounds as the Convention (Article 34). As in the Convention, the foreign judgment cannot be reviewed at the recognition stage (Article 36). Enforcement, provided for in Section 2 'Enforcement' (Arts. 38–52), also sets out the need for an interested party to apply for a declaration of enforceability.

[41] Briggs (n 15) 9. The Regulation for the most part supplants and overrides the Convention, except for the few instances where the Regulation has left a gap for the continued operation of the Convention. For example, the Regulation does not cover non-EU territorialities of Member States, whereas the Convention does.

[42] Article 34 of the 2001 Regulation cf Article 27 of the 1968 Convention.

[43] 'Brussels I Regulation' (Chapter 1, n 36) ch III (Section 2) cf the two-stage enforcement process of the 1968 Convention. In any event, the need for a declaration of enforceability is abolished in the 2012 Recast.

where an interested person may challenge the declaration of enforceability on the grounds set out in the Regulation.[44] These grounds are substantially the same as those set out in the 1968 Convention,[45] and the same general prohibition on reviewing the substance of the judgment coming for enforcement (at either the recognition and enforcement stage) exists.[46]

3.1.4 *The 2007 Lugano Convention ('Lugano II')*

The revised Lugano II Convention entered into force in 2007. It is 'in effect a copy' of the Brussels Regulation,[47] with the main difference being that the word 'Regulation' is replaced with 'Convention' throughout the text.[48] Lugano II was designed to update the original Lugano Convention (itself modelled on the original 1968 Brussels Convention), in line with the updated 2001 Regulation, and to replace the 1968 Brussels Convention (to the extent it still applies – largely to overseas extraterritorialities of EU Members).[49] Formally, the parties are the European Union and the States of Iceland, Norway and Switzerland. Its international significance is thus relatively limited given that all three non-EU Contracting States are based in Europe and relatively small in (economic) size.[50]

The relationship between the Lugano II Convention and its Brussels counterpart largely mimics that of the original Lugano Convention and its relationship with the original Brussels Convention. First, and similar to the original Lugano Convention, there is no substantive difference in terms of the rules relating to recognition and enforcement as compared with the relevant Brussels instrument.[51] Second, similar again to the 1988 Lugano Convention and its relationship with the 1968 Brussels Convention, the primary practical difference between the Lugano II Convention and the Brussels instrument is the absence of a supranational interpretative court for Lugano Contracting States. Third, as with the original Lugano Convention, Lugano II potentially

44 ibid. Art. 38 and following.

45 See Ibid. Arts. 34 and 35 (substantially the same as Arts. 27 and 28 in the 1968 Convention).

46 See ibid. Arts. 29 (recognition) and 29 (enforcement).

47 Briggs (n 15) 6.

48 ibid. 689.

49 ibid. 9.

50 Ulrich Magnus and Peter Mankowski (eds.), *Brussels I Regulation* (2nd ed., Sellier European Law Publishers 2007) chapter I (para 29).

51 The only third State to join the Lugano Convention, Poland, is seen as an exception to the general rule that these procedures are unlikely to be fulfilled and complied with by a third State, as its ascension can be seen as part of the pathway to achieving full EU Member State status (which it achieved in 2004, and hence the Convention no longer applies to it).

further extends the operation of the Brussels Model by opening up the Convention to accession by other States.[52] Similarly, any accession of a third State requires the unanimous agreement of the existing Contracting Parties; and, even after a third State accession, Contracting Parties can still prevent the Convention from coming into force in relation to themselves and the third State. The accession process is further clarified in Lugano II as the Convention now provides further that the third State must submit information on their judicial system, civil procedure and private international law and procedure in order to be considered for invitation for accession. Despite minor changes ensuring compliance with updates to the Brussels Model, Lugano II does not shed significantly more light than the 1988 Lugano Convention on the potential applicability of the Brussels Model globally.

3.1.5 *The 2012 Brussels Regulation Recast*

The 2012 Brussels Regulation Recast came into effect on 10 January 2015 and largely supersedes the 2001 Regulation,[53] reflecting the end result of a project to 'refurbish' the previous instrument.[54] In terms of recognition and enforcement, despite the fact that the 2001 Regulation had worked well, the enforcement of judgments was not 'as smooth and automatic as it was possible for it to be'.[55] As a result, one of the key aims of the process leading to the Recast was to 'make the enforcement of judgments quicker and more straightforward'.[56] However, the reforms proved minimal, representing little movement from the recognition and enforcement framework first established in the 1968 Convention (which itself was little altered in the 2001 Regulation).[57] In addition to a streamlining and reorganisation of recognition and enforcement provisions (with no real substantive change),[58] the 'most significant' change is the abolition of the need to obtain a declaration of enforceability (*exequatur*)

52 'Lugano II' (Chapter 1, n 36) Art 70(c). The procedures for accession by any third State are set out in 'Lugano II' (Chapter 1, n 36) Art 72.

53 *Brussels I Recast* (Chapter 1, n 36) Arts 81 and 80. Except to the extent that it continues to apply to judgments given in proceedings instituted before 10 January 2015: Art. 66.

54 Briggs (n 15) 10.

55 ibid. 6.

56 ibid. 10.

57 Article 33 and following set out the provisions on recognition and enforcement. The now long-standing principle of automatic recognition, limited grounds for refusing enforcement and the prohibition on re-reviewing the merits all remain consistent with previous instruments.

58 See, for example, the 'new' Arts 45(e) and 46, which, respectively, concisely consolidate the grounds for refusing to recognise an award and then make clear these same grounds apply to refusing to enforce an award.

as a pre-condition to taking substantive enforcement measures in another Member State.[59]

The declaration of enforceability was abolished on the basis that it is unduly and unnecessarily cumbersome, and that this procedural hurdle conflicts with the express aims of the Brussels Model by impeding the free movement of judgments.[60] The rationale for its abolition was simply that the declaration of enforceability step is rarely unsuccessful; thus, removing it would have no significant detrimental impact. Instead, removing it would, in the now familiar rhetoric of the Brussels Model terminology, allow for the freer circulation of judgments, help to minimise unnecessary costs and delays for the parties and encourage companies and citizens to pursue cross-border litigation where necessary.[61] Consequently, under the 2012 Recast, a judgment creditor need only present a copy of the judgment of the rendering court and a standard form certificate and can then begin the enforcement process. This certificate is obtained from the Member State of origin (the rendering court) rather than in the Member State of enforcement; a procedure that has not proved controversial.

This procedural simplification has been described as only the 'logical end of a journey' commenced in the 1968 Convention to minimise obstacles to the free movement of judgments within the (now) European Union.[62] Nonetheless, this reform saves a claimant the need to comply with extra formalities, and limits the opportunities for defendants to raise meritless defences in order to delay enforcement. It is premised on the idea that 'judicial cooperation and the level of trust among Member States has reached a degree of maturity which permits the move towards a simpler, less costly, and

[59] Dickinson and Lein (n 16) para 1.02. A further, minor, change with respect to recognition and enforcement is that if a judgment being enforced contains measures that are not known in the State of the enforcing court, the enforcing court can adapt them to a measure used in that State (Article 54).

[60] European Commission, 'Green Paper on the Review of Council Regulation (EC) No 44/2001 on Jurisdiction and the Recognition and Enforcement of Judgments in Civil and Commercial Matters' (Green Paper COM(2009) 175 Final, 21 April 2009). Noting, however, that the push for the gradual abolition of exequatur within the European Union has been on the Brussels agenda across a range of instruments and legal areas (including in family law) for reasons of mutual recognition and trust as 'cornerstones' of European policy. See Xandra E. Kramer, 'Abolition of Exequatur under the Brussels I Regulation: Effecting and Protecting Rights in the European Judicial Area' (2011) 4 *Nederlands Internationaal Privaatrecht* 633.

[61] European Commission, 'Proposal for a Regulation of the European Parliament and of the Council on Jurisdiction and the Recognition and Enforcement of Judgments in Civil and Commercial Matters' (COM(2010) 748 final, 14 December 2010) 2–3 (Explanatory Memorandum).

[62] Dickinson and Lein (n 16) para 1.02.

more automatic system of circulation of judgments':[63] namely, automatic recognition of judgments that should be *prima facie* treated as enforceable (unless proved otherwise). As a result, the 2012 Recast not only upholds but consolidates and strengthens the Brussels Model's ongoing preference for rapid and effective recognition and enforcement of foreign judgments.

3.2 THE BRUSSELS MODEL APPROACH TO RECOGNITION AND ENFORCEMENT OF FOREIGN JUDGMENTS

As the Brussels Model is made up of a series of complex international instruments, negotiated originally in treaty form, it necessarily represents a broad range of competing rationales and interests. Yet, at a high level, it is immediately apparent that the Brussels Model attempts to strike a balance between the interests of defendants and plaintiffs (across many different Member States) by providing a complete 'package' of rules, relating to both direct and indirect jurisdiction, in each constituent instrument.[64] Although not directly impacting on recognition and enforcement, perhaps most prominently the Brussels Model package balances complex jurisdictional concerns, which often directly relate to or mask political concerns. To this end, the Model's rules on direct jurisdiction attempt to minimise discord between States by setting out provisions that assist with ameliorating or avoiding jurisdictional 'battles' and jurisdictional arbitrage between Brussels Model participants. For example, given that jurisdictional bases often overlap across international borders, the Brussels Model provides that if the same claim is litigated between the same parties in the courts of two Member States, the court seized first hears it – the other must decline jurisdiction.[65] This is designed to limit potential unfairness to disputants, by providing that they should only have to defend themselves in jurisdictions that are sufficiently related to the dispute.[66] Another issue that proved controversial, and may yet

[63] European Commission, 'Proposal for a Regulation of the European Parliament and of the Council on Jurisdiction and the Recognition and Enforcement of Judgments in Civil and Commercial Matters' (n 61) 6 (Explanatory Memorandum).

[64] This is a double, closed convention, within the language utilised to describe instrumental features of recognition and enforcement approaches. See further, Section 5.5 and Section 8.2.2.

[65] (see 'Brussels I Regulation' (Chapter 1, n 36) Section 9 (Lis pendens-related actions) and *Brussels I Recast* (Chapter 1, n 36) Arts 29 and 31(2), which alter jurisdictional rules slightly to defuse the so-called Italian torpedo).

[66] Magnus and Mankowski (n 50) Introduction, para 3.

resurface due to the UK's exit from the EU,[67] was the fact the Brussels Model rules on jurisdiction were held to limit the powers of Member States to grant anti-suit injunctions, stopping parties from initiating a legal action in a different jurisdiction.[68] The precise operation of these jurisdictional features is outside of the scope of this book, but it suffices to note they no doubt give participant States a greater degree of comfort to recognise and enforce judgments, as they can be assured that most judgments that eventually come for recognition and enforcement will have complied with jurisdictional limits set out in the Model.[69]

With respect to recognition and enforcement, the Brussels Model package aims to achieve legal certainty with 'highly predictable' outcomes for disputants, enabling them, for example, to know whether any judgment they receive is likely to be given effect to in another Brussels Model State.[70] This is seen in one of the primary objectives of the Brussels Model: the attainment of the maximum acceptable level of judgment recognition and enforcement between signatory States.[71] This objective is given greater latitude where parties exclusively select a court of their own volition, in deference to the principles of party autonomy.[72] Beyond such a choice, the Brussels Model approach relies heavily on mutual trust: that is, an 'expectation' that each Member is willing to strictly obey the operative provisions of the Brussels Model and generally recognise and enforce foreign judgments without

67 As explored in Julio-César Betancourt, 'Anti-Suit Injunctions in the EU: Are They Finally Back on the Menu?' (*Kluwer Arbitration Blog*, 12 February 2021) <http://arbitrationblog.kluwerarbitration.com/2021/02/12/anti-suit-injunctions-in-the-eu-are-they-finally-back-on-the-menu/> accessed 20 August 2021.

68 The treatment of anti-suit injunctions, including how these orders are likely to be recognised and enforced, has also been considered in detail by the Court of Justice in the European Union in the high profile cases of *Allianz SpA and Generali Assicurazioni Generali SpA* v. *West Tankers Inc.* (C-185/07) and *Gazprom OAO* v. *Lithuania* (C-536/13).

69 As Brand notes, when drawing parallels with the 2019 Convention at a global level, the whole idea of regulating jurisdiction within the Brussels Model was originally to facilitate the creation of harmonised rules with respect to recognition and enforcement: Ronald A. Brand, 'Jurisdiction and Judgments Recognition at the Hague Conference: Choices Made, Treaties Completed, and the Path Ahead' [2020] *Netherlands International Law Review*, 17.

70 'Brussels I Regulation' (Chapter 1, n 36) Recital 11. See also *Owens Bank Ltd* v. *Fulvio Bracco and Bracco Industria Chimica SpA (Case 129/92)* [1994] ECR I-155 (para 32), for a statement of the CJEU in a similar vein.

71 Trevor Hartley, 'The European Court, the Brussels Convention/Regulation and the Establishment of an Efficient System for International Litigation in Europe' in Anthony Arnull and others (eds.), *Continuity and Change in EU Law* (Oxford University Press 2008) 386.

72 *Brussels I Recast* (Chapter 1, n 36) Recital 19. See also: Briggs (n 15) chapter 5.

question in their national courts.[73] So long as any judgment coming for enforcement is rendered by a court of a participant State, it will generally be given effect to in other participant States.[74] Procedurally, the Model does so via establishing a general rule in favour of recognition and enforcement,[75] combined with a prohibition on enforcing courts reviewing the substance or merits of the original decision of the rendering court.[76] In these respects, the Model is similar in approach to other international approaches to recognition and enforcement, including the New York Convention and Judgments Conventions.[77] Similar to these instruments, the grounds for refusing recognition and enforcement are enumerated and very limited, and the enforcing court can only refuse to recognise a foreign judgment if one of these limited grounds for refusal exists. As Part II demonstrates, these grounds, despite the passage of almost half a century, remain broadly consistent across all instruments of the Brussels Model. As a result, the Brussels Model consistently offers – and has offered – its participants a harmonised international regime strongly promoting recognition and enforcement.

The mandate for this harmonised pro-recognition and enforcement approach stems from the European Community's decision to seek market integration as part of 'an ever closer union . . . to eliminate the barriers which divide Europe'.[78] One key component of this integration is the 'free movement of judgments', aided by simplifying formalities governing the reciprocal recognition and enforcement of judgments.[79] In other words, a 'true internal market' – as required for effective European economic integration – depends ultimately on a satisfactory judgment recognition and enforcement solution

73 Magnus and Mankowski (n 50) Introduction, para 2. Yet, as Briggs notes, it is somewhat surprising that this obligation of trust and confidence is imposed by the CJEU, rather than deriving from a foundational principle: Briggs (n 15) 34.

74 This approach has, however, been criticised because a judgment rendered under objectionable or exorbitant grounds of jurisdiction can be enforced against a defendant domiciled outside the EU: see, for example, James Fawcett and others, *Cheshire, North & Fawcett: Private International Law* (14th ed., Oxford University Press 2008) 597–98, who question the fairness of this treatment. This outcome is nonetheless consistent with a pro-recognition and pro-enforcement approach within a closed regional grouping, where protections exist solely to protect EU States and defendants domiciled in the EU. As long as those protections are not breached, trust and confidence (and enforcement) must then be given to the judgment of a rendering court by the enforcing court.

75 *Brussels I Recast* (Chapter 1, n 36) Arts 36 and 39.

76 ibid. at Art 52. For example, absent a few enumerated exceptions in the Model, it is not possible for the enforcing court to review the original exercise of jurisdiction by the rendering court.

77 See, further, Chapter 2.

78 'Treaty Establishing the European Economic Community' (1 January 1958) Preamble.

79 This provision stems from ibid. Art. 220 (this became the later Art. 293 of the EC Treaty; but in any event is now deleted from the Treaty on the Functioning of the European Union).

that is both 'rapid' and 'simple'.[80] In the context of the Brussels Model instruments, this ultimately means that the enforcing court in participant States must give due respect to decisions rendered by courts in other participant States, unless there are exceptional reasons (enumerated in the Model) for refusing to do so. The explicit formalisation of these recognition and enforcement rules allows disputants confidence that any judgment they may receive will be readily and predictably enforced across borders within Brussels Model participant States when doing business in other participant States.[81] By contrast, failing to provide a pro-recognition and enforcement ruleset is likely to disturb trade between Brussels Model participants, as private parties will be less likely to transact across borders if they cannot be assured of an effective remedy if their judgment is not given effect to.[82] While the extent to which trade depends on recognition and enforcement is difficult to quantify with 'final precision',[83] each instrument in the Brussels Model nonetheless adopts this rationale to make explicit – and indeed, enshrine – a consistent pro-recognition and enforcement approach to foreign judgments. Consequently, it can be surmised that a primary objective of the Brussels Model is the attainment of the maximum mutually acceptable level of judgment recognition and enforcement between signatory States.[84]

This imperative towards maximal acceptable recognition and enforcement based on mutual trust and confidence has evolved over the history of European Union, and it is now a core shared institutional modality.[85] Not only does it stem from the Brussels Model instruments themselves, but it is an approach shared by the European Commission, the European Council, the Court of Justice of the European Union (CJEU) and even the European Court of Human Rights.[86] Yet, at the same time as the law-making power of the EU has evolved, so too has the expressed rationale for giving effect to foreign judgments. While newer Brussels Model instruments maintain the

80 *Brussels I Recast* (Chapter 1, n 36) Recital 4.

81 This point was made as early as 1959 in a Note from the Commission, quoted in Paul Jenard, 'Report on the Convention on Jurisdiction and the Enforcement of Judgments in Civil and Commercial Matters of 27 September 1968' (1979) No C59/1 *Official Journal of the European Communities*, 3. The original version of the Report was issued in French in 1967.

82 ibid.

83 Magnus and Mankowski (n 50) chapter I (para 36).

84 Hartley (n 71) 386.

85 This approach is described as the one of the 'key' principles governing cross-border movement of judgments in Europe, 'enshrined' in all European texts on this topic: Dickinson and Lein (n 16) 377.

86 Matthias Weller, 'Mutual Trust: In Search of the Future of European Union Private International Law' (2015) 11 *Journal of Private International Law* 64, 65.

rhetoric of the 'free movement of judgments', they are also more explicitly guided by the idea that a straightforward approach to recognition and enforcement streamlines inter-regional trade as well as fulfilling the EU's expanded legislative goal of 'maintaining and developing an area of freedom, security and justice'.[87] As Weller argues, all of these justifications depend on giving effect to foreign judgments being an expression of mutual trust: that is, participant States agree, to some pre-defined limit, to 'allow' their enforcing court to implicitly trust in the decision (or the process) the rendering court has undertaken.[88] This conception of mutual trust as the 'overriding principle'[89] underlying the Model builds on the explicitly shared foundations of 'justice' and the 'rule of law' within the EU.[90] Seen in this light, the Brussels Model further represents the high point of mutual trust between sovereign States.

However, no guidance is provided as to the extent of mutual trust that should be accorded in terms of recognition and enforcement. Do these principles, for example, call for a complete and uncritical acceptance of all foreign judgments between participant States? The practical answer is of course not. Even among EU States – States with the closest degree of shared legal, economic and political institutions – this trust is never granted unconditionally, and remains balanced against forms of residual control by the enforcing court (based usually on grounds for refusing to give effect to a judgment, such as the public policy exception).[91] At least within the confines of the Brussels Model, the practical need to balance trust with control requires that limits are placed upon the scope or extent to which recognition and enforcement can be granted by enforcing courts. It does so in two key ways: first, by excluding from recognition and enforcement some politically sensitive matters that States are likely to want exclusive control and jurisdiction over; and second, by allowing for exceptions to recognition and enforcement if any judgment is rendered contrary to fundamental precepts of procedural fairness.

As to the first exclusion, the Brussels Model limits recognition and enforcement by either removing certain politically sensitive matters entirely from the scope of the Model or, in other cases, by overriding the Model's default rules in favour of recognition and enforcement if a judgment is rendered contrary to

87 See 'Brussels I Regulation' (Chapter 1, n 36) Recitals 1–2 and *Brussels I Recast* (Chapter 1, n 36) Recitals 3–4.

88 Weller (n 86).

89 Geert van Calster, *European Private International Law* (2nd ed., Hart Publishing 2016) 26.

90 European Union, 'Consolidated Versions of the Treaty on European Union and the Treaty on the Functioning of the European Union' (7 June 2016) (Treaty on European Union, Arts 2 and 6), OJ C 202/1.

91 Weller (n 86) 100.

exclusive jurisdiction rules.[92] Consistent with other transnational approaches, the first layer of exclusion from scope is that the Brussels Model only applies to 'civil and commercial' judgments, excluding all others, including 'revenue, customs or administrative matters' and the liability of the State in the exercise of State authority.[93] The second layer excludes from scope further matters that are either handled by other international treaties or implicate concerns that are fundamentally domestic, such that there is a widely accepted preference for only allowing for domestic resolution.[94] These matters include, for example, disputes relating to wills, family law and maintenance obligations, bankruptcy proceedings and social security. In addition to these exclusions from scope, if a judgment is rendered contrary to exclusive jurisdiction rules, the enforcing court must not give effect to it.[95] These jurisdictional exclusions relate primarily to State-specific concerns including insurance, company incorporation, intellectual property and the protection of groups or individuals perceived to be vulnerable (such as consumers and employees).[96]

In addition to excluding via scope and the protection of exclusive jurisdiction, a further brake on the pro-recognition and enforcement approach of the Model is its parallel goal of *limiting* enforcement prospects against defendants facing judgments rendered in breach of fundamental notions of procedural fairness. This is because the principle of 'respect for the rights of the defence' is one of the explicit objectives of the Brussels Model.[97] This principle suggests that even a strongly pro-recognition and enforcement instrument cannot, and indeed should not, solely be about maximising recognition and enforcement by any means. Instead, exceptions exist for breaches of serious procedural grounds – albeit grounds that are particularly carefully crafted and considered to be 'time-proof'[98] – the breach of which is sufficient to *compel* the enforcing court not to give effect to a foreign judgment. Due to the

92 For a detailed overview of these exclusions, their operation and case law on their use, see generally: Calster (n 89) chapter 2 ('The Core of European Private International Law: Jurisdiction').

93 *Brussels I Recast* (Chapter 1, n 36) Art 1(1).

94 ibid. at Art 1(2).

95 ibid. at Art 45(e) (recognition) and Art 46 (enforcement).

96 ibid. at chapter II (Sections 3–6).

97 See, for example: European Commission, 'Proposal for a Council Regulation (EC) on Jurisdiction and the Recognition and Enforcement of Judgments in Civil and Commercial Matters' (n 34) Recital 19. These rights are safeguarded by Art 47 of the 'Charter of Fundamental Rights of the European Union' (2012) OJ C 326/2.

98 Xandra E. Kramer, 'Cross-Border Enforcement and the Brussels I-Bis Regulation: Towards a New Balance between Mutual Trust and National Control over Fundamental Rights' (2013) 60 *Netherlands International Law Review* 343, 363.

principle of 'certainty' and 'predictability', these are cast in mandatory terms: unlike in other regional or global instruments, the enforcing court under the Brussels Model must refuse recognition or enforcement of a judgment if a ground for refusal is found to exist.[99] These grounds are exhaustively set out in each instrument constituting the Brussels Model, formulated to arise in exceptional circumstances where recognising the judgment would offend the public policy of the State of the enforcing court, one of the parties to the litigation was not given proper notice of proceedings or the judgment coming for recognition is 'irreconcilable' with a conflicting judgment.[100] The Brussels Model protections are also bolstered by further European Union treaties and case law. For example, the European Court of Human Rights held in *Avotiņš* v. *Latvia*[101] that the European Convention of Human Rights' right to a fair trial must be considered even in light of 'mechanistic' recognition procedures that derive from the Brussels Regulation (as an incidence of EU law).[102] This serves as a further limit to recognition and enforcement, and has even been criticised on the basis that 'without clear EU rules as to what constitutes a fair trial, mutual trust may be little more than a hollow phrase'.[103]

Consequently, it can be surmised that participants in the Model (as an incidence of being in the EU or as non-EU Lugano State signatories) are concerned primarily with maximising recognition and enforcement prospects. At the same time, however, they also insist upon employing procedural safeguards, so that this level of recognition and enforcement is mutually

[99] Christian Thiele, 'The Hague Convention on Choice-of-Court Agreements: Was It Worth the Effort?' in Eckart Gottschalk and others (eds.), *Conflict of Laws in a Globalized World* (Cambridge University Press 2007) 80 (footnote 127) undertakes a linguistic analysis of the terms 'may' and 'shall', indicating that the former allows discretion globally and the latter removes it. For a comparison between instruments, see, for example, 'Brussels I Regulation' (Chapter 1, n 36) Art 34, as distinct from Hague Conference, 'Choice of Court Convention' (Chapter 2, n 12) Art. 9.

[100] See, for example, Arts 45 and 46 of the 2012 Brussels Recast (which is consistent in approach with all other Brussels Model instruments).

[101] Application no. 17502/07 of 23 May 2016,

[102] See, further, on the interaction between the national law implementation of the Brussels Model procedural justice provisions and how they are supplemented or intersect with the ECHR's interpretation of Article 6 ('Right to a fair trial') of the European Convention on Human Rights: Zvonimir Jelinić and Katarina Knol Radoja, 'Mutual Recognition of Judicial Decisions and the Right to a Fair Trial with Special Focus on the ECHR's Findings in the Case of Avotiņš v. Latvia' in Tunjica Petrašević and Dunja Duić (eds.) (Faculty of Law Josip Juraj Strossmayer University of Osijek) <https://hrcak.srce.hr/ojs/index.php/eclic/article/view/7127>.

[103] Xandra E. Kramer, 'Cross-Border Enforcement in the EU: Mutual Trust Versus Fair Trial? Towards Principles of European Civil Procedure' (2011) 2 *International Journal of Procedural Law* 202, 202.

acceptable by participants. This is achieved by the general pro-recognition and enforcement rules yielding to other fundamental concerns in exceptional cases, for example, where a judgment coming for recognition or enforcement relates to a carved-out political or legal exclusion or does not meet at least minimum standards relating to the proper administration of justice. A similar approach, founded upon a very different regional grouping, is evident in the operation of the Commonwealth Model, to which I now turn.

4

The Commonwealth Model and Common Law Recognition and Enforcement

This chapter analyses the Commonwealth approach to recognition and enforcement of foreign judgments – referred to in this book as the

'Commonwealth Model' – and its common law underpinnings.[1] At its core, the Commonwealth Model is a statutory judgment registration system that is premised upon British dominion, seconded only where historical ties (but not dominion) extend by reciprocity. In this way, shared British or Commonwealth heritage underlies participation in the Commonwealth Model, and its genesis can be traced back to the original statutory implementations in the United Kingdom.[2] The Model offers a method of bypassing traditional common law actions for recognition, in effect 'fast tracking' recognition procedures for participants and ultimately allowing foreign judgments to be treated as if they are domestic. It has been argued that the existence of such a Model adds 'greater predictability and fluidity to the English practice of foreign judgment enforcement',[3] and no doubt this same accolade could be extended to all participating States. Yet, as distinct from a harmonised multilateral treaty, the Model's legal instrumentation is far from clear. This is largely because statutory provisions need to be implemented in each participant State for it receive preferential treatment from other participants. In this complex bilateral manner, a criss-crossing web of preferential and harmonised treatment for Commonwealth and British dominion-linked foreign judgments can be established via domestic statute, supplemented where appropriate with bilateral or regional arrangements. Additionally, whether recourse remains to underlying common law recognition and enforcement rules, where a statutory regime applies, differs across implementations.

Because of this reliance on reciprocal domestic enactment, the approach of the Model is best summarised by considering the originating Acts of the United Kingdom, as the jurisdiction originally exercising influence over States facing British dominion or Commonwealth. These Acts are, respectively, the *Administration of Justice Act* 1920 (UK) (the '1920 Act') and the

[1] Notably, the Commonwealth Model, like the common law from which it derives, focuses only on the recognition and enforcement of monetary judgments, a fact that has been criticised and even overcome in some common law States. See, for example, Kim Pham, 'Enforcement of Non-Monetary Foreign Judgments in Australia' (2008) 30 *Sydney Law Review* 663; Stephen G. A. Pitel, 'Enforcement of Foreign Non-Monetary Judgments in Canada (And Beyond)' (2007) 3 *Journal of Private International Law* 241. See also Lee's comments about the ongoing role of equity in allowing for non-money judgments: Stephen Lee, 'The Equitable Jurisdiction to Enforce Foreign Judgments' (2020) 39 *University of Queensland Law Journal* 313.

[2] Foreign Judgments (Reciprocal Enforcement) Act 1933 (UK) ch 13, 23 and 24 Geo 5; Administration of Justice Act 1920 (UK) ch 81, 10 and 11 Geo 5.

[3] Brian Paige, 'Foreign Judgments in American and English Courts: A Comparative Analysis' (2003) 26 *Seattle University Law Review* 591, 609.

Foreign Judgments (Reciprocal Enforcement) Act 1933 (UK) (the '1933 Act').[4] It has been suggested that the registration procedures established by these Acts marked, at the time, 'a significant step in the evolution toward a more efficient and uniform' judgment recognition and enforcement approach.[5] Yet, apart from reliance on concepts of reciprocity, the Commonwealth Model remains fundamentally premised on the common law approach that preceded it. This is because the Model either refers back to or substantially replicates the common law approach to recognition and enforcement.[6] This approach is nonetheless familiar. Consistent with other transnational approaches, the Commonwealth Model employs a presumption (or rule) in favour of recognition, subject to the 'usual' exceptions for potentially objectionable judgments or classes of judgments.[7] In fact, this presumption is likely strengthened in the Commonwealth Model, as each of its constituent Acts seem to (implicitly) presume that a foreign judgment is recognisable, rather than placing the onus of proving this on the plaintiff (as the common law usually does).

In addition to the two statutory schemes, a Commonwealth Model Law on the Recognition and Enforcement of Foreign Judgments ('2017 Model Law') was adopted by the Commonwealth Law Ministers in 2017.[8] The 2017 Model Law improves significantly on the Commonwealth Model's statutory judgment recognition and enforcement approach. It has, however, not been enacted in any State, and due to the adoption of the 2019 Judgments Convention this state of affairs may not change. For this reason, Section 4.1 focuses primarily on the existing Commonwealth Model in its two original implementing Acts. However, I do nonetheless briefly consider some of the more significant changes, commenting in particular on the increased 'transnationalisation' witnessed through the 2017 Model Law. The chapter concludes by analysing the underlying common law approach to recognition and enforcement, both in theory and as implemented in practice in the exemplar of the United States.

4.1 THE COMMONWEALTH MODEL: STATUTORY JUDGMENT REGISTRATION

The Commonwealth Model is made up of the 1920 and 1933 Acts, explored in Sections 4.1.1 and 4.1.2, respectively. The recognition and enforcement

4 Administration of Justice Act 1920 (UK), s 9(3)(a); Foreign Judgments (Reciprocal Enforcement) Act 1933 (UK), 2(2).

5 Paige (n 3) 613.

6 ibid. 618.

7 ibid. 619.

8 The Commonwealth Secretariat (Office of Civil and Criminal Justice Reform), *Model Law on the Recognition and Enforcement of Foreign Judgments* (2017).

approaches across the Commonwealth are, for the most part, patterned on these Acts. Notably, these Acts – and hence their implementation across the Commonwealth – largely represent a codification of the pre-existing common law. The Acts themselves have remained unchanged for almost a century, despite recurring criticisim that they are, at least in parts, outdated, and are subject to significant divergences across the Commonwealth.[9]

4.1.1 1920 *Act*

The Administration of Justice Act 1920 (UK) is the first of two Acts that constitute the fundament of the Commonwealth Model. Section 9 of the 1920 Act establishes the basic registration system that underlies the Model, relevantly providing that:

> Where a judgment has been obtained in a superior court in any part of His Majesty's dominions outside the United Kingdom to which this Part of this Act extends, the judgment creditor may apply to the [enforcing court] … to have the judgment registered in the court, and on any such application the court may, if in all the circumstances of the case, they think it just and convenient that the judgment should be enforced in the United Kingdom, and subject to the provisions of this section, order the judgment to be registered accordingly.

Given the broad discretion accorded in this provision, the Act simply refers the enforcing court back to the common law approach that favours a presumption in favour of recognition and enforcement. Section 2 of the Act also sets out that the enforcing court must (mandatorily) deny recognition to foreign judgments that breach the now familiar procedural and public policy exceptions associated with recognising foreign judgments.

A careful review of section 9 also discloses two further critical features of the 1920 Act. First, although non-registration must occur where a ground for refusal is proven, registration under the 1920 Act is entirely discretionary. This means that under this Act the enforcing court *may* order the judgment registered but is not obliged to do so. However, if the enforcing court chooses to register the foreign judgment, this gives it the 'same force and effect… as if it had been a judgment originally obtained… in the registering court'.[10] Second, recognition is not an automatic process. Instead, the Executive can

[9] Abubakri Yekini, *The Hague Judgments Convention and Commonwealth Model Law: A Pragmatic Perspective* (Hart Publishing 2021) 87, 99–101.

[10] Section 3.

order that the benefit of recognition and enforcement processes set out in the Act extend to another jurisdiction in two circumstances: in the case of dominions outside of the UK, where the Executive is satisfied that 'reciprocal provisions have been made by the legislature of any part of His Majesty's dominions outside the United Kingdom for the enforcement ... of [British] judgments';[11] or if the order is in respect to any territory in respect of which a UK government mandate or protection is extended.[12] In summary, registration under the 1920 Act – and Acts in other Commonwealth jurisdictions that substantially follow this Act – is discretionary and premised fundamentally on territorial links to, or dominion of, the United Kingdom. It is a pragmatic approach, premised on similar concepts of international comity, that underly the common law discretion with respect to recognition and enforcement.

4.1.2 1933 *Act*

The 1933 Act is 'patterned closely' on the 1920 Act,[13] and provisions modelled on this Act are in force in many Commonwealth countries (including, New Zealand, Singapore and Zimbabwe). To a greater extent than the 1920 Act, the 1933 Act is based on concepts of reciprocity rather than dominion.[14] For example, it allows judgments obtained in specified courts of other Commonwealth States, privileged under bilateral treaties, to be enforced via registration – including in Australia, Canada, Guernsey and India. This shift in emphasis reflects a change in the nature of the United Kingdom and British dominion towards self-governing independent territories. In this way, the 1933 Act represents the Commonwealth Model's first real attempt to engage more consistently with other States as 'equals' rather than subordinates and dominions under United Kingdom direction or control. Registration is premised upon reciprocity, but the Model is strengthened in that enforcement by registration under the 1933 Act is mandatory rather than discretionary.[15] This means that where the reciprocity elements are met, and no grounds for refusal exist, a foreign judgment must be recognised. In addition, unlike the 1920 Act, the 1933 Act provides a comprehensive approach to matters that fall within its

[11] Section 14. The adequacy of this reciprocity is determined entirely at the discretion of the executive in the United Kingdom – and appears largely to be a matter of having reciprocal provisions (and not whether they have been utilised, or how they are utilised in practice).

[12] Section 13.

[13] Paige (n 3) 611.

[14] Section 1 of the Act establishes the requirement for reciprocity.

[15] Section 2 provides that the enforcing court, 'shall [must], subject to proof of the prescribed matters and to the other provisions of this Act, order the judgment to be registered'.

remit by clarifying that it supplants any common law cause of action to enforce a foreign judgment (to the extent that such a judgment is caught by the provisions of the Act).[16]

Departing from the largely discretionary nature of the 1920 Act, s 4 of the 1933 Act provides clear guidance about the '[c]ases in which registered judgments must, or may, be set aside'. Consistent with other transnational approaches, the Model's promotion of recognition and enforcement is not absolute and relevantly provides that:

> (1) On an application in that behalf duly made by any party against whom a registered judgment may be enforced, the registration of the judgment
> (a) shall be set aside if the registering court is satisfied
> (i) that the judgment is not a judgment to which this Part of this Act applies or was registered in contravention of the foregoing provisions of this Act; or
> (ii) that the courts of the country of the original court had no jurisdiction in the circumstances of the case; or
> (iii) that the judgment debtor, being the defendant in the proceedings in the original court, did not (notwithstanding that process may have been duly served on him in accordance with the law of the country of the original court) receive notice of those proceedings in sufficient time to enable him to defend the proceedings and did not appear; or
> (iv) that the judgment was obtained by fraud; or
> (v) that the enforcement of the judgment would be contrary to public policy in the country of the registering court; or
> (vi) that the rights under the judgment are not vested in the person by whom the application for registration was made;
> (b) may be set aside if the registering court is satisfied that the matter in dispute in the proceedings in the original court had previously to the date of the judgment in the original court been the subject of a final and conclusive judgment by a court having jurisdiction in the matter.

In this way, recognition and enforcement can be refused on either mandatory or discretionary grounds. It is also evident that these grounds for refusal seen within the Model substantially replicate or refer back to the common law. For example, the definition of 'fraud' or matters that breach 'public policy' are inherently concerns to be resolved according to the common law of the

[16] Section 6.

enforcing court.[17] Furthermore, acceptable jurisdictional bases under the 1933 Act substantially replicate the narrow and well-trodden jurisdictional bases under the common law, such as deemed or actual submission to jurisdiction, personal ties to the jurisdiction of the rendering court and bases centred upon 'reciprocity'.[18] Additionally, s 4 of the 1933 Act reflects an early instance of the intersection between closed (exhaustive) and open (inclusive) approaches to recognition and enforcement:[19] although non-recognition is mandatory for most grounds of refusal, where the matter in dispute in the foreign judgment can be shown to have already been the subject of a previous final and conclusive judgment, the registering court is accorded discretion to determine whether to allow recognition. For these reasons, the Commonwealth Model reflects, and was a likely progenitor of, a now consistent theme: the general presumption–exception to recognition and enforcement codified or 'statutorised' in a legal instrument. Given that the Commonwealth Model is designed to extend almost exclusively to common law jurisdictions, this means that the Model, for efficacy, clarification and exposition of the concepts within each implementing State, ultimately and explicitly depends upon the underlying common law in each participant State.

4.1.3 2017 *Model Law on the Recognition and Enforcement of Foreign Judgments*

Although the 2017 Model Law is also designed as a statutory Act to be implemented by domestic enactment, in substance it represents a significant departure from prior statutory schemes. In this section, I aim to provide only a brief overview of these changes, noting in particular that the 2017 Model Law has not been enacted in any jurisdiction, and it is possible that it may never come into force. Departing from prior statutory schemes that were conceived of as an incidence of British dominion or lesser ties in the Commonwealth, the Model Law drew heavily for inspiration upon other developments in the recognition and enforcement field. This includes the Hague Conference work on the Judgments Project, demonstrating the close interrelation and

17 See, further, Adrian Briggs, *Civil Jurisdiction and Judgments* (6th ed., Informa Law from Routledge 2015), who explores the common law defence of fraud (at 728–34), and public policy (at 736–37).

18 The range and nature of jurisdictional bases utilised in transnational recognition and enforcement approaches are explored in their comparative context at Section 5.3.3.

19 This terminology and the underlying concepts are explored further in their comparative context at Section 5.4.

fertilisation across modern recognition and enforcement regimes. As noted in the Background to the 2017 Model Law:

> This Model Law fulfils a long-standing mandate from law ministers to address the need to reform the arrangements within the Commonwealth for the recognition and enforcement of foreign judgments. It also reflects the co-operation over many years between the Commonwealth Secretariat and The Hague Conference on Private International Law. The Secretariat participated in The Hague Conference's efforts in the period 1992–2001 to draw up a wide-ranging convention dealing with both jurisdiction and the recognition and enforcement of foreign judgments. The drafting of this Model Law drew upon the experience gained in the earlier Hague Conference project, and also The Hague Convention of 30 June 2005 on Choice of Court Agreements.

The experience sharing of the 2017 Model Law highlights a wider argument made in this book. What we see is that decades of experience with harmonisation and similar rationales for giving effect to foreign judgments and foreign awards have led to a high degree of convergence in recognition and enforcement approaches. Such convergence is explored in a comparative context in Chapter 5, and the way in which perceived hurdles arising from differences in legal tradition have been streamlined is analysed in Chapter 6. This explicit experience sharing also supports the claims made in Chapter 8 that recognition and enforcement practice is increasingly 'transnationalised' and, consequently, must be analysed in a fashion sensitive to this fact.

The precise operation of the provisions of the 2017 Model Law are explored in a comprehensive comparative fashion by Abubakri Yekini.[20] In broad precis, the 2017 Model Law adopts a similar form to other aspects of the Commonwealth Model by first requiring recognition (under s 6) before a judgment can be registered for enforcement (s 7). Once this occurs, the judgment is enforceable in the same way as a domestic judgment (s 9). The 2017 Model Law however modernises and reforms the 1920 Act and 1933 Act statutory regimes by:[21]

- removing any requirement for reciprocity as a condition for recognition and enforcement – a particularly vexed question both under the statutory regimes and the common law;
- providing that the judgments that are to be recognised and enforced no longer need to come from 'superior' courts; and

[20] Yekini (n 9).
[21] ibid. 98–99.

providing that recognition and enforcement extends to both money and non-money judgments.[22]

Like the 2019 Judgments Convention, the 2017 Model Law is single in nature, regulating only recognition and enforcement rather than direct jurisdiction of the rendering court. The Model Law nonetheless still sets out indirect jurisdictional grounds in s 6. These grounds are broader than those seen under prior statutory schemes, as they are made up of a combination of existing codified common law jurisdictional bases, as well as new bases determined by reference to some of the agreed heads of jurisdiction drafted during negotiations towards the Judgments Project.[23] While these jurisdictional filters have been criticised – as 'simplistic', or subject to uncertainties due to an overly broad drafting approach[24] – they go a long way towards harmonising recognition and enforcement on a transnational level. Apart from these changes, s 6 establishes the now familiar presumption–exception framework to recognition and enforcement, with similar grounds for refusing recognition and enforcement, and a strong prohibition on any merits review. Perhaps most notably for the purposes of comparison, the 2017 Model Law is designed in a closed fashion. That is, no residual recourse remains to common law,[25] and if a ground for refusal exists recognition and enforcement must be denied.[26] This diverges from the standard approach on a global level, where open conventions predominate.[27]

The fate of the 2017 Model Law, including whether it will be adopted in any jurisdiction, is, however, unclear. To the extent that current events can be extrapolated into the future, this is unlikely to change. As Yekini notes, the Model Law has not been part of the agenda in Commonwealth meetings, and even though Singapore revised its judgments enforcement statute in October 2019, it did so without considering the Model Law or its approach in

[22] Common law regimes, with notable exceptions, have traditionally enabled only the recognition and enforcement of money judgments: see footnote 1. This extension to non-money judgments is, however, not controversial under global enforcement architecture – see, for example Article 3 of the 2019 Convention, which defines judgment to include any decision on the merits, and hence extends to both money and non-money judgments.

[23] Acceptable jurisdictional bases for the purposes of recognition and enforcement, often referred to in the common law as 'international jurisdiction', are analysed in Yekini (n 9) 109–30.

[24] ibid. 146.

[25] Section 8 is titled 'No other method of enforcement is to be used'. It abolishes the common law action on a judgment debt, and provides that a foreign judgment shall not be enforced 'except by registration under [the Model Law Act]'.

[26] Sub-section 6(3).

[27] As discussed at Section 8.2.1.

introducing revised jurisdictional grounds and overcoming reciprocity.[28] In any event, the Model Law still suffers from the same issues as other statutory schemes in the Commonwealth Model, as it continues to rely on reciprocal implementation of statutory schemes. As this book explores in a range of contexts, unilateral action based solely on a suggested legislative model has long proven a haphazard mechanism for wider harmonisation, due to the very real prospects of divergent implementations. Further, it is likely that the adoption of the 2019 Convention on a global level will act to retard the Commonwealth Model Law's harmonising motive. This represents quite a turnaround in position: recall that in the context of the Brussels Model it was argued that regional harmonisation may have removed the impetus of European States to contribute to or reach global consensus during negotiations towards the Judgments Project. If the 2019 Convention does begin to achieve a critical mass of adoption, the New York Convention experience may also prove telling here: where a global enforcement harmonisation regime is considered appropriate, and receives widespread implementation internationaly, there is little need or impetus for regional harmonisation projects to do the same.

4.2 COMMON LAW RATIONALES UNDERLYING RECOGNITION AND ENFORCEMENT

Having considered the Commonwealth Model and attempts to reform it in the 2017 Model Law, I turn now to analyse the rationales or policies underlying common law recognition and enforcement. This is not intended as an authoritative exposition of the reasons why any particular State or enforcing court gives, or refuses to give, effect to foreign judgments. Instead, the analysis is intended to aide the reader's understanding of the development of harmonised or codified recognition and enforcement schemes, by adopting a broadly historical lens, and by emphasising divergences in approach amongst even very similar common law States.

In broad precis, recognition and enforcement of judgments in the common law is based on a concept, or potential doctrine, of 'comity'. Comity is a flexible notion, which is often relied upon to support a general presumption in favour of giving effect to foreign judgments, in a bid to rationalise and respond to clashes of State sovereignty that arise with the intersection of domestic and foreign laws, judgments and legal systems. Notably, for much of its history,

28 Yekini (n 9) 244.

comity as an explanatory rationale was premised on *State* interests in mutually deferring to the exercise of powers of foreign States, and the acceptable (and unacceptable) parameters for doing so. This stands in stark contrast to the emphasis placed upon the interests of disputants, often reflected in the concept of party autonomy that underlies both the 2005 Choice of Court Convention and the 1958 New York Convention. It should be noted, however, that comity, as a driver of common law recognition and enforcement and practice, has been supplemented, criticised, confused, amended, built upon and reinterpreted to encompass a series of other policies or rationales that stand in favour of recognition and enforcement. To explore these, I first set out the development of comity historically, before considering how comity intersects with enforcement rationales in common law recognition and enforcement practice.

4.2.1 *Principles in Search of a Rule*

The first 'modern' attempt to theorise as to why foreign judgments should be given effect to within the common law built on Ulrich Huber's seventeenth-century conception of comity,[29] which is now commonly referred to as 'prescriptive comity'.[30] This conception refers to a 'comity of nations': that is, the idea that States (via their enforcing courts) should attempt to give effect to foreign judgments – unless doing so offends a State interest or the rule of law – as a matter of respect for other sovereigns.[31] This is for intensely practical reasons: as Huber explains, the 'civility of nations' calls for a general rule in favour of applying foreign laws (and foreign judgments) where necessary, to avoid interference with litigants' legitimate interest in achieving justice, and the flow of international commerce.[32] Prescriptive comity represents the idea

[29] See the translation of Ulrich Huber's seventeenth-century '*Praelectionum Juris Civilis Tomi Tres*' in Ernest Lorenzen, 'Huber's De Conflictu Legum' (1919) 13 *Illinois Law Review* 401 (and following). Huber's approach is discussed further in this chapter.

[30] Prescriptive comity 'is a term used to justify the decision of a sovereign to permit the application of foreign law within its own territory and, by implication, to limit the application of its own law to matters within its jurisdiction.' N. Jansen Calamita, 'Rethinking Comity: Towards a Coherent Treatment of International Parallel Proceedings' (2006) 27 *University of Pennsylvania Journal of International Law* 601, 615.

[31] This conception expressly rejects the earlier idea of 'statutism' that had permeated earlier conflicts of law discussion. See, for a summary exposition: James Allsop, 'Comity and Commerce (Address to the 16th Conference of Chief Justices of Asia & the Pacific)' [2015] *Federal Judicial Scholarship* 27, paras 20–23.

[32] As originally suggested in the late seventeenth century (expressed now in modern terminology) by Ulrich Huber.

that States, despite being territorially sovereign, should generally give effect to foreign laws and judgments out of respect for foreign sovereigns. Comity is thus used as a theoretical construct in the recognition and enforcement context: serving as both a justification for recognising and enforcing in the first place and a reason for preserving a discretion in the enforcing court to determine whether to give effect to a foreign judgment.

Comity, formulated in this way, represents a formalisation of theoretical approach to what is essentially a political concession, and not a matter of binding obligation or duty. As a result, although comity inherently involves matters concerning the interaction and intersection between domestic and foreign law and judgments, it remains, in its original form, entirely a domestic legal concept, such that no foreign State can insist upon comity as a matter of right.[33] Comity should, nonetheless, be accorded as the general rule, so long as – adopting the language of Huber's original formulation – it does not 'cause prejudice to the power or rights of such government or of their subjects', it is not 'revolting' to give effect to the foreign judgment or it does not assist in 'evasion of the local law'.[34] This formalisation of the concept of prescriptive comity represents the same sort of approach as that taken in transnational approaches: a general presumption in favour of giving effect to foreign judgments, subject to limited exceptions where so doing would be particularly objectionable to the enforcing State. Because of the amorphous nature of exceptions to this presumption, it should come as no surprise that comity has been described as 'vague, incoherent, illusory and ephemeral'.[35] For example, Childress, reviewing modern case law relating to comity in the United States, notes that: 'we are left with a situation where comity is being applied in many different situations, but *how* it is to be applied is unclear'.[36] Yet, as Paul argues, it is 'precisely these qualities' that have allowed comity to be used to develop to meet different political circumstances over a number of centuries.[37]

Although originally a product of continental European theoretical thought, the principles of comity expressed in this way first found acceptance in the

[33] Because States who give effect to a foreign judgment are voluntarily choosing to do so as a matter of comity to other nations, this is not an international obligation: see the translation of Ulrich Huber's seventeenth-century '*Praelectionum Juris Civilis Tomi Tres*' in Lorenzen (n 29) 401 (and following).

[34] ibid.

[35] Joel Paul, 'The Transformation of International Comity' (2008) 71 *Law and Contemporary Problems* 19, 20.

[36] Donald Earl Childress, 'Comity as Conflict: Resituating International Comity as Conflict of Laws' (2010–11) 44 *UC Davis Law Review* 11, 53.

[37] Paul (n 35) 20.

common law as a doctrine justifying courts' discretion as to choosing to apply foreign law. Huber's work in relation to prescriptive comity was cited approvingly in Scotland as early as [38] and received English judicial support in subsequent decades.[39] Yet due to the piecemeal nature of common law decision making, the recognition and enforcement practice of the common law remains 'far from settled', with less than full support from then contemporary common law jurists.[40] Nonetheless, a body of common law jurisprudence accepting comity as a starting point to giving effect to foreign judgments began to develop, which eventually reached broad acceptance in the common law. This was assisted by Joseph Story's comprehensive seminal nineteenth-century text *Commentaries on the Conflict of Laws*.[41] Story's text drew heavily upon Huber's conception of comity and its induction into the common law by Lord Mansfield during his Lordship's tenure on the King's Bench. Story, reviewing the common law at the time, noted that the 'true foundation' on which giving effect to foreign laws (and judgments) ultimately rests is a State's 'mutual interest and utility' in avoiding 'a sense of the inconveniences which would result from a contrary doctrine, and from a sort of moral necessity to do justice, in order that justice may be done . . . in return'.[42] According to Story, absent 'any positive rule affirming or denying or restraining the operation of foreign laws' common law courts 'presume the tacit adoption of [foreign laws] by their government, unless they are repugnant to its policy or prejudicial to its interests'.[43] This remains the backbone of present day common law recognition and enforcement approaches.

38 *Ursula Goddart* v. *Sir John Swinton* [1711] Brn 848 cited in Allsop (n 31) para 27 (at footnote 53).

39 See for example late eighteenth-century decisions of the King Bench, cited in Calamita (n 30) 619. As Allsop (n 31) para 29 notes, Lord Mansfield was instrumental in introducing and cementing comity as the basis of common law recognition and enforcement. See, for example, Lord Mansfield's widely cited decision in *Somersert* v. *Stewart* (1772) 98 ER 499 (prohibiting the slave trade in England), explored in its historical and commercial context in Norman S. Poser, *Lord Mansfield: Justice in the Age of Reason* (McGill-Queen's University Press 2013) 292–99. See also *Alves* v. *Bunbury* (1814) 171 ER 10 at 10.

40 For example, Paul notes the 1828 publication of the first American treatise on conflicts, explicitly repudiating Lord Mansfield's idea of comity (built on Huber's original analysis) as a basis for giving effect to foreign law: Paul (n 35) 24.

41 Joseph Story, *Commentaries on the Conflict of Laws: Foreign and Domestic, in Regard to Contracts, Rights, and Remedies, and Especially in Regard to Marriages, Divorces, Wills, Successions, and Judgments* (8th ed., Lawbook Exchange (2007 Reprint) 1887). Lorenzen (n 29) 375 notes, with reference to the work of Laine Clunet in *Journal du Droit International Prive*, XXIII, 486, that Story's work is 'in reality nothing but a "paraphrase" of Huber'.

42 Story (n 41) 33, 35.

43 ibid. 35 cited in Lorenzen (n 29) 397–98.

Story's formulation of comity, drawing together Huber's original formulation and its support in English judgments, largely came to be regarded in the eighteenth and nineteenth centuries as an authoritative exposition on the rationale for giving effect to foreign judgments across the common law, including in both the United States and England.[44] Much of this can be attributed to Story's explicit reference to the development of the common law's presumption in favour of recognition and enforcement, tempered, of course, with exceptions to protect fundamental values of natural justice or public policy in the State in which recognition and enforcement is sought. Thus, Story – consistent with both Lord Mansfield and Huber – conceived of comity as a 'license' empowering enforcing courts to decide whether to defer to foreign law (as represented in foreign judgments) or to allow domestic public policy to trump this courtesy.[45] Aided by Story's exposition, as comity came to be integrated into the common law, jurists maintained a keen understanding of its discretionary roots. From its earliest acceptance into the common law of England and the United States, the decision to extend comity to foreign judgments in individual cases was a discretion entirely – and 'appropriately' – vested in courts as part of their inherent judicial power.[46] Consequently, Huber's original formulation of prescriptive comity assisted in establishing the first general presumption in favour of giving effect to foreign judgments. This presumption – consistent with transnational approaches that have followed since – retains exceptions where doing so is likely to conflict with a State's most fundamental values.[47] I turn now to consider how common law jurists built and extended upon the rationale of comity for giving effect to foreign judgments.

4.2.2 *Developing Conceptions of Comity*

Despite the prominence and acceptance of Huber's concept of comity, it represents only the beginning of the story. This is because, in this form, comity is only an explanatory hypothetical principle aimed at reconciling 'discord between sovereignty and extra-territoriality of laws':[48] in effect, determining

[44] See, for example, the historical commentary noted at footnote 70 in Allsop (n 31) para 31. The adoption of Story's formulation was no doubt assisted by his role as a Justice of the Supreme Court, sitting in the case of *Bank of Augusta* v. *Earle* 38 US [1839] USSC 2 (in which the Court expressly adopted Story's approach to comity as a basis for giving effect to foreign judgments).

[45] Paul (n 35) 26.

[46] Calamita (n 30) 621.

[47] Importantly, this means no State can 'demand' the application of comity as a matter of right; the doctrine nonetheless acts as a mediating force – or 'bridge' between foreign and domestic laws: ibid. 619.

[48] Allsop (n 31) para 23.

the appropriate interplay between national and foreign legal systems when they come into contact.[49] Applied in this way, comity provides only the general theoretical justification for giving effect to a foreign State's power (via recognising and enforcing its judgments). It offers little practical guidance to enforcing courts tasked with giving effect to a judgment.[50] For example, the concept of prescriptive comity does not impact at all on when and in what circumstances an enforcing court should refuse to give effect to a foreign judgment. In other words, prescriptive comity offers no guidance as to when it is appropriate to defer to foreign judgments in individual cases. Consequently, efforts were made to expand this concept of comity, including by incorporating a requirement of reciprocity and developments that aimed to expound an adjudicatory theory of comity.

4.2.2.1 Reciprocity in Common Law Recognition and Enforcement

Reflecting debate subsequently seen in transnational approaches to recognition and enforcement, one of the first conceptual hurdles the common law's conception of comity attempted to resolve was whether comity is or should be built upon a parallel or implicit doctrine of reciprocity. However, it is unclear precisely what is required by this idea of reciprocity. Is it a hypothetical or theoretical exercise to determine if a foreign judgment would be given effect to in similar circumstances by the rendering State?[51] Or is evidence of this reciprocity – for example, in having given effect to a previous judgment – required?[52] The common law approach seems to require an investigation of State practice – supported by expert opinion – that considers both the laws that might apply to recognition and enforcement of a judgment in a foreign State and where evidence of this practice exists, how they have been applied.[53] This

[49] Calamita (n 30) 618.

[50] In other words, comity is (only) a 'theoretical explanation for how an absolutely powerful domestic sovereign could give effect to foreign law within its territory without implicitly diminishing or denying its absolute power': ibid. 616.

[51] As most famously expressed in *Hilton* v. *Guyot* 159 US 113 (1895), discussed further in this chapter.

[52] Requiring evidence of reciprocity may lead to a 'recognition deadlock', which can arise where two States share a requirement for evidence of a judgment being recognised and enforced before giving effect to a foreign judgment (as neither State can act as a 'first mover' in this scenario by giving effect to a foreign judgment of another): Richard Garnett, 'Increasing Co-Operation between Australia and China in the Recognition and Enforcement of Judgments' (2018) 19 *Melbourne Journal of International Law* 1, 7.

[53] See, generally, John Coyle, 'Rethinking Judgements Reciprocity' (2014) 92 *North Carolina Law Review* 1109. Coyle explores the various definitions of reciprocity and the way that such a requirement may manifest (or be adopted) within the common law (in the context of the United States).

means that in circumstances where there is no evidence of any foreign judgment of the enforcing court that has been successfully recognised and enforced by the courts of the rendering State, the reciprocity requirement can still be met (on the basis that recognition and enforcement is contemplated or provided for in the law). Thus, the idea behind common law reciprocity – similar to the idea underlying comity – is that it should encourage mutually beneficial outcomes where States are encouraged to treat the judgments of other States favourably, in return for favourable treatment for their own judgments. Reciprocity, used in this way, is said to accord and assist in generating respect, deference and politeness between States, for largely practical and prudent reasons.[54] Perhaps for these reasons, Justice Gray in *Hilton* 'reinterpreted' the earlier concept of comity (as set out in the immediately preceding section) to require reciprocity as an additional element to satisfy before giving effect to a foreign judgment.[55] The Court notes that reciprocity is a:[56]

> distinct and independent ground upon which we are satisfied that the comity of our nation does not require us to give conclusive effect to the judgments of the courts of France, and that ground is the want of reciprocity on the part of France as to the effect to be given to the judgments of this and other foreign countries.

However, while Justice Gray's approach to reciprocity has received some judicial and academic support in the United States, it has also been criticised extensively.[57] Indeed, given that domestic state courts in the United States are not bound by the Supreme Court's interpretation of their own common law, state courts have pursued a parallel track of *not* requiring reciprocity before giving effect to foreign judgments, dating back to the 1926 case of *Johnston*.[58] Brand, for example, reviewing United States recognition practice, concludes that a consideration of reciprocity has been 'remembered but rejected in all

[54] Ralf Michaels, 'Recognition and Enforcement of Foreign Judgments' [2009] *Max Planck Encyclopaedia of Public International Law* para 7.

[55] *Hilton* v. *Guyot* (n 51) 210–29.

[56] ibid. at 210.

[57] See, generally, Richard H. M. Maloy and Desamparados M. Nisi, 'Message to the Supreme Court: The Next Time You Get a Chance, Please Look at Hilton v. Guyot; We Think It Needs Repairing' (1999) 5 *Journal of International Legal Studies* 1. The authors conclude, at 42, that '*Hilton* needs some repair' as the requirement for reciprocity is 'out of sync with modern times' and has led to 'confusion'.

[58] As the New York Court of Appeals held in *Johnston* v. *Compagnie Generale Transatlantique* (1926) 242 N.Y. 381, 387. For a more recent rejection of the concept of reciprocity see, for example, *Nicol* v. *Tanner* (1976) 256 NW2d 796.

but a handful of subsequent cases and state statutes', and in other cases, where ostensibly required, simply ignored.[59] This is consistent with the Uniform Acts in the United States[60] and the majority common law position summarised in the *Restatement*,[61] both of which represent a move away from prior common law uncertainty regarding requirements of reciprocity.[62] Indeed, upon reviewing recognition and enforcement practice across the United States, drafters of the original Uniform Act decided there was little utility in maintaining a reciprocity requirement, and they expressly omitted to include one within the original Uniform Act approach.[63] Consequently, reciprocity is not a cornerstone of common law recognition and enforcement approaches, and even where approaches purport to provide for or insist upon reciprocity, they are largely 'relaxed' and 'toothless' in the way they are applied.[64] Reciprocity thus cannot be said to represent a significant rationale or driver towards giving effect to foreign judgments. This is further witnessed in the fact that even though strict statutory conceptions of reciprocity are employed in the Commonwealth Model (which is largely a restatement of the common law position), reciprocity does not survive the modernising attempt of the 2017 Model Law.[65]

59 Ronald A. Brand, 'Understanding Judgments Recognition' (2015) 40 *North Carolina Journal of International Law and Commercial Regulation* 877, 895.

60 *Uniform Foreign Money-Judgments Recognition Act* 1962 (the 'Uniform Act') and its 2005 revision, the *Uniform Foreign Country Money-Judgments Recognition Act* ('2005 Uniform Act'); collectively, these are referred to in this book as the 'Uniform Acts'.

61 American Law Institute, 'Restatement (Third) of Foreign Relations Law of the United States' (1987) ('the Restatement').

62 See, further, Juan Carlos Martinez, 'Recognizing and Enforcing Foreign Nation Judgments: The United States and Europe Compared and Contrasted – A Call for Revised Legislation in Florida' (1995) 4 *Journal of Transnational Law & Policy* 49, 65.

63 See, for example, the discussion in Uniform Law Commission, 'Uniform Foreign-Country Money Judgments Recognition Act' (2005) Prefatory Note, where the Uniform Law Commission notes that the conscious act of drafters of the 1962 Uniform Act to not insist upon reciprocity remains the 'wisest course' as it 'creates a stability . . . that facilitates international commercial transactions'. Yet, some states still see value in having a reciprocity requirement, and in implementing the Uniform Act adopt it in a non-uniform way by adopting their own requirement of reciprocity: Paige (n 3) 596 (footnote 7) notes that at least seven of the Uniform Act states continue to insist upon reciprocity, and that even among these states there is a further level of division as six states have incorporated reciprocity as a discretionary basis for non-recognition, whereas two states have made lack of reciprocity a mandatory ground for non-recognition

64 Béligh Elbalti, 'Reciprocity and the Recognition and Enforcement of Foreign Judgments: A Lot of Bark but Not Much Bite' (2017) 13 *Journal of Private International Law* 184.

65 See, for a comparative exposition of reciprocity, Section 5.1.2.

4.2.2.2 Towards Adjudicatory Comity

Beyond reciprocity, one of the key developments with respect to the common law approach to recognition and enforcement is the fledgling concept of what has now come to be termed adjudicatory comity.[66] In summary, the concept of adjudicatory comity represents a development in the idea of comity from a purely theoretical doctrine to a practice, legal rule or standard that can assist (or oblige) enforcing courts to give effect to certain judgments in certain circumstances. The need for such guidance is not new: for example, common law jurists – in line with Huber's comments in the seventeenth century that certain classes of judgments could and should be handled in different ways[67] – began to develop the idea of using comity in a practical way to guide the kinds of judgments that should be given effect to, and in which circumstances. Thus, rather than simply noting that States are free to reject foreign judgments in an entirely arbitrary or capricious exercise of will, as prescriptive comity does, adjudicatory comity outlines the kind of judgments that litigants may 'justly demand' be recognised and enforced.[68] This idea came to prominence in the seminal case of *Hilton*,[69] where Gray J developed an initial sketch of adjudicatory comity by holding that comity extended not only to relations between nations but also to a 'comity of courts' – an idea completely absent from the original works of Huber, Mansfield and Story.[70] Justice Gray reached this view by treating with scepticism claims that a ground for refusal existed on the basis that the foreign court (in that case, a French court) should be presumed to be inadequate to deliver justice; Gray J preferred, instead, a presumption that the French judiciary was capable of administering justice adequately.[71]

66 In a recognition and enforcement context, adjudicatory comity refers to the 'basis for domestic courts to defer or limit the exercise of jurisdiction in deference to the courts of another sovereign' by giving effect to a foreign judgment: Calamita (n 30) 606, 615.

67 As noted in Lorenzen (n 29) 405, 417.

68 Irina Getman-Pavlova, 'The Concept of "Comity" in Ulrich Huber's Conflict Doctrine' (Working Paper, 2013) 8.

69 *Hilton* v. *Guyot* (n 51). This case is discussed extensively when the United States' approach to recognition and enforcement is considered at Section 4.3.

70 For a recent discussion of judicial authorities and a re-exploration of the principles set out in *Hilton*, see, generally: Brand, 'Understanding Judgments Recognition' (n 59). In particular, Brand questions whether lessons beyond the simple 'comity' and 'reciprocity' aspects of *Hilton* have been 'forgotten' (at 897) and attempts to resuscitate other elements of Justice Gray's recognition and enforcement approach that have not received much judicial or scholarly attention.

71 Calamita (n 30) 630–31.

What remains particularly challenging in this context, even to this date, is whether a recognition and enforcement approach should adopt what has been referred to as a 'principle of systemic calibration'.[72] Essentially, this concept calls for allowing a foreign judgment not to be given effect to if it comes from a legal *system* that can be characterised as one with systemic issues in procedural fairness and impartiality. The basis for doing so in United States law stems from *Hilton*, primarily a passage where the Court indicated that recognition and enforcement is premised upon a 'full and fair trial', 'upon regular proceedings', under a system of laws that is 'likely to secure an impartial admistration of justice'.[73] This systemic ground for refusal is codified in the Uniform Acts: §4(a)(1) of the original 1962 Act and §4(b)(1) of the updated 2005 Act. As Dodge notes, however, this systemic calibration ground was:

> incorporated at the height of the Cold War, and included in the 2005 Uniform Act without discussion, apparently to maintain continuity with the 1962 Act. Despite its codification for nearly sixty years, fewer than five cases have refused recognition on this ground[74]

Although it may have been assumed that the case for a systemic calibration ground of refusal could be put to rest – on the basis that it is unique to the law of the United States, and even within that context empirical evidence suggests that the ground is unnecessary and rarely used (even in circumstances which indicate it may be relevant)[75] – the prohibition of systemic inquiries has recently been raised as a 'serious flaw' in the 2005 Choice of Court Convention.[76] I discuss this claim in more detail, in a comparative fashion, at Section 8.3.2. However, for present purposes I note simply that attempts to engage in 'systemic calibration' are usually considered to be counterproductive or too costly to implement, and are rare even within the United States. This is because such investigation and decision making requires significant costs, including the political cost of a United States court having to declare that an entire foreign legal system consistently falls below basic internationally

[72] Christopher A Whytock and Samuel P Baumgartner, 'Enforcement of Foreign Judgments, Systemic Calibration, and the Global Law Market' (2022) 23 *Theoretical Inquiries in Law* 119, 121.

[73] *Hilton v. Guyot* (n 51) 202–03.

[74] William Dodge, 'New York's Appellate Division Holds that Chinese Judgment Should Not Be Denied Enforcement on Systemic Due Process Grounds' (*Conflict of Laws*, 15 March 2022) <https://conflictoflaws.net/2022/new-yorks-appellate-division-holds-that-chinese-judgment-should-not-be-denied-enforcement-on-systemic-due-process-grounds/> accessed 2 May 2022.

[75] Whytock and Baumgartner (n 72) 121 and 146–7.

[76] Gary Born, 'The Hague Convention on Choice of Court Agreements: A Critical Assessment' (2021) 169 *University of Pennsylvania Law Review* 2079, 2122–25.

accepted norms of fairness and impartiality. Furthermore, most courts and court processes are, by design, aimed at resolving the singular case at hand. They are poorly equipped to make sweeping inquiries and investigations into the overall status of entire legal systems and their quality of justice.

What is clear, however, is that the level of judicial deference contained within this form of adjudicatory comity extends far beyond Huber's original exposition. In particular, Huber's exposition does not provide any indication that the enforcing State (via its courts) should be 'circumspect' in inquiring into the nature of the foreign judgment and whether it would offend the values of the domestic forum such as to enliven a ground for refusal.[77] By contrast, Gray J's conception of a comity of courts is not designed to implement a new bar based on systemic calibration; instead, it is merely to set the minimal preconditions for a strong presumption in favour of giving effect to foreign judgments. It does so by encouraging a transition from a concept of solely prescriptive comity to a concept of adjudicatory comity that aims to provide guidance as to the limited circumstances when refusing to give effect to a foreign judgment may be justified.[78] Yet, Justice Gray's 'opaque' judgment in *Hilton* remains one of the only extended discussions of this idea of adjudicatory comity.[79] This judgment has itself been criticised as 'woefully inadequate' in this respect, as it does not squarely and comprehensively address the key issue that adjudicatory comity is designed to address: namely, whether and on what basis prescriptive comity can or should be given effect to.[80] Having set out some of this fledgling concept, and some of its practical challenges, I turn now to consider developments in common law recognition and enforcement that have focused instead on expanding the rationales for so doing beyond comity.

4.2.3 *Extending Comity . . . and beyond?*

The key theme that has allowed recognition and enforcement approaches to evolve and adapt over time is the 'remarkably elastic and adaptive' concept of comity, ranging from its prescriptive origins through to perhaps even integrating a potential legal obligation to apply foreign law.[81] Expanded conceptions of comity – encompassing reciprocity or aspects of adjudicatory

77 Calamita (n 30) 630.
78 ibid. 631.
79 Childress analyses other United States judgments touching on adjudicatory comity, which he ultimately concludes add little to its understanding: Childress (n 36) 51.
80 ibid. 34.
81 Paul (n 35) 38.

guidance – allow for guidance by common law principles, cognisant of prescriptive comity's expressed purpose of doing justice and fostering international trade.[82] Indeed, some authors have argued that the concept of comity can be broadly construed to take into account a range of objectives, including:[83] the 'primary aim' of allowing the enforcing court to achieve justice in individual cases;[84] vindicating fundamental State values (by refusing to enforce a conflicting foreign judgment); and encouraging the 'practical desirability' of courts coming to decisions that further the development of an international system of commerce. This can encompass, as the following section sets out, goals such as finality, or a desire to support party autonomy and in some instances even a broader desire to defer to the amorphous concept of 'the market' or 'market forces'.[85] It has even been argued that comity should be applied broadly to conflicts of law issues outside of recognition and enforcement. For example, in the context of the United States, being adapted to respond to the 'pervasive threat' posed by the Cold War,[86] or through the use of conflicts of laws to minimise the risk of judicial intervention 'embarrass[ing] the conduct of foreign relations by the political branches'.[87]

As Turner noted in 2013, both comity and obligation theory have received varying degrees of approval both over time and across different common law jurisdictions.[88] Indeed, even a cursory analysis of common law jurisprudence suggests that the theory underlying common law recognition and enforcement approaches has shifted full circle in recent decades: from Huber's initial approach of giving effect to judgments as primarily or solely a matter of international deference (as preferred in the United States) to viewing the rationale as one of respecting debt obligations (the preferred English position) to a re-conceptualised middle ground of comity due to the needs of an increasingly globalised society.[89] For example, despite the early English preference for the theory of obligation, recent judgments of English courts suggest judicial acknowledgement that a strict adherence to the common law theory

[82] Calamita (n 30) 618.
[83] ibid. 622–23.
[84] ibid. 623.
[85] It has been argued that if this last formulation – comity as deference to the market – is to gain further traction, this likely represents a 'dangerous and ironic' step, as it does little more than allow courts to shield their own ideological preference for markets from democratic processes and scrutiny: Paul (n 35) 38.
[86] ibid. 28.
[87] *First National City Bank* v. *Banco Nacional de Cuba* 406 US 759 (1972) cited in Paul (n 35) 32.
[88] John Turner, 'Enforcing Foreign Judgments at Common Law in New Zealand: Is the Concept of Comity Still Relevant?' (2013) 2013 *New Zealand Law Review* 653, 687.
[89] ibid..

of obligation is not 'sufficiently explanatory' of the reasons why States give effect to foreign judgments, where, due to sovereignty, giving effect to a foreign judgment could validly be refused.[90] For example, in the English case of *Adams* v. *Cape Industries*, the Court noted that judgment recognition must depend, at least to some extent, on notions of comity (albeit, a re-interpretation of comity based on the effectiveness of access to international assets to satisfy judgment debts).[91]

Part of this reluctance to embrace comity is likely attributable to common law historical developments, as well as judicial pronouncements that may confuse, rather than illuminate, the rationales underlying recognition and enforcement. For example, Justice Gray's potentially misleading definition of comity:[92]

> 'Comity,' in the legal sense, is neither a matter of absolute obligation, on the one hand, nor of mere courtesy and goodwill, upon the other. But it is the recognition which one nation allows within its territory to the legislative, executive, or judicial acts of another nation, having due regard both to international duty and convenience and to the rights of its own citizens or of other persons was are under the protection of its laws.

This phrasing appears to place significant emphasis on the need to respect finality and to defer to foreign legal acts where appropriate. As such, this interpretation of comity appears at first glance to be consistent with prescriptive comity's deference to judicial discretion, but, read closely, it introduces new ambiguity. In particular, attempting to position comity as sitting somewhere between courtesy and obligation establishes a precarious and 'confusing' legal position.[93] Put simply, if comity is not a mere courtesy, and not an obligation, what exactly is its legal impact? In line with Huber's view of prescriptive comity, which has received judicial support in the common law – including in the United States[94] – comity is simply a rule of 'practice, convenience and expedience': a discretionary matter of goodwill.[95] Yet, an alternative reading of Justice Gray's exposition of comity suggests that comity may include some degree of obligation; however, this position is only half-advanced without any significant exploration of the contours this concept of

90 See, for example, *Adams* v. *Cape Industries PLC* [1990] CH 433, cited in ibid. 668.
91 [1990] CH 433, 552.
92 *Hilton* v. *Guyot* (n 51) 163–64.
93 Maloy and Nisi (n 57) 42.
94 See, for an early case, *Mast, Foos & Company* v. *Stover Manufacturing Company* 177 US 485 (1900).
95 Maloy and Nisi (n 57) 42.

comity necessitates.[96] Thus, the rationales underpinning recognition and enforcement in the common law remain contested.

It nonetheless is illuminative to consider the major 'competing' viewpoint to comity, obligation theory, and then consider other administration of justice rationales that can also be said to underly or inform the common law's approach based on comity. Notably, which rationales predominate in giving effect to foreign judgments is still contested, particularly in light of the substantial variance across common law jurisdictions.[97] Indeed, it is even possible to fit both obligation theory and administration of justice rationales within a broad concept of comity. At the least, what these further rationales suggest is that a narrow conception of comity – based upon deference to sovereign power – is not (and cannot be) a complete representation of the reasons why enforcing courts give effect to foreign judgments.

4.2.3.1 Obligation Rather Than Discretion?

As comity came to be increasingly accepted in the common law – particularly in the United States – a 'competing' concurrent theoretical doctrine for giving effect to foreign judgments, based on obligation, also grew in force.[98] Indeed, it has been suggested that over the course of the nineteenth century, comity 'gave way' to a theory of obligation, which provides that enforcing courts should give effect to foreign judgments as they create obligations in judgment debtors that the enforcing court should heed. This is a recognition and enforcement rationale that is 'based upon obligation' rather than the comity's 'doctrine of deference based upon courtesy'.[99] This obligation theory still resounds in many common law jurisdictions.[100] For example, Lord Abinger

96 But see, *Hilton v.Guyot* (n 51) 139 (and following), where Justice Gray attempts to distinguish some basic precepts, or rules of adjudicatory comity, that should be treated with different levels of scrutiny for 'different kind of judgments'.

97 Roodt, for example, considering the South African common law experience refers to 'Hobson's choice [a choice without alternatives] among competing theories' that underly this divergence: Christa Roodt, 'Recognition and Enforcement of Foreign Judgments: Still a Hobson's Choice among Competing Theories?' (2005) 38 *The Comparative and International Law Journal of Southern Africa* 15, 15.

98 For an overview of these perspectives in their historical context, see Paul (n 35) 27–28. See, also, Childress (n 36) 35–43.

99 Paul (n 35) 28. See, for example, the *Restatement (First) Conflict of Laws*, that prominently adopted the 'vested rights' (legal obligation) theory.

100 See, for example, Reid Mortensen and others, *Private International Law in Australia* (3rd ed., LexisNexis Butterworths 2015) 130, who note (in an Australian context) that the common law recognition and enforcement of foreign judgments 'depends on the theory of obligation'.

noted in a nineteenth-century English case that: '[f]oreign judgments are enforced in these Courts, because the parties liable are bound in duty to satisfy them'.[101] This line of reasoning was supported perhaps most prominently by Blackburn J in *Godard* v. *Gray*, who noted that:[102]

> ... in England and in those states which are governed by the common law, such judgments are enforced, not by virtue of any treaty, nor by virtue of any statute, but upon a principle very well stated by Parke, B., in Williams v. Jones ((1845) 13 M & W 628 at 633, 153 ER 262 at 265): 'Where a court of competent jurisdiction has adjudicated a certain sum to be due from one person to another, a legal obligation arises to pay that sum, on which an action of debt to enforce the judgment may be maintained. It is in this way that the judgments of foreign and colonial courts are supported and enforced.' And taking this as the principle, it seems to follow that anything which negatives the existence of that legal obligation, or excuses the defendant from the performance of it, must form a good defence to the action ...

This view of the common law as keeping a promise to pay a debt was (and no doubt still is) part of the prevailing view of the common law to protect commercial relations voluntarily entered into.[103] This approach is given further theoretical support in the form of vested rights theories, which normatively posit that States (via their enforcing courts) should enforce rights validly created by foreign judgments that 'vest' in and travel with the defendant.[104] Conceiving of obligation as a rationale for giving effect to a foreign decision, of course, intersects (or competes) with Huber's conception of discretionary prescriptive comity. Yet, concepts of obligation and 'vested rights' have been criticised as tautological, as although they claim to be based on obligation or rights, they beg the question as to when these obligations or rights are properly 'acquired' (and thus when a court *should* give, or refuse to give, effect to a foreign judgment).[105]

[101] *Russell* v. *Smyth* (1842) 152 ER 343, 346.

[102] (1870) LR 6 QB 139.

[103] See, for a modern English exposition, *Standard Chartered Bank* v. *Zungeru Power Ltd* [2014] EWHC 4714 (QB).

[104] *Schibsby* v. *Westenholz* (1870) 6 LR QB 155, 159. The doctrine was approved in *Adams* v. *Cape Industries Plc* (1990) Ch. 433.

[105] Michaels, 'Recognition and Enforcement of Foreign Judgments' (n 54) para 9. Ho goes further and notes that acceptance of these theories is 'very odd' as it is 'obvious' that these theories are 'inadequate, misleading and simplistic': HL Ho, 'Policies Underlying the Enforcement of Foreign Commercial Judgments' (1997) 46 *The International and Comparative Law Quarterly* 443.

4.2.3.2 The Administration of Justice

A further rationale said to underly common law recognition and enforcement – whether embedded in concepts of comity or acting with distinct force – are concerns with respect to the administration of justice. Ho argues that such concerns independently support a general rule in favour of recognition and enforcement, and reach beyond the merits of any dispute or any interests of the parties therein,[106] based upon two distinct components:[107]

1. Interest in finality: fairness to judgment creditors and the conservation of judicial resources
2. Procedural justice (fairness to the judgment debtor) and public policy

The first component, the interest in finality, is said to be a 'major reason' for allowing recognition and enforcement, which features prominently in the common law.[108] This is reflected in the rule that enforcing courts treat foreign decisions as conclusive: the general presumption in favour of recognition and enforcement (which comity also supports). Giving effect to foreign decisions in this way reflects broader concerns about the private 'fairness' (and expense) to the judgment creditor if a dispute is re-opened and has to be re-decided, as well as public concerns with respect to consistency of decisions and concepts of avoiding waste or promoting efficiency (avoiding the public and private costs of rehearing a dispute). However, finality is not in and of itself a virtue to pursue at all costs, as the second category, procedural justice, highlights. In certain circumstances – such as where a foreign decision is obtained by fraud, or where giving effect to a foreign judgment would offend the public policy of the enforcing State – finality cannot be the only determination. Thus, finality must be tempered by a concern for fairness to the debtor, as well as broader public policy or natural justice concerns arising from giving effect to potentially problematic decisions. The primary difficulty is whether such an inquiry should be only based on evidence proferred in the case at hand, or, as highlighted above, be able to be established by way of some form of 'systemic calibration'.

Read together, it is nonetheless evident that the common law approach to recognition and enforcement – upon which the Commonwealth Model depends – has no universally accepted or singular rationale or policy for giving effect to foreign judgments. Instead, the common law draws on comity,

[106] Ho (n 105) 459–60.
[107] ibid. 460–62.
[108] ibid. 460.

loosely and often inconsistently defined, as well as concepts of obligations based upon debt. These rationales or concepts may also be supplemented by concerns about the effective administration of justice. Given this theoretical indeterminacy, it is useful to consider more closely how the common law approach to recognition and enforcement operates in practice.

4.3 COMMON LAW RECOGNITION AND ENFORCEMENT APPROACHES

Having noted the Commonwealth Model's dependence on its common law underpinnings and having set out the rationales or policies underlying the common law's approach to recognition and enforcement, I now set out what can broadly be described as the common law approach. A broadly coherent and consistent approach can be said to exist in the common law, because many States share a colonial or Commonwealth link with the United Kingdom (or the former British Empire) due to the United Kingdom's most successful export: the common law legal system. Yet, such an exposition is necessarily imprecise due to the 'great' complication of State sovereignty, even within the common law.[109] Because of this sovereignty, each jurisdiction, including those that share a common law tradition, remain governed by their own domestic law, including with respect to recognition and enforcement. In this sense, and as this section progresses, it must be recalled that there is no 'true' common law approach to recognition and enforcement. For this reason, instead of individually considering each recognition and enforcement approach in place in the diversity of common law States,[110] I first briefly set out and analyse the key aspects of the common law's approach, before considering in greater detail the common law's approach in one key jurisdiction: the United States. I highlight the United States as differences in recognition and enforcement approaches witnessed within the federation highlight the sheer potential for variance of recognition and enforcement practice, even

[109] Particularly as compared to the *jus commune* of all 'civilised' Roman countries (which could be treated as functionally equivalent for recognition and enforcement purposes): see, for example, Lorenzen (n 29) 391–92.

[110] The exact approach and rationale of each common law legal system to giving effect to foreign judgments falls outside the scope of this book, as it is jurisdiction-specific and discussed at length elsewhere. See, for example, within the United Kingdom and Australia, respectively, Adrian Briggs, *Agreements on Jurisdiction and Choice of Law* (Oxford Private International Law Series 2008) ch 7; Martin Davies and others, *Nygh's Conflict of Laws in Australia* (10th ed., LexisNexis Butterworths 2019) Part X.

within one federal system where almost all states apply similar common law principles.

4.3.1 *An Overview: The Common Law Recognition and Enforcement Approach*

Consistent with the Commonwealth Model – and global regimes set out in Chapters 2 and 3 – the common law approach is based on a presumption–exception model.[111] First, a presumption in favour of giving effect to foreign judgments; second, despite (or perhaps because of) this presumption, grounds for refusal exist. Again consistent with other transnational approaches, these exceptions are limited. They arise only in circumstances where: proceedings are in some way 'irregular', that is, occasioned by either a breach of due process, such as by fraud, or a breach of natural justice; or, if giving effect to the foreign judgment conflicts with the public policy of the enforcing State, for example in cases where the issue or issues 'resolved' by the foreign judgment have already been decided elsewhere (as giving effect to such judgments offends fundamental moral and legal values).[112] See, for example, the case of *Tahan* v. *Hodgson*, where the Court notes that international commerce requires that foreign judgments be recognised, except where inconsistent with fundamental concepts of justice and fairness in United States law such that it is 'repugnant to fundamental notions of what is decent and just'.[113] Additionally, the 'thrust of English cases', as well as those of jurisdictions that derive approaches from English common law, is that foreign judgments should generally be given effect to, 'unless the foreign judgment contradicts fundamental principles' of the enforcing court.[114]

[111] Consistent with other transnational approaches, the common law also carves out exceptions from recognition and enforcement for matters intimately connected with the rendering court. For example, foreign judgments based on the penal and revenue laws: William Dodge, 'The Penal and Revenue Rules, State Law, and Federal Preemption' in Paul B. Stephan (ed.), *Foreign Court Judgments and the United States Legal System* (Brill 2014) 55.

[112] In the United States, this formulation can be traced back to *Hilton* v. *Guyot* (n 51) 144. This continues to inform current recognition and enforcement practice: Gary Born, *International Civil Litigation in United States Courts: Commentary and Materials* (Kluwer Law International 1996) ch 12, discusses extensively *Hilton's* approach to recognition and enforcement of judgments and the (significant) extent to which it informs modern practice. See, for Australia and the United Kingdom, respectively, Martin Davies and Others, *Nygh's Conflict of Laws in Australia* (9th ed., LexisNexis Butterworths 2014) 895; Briggs (n 110) [7.45] (and following).

[113] 662 F 2d 862 (DC Circuit 1981) at 864-8. See also *In Sik Choi* v. *Kim, Lee & Or* 50 F 3d 233 (3rd Circuit 1995) at 252, where the Court stresses that comity should be accorded to the greatest extent possible to respect foreign laws.

[114] Turner (n 88) 669.

Despite this similarity, there remains potential for a significant degree of latitude and variation in the way in which different common law States handle recognition and enforcement. Part of this latitude is simply because the common law is the ultimate source of authority in each jurisdiction; this has greater impact given that the presumption–exception model of recognition and enforcement necessarily depends upon amorphous exceptions based on the enforcing State's core values. The position is further complicated as often the enforcing court retains residual discretion to give effect to a foreign judgment, even if a ground for refusal is found within the common law. Nonetheless, this apparent discretion – founded upon State sovereignty – must be read in light of the 'reluctance' by common law courts to extend or broadly interpret established refusal grounds, which, absent serious defects, remain 'narrow in scope and sparingly applied'.[115] Because of this, the common law approach to recognition and enforcement of foreign judgments cannot be summarised by a singular neat or coherent rationale. Nonetheless, and at the same time, the broad outline of the common law approach – despite shifting theoretical foundations and developments in jurisprudence relating to the appropriate bounds of giving effect to foreign judgments – has not changed substantially since the rise of individual State sovereignty in the seventeenth century.

At this juncture, it should be noted that perhaps the most significant difference in common law approaches is the acceptable categories of jurisdiction. That is, for the common law to give a foreign judgment effect requires that there be an acceptable – in the eyes of the enforcing court – claim to jurisdiction over the dispute (hence, as in the Brussels Model, establishing a close link between the concepts of recognition and enforcement and jurisdiction). Jurisdictions that have a more expansive concept of jurisdiction thus are likely to give effect to a broader array of judgments. So much is evident in the ongoing negotiations at the Hague Conference, as set out at Chapter 2, where the relationship between direct jurisdiction and otherwise indirect controls on jurisdiction in recognition and enforcement have been explored at length. Suffice to say that in common law recognition and enforcement, jurisdiction has been described as a 'cornerstone',[116] and restrictive approaches that predominate in common law States have been heavily criticised. The United States stands as an outlier in the common law world as it offers an expansive view of general and special jurisdiction. Brand suggests that this is due to jurisdiction being considered a constitutional matter in the United States,

[115] ibid. 688.
[116] Yekini (n 9) 109.

related to due process rights.[117] This leads to the potential for variance within the common law as most other common law States have more limited conceptions of acceptable bases of jurisdiction.[118] Take, for example, Australia, which follows in the English common law tradition of requiring that the rendering court have exercised 'international' or 'traditional' jurisdiction. However, this reference to international jurisdiction is:[119]

> [a] restrictive 19th century jurisdictional standard ... based on the exercise of personal jurisdiction based on no more than the defendant's presence in the jurisdiction, submission to the exercise of jurisdiction, or (in the case of movable or immovable property) presence of the property in the jurisdiction at the relevant time.

This situation has even been described as a 'double standard' in international dealings, as some common law courts will not recognise the long-arm exercise of jurisdiction by foreign courts for the purpose of recognition and enforcement, even though they themselves may exercise similar long-arm jurisdiction over foreign defendants.[120] It is this distinction – between the precise controls applied by the enforcing court to the rendering court's exercise of jurisdiction – that represents the greatest practical divergence in common law approaches. Having set out the contours of the common law's approach to recognition and enforcement, I now consider the United States as an exemplar of this practice.

4.3.2 *Recognition and Enforcement Approaches in the United States*

The complexity of federation in the United States has led to voluminous case law and academic study of what is commonly described as a 'confusing' and 'enigmatic patchwork' of recognition and enforcement approaches.[121] This confusion arises in large part because no federal law in the United States

[117] Ronald A. Brand, 'Jurisdictional Developments and the New Hague Judgments Project' [2013] in, 'A Commitment To Private International Law: Essays In Honor of Hans Van Loon', Intersentia, 2013 University of Pittsburgh Legal Studies Research Paper No 2013-19 91–92.

[118] These approaches are compared and analysed in the context of the Commonwealth Model Law in Yekini (n 9) 109–31.

[119] Timothy McEvoy, 'Common Law versus Statutory Approaches to Enforcing Foreign Judgments: The Australian Experience' in Paul B. Stephan (ed.), *Foreign Court Judgments and the United States Legal System* (Brill, 2014) 179, 180 ('Common Law versus Statutory Approaches to Enforcing Foreign Judgments').

[120] ibid. 184.

[121] Paige (n 3) 593; Ronald Brand, 'Recognition and Enforcement of Foreign Judgments' (International Litigation Guide, April 2012) 1.

governs the recognition and enforcement of foreign judgments.[122] Consequently, as each of the fifty states in the United States has its own recognition and enforcement approach, this results in a potentially 'daunting' 'multiplicity' of laws to consider.[123] Adding to the confusion is the interplay between federal and state courts and law:[124] while the recognition and enforcement of foreign judgments is a state matter, state courts historically remain guided by federal jurisprudence, particularly Justice Gray's judgment in the seminal federal case of *Hilton*.[125] Further confusion arises because of the range of sources of law and the technical delineation between recognition and enforcement – as represented in intra-state variations on *Hilton*'s original common law position,[126] as well as a number of more recent statutes that have different degrees of implementation across each state.[127] This is particularly significant due to the considerable degree of legal powers accorded to each state in the United States,[128] and the United States' active role in international commerce, which potentially calls for a different 'international' approach to giving effect to foreign judgments vis à vis domestic (inter-state) judgments.[129]

Despite all of these confounding factors, the overall practice of the United States towards recognition and enforcement can be summarised as 'quite

[122] This is because there is no federal constitutional requirement to give effect to foreign *international* judgments. Note that the 'full faith and credit' clause, United States Constitution Art IV, §1 (US), applies only to 'foreign' judgments from other states within the United States and does not apply internationally: see, for example *Aetna Life Insurance Company* v. *Tremblay* (1912) 223 US 185 (1912).

[123] Yuliya Zeynalova, 'The Law on Recognition and Enforcement of Foreign Judgments: Is It Broken and How Do We Fix It?' (2013) 31 *Berkeley Journal of International Law* 155.

[124] Even where litigants attempt to exercise procedural mechanisms to enliven federal jurisdiction, federal courts will still exercise state law: ibid. Nonetheless, the *procedures* for recognition and enforcement do differ between court systems. The 'curious history' as to how state law came to govern recognition and enforcement practice is set out in Linda J. Silberman, 'The Need for a Federal Statutory Approach to the Recognition and Enforcement of Foreign Country Judgments' in Paul B. Stephan (ed.), *Foreign Court Judgments and the United States Legal System* (Brill, 2014) 99, 102–4.

[125] *Hilton* v. *Guyot* (n 51).

[126] The term 'common law' has many meanings, depending on what it is defined against. In the context of this section, it is used to refer to judge-made law as opposed to statute.

[127] Brand, 'Recognition and Enforcement of Foreign Judgments' (n 121) 1.

[128] Of which recognition and enforcement is assured by the 'full faith and credit' clause of the Constitution: see n 122. Yet, just as foreign judgments outside of the European Union do not benefit from the Brussels Model, foreign judgments do not benefit from this intra-State recognition and enforcement: Brand, 'Understanding Judgments Recognition' (n 59) 894.

[129] This was noted, in the context of comity, as early as the nineteenth century. Story, for example, notes that 'commerce is now so absolutely universal among all countries that without some common principles there would be utter confusion of rights and remedies': Story (n 41).

liberal' on an international basis.[130] From a political perspective, its liberality in giving effect to foreign judgments is perhaps most surprising as it is not a party to any international treaty compelling such treatment. It thus remains perhaps the only State that almost entirely bases its recognition and enforcement approaches on the common law (or simple codifications or restatements of the common law).[131] Given the size and value of the United States' economy and its federalist structure, which accords significant powers to domestic states, this is perhaps surprising. Additionally, given the United States' critical role as an instigator, and negotiating party, at the Hague Conference on efforts to reach consensus on a multilateral judgments instrument, the way in which it conceives of and gives effect to foreign judgments is particularly relevant for global negotiations to this end.

4.3.2.1 A Shared Common Law Basis in Domestic Approaches

Despite state-based fragmentation, a general approach in favour of recognition and enforcement can be discerned in the United States, as the basic recognition and enforcement principles are substantially the same between states.[132] This 'semblance of uniformity' arises largely due to the shared common law roots of recognition and enforcement in almost every state.[133] Comparability between these approaches is aided by model laws and uniform law statements that restate, codify or attempt to harmonise minor divergences in state approaches: relatively uniform 'model' statutory provisions are implemented in over 60 per cent of states,[134] and the common law approaches of most of the

[130] Brand, 'Recognition and Enforcement of Foreign Judgments' (n 121) 2. While judgments between states within the United States are also referred to as 'foreign' in domestic statutes, the word foreign is herein used to connote an international judgment: that is, a judgment rendered in a court from a State outside of the United States.

[131] Although the United States signed the 2005 Convention in 2009, it has not acceded to it. It has not signed the 2019 Convention.

[132] Paige (n 3) 593.

[133] Zeynalova (n 123) 156. Louisiana, as a jurisdiction heavily influenced by the civil law legal tradition, being the major exception, yet still sharing substantial similarities in ultimate approach.

[134] Uniform Law Commission, 'Uniform Foreign Money-Judgments Recognition Act' (1962); Uniform Law Commission (n 63). I use the term 'Uniform Acts' to refer to both Acts. For a list of jurisdictions that have enacted the 1962 Act see: 'Legislative Fact Sheet – Foreign Money Judgments Recognition Act' (no date) <www.uniformlaws.org/LegislativeFactSheet.aspx?title=Foreign%20Money%20Judgments%20Recognition%20Act> accessed 2 August 2021. For the 2005 Act see: 'Legislative Fact Sheet - Foreign-Country Money Judgments Recognition Act' (no date) <www.uniformlaws.org/LegislativeFactSheet.aspx?title=Foreign-Country%20Money%20Judgments%20Recognition%20Act> accessed 29 August 2021.

remaining states are generally stated in the Restatement.[135] In practice, this means that regardless of the source of law setting out recognition and enforcement principles – state, federal or common law (represented in the Restatement), or statutory (the Uniform Acts) – the question of whether a foreign judgment should be given effect to is relatively straightforward. Recent (and ongoing) efforts to further develop and reform recognition and enforcement approaches in the United States are also consistent with these principles and attempt to further procedurally harmonise approaches to recognition and enforcement.[136] Consequently, this section does not consider the approach in any particular state but instead analyses the widely shared principles of recognition and enforcement and any significant variations across each source of law.[137]

Ultimately, recognition and enforcement approaches can be traced back in their modern incarnation in the United States to Justice Gray's seminal judgment in *Hilton*.[138] This judgment – or at least the portions that are now generally relied upon – continues to serve as the 'historical foundation' for almost all foreign judgment recognition and enforcement approaches in the United States.[139] Since *Hilton*, 'most' United States courts (across both state and federal levels) adhere to the conception of foreign judgment recognition and enforcement as an incident of comity, broadly construed in light of its evolving meaning in the common law.[140] In practice, this means that enforcing courts presume that a foreign judgment should be given effect to, as long as no ground or grounds for refusal exist.[141] As Justice Gray explained in

[135] American Law Institute, 'Restatement (Third) of Foreign Relations Law of the United States' (1987) §§ 482-3.

[136] American Law Institute, *Recognition and Enforcement of Foreign Judgments: Analysis and Proposed Federal Statute* 2005 ('*2005 American Law Institute Proposal*'); American Law Institute, *Tentative Draft No. 1 – Jurisdiction (Covering Part IV Enforcement; Restatement of the Law Fourth: The Foreign Relations Law of the United States)* 1 April 2014 <www.ali.org/publications/show/foreign-relations-law-united-states/>.

[137] It is beyond the scope of this chapter to consider a state-by-state analysis of the differences in recognition and enforcement approach, yet, due to the significant degree of commonality outlined in this section, this does little to limit an understanding of the broad tenor of recognition and enforcement approaches across the United States.

[138] *Hilton* v. *Guyot* (n 51). Despite legally being a state matter, the source of the law of judgments recognition and enforcement in the United States 'draws its genealogy from federal common law, and has clear foreign relations implications' under Article I, § 8 of the United States Constitution: Brand, 'Understanding Judgments Recognition' (n 59) 893. See, further, Childress (n 36) 44.

[139] Brand, 'Recognition and Enforcement of Foreign Judgments' (n 121) 3.

[140] Paige (n 3) 596.

[141] The precise nature and bounds of these grounds for refusal continue to be refined in the common law, but at a high level they include circumstances where: the foreign judgment was

Hilton, judgments are to be given effect to unless there are 'special grounds ... for impeaching the judgment' that mean the judgment should not be recognised.[142] This leads to a presumption that decisions of foreign courts should not be 'tried afresh, as on a new trial or an appeal, upon the mere assertion of the party that the judgment was erroneous in law or in fact'.[143] This means that the presumption in favour of recognition is strong; it can with almost equal force now be termed a rule of law. That is, most enforcing courts in the United States consider themselves as *bound* to recognise a foreign judgment, unless a ground for refusal excuses them from so doing.

Assuming that recognition is granted to the foreign judgment, it is thus considered to be largely 'domesticated'. But this is not the end of the matter for giving effect to foreign judgments in the United States: the judgment usually still requires that it be given effect to via enforcement mechanisms. If enforcement is sought at the same time as recognition (in the same proceedings), and if recognition is granted, enforcement is likely to necessarily and immediately follow.[144] However, there is some uncertainty as to whether a foreign judgment recognised in the court of one domestic state coming for enforcement in another domestic state should be subject to further scrutiny in another or should immediately be enforced according to the principles of 'full faith and credit' that govern the recognition and enforcement of domestic (inter-state) judgments. In other words, will a judgment of a domestic enforcing court recognising a foreign judgment be granted preclusive effect across all domestic jurisdictions?[145] As Silberman notes, the law in the United States remains

obtained by fraud; the foreign judgment was obtained in proceedings in which the defendant was denied natural justice; the recognition or enforcement of the foreign judgment would be contrary to public policy of the judgment-enforcing state; and the foreign judgment is in conflict with a prior final judgment within the judgment-enforcing state, between the same parties and concerning the same issues or is in conflict with a foreign judgment.

142 At the same time, the Uniform Acts – again, like most other international instruments – do not prescribe a uniform enforcement *procedure*, but instead set out that foreign judgments that fall under their remit are to be enforceable in the same (liberal) manner as the judgments of 'sister states' (intra-United States judgments): Uniform Law Commission (n 63) Prefatory Note.

143 *Hilton* v. *Guyot* (n 51) 203.

144 The Uniform Acts, outlined in this section, provide some guidance by noting that 'a judgment entitled to recognition will be enforceable in the same manner as the judgment of a court of a sister state which is entitled to full faith and credit': Uniform Law Commission (n 134) Prefatory Note. See, for example §7(2) of the 2005 Uniform Act, which provides that once recognised, a foreign judgment is 'enforceable in the same manner and to the same extent as a judgment rendered in this state'.

145 Shill, in an article concerned with the practice of 'judgment arbitrage' (recognising a judgment in a state with a particularly accepting recognition practice, and then using this fact of recognition to achieve enforcement in another state that would not have granted recognition in the first place), assumes that once recognised by a domestic court any other domestic enforcing

'unclear and unsettled' on this point, particularly as some judicial decisions have suggested that such acceptance is not necessarily automatic.[146] Consequently, the precise relationship between recognition and enforcement is not fixed or yet certain – and like efforts within the Brussels Model to limit or restrict the degree of marginal review that occurs at the enforcement stage[147] this process remains controversial.[148] This is due to concerns about potential jurisdictional 'forum shopping', which is consistent with concerns in other transnational recognition and enforcement approaches, and it is explored further in its comparative context at Section 6.1.2. Before turning to consider these transnational approaches, it is useful to briefly note the process of statutorisation seen in the United States' approach to recognition and enforcement.

4.3.2.2 Replication of the Common Law via Uniform Act Approaches

The common law's presumption in favour of recognition and enforcement is widely mirrored throughout all major recognition and enforcement statutes and restatements in the United States.[149] Despite the approach to recognition and enforcement differing in each state, coming to this conclusion is aided by the fact that the key legislative approaches to recognition and enforcement in the United States derive from a set of 'Model' laws termed the 'Uniform Acts': the *Uniform Foreign Money-Judgments Recognition Act* ('Uniform Act' or '1962 Act')[150] and its 2005 revision, the *Uniform Foreign Country Money-Judgments*

court must enforce such a judgment: Gregory Shill, 'Ending Judgment Arbitrage: Jurisdictional Competition and the Enforcement of Foreign Money Judgments in the United States' (2013) 54 *Harvard International Law Journal* 459. Cf Silberman (n 124) 108 (footnote 29).

146 Silberman (n 124) 108 (footnote 29).

147 See Section 7.2.1.

148 Silberman (n 124) 108–9 (footnote 29) notes that 'most proponents' of uniform law developments in the United States see as beneficial the fact that a judgment recognised in one state is binding in all other states. This diverges from the book of Shill, that such 'judgment arbitrage' may have significant negative consequences and should be controlled: Shill (n 145) 511.

149 American Law Institute, 'Restatement (Third) of Foreign Relations Law of the United States' (n 135) § 482; Uniform Law Commission (n 134) art. 4; Uniform Law Commission (n 63) art. 5. This approach is also consistent with the American Law Institute's 2005 proposed federal statute on recognition and enforcement (American Law Institute, '2005 American Law Institute Proposal' (n 136) s 5) and attempts to revise the Restatement (see Revision to the Restatement – Tentative Draft 1 2014 (n 136)).

150 For a list of states that have enacted the Uniform Act see: 'Legislative Fact Sheet – Foreign Money Judgments Recognition Act' (n 134).

Recognition Act ('2005 Uniform Act' or '2005 Act').[151] These primarily set out to codify the majority rule arising from common law states, rather than to change recognition and enforcement practice.[152] Additionally, among the remainder of states that do not adopt the Uniform Acts, the overall common law approach remains broadly consistent with the approach in *Hilton*. Hence the common law position in the United States can be readily summarised,[153] as formally occurs in the Restatement.[154] The Restatement has a slightly wider scope than the Uniform Acts in that it extends to matters the Uniform Acts do not reach, for example, to judgments confirming the status of persons or determining interest in property (such as in family law matters).[155] However, both share the same general approach in favour of recognition, as both instruments simply map underlying common law approaches. They do so by fundamentally deriving authority from and relying for efficacy upon the underlying common law. The 2005 Act, for example, consists of only thirteen relatively short sections that codify the common law position that a foreign judgment must be recognised unless an enumerated exception (or ground for refusal) can be proven by the party resisting recognition.[156] Indeed the expressed rationale for the enactment of the original 1962 Uniform Act was not to modify the common law recognition approaches in place at the time, but, as explained at the time of the 1962 Act,[157] to assist judiciaries in civil law States – used to dealing with codes, and not judicial pronouncements in the common law – to understand that the United States does indeed give liberal effect to foreign judgments, and that any requirement for reciprocity would be met in that particular state in the United States.

[151] Uniform Law Commission (n 63). All references in this section are to the 2005 Act, unless otherwise specified.

[152] Indeed, the primary purpose of the original Uniform Act was to provide proof – via this statutory formulation or codification – that recognition and enforcement practice in the United States was particularly liberal, so that judgments of United States courts would gain wider acceptance internationally: see the Prefatory Note to the Uniform Law Commission (n 134).

[153] Martinez (n 62) 64.

[154] The recognition aspects in the Restatement have been re-examined and expressed in a more recent (Draft) Restatement: American Law Institute, 'Tentative Draft No 1 - Jurisdiction (covering Part IV Enforcement; Restatement of the Law Fourth: The Foreign Relations Law of the United States)' (n 136).

[155] American Law Institute, 'Restatement (Third) of Foreign Relations Law of the United States' (n 135) § 481.

[156] §§4 & 5. These provisions represent the bulk of the text (quantitatively) of the Uniform Acts, and act simply to codify the common law.

[157] Uniform Law Commission (n 63) Prefatory Note.

The Uniform Acts share a series of features with the transnational approaches analysed in Chapter 2 (and considered in their comparative context in Chapter 5). I set them out here briefly, before turning in Chapter 5 to consider transnational comparisons more generally. First, the Uniform Acts are not designed to be fully exhaustive (closed): they are instead open, as they set out only a minimum of foreign-country judgments that must be recognised by enforcing courts, leaving those courts free to recognise other foreign-country judgments not covered by the Uniform Acts under principles of comity or otherwise.[158] Second, again modelling concerns seen in transnational approaches to recognition and enforcement, the most significant divergence in common law approaches across the United States is whether a state insists upon reciprocity as a pre-condition for giving effect to a foreign judgment.[159] Third, they share a consistent theme of incremental evolution, whilst attempting to remain consistent with previous recognition and enforcement approach or instruments in force. As indicated, the original 1962 Act did so initially by aiming merely to clarify provisions of the common law. The 2005 Act continues the basic approach of the 1962 Act. Indeed, even the process that led to the 2005 Act was a limited one, concerned primarily with reflecting divergent state 'policy preferences',[160] and clarifying varying divergent interpretations of the original provisions across different state courts since its implementation.[161] Relevantly for the transnational comparison undertaken, the Uniform Act experience also serves to clarify that codifying recognition and enforcement practice does not necessarily stifle or override legal development.[162] Consequently, it may be possible to continue to develop a greater degree of uniformity in recognition and enforcement approaches, over time, by providing further interpretive guidance and clarification where participating jurisdictions have adopted divergent interpretations.[163]

[158] §11 expressly provides: 'This [act] does not prevent the recognition under principles of comity or otherwise of a foreign-country judgment not within the scope of this [act]'.

[159] See Section 5.1.

[160] California Law Revision Commission, 'Recognition of Tribal and Foreign Court Money Judgments (Changes to Uniform Act in Other States)' (17 July 2015) 3.

[161] Uniform Law Commission (n 63) Prefatory Note. The major changes include a clarification of which party bears the burden of proof in establishing the presumption or the grounds for refusal; establishing a recognition procedure under the Act; and, clarifying the grounds for denying recognition, in light of different judicial interpretations.

[162] See, further, Section 7.2.2.2.

[163] The idea of divergent interpretation and its impact on uniformity and harmonisation prospects is discussed further at Section 7.1.

Having set out the Commonwealth Model, as well as the rationale and approach embodied in its common law underpinnings (as set out in the US exemplar), I turn now to directly compare each transnational approach to recognition and enforcement, building upon observations drawn in each of the preceding chapters.

5

Comparative Analysis of Recognition and Enforcement

As is apparent from a review of Part I of this book, there is a significant degree of overlap and interrelation between increasingly transnationalised recognition and enforcement frameworks. In large part this is because negotiators, drafters and implementers of recognition and enforcement frameworks must make similar decisions about how, and the precise extent to which, they will oblige promotion and harmonisation of recognition and enforcement by enforcing courts in participant States. This chapter draws together and comparatively analyses the way each of these frameworks operate, in order to shed light on the essential features of transnational recognition and enforcement.

Based upon the doctrinal and historical analysis in the preceding chapters, I isolate five key design decisions that modern recognition and enforcement frameworks must address:

1. the extent to which reciprocity is relied upon;
2. the liberality of the presumption in favour of recognition and enforcement, and the extent of justified avoidance;
3. the extent of limitations or exclusions on the framework's scope of operation;
4. whether to adopt an 'open' (non-exhaustive) or 'closed' (exhaustive) design; and
5. whether to simultaneously attempt to solve jurisdictional questions.

I define each design decision, and analyse how each framework addresses it, before commenting on the interrelation and interaction of these features in each of the recognition and enforcement frameworks analysed in this book.

5.1 RECIPROCITY AS A CORNERSTONE OF TRANSNATIONAL RECOGNITION AND ENFORCEMENT

International and regional approaches to recognition and enforcement largely – and increasingly over time – rely upon reciprocity. Yet reciprocity is 'susceptible to a variety of shadings and interpretations'.[1] Coyle suggests that in the case of recognition and enforcement, the reciprocity focuses on the rights and liabilities of private individuals.[2] Under this conception, an enforcing court will only give effect to a foreign decision if satisfied that the rendering forum would give similar treatment to its own foreign decisions, thereby preserving private rights. Evidence of this reciprocal treatment can be deemed or actual. Deemed forms of reciprocity can be satisfied based on some external manifestation of the foreign State, such as if the State is a party to a relevant international treaty, or a rule of law or statutory provision in the foreign State suggests that foreign decisions from the enforcing court would be given effect to. By contrast, actual reciprocity is a higher standard, requiring evidence of foreign decisions being recognised (or, at the least, of foreign decisions *not* being refused recognition and enforcement).

I now consider the forms of reciprocity that arise in each of the recognition and enforcement frameworks analysed in this book.

1 John Coyle, 'Rethinking Judgements Reciprocity' (2014) 92 *North Carolina Law Review* 1116.

2 ibid. 1117.

5.1.1 *Deemed Reciprocity in Global Instruments*

Reciprocity is a key feature of all global recognition and enforcement instruments, and reliance on reciprocity has increased in emphasis since the coming into force of the 1958 New York Convention. The New York Convention expressly provides for a possible reservation based on reciprocity.[3] If the reciprocity reservation is chosen by a Contracting State, arbitral awards made in the territory of a foreign State that is not a Contracting State that come before an enforcing court of a Contracting State will not benefit from the pro-recognition and enforcement measures in the Convention. The requirement of reciprocity is only a 'deemed' requirement, as it is satisfied by the foreign State simply being a Contracting State to the Convention: no evidence of the foreign State's treatment of the enforcing court's decisions is required. As Paulsson notes, the idea of embedding reciprocity in this way means that, over time, States that do not become signatory to the Convention become less and less appealing as venues for arbitration.[4] By contrast, if a Contracting State does not implement the reservation, the Convention instead takes on a broad harmonisation aim: obliging its enforcing courts to give effect to all foreign awards that meet the criteria for recognition and enforcement set out in the Convention (irrespective of where they are rendered). Approximately half of the New York Convention Contracting States have made the reciprocity reservation.[5] Over time, however, the reciprocity reservation has become of limited practical use for recognition and enforcement prospects of foreign arbitral awards. As the number of New York Convention signatories has reached critical mass, even States that insist on the reciprocity reservation must give effect to judgments from a wide array of Contracting States who have reciprocally given effect to the Convention.

Both Judgments Conventions take this reciprocity one step further, providing *solely* for reciprocal operation of recognition and enforcement obligations. This reciprocity is also a deemed form of reciprocity, as both instruments are expressed to only apply as between States that have reciprocally given effect to each respective instrument:[6] no evidence of actual recognition and enforcement practice is required. Additionally, the 2005 Convention relies on

3 See Section 2.2.1.

4 Marike Paulsson, *The 1958 New York Convention in Action* (Wolters Kluwer 2016) 37.

5 These States are marked with '(a)' in the Notes section on the UNCITRAL website: 'UNCITRAL: Status of the Convention on the Recognition and Enforcement of Foreign Arbitral Awards (New York, 1958)' <www.uncitral.org/uncitral/en/uncitral_texts/arbitration/NYConvention_status.html> accessed 12 January 2017.

6 See Art 8(1) of the 2005 Convention, and Art 1(2) of the 2019 Convention.

reciprocity to establish a further ground for recognition and enforcement: instances where a *non-exclusive* choice of court agreement is entered into (rather than an exclusive choice of court agreement that the 2005 Convention generally covers).[7] This provision has its genesis in response to discussions internationally that indicated that some industries rely on 'asymmetrical and otherwise non-exclusive choice of court clauses';[8] and reciprocal treatment was taken as a given for creating any additional obligation via the 2005 Convention.

In this way, the Judgments Conventions depart slightly from the broad harmonisation task of the New York Convention by firmly embedding reciprocity as the basis for an obligation to recognise and enforce a foreign judgment. Provision is made in both Conventions for States with a 'strong interest' to not apply the Convention to a specific matter;[9] if this is done, the Convention obligations will not apply to the this matter in the Contracting State that made the reservation, or in other Contracting States where recognition or enforcement of a judgment of the State making the declaration is sought. Article 19 of the 2019 Convention also permits declarations excluding the State or State authorities from its obligations that operate in a similar reciprocal fashion.

Article 29 of the 2019 Convention provides a further procedural safeguard, which is absent from the 2005 Convention: effectively providing an option for States to make a valid declaration that the 2019 Convention obligations will not apply to judgments from a particular excluded State. This operates in the reverse fashion to the 1971 Convention. The 1971 Convention is discussed at Section 2.1.1.1, but it suffices to note here that it required reciprocal bilateral agreements in order for recognition and enforcement obligations to activate between States. In this way the 1971 Convention represented an entirely opt-in system, whereas the 2019 Convention adopts an opt-out approach. Note that the ability to make such a declaration is not a mere procedural technicality. It may be one of the most significant ways of providing procedural protections against judicial systems that are, en masse, considered to lack integrity or independence.[10]

7 Article 22.

8 Ronald A. Brand and Paul Herrup, *The 2005 Hague Convention on Choice of Court Agreements: Commentary and Documents* (Cambridge University Press 2008) 15.

9 Article 21 (2005 Convention) and Article 18 (2019 Convention). These declarations operate on the basis of reciprocity. However, Art 17 2019 Convention also makes allowance for a declaration to not apply the Convention that is not grounded in reciprocity if all elements of the dispute (including the location of the parties, etc), other than the location of the court origin, are connected only with the requested State.

10 This point is lamented in the context of the 2005 Convention by Born, who notes that the lack of an equivalent to Article 29 of the 2019 Convention represents a significant issue and is one reason why States should not ratify the 2005 Convention: Gary B. Born, 'Why States Should

What can be surmised is that all global instruments studied rely on reciprocity as a basis for establishing 'minimum standards' of recognition and enforcement. The greatest variance arises in in the extent to which these obligations can be extended, or limited, by declarations or reciprocal agreement between individual Contracting States.

5.1.2 *The Brussels Model, the Commonwealth Model and the Common Law*

Beyond global approaches, it is also instructive to consider the Commonwealth Model – and the common law that underlies it – as well as the Brussels Model approach to recognition and enforcement. First, with respect to the common law, the reciprocity requirement involves a mixture of deemed and actual evidence of reciprocity, rather than a strict empirical concept of reciprocity. This has been criticised as leading to both harsh and absurd results, such as a 'recognition deadlock' where recognition and enforcement can never occur for the first time between two States if each first requires evidence of the other State's enforcement of its own judgments.[11] Additionally, as Section 4.2.2.1 highlights, the degree to which reciprocity underpins recognition and enforcement under the common law varies significantly. This is seen most clearly in attempts to statutorise and harmonise recognition and enforcement practices in the United States via the Uniform Act approach. When this unification project was attempted, a reciprocity requirement was consciously omitted from the Uniform Act approach.[12] Yet, some states still see value in having a reciprocity requirement and somewhat paradoxically implement this Uniform Act in a non-uniform way by including their own requirement of reciprocity.[13] This analysis is further complicated on a domestic level as it is evident that in some circumstances where reciprocity is

Not Ratify, and Should Instead Denounce, the Hague Choice-of-Court Agreements Convention, Part III' (*Kluwer Arbitration Blog*, 18 June 2021) <http://arbitrationblog.kluwerarbitration.com/2021/06/18/why-states-should-not-ratify-and-should-instead-denounce-the-hague-choice-of-court-agreements-convention-part-iii/> accessed 2 October 2021. See, further, Section 8.3.2.

[11] See the discussion of common law reciprocity at Section 4.2.2.1, focusing on criticisms of practice that may lead to a 'recognition deadlock' (at Chapter 4, n 52).

[12] See, for example, the discussion in Uniform Law Commission 'Uniform Foreign-Country Money Judgments Recognition Act' (2005) Prefatory Note, where the Uniform Law Commission notes that the conscious act of drafters of the 1962 Uniform Act to not insist upon reciprocity remains the 'wisest course' as it 'creates a stability . . . that facilitates international commercial transactions'.

[13] Brian Paige, 'Foreign Judgments in American and English Courts: A Comparative Analysis' (2003) 26 *Seattle University Law Review* 596 (footnote 7). Even among Uniform Act states who require reciprocity, there is a further level of division: six states have incorporated reciprocity as

technically required, it is often ignored or applied in a less than rigorous fashion.[14] This, it has been suggested, has led certain common law reciprocity requirements in recognition and enforcement to be considered 'watered down' to the extent that they have 'become a mere formality'.[15] Broadly, this aligns with the New York Convention approach of leaving it to Contracting States to decide whether they insist on reciprocity.

Second, and reflecting similar concerns as the domestic common law concepts on which it is built, the Commonwealth approach diverges in the extent to which it privileges or insists on reciprocity in recognition and enforcement. While most Commonwealth States insist on reciprocity,[16] some do not.[17] The form of this reciprocity is a deemed one, usually based on a review, either judicially or to the satisfaction of the Executive in the enforcing State, that the foreign jurisdiction is likely to give effect to properly rendered judgments of the enforcing State.[18] By contrast with the common law, however, the statutorisation of reciprocal obligations means that the reliance on reciprocity becomes more than a potentially 'ignorable' legal trifle or formality.[19] In Commonwealth States that implement the Model with a strict reliance on reciprocity, obligations to recognise and enforce under that statutory

a discretionary basis for non-recognition, whereas two states have made lack of reciprocity a mandatory ground for non-recognition of foreign judgments.

14 See, for example, discussion of the common law approach to reciprocity: Section 4.2.2.1.

15 Béligh Elbalti, 'Reciprocity and the Recognition and Enforcement of Foreign Judgments: A Lot of Bark but Not Much Bite' (2017) 13 *Journal of Private International Law* 185.

16 For example, Australia, the United Kingdom, Nigeria and Malaysia. This reciprocity itself has various forms. Some States, for example Nigeria, automatically extend reciprocity to other Commonwealth States. Other States, for example Australia, only extend recognition and enforcement frameworks to other Commonwealth States that apply similar frameworks to their own judgments. See, further: Paper by the Commonwealth Secretariat, 'Commonwealth Practice in the Recognition of Foreign Judgments' (2009) 35 *Commonwealth Law Bulletin* 345; Commonwealth Secretariat, *1999 Meeting of Commonwealth Law Ministers and Senior Officials: Port of Spain, Trinidad and Tobago, 3–7 May 1999: Memoranda* (Commonwealth Secretariat 2001). Oppong, when considering Commonwealth Africa, surmises that, excluding South Africa and Zimbabwe, the requirement of reciprocity lies 'at the heart' of all studied regimes: Richard Frimpong Oppong, *Private International Law in Commonwealth Africa* (Cambridge University Press 2013) 387.

17 For example, Canada (including Ontario and Quebec) and South Africa. Again, this comes in various forms: in South Africa, for example, this is not a matter of right and depends upon the exercise of judicial discretion.

18 Each Commonwealth Model State thus usually has a proscribed lists of countries that are deemed to satisfy reciprocity requirements. See, for example, the approach of the UK in the 1920 Act at Section 4.1.1.

19 It is worth noting in this context that despite the existence of these regimes across many common law jurisdictions, each jurisdiction designates only relatively few others for reciprocal treatment: see, further, Oppong (n 16) 387.

scheme simply do not arise if reciprocity is not deemed to exist.[20] Where this is the case, the Commonwealth Model's approach to reciprocity is similar to the strict focus on reciprocity seen in the Judgments Conventions. However, the 2017 Model Law explicitly aims to overcome the hindrance of inconsistent requirements of reciprocity, doing away with any reciprocity arrangement by which judgments from other Commonwealth states receive favourable treatment as compared to judgments from outside the Commonwealth.[21]

Third, and finally, the Brussels Model also adopts a similar – and strict – focus on reciprocity. However, this is perhaps not surprising given the genesis of the Model in its European context: as between most participants in the Brussels Model, there is an agreed on (and compulsory) degree of integration, cooperation and 'mutual trust' – essentially, in-built controls of EU membership that depend on reciprocity – largely unknown outside of the EU's supranational structure. This concept of mutual trust, and its likely impact on the extensibility of the Brussels Model to other regimes, is considered at Section 6.2.2.1.

Ultimately, despite divergent conceptions of reciprocity, recognition and enforcement frameworks require reciprocity. This likely reflects an evolving idea about the nature of multilateral treaties: rather than serving entirely as tools of legal harmonisation, they instead can be seen to represent a series of mutually bargained for promises between Contracting States. On the domestic level, at least as represented in the common law, concerns about the difficulty in determining reciprocity have largely been managed by ignoring – or treating as a trifling formality – any requirement of reciprocity. However, once recognition and enforcement obligations come to be 'statutorised' or codified – either in the form of statute that is to be promulgated throughout Commonwealth nations, in the form of European directive or via international treaties – this is more difficult to do. This is because the relevant recognition and enforcement regime only 'activates' once reciprocity is met: that is, when the State from which the original decision comes also implements the same instrument into their own laws. This is a much more confined task than the complex evidentiary task of determining whether foreign courts from the jurisdiction where the decision originated, in general, provide reciprocal treatment. Hence, it is less likely to be overlooked or worked around.[22]

20 With the usual proviso being that recognition and enforcement falls to be determined by the surrounding 'default' common law rules of recognition and enforcement.

21 Abubakri Yekini, *The Hague Judgments Convention and Commonwealth Model Law: A Pragmatic Perspective* (Hart Publishing 2021) 98–99.

22 See, for further discussion of the difficulties in determining what reciprocity in this context means (at least in the common law), Section 4.2.2.1.

There is thus less scope to 'water down' discretionary (and contestable) reliance on reciprocity, as may happen in more flexible practice tied into domestic jurisprudence, as seen in the common law. Consequently, reciprocity forms a real cornerstone of international recognition and enforcement.

5.2 A PRESUMPTION–EXCEPTION MODEL OF RECOGNITION AND ENFORCEMENT

Across all approaches analysed in Part I of this book, a common theme is reliance on a broad presumption in favour of recognition and enforcement. This presumption is largely built on restricting review of the merits of the original decision, pre-supposing recognition and enforcement, and, as the immediately following section suggests, strictly limiting the exceptional bases for refusing to do so.

On an international level, the reason for this presumption–exception approach can be attributed to express decisions in each recognition and enforcement approach – both by the original negotiating States and subsequent implementing States – to maximise reciprocal recognition and enforcement prospects for foreign decisions. From an instrumental perspective, this is done via States implementing treaty obligations expressly obliging their respective enforcing courts to presume that foreign decisions should be recognised and enforced, subject only to limited (and enumerated) grounds for refusal. This gives rise to a presumption that should only be overcome in exceptional cases. For example, where there are significant procedural breaches in the original proceedings, or giving effect to the foreign decision would be fundamentally incompatible with the public policy of the State where the enforcing court is located. The fact that exceptions to this presumption are very limited reflects an approach where exceptions operate primarily as a 'safety valve' of last resort. Metaphorically, this serves to release the pressure generated by the general presumption in favour of recognition and enforcement (where necessary to do so, to avoid a breakdown in the use of such a presumption). Including this 'safety valve' allows States greater confidence to reach agreement to giving in-principle (or 'presumptive') effect to foreign decisions, as these exceptions can be used to excuse enforcing courts from obligations to give effect to potentially objectionable decisions or classes of decision.

5.2.1 A *Shared Presumption of Recognition and Enforcement*

The legal technologies or terminologies employed in recognition and enforcement instruments to reach a presumption of enforceability include the requirement that decisions 'shall' be given effect to,[23] without review of the merits of the original dispute,[24] and binding the enforcing court to findings of fact made by the original decision maker (including as to that decision maker's jurisdiction over the matter).[25] This is also supported by obligations to treat the choice of forum independent from other terms of the contract – the concept of separability.[26] Broadly speaking, this presumption reflects the idea that the enforcing court should act in a minimal capacity at the recognition and enforcement stage, based only on a prima facie review of minimal evidence submitted by the successful judgment- or award-creditor, who has a right to execute this decision, with a heavy onus on the party resisting enforcement preventing that party from engaging in delaying tactics at the recognition and enforcement stage.[27] As Baumgartner and Whytock note, such a presumption is the way in which 'recognition-favoring principles' – including comity, efficiency and access to justice – are given effect to.[28] Once this presumption is established, it is only then 'fine tuned' by employing minimal exceptions where necessary.

At a high level, this presumption in favour of recognition and enforcement seen in global instruments is also broadly consistent with the intra-European Brussels Model approach,[29] the Commonwealth recognition and enforcement approach and common law recognition and enforcement approaches

[23] See, e.g., Art 8(1) Hague Conference, 'Convention on Choice of Court Agreements' (1 October 2015) ('Choice of Court Convention' or '2005 Convention'). See also Art III of the New York Convention, which provides that enforcing courts must give effect to foreign awards in the same way, using national procedural rules, as if enforcing a domestic award. The New York Convention also expressly precludes the imposition of more onerous conditions or higher fees than would be imposed on domestic arbitral awards, while the Hague Convention does not impose this restriction on national courts.

[24] See, e.g., Art 8(2) of the 2005 Choice of Court Agreements Convention, which provides that there is to be no review of the merits. This is expanded upon in Art 4(2) of the 2019 Convention, which provides that review of the merits can only occur where 'necessary' in applying any inbuilt exceptions to recognition and enforcement. This idea of limiting the review of the merits – *révision au fond* – as Brand and Herrup note, is a 'standard provision' in recognition and enforcement conventions: Brand and Herrup (n 8) 273.

[25] In the context of foreign judgments, this applies so long as the judgment was not given in default: Art 8(2) of the 2005 Choice of Court Agreements Convention.

[26] As enshrined in Art 3(d) of the 2005 Conventon, and Art II of the New York Convention. See, for further discussion of the concept of separability in an arbitral context: Croft, Stamboulakis and Warren, *International and Australian Commercial Arbitration* [3.70]–[3.74].

[27] Paulsson, *The 1958 New York Convention in Action* (n 4) 96.

[28] Samuel P Baumgartner and Christopher A Whytock, 'Enforcement of Foreign Judgments, Systemic Calibration, and the Global Law Market' (2022) 23 *Theoretical Inquiries in Law* 1, 119–20.

[29] As Stone notes, only in 'exceptional cases' is the enforcing court able to review the rendering court's jurisdiction, and it is 'never' allowed to review the substance or merits of the foreign

built upon concepts of comity.[30] Additionally, as years of practical experience in the context of the New York Convention have demonstrated, the instrumental presumption in favour of recognition and enforcement often permeates surrounding enforcement procedure that the Convention does not expressly cover. For example, a number of Convention jurisdictions provide, in light of the Convention's presumptive approach to facilitate expeditious enforcement, that any unsuccessful attempt to resist the enforcement of an arbitral award should, in the usual course, result in indemnity costs against the debtor.[31] Across a range of recognition and enforcement levels, there is a significant degree of doctrinal uniformity for the continued operation of a recognition and enforcement presumption.[32]

5.2.2 *Strictly Limited 'Safety Valve' Exceptions, and Residual Discretion to Enforce*

There are few, and narrow, exceptions to the presumptions that a foreign decision should be recognised and enforced. To stretch a metaphor, these exceptions operate as a limited 'safety valve', in that they are designed (and are to be construed) in the narrowest possible way to 'vent' pressure that may arise from enforcing courts being obliged to give effect to particularly objectionable foreign decisions. This deference to enforcement being the usual course, represented by the presumption in favour of it, is also reinforced in the permissive nature of the global approaches (the Convention and the Judgments Conventions), as well as the common law, all of which allow but do not compel enforcing courts to refuse recognition and enforcement where an enumerated exception is proven.[33] This stands in stark contrast to the Brussels Model approach whereby recognition and enforcement must be

judgment: Peter Stone, *EU Private International Law* (Elgar European Law Series, Edward Elgar Publishing 2014) 28.

30 See Section 4.3.1.

31 See, for example, the practice of Hong Kong: David Kwok, 'Pro-Enforcement Bias by Hong Kong Courts: The Use of Indemnity Costs' (2015) 32 *Journal of International Arbitration* 677.

32 Noting the perennial concern that any doctrinal or instrumental analysis, 'must be tempered by a trebled measure of realism' as to what actually occurs in practice: Paulsson, *The 1958 New York Convention in Action* (n 4) xxii.

33 Using some formulation such as 'recognition and enforcement *may* be denied if': see, for example, Art 7(1) of the 2019 Convention. As Section 4.1 explains, the Commonwealth Model (and the common law that underpins it) has largely discretionary grounds for refusing enforcement; however, a few mandatory grounds – where enforcement must be denied – have developed over time in the statutory frameworks.

denied.[34] As Paulsson notes in the context of the New York Convention, the idea of significantly restricted grounds for rebutting the presumption in favour of recognition and enforcement derives from six 'canons' of interpretation drawn not only from the text of the Convention but also from its 'context, purpose and drafting history and judicial application', that:[35]

1. The listed grounds for refusal are fully exhaustive (hence, enumerated grounds for refusal);
2. A court may not review foreign decisions that come for enforcement on their merits, outside as provided for within the recognition and enforcement instrument itself;
3. The burden of proving the existence of a refusal ground rests on the respondent, and this onus is heavy;
4. Courts must construe the refusal grounds narrowly;
5. Refusal should only be granted in 'serious cases' not on the basis of a *de minimis* defect; and
6. These grounds for refusal must be read in light of a pro-enforcement 'stance', 'bias' or 'attitude' embodied in global recognition and enforcement instruments.

Although many of these canons do not expressly derive from a literal textual analysis of recognition and enforcement instruments – and hence cannot be applied directly to the Hague Conference instruments that have little or no judicial application[36] – they are still likely to be applicable to the Judgments Conventions. First and foremost, this is because the grounds for refusal, and the way in which they are construed in a pro-enforcement manner, are (and are likely to remain into the foreseeable future) broadly consistent and standardised across international recognition and enforcement instruments. Indeed, all instruments expressly limit the grounds for refusing recognition and enforcement to a very similar and restrictive set of exceptions, premised on invalidity of the original decision, party incapacity, egregious procedural

[34] As exemplified by Arts 27 and 28 of the Brussels Convention, which provide that 'a judgment shall not be recognized . . . '.

[35] Paulsson, *The 1958 New York Convention in Action* (n 4) 165–66. These canons are adopted from Paulsson's application to the New York Convention but modified slightly to apply to foreign decisions generally. See also, for a detailed overview of a range of judicial interpretations in light of these canons, Gary Born, *International Commercial Arbitration* (KluwerArbitration, Third edition, Kluwer Law International BV 2020) §26.03 (and following).

[36] This is because the 2005 Convention only recently came into force, has only a limited signatory pool and has not yet come to be applied by an enforcing court of record. Clearly, there is no judicial application of 2019 Convention, as it has not entered into force.

breaches and fraud, or breaches of public policy or fundamental principles of procedural fairness.[37]

However, strident criticism has arisen due to the way in which certain grounds of refusal are narrowed or removed in the 2005 Convention, as distinct from the New York Convention.[38] Unlike under the New York Convention, there is no express ground under the 2005 Convention for an enforcing court to deny recognition based on the fact that a chosen court has exceeded its authority or determined matters beyond the consensual submission (unless this constitutes a breach of public policy).[39] Perhaps most notably, the enforcing court has no ability to reconsider the validity of any exclusive choice of court agreement if it is ruled valid by the court putatively chosen under such an agreement.[40] This differs from the New York Convention experience, where the enforcing court is not bound by the tribunal's decision with respect to the validity of the arbitration agreement.[41] Concerns have also been raised about whether the grounds of refusal based on fraud in the Judgments Conventions are as broad as the procedural fairness protections in the New York Convention.[42] Both Judgments Conventions provide that recognition and enforcement may be refused if the judgment coming for recognition and enforcement was obtained 'by fraud'. According to the respective Explanatory Reports for these Conventions, fraud so understood

[37] See: Art V (New York Convention); Art 9 (2005 Convention); Art 7 (2019 Convention). For completeness, it should be noted that the Judgments Conventions provide an additional ground for refusal – that the New York Convention does not – that arises in circumstances where the judgment coming for recognition or enforcement is 'inconsistent' with another judgment involving the same parties (regardless of the subject matter or cause of action): Art (9)(f)–(g) (2005 Convention); Art 7(1)(e)–(f) (2019 Convention). The inclusion of such a ground for refusal stems from Commonwealth practice in reciprocal recognition and enforcement acts: see Foreign Judgments (Reciprocal Enforcement) Act 1933 (UK), 4(1)(b).

[38] Many of these critiques are raised by Born in relation to the 2005 Convention, as discussed at Section 6.2.1.

[39] Gary Born, 'The Hague Convention on Choice of Court Agreements: A Critical Assessment' (2021) 169 *University of Pennsylvania Law Review* 2079, 2118. The reasons for this are discussed further at Section 6.2.1, and stem from a privileging of the putatively chosen court's determination, presumably for reasons of certainty and predictability.

[40] Art 9(a) (2005 Convention). Additionally, there is no analog to Art V(1)(c) of the Convention in the 2005 Convention. This ground of refusal allows an enforcing court to refuse enforcement if the tribunal has ruled upon matters beyond the scope of submission to arbitration.

[41] Art V(1)(a) (New York Convention). This provision is silent as to the standard of judicial review, but it has been accepted in some jurisdictions that a review of the validity of the award should be considered *de novo*: UNCITRAL, *UNCITRAL Secretariat Guide on the Convention on the Recognition and Enforcement of Foreign Arbitral Awards* 148–50 (2016).

[42] Art 7 (2019 Convention); Art 9 (2005 Convention); Art V(1)(b) and (d) (New York Convention).

relates to 'deliberate dishonest or deliberate wrongdoing',[43] that is, 'behaviour that deliberately seeks to deceive'.[44] The 2019 Convention removes the extra stricture contained within the 2005 Convention, that the fraud must arise 'in connect with a matter of procedure'. Notably, neither ground for refusal under the Judgments Conventions covers the same ground as the 'full' or 'reasonable' opportunity to be heard provisions of Art 18 of the United Nations Commission on International Trade Law, 'Model Law on International Commercial Arbitration (with Amendments as Adopted in 2006)' (1985), which often accompany claims under the New York Convention. These changes are perhaps explicable on the basis that courts are presumed to provide, by default, a greater standard of natural justice than arbitral tribunals. Born notes that the 2005 Convention's relegation of natural justice concerns to merely a sub-set of policy represents a dilution of the protections that the New York Convention offers.[45] However, as noted expressly in the 2019 Convention Explanatory Report, because of the existence of the public policy exception and the overlap of procedural claims in that ground for refusal, any differences in approach in this respect are 'unlikely to have an impact in practice'.[46] This is consistent with arbitral case law around the world, which has regularly reinforced the understanding that grounds of refusal can and do necessarily overlap in many factual scenarios, and nothing turns on a particular ground of refusal being pled or activated.[47]

It follows that each of these Conventions, despite differences in their precise formulation of the grounds of refusal, must nonetheless be understood as similarly ensuring that fundamental principles of procedural fairness are upheld. To this end, the interpretative canons of the New York Convention are likely to be of guidance also to the Judgments Conventions because of the significant degree of explicit overlap and experience-sharing adopted in them.

43 Trevor Hartley and Masato Dogauchi, 'Explanatory Report on the Convention of 30 June 2005 on Choice of Court Agreements' (Explanatory Report, 2007) [188].

44 Francisco Garcimartín and Geneviève Saumier, 'Explanatory Report on the HCCH 2019 Judgments Convention' [2020] 118 ([255]).

45 Born (n 39) 2122.

46 Garcimartín and Saumier (n 44) 118 [257].

47 See, for example the range of Singaporean, English and Australian arbitration cases cited in Croft, Stamboulakis and Warren, *International and Australian Commerical Arbitration* (2021, LexisNexis) at [11.23] and following. Noting in particular the comments of the Full Federal Court of Australia in *TCL Air Conditioner (Zhongshan) Co Ltd v Castel Electronics Pty Ltd* (2014) 232 FCR 361 at 376–7.

Reflecting this idea, both Judgments Conventions are expressly modelled on, and attempt to build and improve on, the New York Convention provisions, which have had the benefit of many years of judicial interpretation across a range of implementing jurisdictions.[48] The Judgments Conventions have also been crafted to provide further express guidance where there may be identified uncertainties or deficiencies in the New York Convention approach. The 'public policy' exception is a good example of where this has occurred in the drafting history of the Judgments Project negotiations.

The public policy ground of refusal serves as one of the key 'safety valves' in recognition and enforcement practice: the presumption in favour of giving effect to a foreign decision is overcome where doing so is incompatible with the public policy of the enforcing State. The New York Convention simply provides that a ground for refusing recognition and enforcement arises when 'the recognition or enforcement of the award would be contrary to the public policy of [the enforcing State]'.[49] By contrast, drawing on perceived issues with the application of the exception under the New York Convention, and using wording from other Hague Conference instruments,[50] the Judgments Conventions explicitly provide greater guidance in the context of foreign judgments. To clarify the intent of this exception, the Judgments Conventions provide that for a public policy ground of refusal to arise, recognition and enforcement must be 'manifestly incompatible' with an enforcing State's public policy.[51] This implies that there must be a 'clear' and 'extremely serious' breach,[52] and that the exception should be 'rarely

[48] For example, a general preference observed globally is the narrow construal of such grounds, with enforcing courts only refusing to give effect to a foreign judgment in 'serious cases': Albert Jan van den Berg, *The New York Convention of 1958: An Overview* (Brussels 2008), available at <www.arbitration-icca.org/media/4/69405158666624/media012125884227980new_york_convention_of_1958_overview.pdf> (accessed 28 September 2016). See, for example, the seminal United States Court of Appeals case *Parsons & Whittemore Overseas Co Inc* v. *Société Générale de l'Industrie du Papier RAKTA* 508 F 2d 969 (2nd Circuit 1974), at 974, where the Court notes: '*[t]o read the public policy defence as a parochial device protective of national political interests would seriously undermine the Convention's utility. This provision was not meant to enshrine the vagaries of international politics under the rubric of "public policy"*'. This narrow interpretation has been consistently adopted across the grounds for refusal in many other jurisdictions. See, for example, the Singaporean case of *Re An Arbitration between Hainan Machinery Import & Export Corporation and Donald & McArthy* [1996] 1 SLR 34, which takes a similarly narrow view of the ambit of the public policy exception.

[49] Article V(2)(b). Albeit, most enforcing courts – and much academic literature – stresses the need for a serious rather than trifling breach of public policy.

[50] Brand and Herrup (n 8) 92.

[51] See: Art 9(e) (2005 Convention); Art 7(1)(c) (2019 Convention).

[52] Brand and Herrup (n 8) 92.

invoked and only as a last resort'.[53] The further guidance in the Judgments Conventions is designed to assist in avoiding issues with the 'misuse' of the New York Convention as it applies to arbitral awards, via a too-broad or 'erratic' interpretation of the public policy exception.[54] Further to this end, the 2019 Convention builds on the additional language of 'manifest incompatibility' that is also seen in the 2005 Convention, and clarifies that this includes 'situations where the specific proceedings leading to that judgment were incompatible with fundamental principles of procedural fairness of that State and situations involving infringements of security or sovereignty of that State'.[55]

Third, and additionally, as the Judgments Conventions are inspired by other international and domestic approaches to recognition and enforcement, the so-called canons that provide for restrictive application of any refusal in the context of the New York Convention are likely to continue in the Judgments Conventions. This is because these other recognition and enforcement approaches, on a 'relatively standard' basis, provide for similar approaches to the presumption in favour of recognition and enforcement, as well as the existence of any grounds for refusal.[56] Perhaps most prominently, the Brussels Model provides even more limited exceptions than those available on a global level, relating only to 'public policy, insufficient service or irreconcilability with another judgment'.[57] As the European Court of Justice has 'consistently emphasised', these limited grounds for refusal – including the public policy ground – should only be applied in 'exceptional cases', and must be read and applied in light of the pro-recognition and enforcement approach of the Model.[58] This narrow view of any exceptions to recognition and enforcement is consistent with the global experience, and also with the common law approach to recognition and enforcement in various jurisdictions,[59] including the way in which it is embodied in the Commonwealth Model.[60] Under both approaches, the grounds for refusal are construed in a similar fashion to

53 Peter Nygh and Fausto Pocar, 'Report by Peter Nygh & Fausto Pocar (Annexed to the 1999 Preliminary Draft Convention)' (Report, August 2000) 114.

54 Born (n 35) §26.05[C][9], citing Jan Paulsson, 'The New York Convention in International Practice: Problems of Assimilation' in Mark Blessing (ed.), *The New York Convention of 1958* (ASA Special Series 9, 1996) 113.

55 Art 7(1)(c) (2019 Convention).

56 Brand and Herrup (n 8) 14.

57 Stone (n 29) 28.

58 ibid. 235. See, further, Section 3.2.

59 See, further, Section 4.3.1.

60 As Chapter 4 explores, this idea survives the transition from the common law into the Commonwealth statutory regime, and can be dated back to the original English

instrumental exceptions: 'narrow in scope and sparingly applied'.[61] Notably, under common law and Commonwealth approaches, 'no account appears to be taken' of the way in which the foreign court achieved jurisdiction in analysing whether an exception should apply, whether this was by party choice or the operation of default jurisdictional rules.[62] As a result, the grounds for refusal can be seen to be similarly restricted across all levels of recognition and enforcement ordering analysed in this book.

5.3 LIMITATIONS OR EXCLUSIONS FROM THE SPHERE OF APPLICABILITY

This section considers the key limitations on recognition and enforcement, representing perhaps the greatest divergence between recognition and enforcement instruments. First, I consider the exclusions from scope in the instruments themselves, including the 'carve out' of certain sensitive matters from the scope of obligations to recognise and enforce. The second limitation or exclusion considered is the use of jurisdictional bases, filters or controls to limit the kinds of foreign decisions that will be eligible for recognition and enforcement at first instance. I consider each in turn.

5.3.1 *Exclusions from Scope*

All recognition and enforcement instruments have a certain instrumental scope with respect to recognition and enforcement, and provide for certain exclusions from this scope. As a starting basis, this scope is broad. For example, the 2005 Convention applies only in 'international cases', which in the case of recognition and enforcement is satisfied as soon as a judgment is rendered by a foreign court (Art 1(3)).[63] This is similar to the approach of Art 1 of the New York Convention, which specifies that the Convention applies to any awards made in States outside of the recognition and enforcement State, and to any

Administration of Justice Act 1920 (see s 9), as well as the *Foreign Judgments (Reciprocal Enforcement) Act 1933* (see s 4).

61 John Turner, 'Enforcing Foreign Judgments at Common Law in New Zealand: Is the Concept of Comity Still Relevant?' (2013) 2013 *New Zealand Law Review* 688.

62 Albeit, Briggs notes that it 'is possible . . . that at a subliminal level this is already happening', but that 'no case has yet admitted it openly': Adrian Briggs, *Civil Jurisdiction and Judgments* (6th ed., Informa Law from Routledge 2015) 718–19.

63 Convention declarations may further narrow this definition – see, for example, the discussion of the Article 19 declaration below.

non-domestic (hence, foreign) awards in the State where recognition and enforcement is sought. Article 1 of the 2019 Convention simply notes that it applies to the recognition and enforcement 'of a judgment given by a court of another Contracting State'. Further shared limitations on scope in all global instruments are that the foreign decision must relate to 'civil or commercial' matters ('commercial', Art 1(3) of the New York Convention).[64] More recent instruments, including both of the Judgments Conventions, demonstrate a trend towards greater specificity, with prescribed instrumental exclusions of controversial or sensitive matters from the scope of the instrument. This represents a change from the earlier New York Convention approach, which broadly leaves the determination of these exclusions to the national law of the enforcing court. The most contentious of these matters are those involving consumer jurisdiction, employment contracts and intellectual property rights. These matters have been the subject of many years of debate at the multilateral level.[65]

The New York Convention approach to the recognition and enforcement of arbitral awards reflects the highpoint of transnational cooperation and allows these carve outs to be determined according to the national law of the enforcing State. Although it obliges enforcing courts to presumptively give effect to foreign arbitral awards, the major caveat is that this obligation only extends to subject matter that is 'capable of settlement by arbitration under the law [of the enforcing court]'.[66] The question of whether a subject matter falls outside the scope of the Convention – and hence is non-arbitrable and gives rise to no obligations to recognise and enforce a resulting award – is determined by the national law of the enforcing court.[67] This mirrors the common law approach to foreign judgments where exclusions have been carved out over time for matters that are intrinsically linked to the rendering State, including exclusions carved out for judgments relating to 'taxes', 'a fine or

[64] As explored in Section 1.3.4, the scope of this book is confined to a consideration of civil and commercial matters. In brief, the terms 'civil' and 'commercial' are intended to be autonomous, with the primary goal of excluding public and criminal law. See, for a further discussion of the width and breadth of these terms in the context of the Judgments Project: Trevor Hartley and Masato Dogauchi, 'Explanatory Report on the Convention of 30 June 2005 on Choice of Court Agreements' (Explanatory Report, 2007) [49].

[65] Allan Phillip, 'The Global Hague Judgments Convention' in Talia Einhorn and Kurt Siehr (eds.), *Intercontinental Cooperation Through Private International Law: Essays in Memory of Peter E. Nygh* (TMC Asser Press 2004) 300.

[66] Enforcing courts giving effect to the Convention face no obligation to recognise such arbitration agreements (Art II(1)), or to recognise or enforce the resulting awards (Art V(2)(a)).

[67] Born (n 35) §26.05[C][10].

other penalty' or a 'judgment for divorce, support, or maintenance'.[68] What is unique about the approach to recognition and enforcement of arbitral awards is the degree to which jurisprudence has arisen about the nature of interpreting grounds for refusal (see Section 5.2.2). Consistent with the pro-arbitration 'bias' implicit in the New York Convention, enforcing courts approach this task with a 'general approach of restraint', as excluding a matter from scope is considered to be an 'exceptional escape mechanism'.[69] This is reflected in practice, as there are 'relatively few' decisions denying recognition or enforcement of awards on the basis of non-arbitrability.[70] The Brussels Model experience is also instructive. The most recent instrument in the Brussels Model – the 2012 Recast – shares most of the key exclusions from scope seen in global instruments (such as family law matters and insolvency) but otherwise has a much narrower set of exclusions, allowing recognition and enforcement obligations to extend, for example, to consumer and employment matters.[71]

By contrast, the Judgments Conventions take a more prescriptive approach, rather than leaving exclusions to be determined as a matter of national law. Similar to the Brussels Model, the scope of these instruments has been carefully crafted – and limited in some key respects – to attempt to overcome impasses in global negotiations by excluding contentious matters that may limit the instruments' appeal. For example, the 2005 Convention excludes all agreements that are non-business (consumer) or relate to employment contracts, and it contains a broad list of excluded matters, including family law matters, insolvency, anti-trust, personal injury claims made by natural persons, *in* rem property claims and intellectual property matters.[72] Many of these exclusions draw directly from the Brussels Model text and experience. While several matters are excluded either because they are covered under other international instruments or subject to mandatory laws in other States – and would likely also be non-arbitrable under the New York Convention – these exclusions, particularly with respect to employment and consumer matters, are still broader than the national law positions reached via application of the

68 §3(b). See also the distinction between a pecuniary penalty and a compensatory judgment explored in Francisco Garcimartín, 'The Judgments Convention: Some Open Questions' (2020) 67 *Netherlands International Law Review* 19, 21–25.

69 See the authorities in various New York Convention Contracting States, cited in Born (n 35) §26.05[C][10].

70 Born (n 35).

71 Article 1(2).

72 Art 2(1)–(2). Note, however, that certain counter-exceptions exist in Art 5; for example, if the judgment rules on a contractual obligation secured by rights *in rem*: Art 5(1)(i).

New York Convention.[73] The 2019 Convention takes a similar approach. While it has some additional exclusions from scope beyond those provided for under the 2005 Convention – such as defamation – it brings back consumer and employment contracts into scope (subject to certain additional controls), drawing on significant drafting efforts that happened before the downsized agreement on the 2005 Convention.[74]

Both Judgments Conventions remain narrower than the New York Convention in this sense, as many of these kinds of matters (such as competition or anti-trust matters, and certain aspects of insolvency) are arbitrable, rather than excluded, under national law in many jurisdictions.[75] Indeed, we see that broader attempts to return several areas excluded from scope by the 2005 Convention back into scope largely did not succeed. For example, the 2018 Draft Convention moved a series of exclusions to a draft option that could potentially be exercised, including in sensitive matters such as privacy, intellectual property rights and competition (anti-trust) matters.[76] These options were removed, and matters simply excluded, in the final 2019 Convention.[77] This means that the scope of the Judgments Conventions are more restrictive in these respects than the New York Convention.

Further, because of the broad-based nature of the 2019 Convention – untethered from a contracting party's choice of forum – additional 'innovative' exclusions are included in the treaty to clarify the Convention's precise reach.[78] This is particularly important in the case of issues considered governmental or political in nature, including exclusions for the activities of law enforcement and armed forces, and unilateral sovereign debt restructuring.[79] Under the Judgments Convention (Art 18 of the 2019 Convention; Art 21 of the

[73] Albeit, consistent with arguments made in favour of a 'closed' Brussels Model approach, this prescriptive approach is likely to provide greater certainty and predictability, as distinct from relying on potentially divergent and pluralistic national law approaches.

[74] See, for example, the options explored with respect to consumer and employment matters in earlier drafts, such as: Hague Conference, 'Preliminary Draft Convention on Jurisdiction and Foreign Judgments in Civil and Commercial Matters' (Preliminary Document, August 2000). An additional jurisdictional filter is introduced in Art 5(2) of the 2019 Convention, for consumers and employees.

[75] See, for a discussion of arbitrability in the context of international commercial arbitration, Croft, Stamboulakis and Warren, *International and Australian Commercial Arbitration* (2021, LexisNexis) [5.26]–[5.30].

[76] See Art 2 for the matters excluded from scope – in particular, sub-ss. (k) and (l); Art 5(2) sets outs the additional controls applicable in employment and consumer agreements.

[77] But see Art 2(1)(p) where some competition matters remain within scope of the instrument.

[78] Paul R. Beaumont, 'Judgments Convention: Application to Governments' [2020] *Netherlands International Law Review*, Section 7 ('Conclusion').

[79] These exclusions, and their rationales, are discussed in ibid.

2005 Convention), discussed at Section 5.1.1, States may declare that the Convention will not apply to a specific matter if they have a 'strong interest' in not doing so. Article 19 of the 2019 Convention also provides an avenue for States to provide a declaration that they will not apply the Convention to judgments arising from proceedings to which the State, or a government agency of the State, are party. While there may be justifiable concerns about the potential width of these exclusions created by declaration – potentially being used by some States to extend to State-owned enterprises or exempt broad matters from the operation of Convention obligations – these declarations are corralled by the concept of reciprocity (set out at Section 5.1). The reciprocal nature of these declaratory provisions is perhaps the 'strongest deterrent' against a State acting in this manner.[80]

The 2019 Convention, however, also has the potential not just to narrow but, in certain narrow respects, 'flip' or overcome the enforcement gap as distinct from foreign decisions rendered under the head of party autonomy. This is because certain matters may only be resolved judicially pursuant to default jurisdictional rules, such as instances where the subject matter of a dispute in question is non-arbitrable. Such a dispute may have to be heard in judicial proceedings; and, if a jurisdictional base supports doing so, the judgment can be enforced under the Judgments Convention. The gap may also narrow with respect to claims that are more effectively resolved in a judicial forum, such as claims that would benefit from judicial processes to allow for compulsory joinder or to promote third party involvement,[81] as well as claims that may be conveniently or cost-effectively resolved by a court (particularly as private disputants do not usually bear the full cost of judicial determination, unlike in arbitration).

5.3.2 *Enforcing Foreign Decisions That Are Ineffective or Set Aside*

One of the primary divergences in the recognition and enforcement of foreign decisions is the extent to which enforcing courts will give effect to a decision that is, or is likely to be, ineffective or annulled in their state of origin. This is very much a live issue with respect to enforcing arbitral awards. Even though the fact the award has been set aside is a ground for refusal under the New York Convention (Art V(1)(e)), this does not compel refusal. As explained at Section 5.2.2, the enforcing court 'may' refuse recognition and enforcement

80 ibid. Section 6 ('Article 19 Declaration').

81 Michael Hwang, 'Commercial Courts and International Arbitration: Competitors or Partners?' (2015) 31 *Arbitration International* 195.

but is not compelled to do so. Consequently, national law practice diverges significantly with respect to how an enforcing court will treat any such set aside decision, and whether it will, or might, give effect to the award in any event.[82]

This distinction was highlighted by the controversy sparked by the 1996 decision of the United States District Court (District of Columbia) in *Chromalloy*,[83] where the Court decided to enforce an arbitral award, even though it had been set aside in the country of the arbitration (Egypt). The opposite has also occurred, where the enforcing court has gone on to deny recognition and enforcement to an award, even though set aside applications have been heard and refused based on the same refusal factors in supervisory courts of the seat of arbitration.[84] As Rana notes, the idea that an award that has been set aside might still be recognised and enforced, and indeed vice versa, also permeates French enforcement practice, whereby enforcing courts 'disregard the decisions of seat courts altogether' when considering whether to give effect to an award.[85] By contrast, in England and Wales, the set aside decision is considered to be so persuasive that for enforcement to be granted in any event, the 'decision of the foreign court must be deliberately wrong, not simply wrong by incompetence'.[86] Herein lies the tension between promoting recognition and enforcement by allowing enforcing courts to give effect to decisions even when they are not operable in the 'original' jurisdiction and the

[82] Karl-Heinz Bockstiegel, 'Summary of Discussion in the Third Working Group' in Albert Jan van den Berg (ed.), *Improving the Efficiency of Arbitration Agreements and Awards: 40 Years of Application of the New York Convention* (KluwerArbitration, Kluwer Law International 1999) 434–35.

[83] *Chromalloy Aeroservices* v. *The Arab Republic of Egypt* 939 F Supp 907 (District Court of Columbia) (District Court 1996).

[84] As occurred in the high profile *Dallah Real Estate* cases (*Dallah Real Estate and Tourism Holding Co* v. *Ministry of Religious Affairs of the Government of Pakistan* [2011] 1 AC 763; Cour d'appel de Paris, 17 février 2011, *Gouvernement du Pakistan – Ministère des Affaires religieuses c. Société Dallah Real Estate and Tourism Holding Company*, R/G 09/28533), discussed at Section 7.1.1.

[85] For example, French arbitral practice: see, generally, Emmanuel Gaillard, 'Enforcement of Awards Set Aside in the Country of Origin: The French Experience' in Albert Jan van den Berg (ed.), *Improving the Efficiency of Arbitration Agreements and Awards: 40 years of Application of the New York Convention* (KluwerArbitration, Kluwer Law International 1999). See for a more recent comparative exposition that considers France and several other jurisdictions: Rashda Rana, 'The Enforceability of Awards Set Aside at the Seat: An Asian and European Perspective' (2017) 40 *Fordham International Law Journal* 813, 813–15.

[86] *Nikolay Viktorovich Maximov* v. *Open Joint Stock Company 'Novolipetsky Metallurgichesky Kombinat'* [2017] [EWHC 1911 (Comm) (at [15]), which is discussed in detail in Philip Devenish, 'Enforcement in England and Wales of Arbitral Awards Set aside in Their Country of Origin' (2018) 18 *Oxford University Commonwealth Law Journal* 143.

inevitable lack of harmonisation that happens when differing positions are taken by enforcing courts. The ability for an enforcing court to give effect to an award even if it has been held to be invalid in the seat of the arbitration (or indeed denied enforcement in another State) has been criticised as a 'potential weakness' in the Convention's design as it allows recognition and enforcement of an award to be 'subject to the local peculiarities of the country where the award was rendered – including eccentricities, or whims, or even xenophobia'.[87] This is because, it is argued, that it is 'too radical, and contrary to current expectations' for enforcing courts to simply ignore a setting aside of an award, even where so doing promotes recognition and enforcement prospects.[88]

This residual discretion is primarily an issue that impacts the enforcement of arbitral awards, as distinct from judgments, however. This is because the decision maker with respect to awards, the arbitrator, exercises private power. The exercise of this private power is often supported in and by the State of origin, but the arbitrator's decision is not an emanation of the power of the State. Much of the permissive national law responses outlined earlier – particularly in France – thus stress that arbitration is in a sense 'delocalised' or, at least, somewhat removed from the legal apparatus of the State. By contrast, the Judgments Conventions are instruments designed to give effect to emanations of state power, in the form of judgments, from one legal system into another. This concept harkens back to the idea of comity, which, as outlined in Section 4.2, originated as a political concept, calling for a deferral to a State's exercise of power (through its judicial organs). Thus, there is little need to allow a judgment that is ineffective in the State of origin to be given effect to. For this reason, and no doubt mindful of the difficulties experienced under the New York Convention, it is uncontroversial that the Judgments Conventions remove any residual discretion of the enforcing court. Both share a provision that:[89]

> A judgment shall be recognised only if it has effect in the State of origin, and shall be enforced only if it is enforceable in the State of origin.

As emphasised in the Explanatory Report to the 2019 Convention, this simply reflects the 'corollary' to the idea that recognition and enforcement under the Convention is simply a way to confer on the foreign judgment

87 Jan Paulsson, 'Awards Set aside at the Place of Arbitration' in *Enforcing Arbitration Awards under the New York Convention: Experience and Prospects* (United Nations 1999) 25.
88 ibid.
89 Article 4(3) 2019 Convention; Article 8(3) 2005 Convention.

'the authority and effectiveness accorded to it in the State of origin' within the enforcing State.[90]

5.3.3 *Jurisdictional Bases for Recognition and Enforcement*

Perhaps the greatest conceptual divergence in recognition and enforcement approaches and instruments internationally arises with respect to jurisdictional bases. The need to prove a jurisdictional base before recognition and enforcement is granted has meant that these bases are often described as 'jurisdictional filters', as they 'filter out' decisions that would otherwise be enforceable but for the lack of an acceptable jurisdictional base. Implementation of such filters, as canvassed in Chapter 2, had been one of the key drivers behind attempts to overcome impasses in global negotiations in the Judgments Project. For example, as set out at Section 2.1.2, the 2005 Convention came about due to a desire to 'save' the substantial work product that had been invested in negotiations towards a broad-based judgments instrument. This was done as the jurisdictional base of an exclusive choice of court by the parties is considered to best represent the widely shared principle of party autonomy, and negotiating parties were more readily able to come to agreement on jurisdictional matters with respect to this base.[91]

It is useful here to briefly introduce a trifold categorisation for the way that jurisdictional bases can be conceptualised and implemented in an instrument: either as *required*, *excluded* or *permitted*.[92] Traditionally, in the context of negotiations over the Judgments Project, these categorisations have also been expressed as, respectively, a 'white list', 'black list' and 'grey area'

[90] Francisco Garcimartín and Geneviève Saumier, 'Explanatory Report on the HCCH 2019 Judgments Convention' [2020] 83.

[91] See, generally, Brand and Herrup (n 8), who, at numerous junctures, review the meaning of party autonomy and its use in the 2005 *Convention*, as well as its interaction with the sovereignty of States.

[92] Ralf Michaels, 'Some Fundamental Jurisdictional Conceptions as Applied in Judgment Conventions' in Eckart Gottschalk (ed.), *Conflict of Laws in a Globalized World* (Cambridge University Press 2007) 32–35. For the purposes of this section, I deal only with 'indirect' jurisdiction – see the discussion of the differences between direct and indirect at Section 5.5. Although not the focus of this book, I also note that attempts to regulate direct jurisdiction (the jurisdiction of the rendering court) work in a conceptually similar manner. That is, regulating jurisdiction directly can occur via some combination of the following: (1) *requiring* jurisdiction, meaning that a rendering court must exercise jurisdiction; (2) *excluding* jurisdiction, meaning a rendering court must not exercise jurisdiction; or (3) *permitting* jurisdiction, meaning that a rendering court's decision to exercise jurisdiction remains at the discretion of the State and is not affected by the attempts to regulate jurisdiction.

(or 'grey zone').[93] As to the first, if a jurisdictional base is *required*, an enforcing court must recognise or enforce a foreign decision rendered under that jurisdictional head (assuming, of course, that the decision meets all other criteria for recognition and enforcement). Second, if a jurisdictional base is expressly *excluded*, an enforcing court must not recognise or enforce a judgment rendered under such jurisdiction. Third, and finally, a jurisdictional base is *permitted*, the base is neither excluded or required, and it falls to the national law of the enforcing court to determine whether a foreign decision should be given effect to. This is the so-called default position, where if a foreign decision is rendered under a jurisdictional head that is not excluded or required, its enforcement remains within the 'state of nature' (within the ambit of national law of the enforcing State, which usually defers to court discretion).[94] This third category can have a particularly wide ambit, as if a convention is intentionally limited in scope or neglects to outline how it treats a jurisdictional base (whether by design or not) it will be treated as permitted.

Global approaches to recognition and enforcement employ some combination of these required, excluded or permitted features, often in ways that are not explicit. For example, both the 2005 Convention and the New York Convention set out only required jurisdiction – broadly speaking, where disputants have selected an exclusive choice of forum. All categories of decision involving a choice of forum – so long as the requisite evidence of this choice, as required by the instrument, are met – thus benefit from the presumption in favour of recognition and enforcement. Yet neither instrument excludes any jurisdictional bases, and hence, all jurisdictional bases not covered remain permitted within the remit of domestic law. Similarly, because the 2019 Convention is designed to apply to scenarios where no such agreement has been reached, foreign judgments only become 'eligible' for recognition and enforcement if the enforcing court finds that a required jurisdictional base exists.[95] These bases in the 2019 Convention reflect a broad array of jurisdictional grounds, stemming from efforts to harmonise and consolidate national law approaches, including, for example, the 'habitual

[93] Arthur von Mehren, 'Recognition and Enforcement of Foreign Judgments: A New Approach for the Hague Conference?' (1994) 57 *Law and Contemporary Problems* 283.

[94] Michaels, 'Some Fundamental Jurisdictional Conceptions as Applied in Judgment Conventions' (n 92) 24–25.

[95] Art 5 of the 2019 Convention. This is consistent with the 1971 Convention, albeit, for conceptual clarity, the 2019 Convention departs from the language of 'jurisdiction' used therein, and attempts to further harmonise these 'bases': see Arts 4 and 10 of the Hague Conference, 'Convention on the Recognition and Enforcement of Foreign Judgments in Civil and Commercial Matters' (1 February 1971) ('1971 Convention').

residence' of a judgment debtor, choice of law rules applicable to contracts and tortious obligations, the defendant's 'presence' in the State of origin and even through to party autonomy-based grounds premised upon the defendant's express consent to the rendering court's jurisdiction or implied consent based on the defendant's failure to contest jurisdiction.[96]

For present purposes, it suffices to note that the aim in explicitly setting out these bases is to move the recognition and enforcement of foreign judgments towards a standardised set of bases that are broader than many jurisdictions presently offer in national law.[97] Although the 2019 Convention goes further than the 2005 Convention or the New York Convention and excludes a very limited number of jurisdictional bases,[98] all other jurisdictional bases remain permitted. As a result, it can be surmised that global approaches broadly rely on the use of permitted jurisdictional filters to activate recognition and enforcement obligations, with limited recourse to excluding matters from recognition and enforcement. This reflects a conscious decision to pursue an 'open' approach built on minimum standards in transnational approaches. That is, unlike in the Brussels Model, the goal of harmonisation globally takes second place to the goal of promoting recognition and enforcement by allowing recourse to domestic law that may be more open to recognition and enforcement than can be expressly agreed in a global instrument.[99]

5.4 'MINIMUM STANDARDS': OPEN VERSUS CLOSED APPROACHES

A critical design decision in any recognition and enforcement framework is whether it will be 'open' or 'closed'. Closed approaches provide a fully

[96] The vexed nature of submission as a jurisdictional base in the context of the 2019 Convention is explored comprehensively in Geneviève Saumier, 'Submission as a Jurisdictional Basis and the HCCH 2019 Judgments Convention' (2020) 67 *Netherlands International Law Review* 49.

[97] See, for example, restrictive approaches to jurisdiction in the context of common law approaches analysed in Chapter 4 of this book.

[98] Article 6 of the 2019 Convention, which has no parallel in the 2005 Convention or the New York Convention, provides that in very limited circumstances, if a judgment rules on rights *in rem*, then it 'shall be recognised and enforced *if and only if* the property is situated in the State of origin'. This provision serves to *limit* recognition and enforcement under the 2019 Convention; hence, departing from the absolute 'all else is permissible' minimum standards approach in both the New York Convention and 2005 Convention. Nonetheless, the 2019 Convention's approach is consistent with earlier multilateral broad-based judgments harmonisation attempts. For example, Art 4(1) of the 1971 Convention mentions only required bases of indirect jurisdiction, supplemented by some excluded bases in Art 4. As with the 2019 Convention, all other bases that are not canvassed remain permitted: Michaels, 'Some Fundamental Jurisdictional Conceptions as Applied in Judgment Conventions' (n 92) 35.

[99] But see the limited nature of residual recourse to national law, analysed at Section 8.2.4.

exhaustive basis for recognising and enforcing foreign decisions and remove any avenue for enforcement outside of the provided bases. This leaves no room for any residual recourse to national law, outside of the implementing instrument. This is because closed approaches aim to exclusively set out all required (acceptable) bases for recognition and enforcement, *as well as* any allowable grounds for refusal: any matters or jurisdictional bases that are not enumerated in this approach, or fall foul of a ground of refusal, are excluded and the foreign decision cannot be recognised and enforced in that jurisdiction at all. By contrast, open approaches reflect only a 'baseline' or 'minimum standards', allowing an enforcing court to adopt a more permissive stance towards recognition and enforcement. The concept of 'minimum standards' means that an enforcing court can never violate any instrumental obligations by giving effect to a foreign decision; instead, 'only by failing to do so'.[100]

The difference between closed and open approaches can be illustrated simply. Consider, for example, enforcement proceedings where a ground for refusal is proven. Under a closed approach, this is the end of the matter: the decision must be denied recognition and enforcement. Being overly prescriptive can be problematic for global approaches in these circumstances, as any base for enforcement that is unable to be negotiated and agreed within a particular legal instrument will likely simply be excluded. Where this is the case, a treaty that is designed to *promote* recognition and enforcement may serve to limit it by setting out expansive categories of foreign decisions that must *not* be given effect to. By contrast, under an open approach, enforcing courts are not compelled to refuse recognition and enforcement.[101] A similar approach can be discerned when considering any limitations or exclusions from the sphere of applicability: if a matter falls outside the scope of a particular recognition and enforcement instrument or there are no required jurisdictional bases available, it is open to the enforcing court to apply a more liberal domestic regime.

Despite the conceptual and practical attractiveness of a closed (exhaustive) approach, global instruments almost exclusively favour an open approach based on the pursuit of minimum standards.[102] This can be discerned from explicit provisions – such as Art VII of the New York Convention and Art 15 of the 2019 Convention – which confirm that convention obligations do not

[100] Paulsson, *The 1958 New York Convention in Action* (n 4) 124.

[101] As reinforced by the discretionary and permissive language of 'may': Section 5.2.2.

[102] See, as an example of this shared approach, Art 7 of the 2019 Convention, which provides, permissively, that recognition and enforcement *may* be refused based on the enumerated grounds in that article; there is no obligation to refuse. Note, *contra*, n 89.

prohibit the application of more liberal recognition and enforcement approaches at national law. As set out at Section 8.2.1, this has led to a practice where States are free to – and indeed do – apply more liberal recognition and enforcement practices than required under treaty law. Indeed, the space reserved by 'open' approaches features most prominently in pro-arbitration jurisdictions, such as France. In this context it has been noted that reference is rarely made to the New York Convention in enforcement proceedings, as more expansive national law concepts are applied instead.[103]

It is at this point instructive to consider the divergence seen in the other regional and international recognition and enforcement approaches analysed in this book. First and foremost, the open approach that prevails globally diverges significantly from the Brussels Model approach. The Brussels Model adopts a closed system that is fully exhaustive: so long as the judgment coming for recognition and enforcement is from another Brussels Model participant, its provisions fully regulate this process. Enforcing courts are compelled to either give or refuse effect to foreign judgments based entirely on the provisions in the Model and not their own national laws. In this sense, the Brussels Model's strong pro-recognition and enforcement framework is facilitated by its exhaustive nature; because if the Model does not apply, there is no residual national law to fall back upon that may aid a party aiming to recognise and enforce a judgment.[104] Assuming a relatively equal and uniform interpretation of the Brussels Model, an improperly rendered foreign decision will not be recognisable or enforceable in any jurisdiction to which the Brussels Model extends. By contrast, on a global level, a defendant seeking to resist recognition or enforcement does not have the same certainty.

Second, and remaining on the international level, the Commonwealth approach is also designed in a relatively closed fashion. As Chapter 4 elaborates, the Commonwealth Model provides a largely mechanistic form of foreign judgment registration (a precursor to enforcement under the Commonwealth approach). In this sense, the Commonwealth Model is similar to the Brussels Model, in that they both largely determine when a foreign judgment must be given effect to.[105] This is so despite the greater 'openness' in the part of the Model constituted by the 1920 Act. The 1920 Act

[103] Emmanuel Gaillard, 'Comment: The Urgency of Not Revising the New York Convention' in Albert Jan van den Berg (ed.), *50 Years of the New York Convention: ICCA International Arbitration Conference* (ICCA Congress Series 14, Kluwer Law International 2009) 692.

[104] Maryellen Fullerton, 'Enforcing Judgments Abroad: The Global Challenge: Introduction' (1998) 24 *Brooklyn Journal of International Law* 1, 2.

[105] See Administration of Justice Act 1920 (UK), s 9. Foreign Judgments (Reciprocal Enforcement) Act 1933 (UK), s 4.

can be seen as more open as it allows residual recourse to the common law if the statutory regime does not apply or is excluded, as the registering court retains ultimate discretion,[106] based upon a catch-all provision 'if it is just and convenient that the judgment should be enforced in the United Kingdom'.[107] The 1933 Act, however, moves the Model closer to a closed basis: it expressly provides that foreign judgments that can be registered pursuant to that Act cannot be enforced in any other way, and it also shifts from an entirely discretionary basis of recognition and enforcement to a basis where certain judgments 'must' be set aside.[108]

Consequently, one of the key differentiating features is the greater extent to which global approaches utilise an open framework. An open framework – cognisant of pro-harmonisation and pro-recognition and enforcement rationales – leaves open the prospect for enforcing States to provide greater recognition and enforcement prospects for foreign decisions than they are instrumentally obliged to. If the pro-recognition and enforcement message of these approaches comes to be regarded as authoritative and legitimate by implementing courts, it is possible that, over time, this may lead to a practice of increased recognition and enforcement prospects in domestic law that operate in addition to the minimum instrumental baseline. As set out earlier, this is precisely what occurs in pro-arbitration jurisdictions such as France with respect to obligations to recognise and enforce foreign arbitral awards.

5.5 TYING TOGETHER JURISDICTION AND RECOGNITION AND ENFORCEMENT

Historically, attempts have been made to harmonise recognition and enforcement with the approach taken to regulating the original jurisdiction of the rendering court. Before considering these linkages, it is useful to clarify some terminology that will be used in this section. In particular, it assists to note that the term 'jurisdiction' used alone masks a conceptual difference between direct jurisdiction (*compétence directe*) and indirect jurisdiction (*compétence indirecte*).[109] Direct jurisdiction refers to the rules 'applicable in the [fora] in which the case is first brought',[110] namely, the *rendering* court (or arbitral

[106] Briggs (n 62) 759.
[107] Administration of Justice Act 1920 (UK), s 9.
[108] See Section 4.1.2.
[109] This distinction stems from French law, which has developed particularly successful terminology to resolve this concern by distinguishing between these two concepts.
[110] Brand and Herrup (n 8) 7.

tribunal).[111] By contrast, indirect jurisdiction refers to 'jurisdictional criteria for recognition and enforcement of judgments' (also termed 'jurisdictional filters') that apply to the *enforcing* court.[112] The 'indirect' in this formulation refers to the fact that the instrument does not attempt to govern the way in which an original rendering court accepts or rejects jurisdiction. Instead, the only time jurisdiction stands to be considered is on an application for recognition and enforcement when the enforcing court considers the rendering court's exercise of jurisdiction to determine if it is in line with the acceptable jurisdictional bases or filters (as set out at Section 5.3.3).

As is set out at Section 2.1.1.1 in a summary fashion, instruments that attempt to regulate both recognition and enforcement and also concurrently regulate the rendering fora's original exercise of jurisdiction can be categorised as 'double'.[113] The most important consequence of this dichotomy between 'single' and 'double' is the lack of direct jurisdictional rules arising under the former. This means that jurisdictional 'protections' only arise indirectly, and the enforcing court becomes the sole guardian of perceived jurisdictional excesses internationally.[114] The 'single' approach, where only the behaviour of enforcing courts (rather than rendering courts) is regulated, remains favoured in broad-based approaches to recognition and enforcement. This is reflected in the return to a 'single' approach of the 2019 Convention,[115] consistent with prior experience with the 1971 Hague Convention approach.[116] This single approach is also consistent with the Commonwealth Model, which due to its origins and intended implementation as domestic legislation does not attempt or purport to have extraterritorial effect: instead, the only consideration of jurisdiction can be indirect.[117]

[111] This includes the forum selection clause (if any) and the original decision made as to which forum will hear and determine the dispute.

[112] Hague Conference, 'Report of the Fifth Meeting of the Working Group on the Judgments Project (26–31 October 2015) and Proposed Draft Text Resulting from the Meeting' (Preliminary Document, November 2015) 2 (footnote 3).

[113] Note, however, that a second meaning of these terms also exists, whereby the terms are used to refer to the 'open' and 'closed' conventions: Michaels, 'Some Fundamental Jurisdictional Conceptions as Applied in Judgment Conventions' (n 92) 40.

[114] This, in turn, places greater pressure on any States to a harmonisation attempt to leave a sufficiently wide 'safety valve' open in terms of the presumption–exception paradigm in recognition and enforcement: see Section 5.2.2.

[115] See Section 2.1.2.2.

[116] See Section 2.1.1.1.

[117] See, for example, s 4(2) of the 1933 Act, set out at Section 4.1.2. The 1920 Act similarly is designed only to extend to recognition and enforcement and does not purport or attempt to extend to direct jurisdiction.

Although the New York Convention and the 2005 Convention are 'double' in nature, this presents few hurdles in that they are premised on a single jurisdictional head: agreement based upon party autonomy. For these reasons, these Conventions can summarily dispense with complexities in direct jurisdiction (the jurisdiction of the rendering court) by providing that an exclusive choice of forum suffices. Beyond this jurisdictional base, both Conventions are almost exclusively concerned with matters relating to the recognition and enforcement of foreign decisions.[118] Although this double approach is not controversial where an exclusive choice of forum is relied on, a double approach was also the basis of broad-based negotiating efforts, as demonstrated by the 1999 and 2001 Drafts. Section 2.1.1 sets out the reasons for this in the historical context of negotiating efforts, and Section 8.1 sets out the various conceptual methods adopted to overcome impasses in this area.

For the present purposes of comparison, it suffices to note that the double approach was strongly promoted by European negotiating States at the Hague Conference, likely because such an approach found favour and use in the Brussels Model. The Brussels Model is the most prominent international example of a 'double' approach, as it provides strict and exhaustive rules for when a rendering court must accept or decline original jurisdiction, in addition to rules relating to recognition and enforcement of foreign judgments.[119] Consequently, a significant point of variance in international approaches to recognition and enforcement is whether they attempt to simultaneously regulate (direct) jurisdiction.

[118] See, further, Sections 2.2 and 2.1.2.1.

[119] The reasons for this – the use of 'single' versus 'double' approaches transnationally – are explored at Section 8.2.2.

PART II

Towards Increased Prospects for Judgments Recognition and Enforcement?

The historical analysis in Part I grounds a comparative analysis of present-day recognition and enforcement regimes. Doing so offers preliminary steps to understanding, on a transnational level, the boundaries of what is likely to constitute a properly rendered decision to which enforcing courts are obliged to give effect. Yet, examining this historical and doctrinal basis for recognition and enforcement is not the end of the story. Despite the apparent similarities between approaches, significant differences and complexities still arise in the way in which recognition and enforcement approaches are implemented or are likely to be implemented. Part II of this book considers broader lessons about how enforcement frameworks are designed, applied and likely to develop or evolve over time. This is particularly important given that many States are now faced with the decision of whether to give effect to one or both of the Judgments Conventions, and, even in the jurisdictions where the 2005 Convention has been implemented, there is little case law that has arisen to provide direct judicial guidance.[1] To this end, this part considers the future lessons that transnational recognition and enforcement may offer. While these lessons are likely to impact on all recognition and enforcement approaches, the focus in this part is on foreign judgments at a global level, given the recent genesis and incipient status of the Judgments Conventions. Chapter 6 first considers the hurdles that have been faced at the global level when attempting to reach consensus in the context of the Judgments Project. Chapter 7 then takes a step back to consider how legal development and uniform and autonomous application and interpretation of transnational approaches are managed, and are likely to be managed in future. Chapter 8 concludes this

[1] Noting that the first judgment to consider a domestic implementation of the 2005 Convention was the 2018 Singaporean case of *Ermgassen & Co Ltd* v. *Sixcap Financials Pte Ltd* [2018] SGHCR 8, where a UK summary judgment was enforced.

part by drawing out the lessons that can be derived from the 'transnationalisation' of recognition and enforcement instruments and experience, including responding to critiques of the Judgments Conventions. The ultimate thrust of Part II is to demonstrate that the Judgments Conventions are appropriate and adapted to the task of making recognition and enforcement more certain and predictable globally; and hence, should be ratified or acceded to and implemented by States.

6

Overcoming Hurdles to Transnational Recognition and Enforcement

This chapter analyses the key hurdles that historically were perceived to limit consensus on a harmonised recognition and enforcement instrument on a global level and the steps taken to overcome them. I consider these hurdles from two perspectives. First, I dispute that there are truly intractable differences in legal approaches and traditions across domestic approaches to recognition and enforcement. It has been suggested, for example, that the difference in 'starting position' between different domestic approaches may lead enforcing courts to limit the recognition and enforcement of foreign judgments that fundamentally diverge from their own public policy. Reserving this power to refuse recognition and enforcement is important to many States due to the importance of their own legal sovereignty.[1] Thus, it is necessary to consider how and whether these differences impact on recognition and enforcement, based predominantly on the desire to minimise 'forum shopping', 'jurisdictional arbitrage' or the possible 'importation' of foreign concepts that may be anathema to the public policy of the enforcing court. Although these obstacles can be seen to permeate all recognition and enforcement approaches studied in this book – for example, motivating aspects of the Brussels Model and the Commonwealth Model, as seen in Chapters 3 and 4, respectively – this chapter focuses on the way in which these issues have potentially limited the prospects of achieving a global judgments convention, and the steps taken to address these obstacles.

Second, I analyse the rationales that are said to be unique to certain transnational recognition and enforcement approaches, and whether they are indeed likely to limit the extensibility of one transnational regime to another. This argument is captured in two concerns with respect to the success of the Judgments Conventions. The first of these concerns is that there is perhaps a fundamental divergence in rationale that allows States to agree to give effect to foreign decisions rendered by an exclusive choice of forum over decisions engendered by no such choice. The second concern is that different regional groupings – exemplified in this book by the Commonwealth Model and the Brussels Model participants – have distinct rationales for giving effect to decisions from their own participants that are unlikely to extend to a more arms-length relationship that a global convention open for accession or ratification by any State may offer.

6.1 DIFFERENCES IN LEGAL TRADITION AND APPROACH ACROSS STATES

I commence by setting out the perceived differences in legal tradition and approach to recognition and enforcement before considering how these differences have been encountered and potentially bridged. Doing so is

[1] The term 'sovereignty' here refers to its use in an external sense – where it connotes independence, entailing 'freedom from unwarranted judicial intervention, including interference by a foreign judicial authority': HL Ho, 'Policies Underlying the Enforcement of Foreign Commercial Judgments' (1997) 46 *The International and Comparative Law Quarterly* 447–50.

necessary when considering the prospects of transnational agreement on recognition and enforcement as there is an underlying concern that these hurdles derive from potentially intractable differences. For example, prior to the introduction of the 2019 Judgments Convention, it was argued that:[2]

> The diversity of procedural and substantive laws and of legal cultures is such that a global multilateral treaty on recognition of foreign judgments has never proven to be feasible. This is unlikely to change. Bilateral treaties or regional arrangements may be feasible in some cases.

Brand and Herrup, continuing in this theme, suggest that it was indeed the 'variation in national practice – and in the values and policies underlying that practice' that frustrated early efforts to reach consensus on a broad-based judgments instrument.[3] Perhaps most prominent in this respect are the differences in jurisdictional theory and practice in the United States compared with the European approach. Because of these differences, recognition and enforcement approaches that have been modelled too closely on the European regime are sometimes seen as 'theoretically flawed' and, for example, potentially unconstitutional if implemented in some federalist systems such as the United States.[4] At the same time, other approaches may potentially conflict with constitutional rights and human rights standards. For example, in the European Union, there is a right to the enforcement of a judgment obtained abroad where it involves a fundamental right.[5] Rather than consider a series of isolated domestic or European developments, in this section I use the history of negotiations on the Judgments Project over many decades at the Hague Conference (as set out in its historical context in Section 2.1.1) to analyse these differences. The Judgments Project's history serves as a particularly clear exemplar, due to the persistent argument that different legal

2 James Spigelman, 'Transaction Costs and International Litigation' (2006) 80 *Australian Law Journal* 438, 450.

3 Ronald A. Brand and Paul Herrup, *The 2005 Hague Convention on Choice of Court Agreements: Commentary and Documents* (Cambridge University Press 2008) 4. See also Section 2.1.1, where these efforts are analysed in their historical context.

4 Arthur T. von Mehren, 'Drafting a Convention on International Jurisdiction and the Effects of Foreign Judgments Acceptable World-Wide: Can the Hague Conference Project Succeed?' (2001) 49 *The American Journal of Comparative Law* 191, 196.

5 European Court of Human Rights case law has established a right to the enforcement of judgments obtained abroad, when they implicate a fundamental right under the European Convention on Human Rights: Patrick Kinsch, 'Enforcement as a Fundamental Right' (2014) 32 *Nederlands Internationaal Privaatrecht* 540. The kind of rights implicated are generally outside the commercial realm – for example, rules on marriage and adoption – however, this example still serves to highlight the range of legal hurdles negotiating parties must traverse in reaching consensus on a broad-based instrument.

systems or families underpinning the two key negotiating blocs – European States (now largely represented by the European Union) and the United States – would serve to limit the success of any negotiations towards a harmonised broad-based Judgments Convention. This, it is said, is because the majority of European legal systems originate from a civilian-law tradition,[6] whereas almost every state in the United States dates its legal approaches back to the English-inspired common law.[7] The argument is that these traditions have led to disparate domestic practices with respect to recognition and enforcement, the unpacking of which requires understanding a complex combination of historical, political, social and economic concerns. Hence, efforts to negotiate approaches to harmonise and promote transnational recognition and enforcement raise the potential for a clash in these values.

First, with respect to the common law, it is argued that the common law tradition of adjudication depends in large part upon reserving at least some degree of judicial discretion in interpreting and developing legal doctrine.[8] This power extends to courts choosing both to recognise and enforce a foreign judgment, and also to the decision to grant (or refuse) adjudicatory jurisdiction in the first instance.[9] This common law discretion is not displaced even though the Commonwealth Model codifies a judgment registration system; because, as Section 4.1 explores, this Model either replicates or defers to pre-existing common law approaches. Thus the common law system is said to focus on achieving 'equitable results in judicial decisions applied to specific

6 Europe is not, and of course never has been, a fully civilian-law driven system, and the utility of this classification has been disputed: Konrad Zweigert and Hein Kötz, *An Introduction to Comparative Law* (Clarendon Press, 3rd ed., 1998). See also John Henry Merryman and Rogelio Pérez-Perdomo, *The Civil Law Tradition: An Introduction to the Legal Systems of Europe and Latin America* (Stanford University Press 2007) ch. I. The broad membership of the European Union also represents States utilising common law legal systems (for example, Ireland and Cyprus) and others that can perhaps be described as 'hybrid' systems (for example, Sweden). The Court of Justice of the European Union further blurs these distinctions, due to its role as a supranational court tasked with harmonising the interpretation of European Union law.

7 Zweigert and Kötz (n 6) ch. 17.

8 ibid. Michaels also criticises other distinctions ostensibly based upon inherent differences in the common law and civil law – such as linkages of the common law to 'private market outcomes', and the civil law with State-desired allocations – as 'deeply problematic': Ralf Michaels, 'The Second Wave of Comparative Law and Economics?' (2009) 59 *University of Toronto Law Journal* 197, 201–2.

9 Ronald Brand, 'Recognition and Enforcement of Foreign Judgments' (International Litigation Guide, April 2012) 3–13.

parties and circumstances'.[10] Second, and in contrast, due to historical and legal differences,[11] States in the European civilian tradition have largely prescribed more limited power for judges due to concerns of uncertainty, arbitrariness and oppression that may arise from the exercise of discretion.[12] Judges are largely versed in the task of following and closely interpreting fixed legislative rules in determining jurisdiction and whether to recognise and enforce foreign judgments, rather than exercising open-ended discretion (contra the approach in common law systems). As a result, it has been suggested that States versed in and familiar with the European civil law tradition have largely sought to set out exhaustive and comprehensive rules that limit discretion on whether to grant or decline jurisdiction and prescribe exhaustive rules on the recognition and enforcement of judgments.[13] This approach is represented in the uniform 'Brussels Model' approach to recognising judgments of other European Contracting States.[14] Yet, as the following section explores when considering the extensibility of transnational approaches, it remains an open question the extent to which the success of the Brussels Model approach depends upon the closer 'economic, political, social and legal proximity' in the region.[15] At the least, it can be said that absent such homogeneity, it proved difficult historically to align the differing traditions and approaches of States into an exhaustive and extensive globally

[10] Ronald A. Brand, 'Jurisdictional Developments and the New Hague Judgments Project' [2013] in, 'A Commitment to Private International Law: Essays in Honor of Hans van Loon', Intersentia, 2013 University of Pittsburgh Legal Studies Research Paper No 2013-19 91.

[11] These differences are themselves complex and stem from different approaches to the idea of law and justice, including the role of judges as interpreters or law-makers and the role of judgments and precedential value of superior courts.

[12] For example, the French *Code Civil* and the German Civil Code (BGB) both attempt to simultaneously guide and limit judicial decision making and discretion: Zweigert and Kötz (n 6) chs. 7 and 11.

[13] For example, it is argued that States that follow at least in part in the civilian law tradition do not share the same trust of case law, compared to States from common law countries: Juan Carlos Martinez, 'Recognizing and Enforcing Foreign Nation Judgments: The United States and Europe Compared and Contrasted – A Call for Revised Legislation in Florida' (1995) 4 *Journal of Transnational Law & Policy* 64. See also Spigelman, who notes that 'the civil law tradition remains comparatively inclined to proceed on the basis that the law, both substantive and procedural, is set out with perfect clarity in a code or equivalent document requiring merely its application by a judge without the judge making a policy choice or exercising a discretion': James Spigelman, 'The Hague Choice of Court Convention and International Commercial Litigation' (2010) 9 *The Judicial Review* 389, 394.

See, for an overview of the approaches and instruments contained within the Brussels Model, and the extent to which they likely reflect the civilian law tradition, Chapter 3.

[14] Discussed further in Chapter 3.

[15] Jie Huang, 'Interregional Recognition and Enforcement of Civil and Commercial Judgments: Lessons for China from US and EU Laws' (2010) 6 *Journal of Private International Law* 109.

harmonised recognition and enforcement approach, as the history of the Judgments Project (set out at Section 2.1.1) suggests.[16]

Unpacking the Brussels Model experience further – as Chapter 3 sets out in its historical context – however, suggests that the touted divide between civil and common law does not necessarily hamper States' agreement to, or implementation of, liberal or harmonised recognition and enforcement rules. At this juncture, it assists to recall that the Brussels Model approach sets out exhaustive rules for both direct jurisdiction (jurisdiction) and indirect jurisdiction (recognition and enforcement). With respect to the former, it is likely that reaching agreement on jurisdictional issues was greatly aided by the closely aligned legal cultures of the six original Member States of the EU, which at the time shared a relatively consistent approach.[17] However, the same could not be said for recognition and enforcement rules of Member States at the time, which diverged significantly both in approach and underlying rationale.[18] Upon the coming into force of the 1968 Brussels Convention, these divergent approaches – at least with respect to other Brussels Model participants – were all harmonised in favour of the Model's pro-recognition and enforcement approach. Despite this operative harmonisation, it has been suggested that a further hurdle arises. Namely, because the Model was originally drafted by negotiating parties steeped in the civilian legal tradition, it 'has to be understood' in accordance with European civil law canons of purposive

[16] The European Union approach also proves instructive here: despite the exhaustive jurisdiction and recognition and enforcement rules in place within Europe, judgments that originate from outside of this grouping remain subject to national laws: *Regulation (EU) No 1215/2012 of 12 December 2012 on Jurisdiction and the Recognition and Enforcement of Judgments in Civil and Commercial Matters (Recast)* (2012) Arts 4(2), 36, 39.

[17] Arthur von Mehren and Eckart Gottschalk, *Adjudicatory Authority in Private International Law* (The Hague Academy of International Law Monographs 5, Martinus Nijhoff Publishers 2007) 357. Common law States that subsequently joined the Model and the European Union – including the United Kingdom, Ireland and Cyprus – had to accept this version of the Model as an incident of Membership, and had limited ability to alter its fundamental features.

[18] In precis, national laws among the original EC Member States provided at the time that: in Italy, foreign judgments were, in principle, to be recognised and enforced; courts in France, Luxembourg and Belgium, however, would regularly review the merits of foreign judgments coming for recognition and enforcement; German law insisted upon strict requirements of reciprocity in recognition and enforcement process; and the Code of Civil Procedure in the Netherlands provided that foreign judgments are not enforceable at all but that these matters may be reconsidered afresh by Dutch courts. See, for a more detailed overview of the existing recognition and enforcement approaches of the six original Member States of the European Commission: Paul Jenard, 'Report on the Convention on Jurisdiction and the Enforcement of Judgments in Civil and Commercial Matters of 27 September 1968' (1979) No C59/1 *Official Journal of the European Communities* ch II (Part A).

interpretation.[19] However, this form of purposive interpretation is not a unique element of civilian law legal systems: while it can be surmised that the common law favours literal interpretation of domestic law,[20] purposive interpretation is, broadly speaking, the preferred approach of common law courts interpreting international treaties.[21] In other words, even though the original drafters of the Brussels Model were schooled in civilian law tradition, and the majority of the EU's current Member States are of civilian law training, this has little operative impact on the Model's interpretation. The Brussels Model experience of harmonisation is also consistent with the experience of other States outside of the European bloc that encompass both civil and common law traditions. For example, the 'bijuralism' in Canada has not acted as an impediment to 'bridg[ing]' the so-called divide in the field of recognition and enforcement, as common law and civil law approaches have been able to be reconciled.[22]

For these reasons, it possible to overcome traditional divides in legal systems to achieve consensus on recognition and enforcement of foreign judgments. It has even been argued that despite civil law and common law traditions with respect to private international law maintaining 'integrity' for a period roughly corresponding to the second millennium of the Christian era, their efficacy and distinction is being eroded in recent decades as the two traditions interpenetrate and create new legal traditions.[23] Indeed, since the 1968 Brussels Convention entered into force,[24] the Brussels Model has remained largely unchanged, and it is broadly considered to be successful.[25] Although not

[19] Adrian Briggs, *Civil Jurisdiction and Judgments* (6th ed., Informa Law from Routledge 2015) 28.

[20] See, in an English law context, the seminal text of Kim Lewison, *The Interpretation of Contracts* (6th ed., Sweet & Maxwell 2015).

[21] Briggs (n 19) 28. See also Eirik Bjorge, *The Evolutionary Interpretation of Treaties* (Oxford University Press 2014) 104 and following.

[22] Maryellen Fullerton, 'Enforcing Judgments Abroad: The Global Challenge: Introduction' (1998) 24 *Brooklyn Journal of International Law* 3.

[23] von Mehren and Gottschalk (n 17) 353. But see Pierre Legrand, 'European Legal Systems Are Not Converging' (1996) 45 *International and Comparative Law Quarterly* 52, where Legrand criticises the idea that civil and common law systems are converging.

[24] See Section 3.1, which sets out the instruments constituting the Brussels Model and notes that the 'core' of the Model has remained unchanged since the coming into force of the 1968 Brussels Convention.

[25] Hartley describes the Brussels Convention in the Model as the 'greatest achievement' of the community in conflict of laws, and notes that no other text, anywhere in the world, has achieved such sophistication; for this reason, it was taken as the model for the Hague Conference's original broad-based Judgments Project re-commencement in 1992: Trevor Hartley, 'The European Court, the Brussels Convention/Regulation and the Establishment of an Efficient System for International Litigation in Europe' in Anthony Arnull and others (eds.), *Continuity and Change in EU Law* (Oxford University Press 2008) 385.

directly relevant now that the UK has left the EU, much can be gleaned from the fact that English scholars, such as Briggs,[26] considered that moving from the simplicity of the common law to an 'elaborate' Brussels Model approach – including its exhaustive rules on jurisdiction – were 'justified, by the increased degree of harmonisation of the law of civil jurisdiction and the enforcement of judgments across the European Union'.[27] Despite the obvious issues raised by the UK exit from the EU, it can still be surmised, as Beaumont notes, that the 2019 Convention goes 'significantly beyond' any common law approach to recognition and enforcement based upon the reliance on jurisdictional filters.[28]

Taken further, it also suggests that the traditional common versus civilian law divide has little to say on the issue of recognition and enforcement. For example, the Brussels Model has inspired a number of Member States to revise their own national rules on the recognition and enforcement of foreign judgments to match the Model's approach, even where they are not compelled to do so under the Model itself, and this approach does not necessarily accord with the State's pre-Brussels Model approach. This has led to an 'increasingly harmonized body of law' with respect to recognition and enforcement.[29] Consequently, the Brussels Model experience suggests that whatever differences in legal tradition and approach may exist, these are not likely to be intractable or insurmountable. I turn now to consider how these differences have arisen, and been addressed, in negotiations towards the Judgments Conventions.

6.1.1 *The 'Uneven' Starting Point for Approaches to Recognition and Enforcement*

Absent convention obligations, the national laws of States can – and do – vary significantly as to how they approach recognition and enforcement of foreign

[26] Briggs (n 19) 1. Noting that the core of this lament, and others, broadly relates to the existence or operation of jurisdictional rules – not the rules relating to recognition and enforcement directly.

[27] ibid. 7. See also Paul Beaumont, 'United Kingdom Perspective on the Proposed Hague Judgments Convention' (1998) 24 *Brooklyn Journal of International Law* 75, 109, who laments the loss of discretion (relating to jurisdiction) but notes that the UK had 'come to live with the certainty' offered by the Brussels Model. Due of course to the UK exit from the EU, this longed-for 'simplicity' may yet return to the UK. See, for some possible pathways forward in this respect: Paul Beaumont, 'Some Reflections on the Way Ahead for UK Private International Law after Brexit' (2021) 17 *Journal of Private International Law* 1.

[28] Beaumont, 'Some Reflections on the Way Ahead for UK Private International Law after Brexit' (n 27) 4.

[29] von Mehren and Gottschalk (n 17) 69.

judgments.[30] This divergence is particularly stark, given the extent to which the New York Convention has successfully harmonised a pro-recognition and enforcement approach towards arbitral awards.[31] This heterogeneity of original position presented difficulties for negotiation over the lifetime of the Judgments Projects, as some parties had more to give up or change than others pursuant to any negotiated global standard. For example, it is likely that the current recognition and enforcement practice in the United States already exceeds the Judgments Convention obligations, as the law in most of its states is 'relatively generous' to giving effect to foreign judgments – even absent any treaty obligations.[32] This has two key consequences. First, when negotiating a global instrument, States such as the United States (and States with a similar original position) are more likely to push for international practice that, at the least, goes as far as they already do. This is because States in this position are unlikely to agree to an exhaustive recognition and enforcement framework that is more restrictive than their existing practice. Instead, they are likely to insist upon a framework that meets their own existing approach, or, at the least, does not limit States' discretion to recognise and enforce judgments (absent a treaty obligation). The risk is then that the Judgments Conventions go further than other nations may be willing to go with respect to promoting recognition and enforcement. The second consequence is less significant but speaks to the challenges with respect to implementation: it is, at least relatively, easier for States with more accommodating domestic law enforcement schemes to expeditiously implement the Judgments Conventions.[33]

Experience with other recognition and enforcement regimes – in particular, the New York Convention and the Brussels Model, given the diversity of

[30] The United States is the 'most generous' due to the principles of comity employed by its courts; countries inspired by English common law sit somewhere in the middle; and some European and Asian States have particularly restrictive national law approaches towards judgments outside of their national or regional borders – for example, some jurisdictions do not recognise foreign judgments at all: Peter Nygh, 'Towards a Global Judgments Convention: The Proposed New Hague Convention on the Recognition and Enforcement of Judgments in Civil and Commercial Matters' (1997) 7 *Australian International Law Journal* 100.

[31] See Section 2.2, where it is noted that the New York Convention approach has been widely lauded internationally as a success.

[32] Yuliya Zeynalova, 'The Law on Recognition and Enforcement of Foreign Judgments: Is It Broken and How Do We Fix It?' (2013) 31 *Berkeley Journal of International Law* 154. The United States is likely the most liberal country in the world when it comes to the recognition and enforcement of foreign judgments.

[33] With the proviso that this is subject to key constitutional concerns in the United States. See, for example: Audrey Feldman, 'Rethinking Review of Foreign Court Jurisdiction in Light of the Hague Judgments Negotiations' (2014) 89 *New York University Law Review* 2190.

their participant States – will likely prove instructive. The experiences in both Models suggests that while 'uneven' starting points of national approaches may affect negotiating parties' expectations and negotiating frameworks, they can be overcome in implementation. This is so even in circumstances where parties are usually required – and often encouraged – to employ diverse procedural and substantive laws and rules that are best tailored towards resolving their particular disputes.[34] Perhaps most pertinently, it must be recalled that prior to the commencement and wide acceptance of the New York Convention, the footing upon which arbitral awards were recognised and enforced was susceptible to the same, if not greater, critique of coming from an 'uneven' starting position. Indeed, an early edition of the seminal text *Dicey's Conflict of Laws* notes the uncertainty surrounding the recognition and enforcement of arbitral awards, prior to the success of the New York Convention, within England, by noting that:[35]

> A foreign arbitration award has no direct operation in England, but, if it fulfils the conditions requisite for the validity of a foreign judgment, it may be enforced by an action at the discretion of the court . . . authority regarding the right to enforce by action in England a foreign arbitration award is scanty, [however] it seems on principle that such an award duly pronounced in a foreign country, if it fulfils the conditions, as to validity affecting foreign judgments, should be allowed to be enforced by an action, and this principle has been adopted by the legislature.

This extract highlights that prior to the widespread acceptance of the New York Convention there was even greater ambiguity as to the likely recognition and enforcement of arbitral awards. This implies that there was then more 'unevenness' than is presently seen in approaches to the recognition and enforcement of foreign judgments. Yet, over the long run, this has not impacted on the success and widespread appeal of the New York Convention. Additionally, as the immediately preceding section sets out, this uneven starting point for approaches to recognition and enforcement also has not ultimately impacted on either the initial agreement or the ongoing success of the Brussels Model. The experience of the 2005 Convention is also instructive: at least with respect to the jurisdictional head of an exclusive choice of forum, participant States have not been hampered in reaching

[34] See, generally, Christopher R. Drahozal, 'Why Arbitrate? Substantive versus Procedural Theories of Private Judging' (2011) 22 *American Review of International Arbitration* 163, who explores the diverse rationales underpinning the choice of both procedure and substance in arbitration.

[35] Albert Venn Dicey and J. H. C. Morris, *Dicey's Conflict of Laws* (6th ed., Stevens 1949) 433.

agreement despite a diversity of starting points in domestic approaches to recognition and enforcement. This is no doubt because of the greater ease of being able to seek agreement on a narrower domain of jurisdictional bases, premised upon party autonomy.[36] However, on its face, the 2005 Convention experience at least suggests that divergent national law approaches are not inimical to harmonisation in favour of greater recognition and enforcement prospects.

6.1.2 *'Exorbitant' Approaches, 'Forum Shopping' and 'Jurisdictional Arbitrage'*

A further practical hurdle arising from differences in legal tradition and approach may be that States are hesitant to agree to implement the Judgments Conventions if they allow for a wholesale 'importation' of legal doctrines that they do not agree with for fundamental policy reasons. This concern arises around convention obligations that compel national enforcing courts to recognise and enforce a judgment obtained in another jurisdiction in certain circumstances. Reflecting this concern, many States consider it paramount that a foreign judgment should only be given effect if the judgment coming for enforcement was 'properly' obtained. The concern is not simply that foreign laws, doctrines and remedies differ; this is inevitable across diverse and pluralistic transnational legal orders.[37] Instead, the objection of States arises with force in situations where the approach taken by the rendering court is disallowed in the jurisdiction of the enforcing court domestically for fundamental legal or policy reasons. This objection is not solely about parochial domestic concerns but also extends to fairness and efficiency concerns about the global dispute resolution system arising due to the diffuse nature of international disputes that intersect with a range of legal jurisdictions.

The core of the concern is that any enforcement architecture that compels giving effect to exorbitant foreign decisions may 'invite forum shopping'.[38]

[36] This reliance on party autonomy to underpin jurisdictional claims under the 2005 Convention and the New York Convention – as opposed to the broader remit of the Brussels Model, the Commonwealth Model and the proposed broad-based judgments Convention – is discussed further at Section 6.2.1.

[37] Some States adopt a relatively more liberal approach to the recognition and enforcement of judgments and may be more likely to accept differing approaches – perhaps out of deference or respect to the State (and the judiciary) from which the original judgment originates. This can occur even where the foreign approaches differ significantly from that taken in the local legal system. For a comprehensive analysis of why the enforcing courts of States who face no international law compulsion recognise and enforce judgments, see, generally: Ho (n 1).

[38] Nygh (n 30) 98.

This 'forum shopping' (or 'jurisdictional arbitrage') can occur on one or more levels. At its simplest, plaintiffs can seek out jurisdictions that provide exorbitant bases or legal approaches or remedies that are particularly favourable to them. For example, disputants may first 'shop' to find an exorbitant base favourable to them, possibly even in a 'weak or corruptible' foreign court. After that judgment is obtained, they may then continue to 'shop' for the enforcing court and select a jurisdiction with liberal rules that favour the recognition and enforcement of foreign judgments.[39] If an obligation exists to recognise and enforce these kinds of judgments internationally, this will act to 'export' the objectionable approaches to the State of the enforcing court. This situation becomes particularly problematic when standards relating to the recognition of foreign judgments, as opposed to enforcement, are more liberal. These liberal recognition practices may allow plaintiffs to 'effectively launder' a foreign judgment by first getting it recognised in one jurisdiction and then enforcing it in another that would have rejected it if it had not already been recognised.[40] Yet it must also be noted that there is increasing recognition that the idea of forum shopping is 'no longer universally regarded as a term of abuse': that is, while there may be objectionable selections of certain fora, there are and can be legitimate motivations for the selection of a particular venue.[41]

Nonetheless, these concerns about 'exorbitant' (or objectionable) bases or legal areas presented difficulties during the Judgments Project negotiations, as States remained reluctant to accept obligations to recognise and enforce judgments without appropriately wide safeguards. At their core, these perceived exorbitant approaches are based on fairness and efficiency concerns. Over the course of the negotiating history of the Judgments Project, there were three primary types of judgments that States were concerned about being compelled to recognise and enforce:[42] exorbitant exercises of jurisdiction by the rendering court; exorbitant or excessive types or measures of damages; or, unfairly plaintiff-friendly cost regimes, for example in class actions or where plaintiffs do not have to pay their own costs (potentially leading to concerns as to fairness or frivolous or vexatious litigation). A recent example, explored in

39 In the tortious context this has often been termed 'tort tourism'. See, for example: John Bellinger and Reeves Anderson, 'Tort Tourism: The Case for a Federal Law on Foreign Judgment Recognition' (2014) 54 *Virginia Journal of International Law* 501, 503.

40 Gregory Shill, 'Ending Judgment Arbitrage: Jurisdictional Competition and the Enforcement of Foreign Money Judgments in the United States' (2013) 54 *Harvard International Law Journal* 459.

41 Spigelman (n 13) 395.

42 Adapted from Nygh (n 30) 97–101.

the context of the 2019 Convention negotiations, is the idea of whether pecuniary penalties – which in character reflect civil fines, and differ from the compensatory nature of damages – will qualify as a 'judgment' and hence activate the convention obligations.[43] Differences in legal tradition and approach have some explanative force here, as the need for safeguards in recognition and enforcement practice is particularly acute for civil law jurisdictions that either severely limit or do not allow judicial discretion in either compelling or declining to recognise and enforce a foreign judgment.[44] On the other hand, States that already adopt a more liberal approach to the recognition and enforcement of foreign judgments, premised on judicial discretion to avoid abuses, are less likely to take issue with these practices. I turn now to consider each of the three factors that were critical in the history of the Judgments Project, in terms of how they are perceived to have limited transnational agreement and also with respect to the steps taken to remedy or address these concerns.

6.1.2.1 Exorbitant Jurisdiction

The first concern, of exorbitant jurisdiction, arises because many States are reluctant to recognise and enforce foreign judgments where the jurisdiction to adjudicate the original matter was obtained by what the enforcing court considers to be exorbitant and unwarranted jurisdictional reach. It has been argued that most States 'exercise a good deal of exorbitant jurisdiction' by agreeing to hear disputes that lack a significant connection between the rendering State and either the parties or the dispute.[45] The kinds of exorbitant jurisdiction that States have identified as problematic include, for example, opt-out class actions (particularly when combined with a plaintiff-friendly cost regime, as the third concern discusses);[46] extraterritorial jurisdictional

43 Francisco Garcimartín, 'The Judgments Convention: Some Open Questions' (2020) 67 *Netherlands International Law Review* 21–25.

44 For example, many of these States have principled conflict of law rules on jurisdiction that avoid the need for recourse to judicial discretion, particularly in instances where there is a risk of parallel litigation (*lis pendens* rules). This approach is represented in the Brussels Convention and subsequent Brussels Regulations, which provide only for very limited discretion in accepting or declining jurisdiction, which occurs primarily on a rule-driven basis: Peter Nygh and Fausto Pocar, 'Report by Peter Nygh & Fausto Pocar (Annexed to the 1999 Preliminary Draft Convention)' (Report, August 2000) citing the Restatement (Second) Conflict of Laws 30.

45 Kevin Clermont and John Palmer, 'Exorbitant Jurisdiction' (2006) 58 *Maine Law Review* 474.

46 For further discussion on the nature of transnational class actions, see: Zachary Clopton, 'Transnational Class Actions in the Shadow of Preclusion' (2015) 90 *Indiana Law Journal* 1387.

claims;[47] and, so-called tag jurisdiction (based on the transient or temporary presence of a defendant in the jurisdiction).[48] Although not technically necessary to recognise and enforce a foreign decision, almost every enforcing court attempts to assure itself in some way of the suitability of the rendering forum's jurisdiction. 'Controlling' rendering courts' jurisdiction in this way is relatively simple to do, as jurisdictional standards are usually not connected with the matter in dispute, avoiding the need for an extensive exploration of the merits of the underlying litigation.[49] This control can most readily be seen in the application of transnational instruments that depend on party autonomy: namely, the New York Convention (for arbitral awards where parties have selected arbitration) and the 2005 Convention (for judgments where parties have selected an exclusive choice of court).[50]

Where the foreign decision is not brought about by an exclusive choice of forum, however, it is harder to control potentially objectionable exercises of exorbitant jurisdiction. For these reasons, the control of exorbitant jurisdiction was one of the primary negotiating hurdles over the life of the Judgments Project.[51] However, as Section 2.1.2.2 sets out, a range of compromises was worked out over several decades, in a bid to attempt to address these concerns. First and foremost, the 2019 Convention now sets out required jurisdictional bases before it applies; this feature was not always present across the negotiating history. Second, and no less important, States at the time of negotiations, agreed to 'hive off' and postpone efforts to to directly regulate jurisdiction via treaty until and unless work towards an agreement on recognition and

[47] The most 'outrageous' example is Article 14 of the French *Code Civil*: Nygh (n 30) 97. As the *Cour de cassation* (the French supreme court for civil and commercial matters) emphasised in its judgment in 2012, this Article no longer operates to bar the recognition and enforcement of judgments but allows French courts, with no otherwise acceptable ground of jurisdiction, to exercise jurisdiction over matters involving French plaintiffs: (France), 29 February 2012, Case No. 11-40.101, Inédit.

[48] Phillip describes the differences in European and American law on the acceptability of this jurisdiction as the 'biggest difficulty' in progressing the judgments instrument: Allan Phillip, 'The Global Hague Judgments Convention' in Talia Einhorn and Kurt Siehr (eds.), *Intercontinental Cooperation Through Private International Law: Essays in Memory of Peter E. Nygh* (TMC Asser Press 2004) 300.

[49] *Recognition and Enforcement of Foreign Judgments: General Theory and the Role of Jurisdictional Requirements* (Martinus Nijhoff Publishers 1981) 39.

[50] The concept of party autonomy – and the extent to which it stands as an inextensible component of the recognition and enforcement of foreign decisions – is discussed further, below, at Section 6.2.1.

[51] See, further, Trevor Hartley and Masato Dogauchi, 'Explanatory Report on the Convention of 30 June 2005 on Choice of Court Agreements' (Explanatory Report, 2007) [203].

enforcement succeeded.[52] It is likely that these compromises, in addition to any specific measures explored later, will go some way in ameliorating concerns with respect to recognition and enforcement arising from the potential exercise of exorbitant jurisdiction of the original rendering forum, and, hence, not stand as a bar to States acceding to the 2019 Convention.

6.1.2.2 Objectionable, Punitive or 'Grossly Excessive' Damages

A second concern arises because States are often concerned about what are deemed to be excessive or exorbitant types or amounts of damages contained in some categories or kinds of judgments. This concern arises primarily in two instances. The first instance, perceived 'excessive' damages awards, arises where judges or juries return verdicts for large amounts of damages (primarily in tort actions, although this can also occur in contract claims) and the resulting judgment comes for recognition and enforcement in a jurisdiction that considers this award grossly excessive pursuant to its own domestic standards. The second instance arises where the type of damages, for example non-compensatory damages such as punitive (exemplary) damages,[53] are awarded in the foreign decision but are prohibited or severely limited by domestic standards in the jurisdiction of the enforcing court.[54] For example, as noted by the Working Group at the Diplomatic Session to approve the 2005 Choice of Court Agreements Convention:[55]

> During the negotiations, it has become obvious that some delegations have problems with judgments awarding damages that go far beyond the actual loss of the plaintiff. Punitive or exemplary damages are an important example. Some delegations thought that the public policy exception in Article 9(e) could solve those problems, but others made it clear that this was not possible under their limited concept of public policy. Therefore it was agreed that there should be an additional ground for refusal for judgments on damages. This is the new Article 11. As in the case of all other

[52] Hague Conference, 'Report of the Fifth Meeting of the Working Group on the Judgments Project (26–31 October 2015) and Proposed Draft Text Resulting from the Meeting' (Preliminary Document, November 2015) 5.

[53] Punitive damages are damages awarded to 'punish' the defendant for particularly egregious conduct, with the aim of both specific and general deterrence.

[54] For example, German law (contra the United States), for the most part, considers that punitive damages should only be awarded in criminal, not civil, matters: Gralf-Peter Calliess, 'Value-Added Norms, Local Litigation, and Global Enforcement: Why the Brussels-Philosophy Failed in The Hague' (2004) 05 *German Law Journal* 1496.

[55] Hague Conference Working Group, 2005 Diplomatic Session, Minutes No 19 of the Twentieth Session, Commission II, at para 14.

grounds for refusal, this provision should be interpreted and applied in as restrictive a way as possible.

Yet, at the same time, States that do allow such damages – and key stakeholders who will lose out by such prohibitions and not gain corresponding advantages by other parts of the convention[56] – often consider a refusal to recognise and enforce a foreign decision on its terms to be an unwarranted criticism and imposition on the law-making power of the rendering forum and the sovereignty of any State sanction that underlies it. It has been nonetheless suggested, at least in the context of enforcing arbitral awards under the New York Convention, that despite a range of theoretical criticisms, concerns about forms of punitive damage are 'much ado' about a 'virtually inexistent' problem in international commercial dispute resolution.[57] This, Petsche argues, is because very few laws authorise the award of punitive damages, particularly where contract claims are involved. Indeed, it is only very few courts – predominantly in common law jurisdictions – that allow for or recognise punitive damages.[58] The New York Convention and the 2005 Convention alike also have the further comfort of giving effect to the autonomy of the parties' choice of law; and hence, in theory at least, it should be less objectionable to give effect to a particular law that allows for more than compensatory damages. These approaches differ from enforcement under the 2019 Convention, which applies to judgments rendered by default rules.

Although attempts have been made to resolve this impasse – as the long negotiating history of the broad-based Judgments Project suggests – this polarisation of the role and use of damages in a legal system remains a live issue that arises in exceptional circumstances. This means that it cannot readily be solved on a transnational level without compromise by States. Compromise in this instance means that some States will either need to accept that some judgments that are rendered will be enforced (even with perceived exorbitant or excessive damages) or the States of rendering courts accept that some types or amounts of damages may be limited or 'carved out'

[56] David Bennett, 'The Hague Convention on Recognition and Enforcement of Foreign Judgments: A Failure of Characterisation' in Talia Einhorn and Kurt Siehr (eds.), *Intercontinental Cooperation Through Private International Law: Essays in Memory of Peter E Nygh* (TMC Asser Press 2004) 20.

[57] Markus A. Petsche, 'Punitive Damages in International Commercial Arbitration: Much Ado about Nothing?' (2013) 29 *Arbitration International* 89, 90–91.

[58] As Petsche notes, punitive damages are most notably awarded by courts in the UK, the United States, Canada, Australia and New Zealand, and, as a general rule, punitive damages are 'generally not available' in civil law jurisdictions: ibid. 94.

from a potential global instrument.[59] Traditionally, the New York Convention approach has made no particular carve out for these kind of objectionable decisions; instead, if there is an objectionable quantum or head of damages awarded, the award can be refused recognition and enforcement under the public policy exception.[60] However, doing so is rather a blunt approach: the entire award is then refused recognition and enforcement, including the part of the award that awards compensatory damages (which are usually not objectionable).

Rather than leaving resolution to the blunt tool of public policy, the Judgments Conventions expressly address this issue by providing an exception to recognition and enforcement in the following terms:[61]

(1) Recognition or enforcement of a judgment may be refused if, and to the extent that, the judgment awards damages, including exemplary or punitive damages, that do not compensate a party for actual loss or harm suffered.

This provision must then be read together with provisions that compel enforcing courts to sever any part of the foreign judgment that is objectionable, and continue to recognise and enforce the remainder.[62] Indeed, this approach is designed to improve recognition and enforcement outcomes as:[63]

> Recognition and enforcement may only be refused to the extent that the judgment goes beyond the actual loss or harm suffered. For most delegations, this might already be a logical consequence of the limited purpose of this provision. However, it is useful to state this expressly. This avoids a possible 'all or nothing approach' some legal systems apply to the public policy exception.

Noting the exceptional nature of awarding these kinds of non-compensatory damages in domestic legal systems,[64] it is likely that the control introduced by

59 von Mehren (n 4) 195–96.

60 Punitive damages are expressed to be 'incompatible' with the public policy of most jurisdictions, and hence face limited enforcement support internationally: Petsche (n 57) 97 (and following).

61 Article 11(1) of the 2005 Convention; Article 10(1) of the 2019 Convention. The desire of these provisions to avoid a 'possible "all or nothing approach"' is the expressed rationale of these provisions, as set out in Hartley and Dogauchi (n 51) para [203]–[205].

62 Article 15 of the 2005 Convention; Article 9 of the 2019 Convention.

63 This statement was agreed by the members of the Working Group that drafted this article and adopted by the Diplomatic Session that agreed to the 2005 Convention: as recorded in Hague Conference, 'Statement of the 2005 Convention Working Group Drafters (Adopted by the Diplomatic Session)' (no date) [14].

64 Petsche (n 57) 94–95.

these provisions – essentially allowing the enforcing court to sever non-compensatory damage – will meet the needs of States that object to their grant.[65] Notably, it does so in a manner that continues to support a pro-recognition and enforcement approach towards foreign decisions, as it does not compel non-enforcement and provides an avenue for States to avoid giving effect only to the objectionable portion of a foreign decision that awards non-compensatory damages. As the Explanatory Memorandum to the 2019 Convention sets out, these provisions are intended to be used instead of the public policy exception where non-compensatory damages are objectionable in the jurisdiction of the enforcing court.[66] Additionally, it has been stressed that this provision is not intended as a general review of whether the enforcing court would have awarded the same amount of damage; instead, it only operates 'when it is obvious from the judgment that the award appears to go beyond the actual loss or harm suffered'. This assists in minimising the observed risk, as seen in the context of the New York Convention, of enforcing courts potentially extending the reach of the general public policy exception in a manner that is not consistent with pro-recognition and enforcement obligations in that instrument.[67]

6.1.2.3 'Importation' of Plaintiff-Friendly Cost Regimes

The third concern arising in negotiations towards a global judgments recognition and enforcement instrument is the risk of allowing the import of plaintiff-friendly cost and expense regimes. In the context of recognition and enforcement, this concern has the greatest force in the context of the unique cost practice of the United States. This is because its practice diverges from most other modern legal systems.[68] The American practice, decried as 'incredible, strange, terrible and intolerable' to the foreign jurist, can be referred to as

65 What remains to be seen is the extent to which this approach will be supported by States and key interest groups within certain States (such as trial lawyers in the United States). This, of course, is a key concern, as it is argued that this was a key reason why early efforts to reach consensus on the 1999 Draft and the 2001 Draft of the broad-based judgments project failed: see Section 2.1.1.

66 Francisco Garcimartín and Geneviève Saumier, 'Explanatory Report on the HCCH 2019 Judgments Convention' [2020] 131–33.

67 For a detailed exposition of the New York Convention and the interpretation and application of the public policy exception see generally: Anton G. Maurer, *Public Policy Exception Under the New York Convention: History, Interpretation, and Application* (Revised, Juris Publishing, Inc 2013).

68 James Maxeiner, *Failures of American Civil Justice in International Perspective* (Cambridge University Press 2011) 32–35.

the 'no indemnity practice' (or the 'American rule').[69] It stipulates that each party must bear their own legal costs, irrespective of whether they ultimately fail or succeed in the litigation. In almost every other legal system, plaintiffs who succeed in their claim are entitled to some indemnity for their legal costs incurred from the losing parties who resisted the claim. If the plaintiff's claim is found unmeritorious, it will have to contribute to the legal costs of the defending party.

The responsibility for legal costs is also controversial, as some States object to other States allowing the costs of litigation to be borne by a representative class or by litigation funders who bankroll legal proceedings. The concern is that this encourages what can perhaps charitably be described as 'marginal' litigation, where the prospects of success are not particularly strong.[70] This is costly for the judiciary and individual defendants to respond to, and is perceived to be unfair for a range of reasons, including the perception that these rules may be used to place unfair pressure on defendants in commercial matters to settle even unmeritorious claims.[71] In summary, these two cost rules give rise to concerns that parties with frivolous or vexatious claims may choose to litigate in jurisdictions that follow the American rule or that the rules allow them to bring proceedings without facing legal costs themselves (funded by the class, or a litigation funder). After so doing, they can then seek recognition and enforcement of the resulting judgment and its costs component,[72] even in jurisdictions that do not agree with the award of costs on this basis.

Because of a concern that they may be compelled to recognise and enforce judgments with such costs orders, States are sometimes reluctant to agree to transnational obligations that compel recognition and enforcement. The way this is handled in the recent Judgments Conventions – departing from the New York Convention approach, which remains silent on this issue – is indirectly and only partially. That is, by using the provisions set out in the

69 ibid. 33.

70 A. Mitchell Polinsky and Steven Shavell, *Handbook of Law and Economics* (Elsevier 2007) 307.

71 Lang Thai, 'Commercial Litigation Funding: The Need to Impose Regulations to Improve the Outcome of the Shareholder Class Actions' (2011) 4 *Journal of the Australasian Law Teachers Association* 1, 14.

72 Courts around the world vary in how the costs determination is made, and thus both the 2005 Convention and the broad-based Judgments Draft Convention define a judgment broadly to cover these situations by providing, in Art 4(1) and Art 3(1), respectively, that 'judgment means any decision on the merits given by a court, whatever it may be called, including a decree or order, and a determination of costs or expenses by the court (including an officer of the court), provided that the determination relates to a decision on the merits which may be recognised or enforced under this Convention'.

immediately preceding section to allow courts to avoid giving effect to excessive or punitive damages but at the same time compelling enforcing courts to 'take into account whether and to what extent the damages awarded by the court of origin serve to cover costs and expenses relating to the proceedings'.[73] As Nygh and Pocar note, this practice allows judgments that contain some potentially objectionable category of damage, such as punitive damages, to be recognised and enforced where such damage can be seen as intended to cover the costs and expenses of the successful party.[74] This reflects global agreement upon the usual function of damages (and the award of costs) as compensatory[75] and allows for as broad as possible a category of judgments to be recognised and enforced while still respecting this idea. Beyond the compensatory nature of damages (and the award of costs), the broader question – as to whether differences in rationales underlying recognition and enforcement of different categories or types of foreign decisions may impact on the success of the Judgments Conventions – remains unanswered.

6.2 DIFFERENCES IN RATIONALES UNDERLYING RECOGNITION AND ENFORCEMENT APPROACHES

In this section, I consider how likely it is that experiences or lessons learnt in one transnational approach may extend to others. This inquiry arises given recurring suggestions that experience from other transnational recognition and enforcement approaches may have either no or limited applicability beyond their own domains. As with the Section 6.1, the focus is on assessing whether and to what extent these perceived differences are likely to limit or serve as a hurdle to efforts to promote harmonised pro-recognition and enforcement approaches towards foreign judgments.

6.2.1 *Transnational Divergence: Methods of Achieving Jurisdiction*

The widespread success of the New York Convention, coupled with eventual transnational agreement to the 2005 Convention (and its coming into force in 2015), gives rise to the suggestion that the jurisdictional head of party autonomy may be a key driver facilitating harmonisation and promotion of recognition and enforcement prospects. This is because the New York Convention is

[73] Article 11(2) of the 2005 Convention. This provision is duplicated in its entirety in Article 10(2) of the draft Convention.

[74] Nygh and Pocar (n 44) 119.

[75] Hartley and Dogauchi (n 51) [205].

said to have the same 'core justification' as the 2005 Convention: both give effect to parties' choice of forum, with the only difference between an arbitration agreement and a choice of court agreement being that in one case the parties select a private forum and in the other case the parties select a public forum.[76] In large part, this is because the jurisdictional head of party autonomy is considered less controversial than a Convention that applies in default of choice, as it accords with the concept of party autonomy that most States allow for within the realm of private contractual obligation.[77] Of course, this support for autonomy is not absolute.[78] As Brand and Herrup suggest in the context of the 2005 Convention, private choices of law and policy must be subordinate to public institutions; a rule that ranges from a 'strong' tradition in many jurisdictions to a 'rigid rule' in others.[79] Yet the suggestion remains that the 2019 Convention should be distinguished from the 2005 Convention and the New York Convention, as it alone does not require the active choice of disputants to select a mutually agreeable forum. This is what underlies the suggestion that it was more 'realistic' to agree to the 2005 Convention rather than the 2019 Convention, which requires no such choice.[80]

As Chapter 2 analyses in some detail, the issue of jurisdiction stood as a key negotiating impasse with respect to a broad-based Judgments Project. Jurisdictional issues were finally addressed in the 2019 Convention by predicating the application of obligations to recognise and enforce upon finding an acceptable jurisdictional base.[81] This requires that an identified jurisdictional base (also termed a 'jurisdictional filter') be applied, or else the obligation of States to give effect to foreign decisions does not activate. It bears noting, however, that the mere existence of jurisdictional filters – rather than a permissive approach that does not rely upon such filters – does not necessarily mean that a broader array of foreign decisions is likely to be excluded. Instead, this reliance can be seen as merely a mechanism for making explicit the

[76] Jason Yackee, 'A Matter of Good Form: The (Downsized) Hague Judgments Convention and Conditions of Formal Validity for the Enforcement of Forum Selection Agreements' (2003) 53 (3) *Duke Law Journal.*

[77] See, for example, Marta Pertegás and Brooke Marshall, 'Party Autonomy and Its Limits: Convergence Through the New Hague Principles on Choice of Law in International Commercial Contracts' (2014) 39 *Brooklyn Journal of International Law* 975.

[78] See, for example, the range of limitations placed on the sphere of application that are broadly consistent across transnational approaches: Section 5.3.

[79] Brand and Herrup (n 3) 23.

[80] See for example, Yackee (n 76) 1178, who, prior to the carving out of the work that eventually formed the 2005 Convention, posed the question: 'Can the Hague Judgments Convention be saved through radical downsizing?'

[81] This is set out in its comparative context at Section 5.3.3.

reason for refusing to give effect to judgments. If the filters are sufficiently broad to encapsulate the 'generally accepted' heads of jurisdiction on an international level, then this approach is little different to the exceptions already in place in most transnational frameworks. For example, exceptions or limitations on recognition and enforcement, as set out in the immediately preceding section, as well as the 'safety valve' of the public policy exception in the presumption–exception model, are contained in all transnational approaches. These grounds of exception could apply to excuse an enforcing court from giving effect to a foreign decision – even absent any need for reference to or reliance upon jurisdictional filters – on the basis that if there was no accepted basis for the rendering court's jurisdiction, giving effect to a resulting judgment would offend the public policy of the enforcing States (and hence an enforcing court would not be compelled to give effect to a resulting judgment). The extent to which any perceived reliance on lack of a jurisdictional head of party autonomy will, in practice, impact or change the general approach to recognition and enforcement thus remains unclear.

Considered from the perspective of the broad-based Judgments Project, this concern suggests that the exercise of jurisdiction of a foreign court that is not achieved by party choice may lead to a broader array of less than desirable decisions coming for recognition and enforcement. Given that international arbitration is a completely voluntary process, built upon party autonomy, this choice must always be made. While international litigation can be a product of voluntary party choice – as seen where parties select a court to hear their dispute, and hence potentially activate the 2005 Convention provisions on recognition and enforcement – litigation is often used as a dispute resolution mechanism pursuant to a court's exercise of its jurisdictional rules (often under objection by the defendant to proceedings). It has, for example, been suggested that:[82]

> One of the difficult issues which impedes further development in this field, is the variation in the quality, independence and impartiality of the judiciaries of different nations. To a substantial degree, again setting aside the particular situation of government controlled entities and cases of unequal bargaining power, the choice can be left to bargaining between parties to a commercial relationship.

In other words, where parties have not themselves taken on the risk of any 'variation in the quality, independence and impartiality' of their decision maker, it is more difficult to justify the existence or maintenance of

[82] Spigelman (n 13) 452.

transnational obligations that presume recognition and enforcement. Yet this same concern resounds in equal force to contracts that are not fully negotiated. This is seen, for example, where parties do not turn their mind to the dispute resolution procedures in their dealings and adopt a particular forum or dispute resolution mechanism as a default as it arises in an existing template or standard form contract.[83] Of course, the jurisdictional heads addressed in the 2019 Convention are much broader than this category: as Section 5.3.3 canvasses, these heads include a range of tortious and other default claims that do not require any contractual dealing, and hence lose any claim to justification based upon the autonomy of parties. These situations are what most likely give rise to the concerns expressed in the immediately preceding section, predominantly to do with concerns about importing perceived exorbitant, objectionable or unsupported categories of foreign decision.

More broadly, the way that States may rely upon party autonomy to engender transnational co-operation agreement remains an open question. Brand and Herrup argue that the experience of the New York Convention – premised upon selection of a private neutral arbitral panel – is distinct as it does not raise the same issues of 'sovereign function' that underlie requests for recognition and enforcement of foreign judgments.[84] A recent line of critique has also emerged in a series of blog posts by Gary Born, who strongly opposes the 2005 Convention.[85] This critique is discussed further at Section 8.3.2, but for present purposes I note that Born's view is that party autonomy is not comparable under the 2005 Convention vis à vis the New York Convention, as parties to the former cannot select their decision makers and the procedures that they face. Born emphasies that the New York Convention allows the arbitration agreement's existence, validity and scope to be determined *de novo* in three occasions (at initial stages, at set aside and in enforcement proceedings).[86] This can be contrasted with the 2005 Convention which privileges the decision of the putatively chosen legal system in this respect, and does not

[83] This is consistent with the views of Korobkin, who takes issue with the idea that arises according to basic economic theory that standard form terms – which include the choice of any dispute resolution mechanism or forum – will come to a socially efficient equilibrium: Russell Korobkin, 'Bounded Rationality, Standard Form Contracts, and Unconscionability' (2003) 70 *The University of Chicago Law Review* 1203.

[84] Brand and Herrup (n 3) 23.

[85] Gary B. Born, 'Why States Should Not Ratify, and Should Instead Denounce, the Hague Choice-of-Court Agreements Convention' (Parts I, II and II) and 'Why It Is Especially Important That States Not Ratify the Hague Choice of Court Agreements Convention' (Part I and II) (*Kluwer Arbitration Blog*, 2021).

[86] Gary Born, 'The Hague Convention on Choice of Court Agreements: A Critical Assessment' (2021) 169 *University of Pennsylvania Law Review* 2079, 2115.

allow further review. It is true that this limits the options for review in subsequent proceedings, and that this is likely to be particularly problematic where the putatively chosen court is 'of doubtful integrity, independence, and competence'.[87] However, there are good reasons why judgments should be enforced above and beyond reasons of party autonomy, and a certain and predictable rule that promotes finality is a justifiable option for the 2005 Convention to adopt. It can be justified for a host of reasons – perhaps inspired by the experience of the Brussels Model or the common law – including developing conceptions of comity and deepening relationships between States and enforcing courts. Such a rationale is expressly seen in discussions of the common law's approach to comity, including in particular, analysis of the development of adjudicatory comity (a 'comity between courts'), as explored in Section 4.2.2.2.[88] Perhaps more pressingly, concepts of finality, efficiency or fairness rooted in the administration of justice, may also take on greater precedence in the context of foreign judgments.[89] At this juncture it suffices to note that these kinds of rationales call for foreign judgments to be given effect to in a broader variety of circumstances, even where party autonomy to select a dispute resolution forum does not apply. These rationales may support a more certain and predictable rule that, departing from the New York Convention, privileges the putatively chosen legal system in a choice of forum agreement; even where doing so may, in exceedingly rare cases, mean that enforcing courts are bound to give effect to judgments where they disagree with the putatively selected forum's exercise of jurisdiction.

87 ibid. 2120.

88 João Ribeiro-Bidaoui, 'Hailing the HCCH (Hague) 2005 Choice of Court Convention, A Response to Gary Born' (*Kluwer Arbitration Blog*, 21 July 2021) <http://arbitrationblog.kluwerarbitration.com/2021/07/21/hailing-the-hcch-hague-2005-choice-of-court-convention-a-response-to-gary-born/> accessed 2 October 2021. Cf Born, who stresses that providing a more liberal avenue to enforce judgments, including judgments from corrupt or politicised judiciaries, will encourage illegally-procured judgments: Gary B. Born, 'Why It Is Especially Important That States Not Ratify the Hague Choice of Court Agreements Convention, Part II' (*Kluwer Arbitration Blog*, 23 July 2021) <http://arbitrationblog.kluwerarbitration.com/2021/07/23/why-it-is-especially-important-that-states-not-ratify-the-hague-choice-of-court-agreements-convention-part-ii/> accessed 2 October 2021.

89 These rationales are explored in the context of common law jurisdictions at Section 4.2.3.2, but are likely equally applicable to all States considering whether to give effect to a foreign decision – whether in the form of an award or a judgment. See, for example, Thieffry, who discusses the practical need for the finality that enforcement proceedings give to support the otherwise consensual process of arbitration: Jean Thieffry, 'The Finality of Awards in International Arbitration' (1985) 2 *Journal of International Arbitration* 27.

It has also been argued that the distinct nature of judgments, compared to awards, means that the success of the 2005 Convention – and, by analogy, the 2019 Convention – should not be measured solely with respect to how far and to what extent these instruments promote recognition and enforcement or make national courts 'as efficient as arbitration'.[90] Instead, 'the proper measure of success' is a lesser measure, based upon the extent to which these approaches improve the status quo with respect to the recognition and enforcement of foreign judgments.[91] This modest aim is likely informed by suggestions that the 'degree of liberalism' achieved in the New York Convention may not be attained again if the Convention had to be negotiated closer to today.[92] At the least, additional concerns with respect to judgments suggest that party autonomy is not, and for the 2019 Convention cannot be, fully explanatory as to why States may wish to implement one or both of the Judgments Conventions.

6.2.2 *Beyond Global: Divergent Conceptions of 'Trust' in Sovereign Relationships*

One of the key divergences said to underlie differences in recognition and enforcement approaches is the potentially unique conceptions of sovereign trust that exist between certain States. To explore this juxtaposition, I explore the relationships between States in the two key non-global transnational approaches analysed in this book: the Commonwealth Model and the common law that underlies it (as set out in Chapter 4), and the Brussels Model (as set out in Chapter 3). A consideration of these approaches is particularly illustrative as these two Models have distinct rationales that are absent on the global level. Consequently, I analyse these approaches with respect to whether the conceptions of sovereignty they build upon are likely to limit or impact upon their extensibility to global approaches to recognition and enforcement.

It is useful to also recall the point, discussed at Section 5.1.1, that Article 29 of the 2019 Convention allows States to effectively make a declaration that the Convention obligations will not apply to judgments originating from particular States. This has the ability to act as a hard brake on any conceptions

[90] Brand and Herrup (n 3) 24.

[91] ibid. 23.

[92] Emmanuel Gaillard, 'Enforcement of Awards Set Aside in the Country of Origin: The French Experience' in Albert Jan van den Berg (ed.), *Improving the Efficiency of Arbitration Agreements and Awards: 40 years of Application of the New York Convention* (KluwerArbitration, Kluwer Law International 1999) 692.

of mutual trust globally, although it should be reserved for application to States that have a systemic pattern of bias or corruption in judgments. No equivalent to Article 29 exists within the 2005 Convention.

6.2.2.1 The Brussels Model Concept of Sovereign Relationships

The Brussels Model, as Chapter 3 illustrates, is often heralded as a success due to its widespread adoption among participants and its ongoing evolution. For this reason, it has been studied extensively, particularly with a view to facilitating transnational consensus on global negotiations towards the Judgments Project.[93] Yet, a recurring concern in considering the Brussels Model is the concern that it is 'unlikely to be instructive' for other transnational recognition and enforcement efforts, as it is premised on the basis of the EU's extraordinary degree of mutual trust and cooperation among Member States.[94] That is, the extent of harmonisation in the Brussels Model, and for present purposes the strong balance in favour of recognition and enforcement, is unlikely to extend to 'sovereign relationships of a very different kind' that exist between States worldwide.[95] Thus, it has been suggested that it is 'hardly possible' to transplant the Model outside the EC/EU as it is 'primarily conceived' to facilitate the common market – within the context of the EC/EU's unique institutional setup.[96] Indeed, it has even been argued that the Brussels Model approach, as embodied in the original 1968 Convention, would be unlikely to be obtained even on a more limited regional basis, such as the Asia Pacific, 'even in the core ASEAN grouping of nations, let alone on a broader regional basis'.[97] Thus, it is argued that the Brussels Model's success is inexorably tied to the nature of European co-operation in various groupings.

As Chapter 3 discusses, the Brussels Model achieves harmonised private international law rules by 'distributing' power as a matter of regional governance'[98] extending far beyond the political mandate accorded to global harmonisation projects based on private international law harmonisation in the

93 See Chapter 2, where this overlap is noted, particularly with respect to the 1971 Convention.

94 Andrew Dickinson, 'What, If Anything, Can Australia Learn from the EU Experience?' in Andrew Dickinson and others (eds.), *Australian Private International Law for the 21st Century: Facing Outwards* (Hart 2014) 183.

95 ibid.

96 José Angelo Estrella Faria, 'Globalisation, Legal Identity and Regional Integration: Complementarity or Conflict?' (2013) 18 *Uniform Law Review* 435, 442.

97 Spigelman (n 13) 450.

98 Andrew Dickinson and Eva Lein (eds.), *The Brussels I Regulation Recast* (Oxford University Press 2015) 384–85.

context of the sovereign prerogative of individual nations. For example, as the drafters of the Brussels Model sought 'a genuine legal systematization',[99] there was little interest in maintaining distinct legal traditions, nor in securing the national interests of negotiating parties – as these 'preoccupations' are 'inconsistent with the philosophy of the common market'.[100] As a result, the Brussels Model, in its very design, relies upon a thread of mutual trust and reliance on the capacity of participants' courts.[101] This thread is what unifies the concepts of prescriptive versus adjudicatory comity, which are explored in the section that follows with respect to common law conceptions of sovereign law relationships. For the purposes of the Brussels Model, this mutual trust serves these two roles by calling for sovereignty to be overridden and for the existence of clear and consistent rules on both direct jurisdiction and indirect jurisdiction (recognition and enforcement) for precisely when a judgment should or should not be given effect to. This is, of course, more readily achieved among States that share values and traditions – particularly where they aspire to an 'ever closer union' and undertake to harmonise not only jurisdiction and recognition and enforcement but many other areas of substantive and procedural law as well.

Consequently, the Brussels Model's approach favours mutual trust to a greater degree than a general global instrument is likely to, based on its design goals of supporting and promoting intra-European trade.[102] This is no doubt assisted by other unique factors underpinning European union, including the fact that the EU Member States are a 'manageable' number of sufficiently developed countries, the courts of all are theoretically considered to be equally capable and competent in applying the rules of the Model, and the interpretive assistance of the CJEU can be called upon where necessary or required.[103] As a result, this compulsion towards greater mutual trust is both an imperative and simply a fact of EU membership: Member States, by incidence of being in the EU, must 'take the rough with the smooth, the bitter with the sweet, and not always in balanced or measured quantities'.[104] Yet, even among closely linked EU Member States, this underlying thread in favour of mutual trust in the rendering court's administration of justice has at times been

99 Jenard (n 18) 15.
100 von Mehren and Gottschalk (n 17) 75.
101 Yet, as Briggs notes, it is somewhat surprising that this obligation of trust and confidence is imposed by the CJEU, rather than a foundational principle: Briggs (n 19) 34. The principle stems from the seminal case of Case C-116/02 *Erich Gasser GmbH* v. *MISAT Srl* ECR I-14693.
102 Matthias Weller, 'Mutual Trust: In Search of the Future of European Union Private International Law' (2015) 11 *Journal of Private International Law*.
103 Briggs (n 19) 632.
104 ibid. 34.

controversial. This is because some courts in parts of the EU are, to put it politely, not known for 'impartial excellence and adjudicatory expertise'.[105] In this sense, the unifying powers of the 'myth' of mutual trust between EU Members serves a similar function to the role of comity in the common law: attempting to expand the sovereign relationship but generally stopping at a presumption–exception model. The difficulty in extending mutual trust in favour of recognition and enforcement of foreign judgments – absent such a close relationship between States – is exemplified even in the design of the Brussels Model. Despite comprehensively harmonising both jurisdiction and recognition and enforcement between participants, it does not at all impact on participants' national recognition and enforcement rules for foreign judgments rendered by courts *outside* of the Brussels Model.[106] In this sense, the Brussels Model is facilitated by its explicit design in favour of its European participants only,[107] carried out by privileging only the recognition and enforcement of judgments coming from courts of its participant States, and not at all regulating judgments rendered by a non-Brussels Model court.[108]

At the same time, however, the extension of the Model to non-EU Lugano States – who do not share the EU's conception of common market – suggests that the Brussels Model approach is not entirely unique as a product of the European integration project; a common reason for dismissing recognition and enforcement harmonisation as a utopian endeavour outside of the EU. This extension is aided by the potential guidance that the CJEU can provide to Lugano States on a non-binding basis.[109] However, the practical reach of the Lugano Convention is limited, given that it extends to only three small 'pure' (non-EU) States, which can be criticised on a similar basis: being closely aligned to the EU and primarily concerned with attracting and engaging in intra-European trade.[110] This limited adoption may, at first glance,

[105] ibid.

[106] Procedurally, it does so by defining a judgment only to mean 'any judgment given by a court or tribunal *of a Member State*' (emphasis added): *Brussels I Recast* (Chapter 1, n 36) Art 2(a).

[107] See the Preamble of the various Brussels Model instruments. For example, the Preamble of the 1968 Convention makes clear that it is designed to 'strengthen in the Community the legal protection of persons'.

[108] Perez argues further that the Brussels system 'discriminates against judgments rendered by foreign states', leaving non-EU trading partners at a relative disadvantage: Antonio Perez, 'The International Recognition of Judgments: The Debate between Private and Public Law Solutions' (2001) 19 *Berkeley Journal of International Law* 44, 65.

[109] The role the CJEU plays in attempting to ensure uniformity of interpretation between EU Member States and Lugano States is discussed further at Section 7.1.2.

[110] Ulrich Magnus and Peter Mankowski (eds.), *Brussels I Regulation* (2nd ed., Sellier European Law Publishers 2007) Chapter I (para 29).

suggest that the Brussels Model balance is so inexorably tied to the European ideal that despite being open to third State accession or ratification in the Lugano Conventions, it has had limited success in so doing. However, the sheer growth in the number of EU members – from six to a highpoint of twenty-eight – has largely stalled the impetus or need for the Lugano Convention among European States (as most of these States have now joined the EU). Nonetheless, in this way, the balance struck by the Brussels Model participants can – and indeed does – extend beyond the unique relationship between EU Member States.[111] Consequently, while the precise balance in favour of mutual trust over residual control is a deeply political concern intimately concerned with conceptions of sovereign relations, the mere fact of the Brussels Model's extension to non-EU Lugano States, coupled with the Brussels Model's harmonising mission, indicates that it is not uniquely and inextricably tied to the EU.[112] On this basis, the Brussels Model is likely to continue to both draw on and contribute to global developments in recognition and enforcement, and is likely to remain instructive as long as mutually acceptable harmonised instruments on recognition and enforcement are sought.[113]

6.2.2.2 The Commonwealth Model and Concepts of Sovereign Relationships in the Common Law

By contrast to the Brussels Model, the Commonwealth Model – which relies heavily on the common law foundations underpinning it – does not insist upon any special conception of 'mutual trust'. Nonetheless, having its origin in British dominion and Commonwealth ties, it can be posited that participant States

[111] This of course begs the question that remains yet without answer: if the Model is so adaptable and worthwhile, why has it not been exported to States outside of Europe? No doubt part of this answer has been a reluctance to act pending a continued expectation that global negotiations will succeed, premised on the idea that it is preferable to act globally (rather than regionally or unilaterally) as the controversies that arise are 'widely and randomly distributed' in the recognition and enforcement sphere: von Mehren and Gottschalk (n 17) 376. In this sense, these complex policy concerns may encourage individual States to proceed with harmonisation 'by reciprocal agreement [globally] rather than unilaterally': Dickinson (n 94) 183.

[112] Extending the operation of the Brussels Model to the Lugano States also requires 'tweaks' to the Model. See, for example, the different pathways of uniform interpretation that Lugano participants face compared to European Member States, as set out in Section 7.1.2.

[113] I note in passing at this juncture that as the Brussels Model and its surrounding instruments continue to evolve, its direct applicability to other States outside of the EU is likely to diminish: see, further, Section 7.2.1 for an exposition of recent trends in the Brussel Model's evolution, which increasingly draw on a stronger core of mutual trust, and hence tend towards this conclusion.

share a degree of commonality. This commonality extends in many cases to both the institutional structures employed in particular jurisdictions and the common law itself. Indeed, the very genesis of the Commonwealth Model is premised on the idea that States that share a Commonwealth heritage are more likely to have some familiarity and potential legal and institutional similarity, allowing them comfort in giving preferential treatment to foreign judgments originating from the 'recognised' courts of most other Commonwealth nations.[114] Thus, this Model serves as another example of international recognition and enforcement efforts between States but with a much lesser conception of similarity and economic homogeneity than Brussels Model participants.

At the same time, however, British-inspired legal and institutional frameworks (including the legal backbone of the common law approach) remain a shared feature among participants, meaning that the Model may not be fully adaptable or appropriate for States without any historical or present ties to the Commonwealth. Despite the potential breadth and reach of the Commonwealth Model, the extent to which this Model is extensible outside of the Commonwealth is perhaps limited. What allowed this approach to flourish initially was the sheer size and impetus of the British Empire, which created strong ties both legally and politically back to the Empire. Despite decolonisation leading to weaker Commonwealth ties in the mid-twentieth century, its (presently) fifty-three members still share some degree of common language, historical, economic and cultural links with the United Kingdom, as well as adherence to shared values of democracy, human rights, international peace and security, governance and the rule of law.[115] In this way, a unilateral legislative scheme, premised at least upon the genesis of the Model, on dominion and central review of reciprocity accorded by dominions, perhaps has little direct explanatory value for States that do not share this history.

To continue to explore the way in which transnational approaches potentially inform each other – and thus the extent to which they can be considered 'extensible' – I now turn, in Chapter 7, to consider the way in which uniformity and legal development is promoted or compelled.

[114] Previously referred to as 'superior' courts: Civil Jurisdiction and Judgments Act 1982 (UK) Sch 10.

[115] See, for a summary of the shared Commonwealth values, the *Charter of the Commonwealth* (Signed by Her Majesty Queen Elizabeth II, Head of the Commonwealth, Commonwealth Day 2013), available at <http://thecommonwealth.org/our-charter> (accessed 24 September 2016). The extent to which this Charter reflects a shared reality, rather than aspiration and general puff, however, is open to argument.

7

Legal Development

Uniformity, Divergence and Evolution

In this chapter, I analyse legal development in transnational recognition and enforcement approaches. I commence by considering measures designed to address the inherent lack of uniformity presented by potentially divergent national application of rules with an international origin. The more effective these measures are, the more coherent and effective the harmonisation and promotion of recognition and enforcement. The second half of this chapter analyses how recognition and enforcement frameworks may develop; either via revisions to the implementing architecture or by surrounding legal evolution.

In order to draw out lessons for the Judgments Conventions, I focus on the divergences between recognition and enforcement approaches. Part of this divergence can be explained by the differing underlying legal form: in the Commonwealth Model (a reciprocal statutory regime), the Brussels Model (now predominantly the product of EU Regulations) and the global instruments (treaties, requiring domestic implementation). Furthermore, the Brussels Model experience demonstrates a series of ongoing evolutions, modelling the process of building closer ties stemming from the underlying project of European integration. This can be contrasted with the weaker ties between States associated with the Commonwealth. The New York Convention approach – premised upon obtaining agreement of States that do not necessarily share any such degree of homogeny or conception of closer union – offers an alternative perspective. It is likely that aspects of these approaches will prove instructive for the Judgments Conventions.

7.1 ENCOURAGING UNIFORMITY AND MANAGING DIVERGENT INTERPRETATION

A key driver of legal development across many harmonisation projects, including in the field of recognition and enforcement, is the desire to encourage uniform interpretation or application across jurisdictions. That is, irrespective of the degree of specificity of harmonised recognition and enforcement rules, there also remains an inherent lack of uniformity by potentially divergent national application of transnational rules. This risk is substantial. The 'utmost importance' of uniformity in this respect was emphasised throughout the modern Judgments Projects efforts, as without it, the 'hoped for advantages of certainty and predictability [that a convention would bring] will be lost'.[1] It was also noted in the context of early negotiations towards the Judgments Project that:[2]

[1] Peter Nygh and Fausto Pocar, 'Report by Peter Nygh & Fausto Pocar (Annexed to the 1999 Preliminary Draft Convention)' (Report, August 2000) citing the Restatement (Second) Conflict of Laws 124.

[2] Antonio Perez, 'The International Recognition of Judgments: The Debate between Private and Public Law Solutions' (2001) 19 *Berkeley Journal of International Law* 68.

> To the extent that judicial interpretation reflects changing political consensus in a particular country, the implementation of the treaty would vary substantially. This variation would defeat the treaty's chief objective of overcoming disincentives to cooperation among states in their pursuit of global free trade goals. In the absence of an agreed upon final interpreting mechanism, auto-interpretation of [the then proposed broad-based Judgments Project instrument] would erode its value in assuring a stable set of commitments, even if cabined by the doctrine of good faith.

In other words, divergent interpretation of harmonised provisions could undermine the harmonisation and promotion project that underlies private international law efforts internationally.[3] As Brand and Herrup modestly suggest, the Judgments Conventions are, if widely implemented, increasingly likely to face 'some variations' in both interpretation and application.[4]

Beyond the general preference for uniform and equal interpretation across States, there is also a critical role for uniform interpretation to ensure that signatories do not liberally interpret what are intended to be construed as narrow exceptions to recognition and enforcement.[5] The public policy ground for refusal – the interpretation of which has plagued other international recognition and enforcement instruments[6] – serves as an illuminating example. The public policy exception allows (and in the Brussels Model compels) the enforcing court to refuse to recognise or enforce a foreign decision on the basis that doing so is contrary to 'public policy' of the enforcing State. This exception exists in every instrument constituting the Brussels Model, as well as every global recognition and enforcement approach, as it is an important safeguard for the enforcing court to exercise discretionary control over matters that are fundamental to the legal system in which it operates. The difficulty arises not so much in the existence of the

3 João Ribeiro-Bidaoui, 'The International Obligation of the Uniform and Autonomous Interpretation of Private Law Conventions: Consequences for Domestic Courts and International Organisations' (2020) 67 *Netherlands International Law Review* 139.

4 Ronald A. Brand and Paul Herrup, *The 2005 Hague Convention on Choice of Court Agreements: Commentary and Documents* (Cambridge University Press 2008) 24.

5 See, for example, the common concept of 'manipulation' that State courts are able to engage in to avoid enforcing arbitration awards by interpreting the public policy exception: Emmanuel Gaillard, 'Enforcement of Awards Set Aside in the Country of Origin: The French Experience' in Albert Jan van den Berg (ed.), *Improving the Efficiency of Arbitration Agreements and Awards: 40 years of Application of the New York Convention* (KluwerArbitration, Kluwer Law International 1999) 691.

6 Inspiring numerous scholarly writings on this point. See, for a representative example of the depth of scholarship on its interpretation, Anton G. Maurer, *Public Policy Exception Under the New York Convention: History, Interpretation, and Application* (Revised, Juris Publishing, Inc 2013).

ground but the extent to which it is interpreted as a basis to refuse to give effect to a foreign decision. Few States would take issue with an enforcing court refusing to give effect to a foreign decision on the basis, for example, that it was rendered by gross fraud or bribery. However, significant interpretive differences in the width of this provision have arisen: for example, by national courts applying the New York Convention, particularly as the concept of public policy cannot be fully autonomous, as it requires, by definition, some contact with the national law of the enforcing court.[7]

7.1.1 *The New York Convention Approach to Uniformity and Divergence*

Over time, since the adoption of the Convention in 1958, there have been significant criticisms about divergences in interpretation – and outcome – that, somewhat paradoxically, arise by enforcing courts all purporting to apply the same text. These range in form and format from minor textual ambiguities or drafting omissions that are perhaps inherent in the Convention (complicated by the authoritative status of different language versions of the Convention) to significant issues to do with the degree of State support for enforcing foreign awards. These concerns with the Convention are explored as examples of the potential for divergence in interpretation or application of recognition and enforcement obligations generally, but this section is not designed to reflect all concerns seen in practice comprehensively.[8]

At a high level, most criticisms can be attributed to the fact that the New York Convention does not offer a global binding interpretive mechanism or body – such as the supranational court system that Brussels Model participants can rely on. The idea of empowering a body, such as the International Court of Justice, was considered but ultimately dismissed in negotiations toward the

7 See, for example, the review of Peter Gillies, 'Enforcement of International Arbitration Awards: The New York Convention' (2004) 9 *International Trade and Business Law Review* 19, under the heading 'Public Policy'.

8 See, for a summary exposition of these concerns, Albert Jan van den Berg, 'Striving for Uniform Interpretation' in *Enforcing Arbitration Awards Under the New York Convention: Experience and Prospects* (United Nations 1999) 41–42. Various solutions have been proposed, and extend to the suggestion that a new convention 'complementary' to the New York Convention be created: Werner Melis, 'Considering the Advisability of Preparing an Additional Convention, Complementary to the New York Convention' in *Enforcing Arbitration Awards Under the New York Convention: Experience and Prospects* (United Nations 1999) 44. This has received support but also received extensive criticism. See, generally, for an overview of both views, Albert Jan van den Berg (ed.), *50 Years of the New York Convention: ICCA International Arbitration Conference* (ICCA Congress Series 14, Kluwer Law International 2009).

Convention. As was noted by the Committee tasked with drafting the Convention at the time:[9]

> 64. Paragraph (1) of this Article provides that any dispute which may arise between contracting States concerning the interpretation or application of the Convention shall be referred to the International Court of Justice at the request of any one of the parties to the dispute, unless the parties agree to another mode of settlement, It was noted by the Committee that this provision is substantially the same as articles on settlement of disputes customarily included in conventions adopted by or under the auspices of the United Nations. The Representative of the USSR opposed the adoption of this article on the grounds that it would mean (1) a violation of the sovereign rights of States with respect to the principle of voluntary recognition of the binding character of the jurisdiction of the International Court of Justice, and (2) a limitation of the sovereign rights of States to make reservations on any article of the Convention.

Without such a body, even where enforcing courts approach their Convention obligations in good faith, there is no guarantee of 'outcome uniformity'[10] where two courts, deciding the same facts under the same law, will come to the same decision. This is despite general principles of international law favouring a uniform interpretation of treaties and the widespread adoption of the *Vienna Convention on the Law of Treaties*.[11] The Vienna Convention creates instrumental obligations that States interpret 'in good faith' and 'in accordance with the ordinary meaning' terms within a treaty, 'in their context and in light of its object and purpose'. The Vienna Convention has broadly been read to support the idea that enforcing courts should refer to foreign judgments to provide and develop 'consistent jurisprudence'.[12]

9 United Nations Economic and Social Council, Report of the Committee on the Enforcement of International Arbitral Awards, 28 March 1955, UN Doc. E/2704, at http://undoc s.org/E/2704, at [64].

10 This term is drawn from Kevin Cope, 'Reconceptualizing Recognition Uniformity' in Paul B. Stephan (ed.), *Foreign Court Judgments and the United States Legal System* (Brill 2014).

11 'Vienna Convention on the Law of Treaties' (27 January 1980) vol 1155. Part III of the Vienna Convention, entitled 'Observance, Application and Interpretation of Treaties', sets out interpretive approaches in Arts 31–33. By 1970, only three of the six original EC members had signed the Vienna Convention; the Netherlands and Belgium followed in 1985 and 1992, respectively; France has not signed the Convention.

12 Mills notes that any new law reform – which extends not just to the implementation of the 2005 Convention but also any draft broad-based Convention – 'inevitably also has the effect of decreasing certainty in the short term until a consistent jurisprudence has developed around the interpretation of the rules': Alex Mills, 'The "Hague Choice of Court Convention" and Cross-Border Commercial Dispute Resolution in Australia and the Asia-Pacific' (2017) 18 *Melbourne Journal of International Law* 1, 14.

The case of *Dallah* serves as an example.[13] In this case, the French court tasked with considering whether to set aside an award, and an English enforcement court, came to opposing conclusions on the same foreign awards, despite facing the same facts and legal issues (and both purporting to apply the same law). This was not due to differing views on the interpretation of the provisions in the Convention but on different characterisations of the evidence presented. The UK Supreme Court accepted that under its understanding of French law there was no common intention that the Pakistani government should be a party to the contract; compared to the Paris Court of Appeal, which held that it was a party as it 'behaved as if it were the true Pakistani party'. This disconnect represents a significant hurdle to international uniformity. Nonetheless, efforts have been made to rationalise and reconcile the decisions. Khanna, for example, suggests that even though the decision of the English court refusing enforcement has been criticised, such criticism should perhaps be reconsidered. This is because the decision to refuse to give effect to the award can be seen as a positive development for arbitration and the Convention, as while the Convention is largely designed to promote recognition and enforcement, it is not designed to do so at all costs.[14] In other words, refusing to give effect to awards that are not properly rendered subject to the grounds for refusal provided in the Convention acts to enhance legitimacy in the enforcement process, serving the interests of justice *and* of international arbitration in the long run.[15]

The difficulty with this argument is that without a uniform interpretation there is no authoritative way of determining which foreign decisions are properly rendered. No doubt, the canons of interpretation, set out at Section 5.2.2, provide significant guidance to enforcing courts in any genuine interpretive complexities they may face. Read together, they combine to favour a strong pro-recognition and enforcement outlook. Yet there is no guarantee of outcome uniformity under the Convention between the supervisory courts where set aside is sought, or even between two courts where both are asked to enforce the same award between the same parties.[16] Additionally, to the extent that divergences between enforcing courts are genuine – rather than a policy

[13] *Dallah Real Estate and Tourism Holding Co* v. *Ministry of Religious Affairs of the Government of Pakistan* [2011] 1 AC 763; Cour d'appel de Paris, 17 février 2011, *Gouvernement du Pakistan – Ministère des Affaires religieuses c. Société Dallah Real Estate and Tourism Holding Company*, R/G 09/28533.

[14] Devika Khanna, 'Dallah: The Supreme Court's Positively Pro-Arbitration No to Enforcement' (2011) 28 *Journal of International Arbitration* 127, 127–29.

[15] ibid. 129.

[16] Explored further at Section 5.3.2.

decision of States not to give effect to certain kinds of awards via misinterpreting or misapplying Convention provisions – they can largely be cured by States' unilateral implementation or amendment of domestic laws, aided in many instances by supplementary interpretive or explanatory instruments (such as the UNCITRAL Model Law). Developments in national law are entirely consistent with the 'minimum standards' approach of the New York Convention, as set out at Section 5.4. As the Judgments Conventions broadly adopt a similar open approach to recognition and enforcement, the same is likely to be true when considering uniformity under these Conventions.

7.1.2 *The Brussels Model: Equal and Uniform Interpretation*

An alternative approach to interpretative difficulties is the Brussels Model's explicit reliance on legal machineries designed to assist with a common and unified interpretation across national courts in different States. The need for such an approach was foreshadowed in the context of recognition and enforcement at the time of the original 1968 Brussels Convention to 'prevent differences of interpretation of the Convention from impairing its unifying effect' and to 'ensure that the Convention is applied as effectively as possible'.[17] Increasingly, as the Brussels Model has evolved, the approach taken is a purposive one – a view that gives predominant weight to achieving the purpose of the instrument as a whole instead of ascertaining the natural meaning of a provision in isolation from the rest of the instrument. The Brussels Model 'must be interpreted independently, by reference to its scheme and purpose'.[18] This is now aided by the existence, composition and operation of the Court of Justice of the European Union (CJEU). As judges come from all Member States, this safeguards against the interpreter being unduly focused on a single national perspective and ensures that other views have been taken into account.[19] The utility of the role of the CJEU has been stressed, as the Brussels Model is likely to have limited efficacy if despite

[17] In a document signed by all members of the then European Community, and termed the European Economic Community, 'Joint Declaration of 27 September 1968'. This declaration was signed at the time of entering into the original instrument constituting the Brussels Model, European Economic Community, 'Brussels Convention on Jurisdiction and the Enforcement of Judgments in Civil and Commercial Matters' (1 February 1973).

[18] Adrian Briggs, *Civil Jurisdiction and Judgments* (6th ed., Informa Law from Routledge 2015) 29, citing the decision in Case C-45/13 *Andreas Kainz* v. *Pantherwerke* AG [2014].

[19] Ulrich Magnus and Peter Mankowski (eds.), *Brussels I Regulation* (2nd ed., Sellier European Law Publishers 2007) Chapter I (para 106).

identical provisions, these are interpreted to mean something slightly different in every Contracting State.[20]

The need for a uniform interpretation has permeated the Brussels Model since its inception. Soon after the 1968 Convention was negotiated, a supplementary Protocol was negotiated to minimise the risk of divergent or conflicting decisions on the Convention.[21] It is designed to guide enforcing courts of participant States in their task of interpreting the 1968 Convention. This Protocol provides that the Court of Justice of the European Communities (the equivalent body is now the CJEU) has jurisdiction to give rulings on the interpretation of the Convention, to which, under certain circumstances, the courts of Member States either may or must refer.[22] At the time the protocol was entered into the *Vienna Convention on the Law of Treaties* was not yet in effect,[23] and despite general principles of international law favouring a likely uniform interpretation of treaties,[24] there were no binding rules of law to ensure a uniform and harmonised interpretation legally across the then EC.[25] Nonetheless, by virtue of the 1968 Convention's international treaty status with express and implied goals for harmonisation, combined with the assistance of provisions of the Protocol, an autonomous and 'to some extent' supra-national interpretive approach is necessitated.[26] This autonomous interpretation is aimed at further improving legal certainty and transparency, as disputants or potential disputants should be able to ascertain under which circumstances they can enforce (or must obey) judgments from other Convention States in

[20] Briggs (n 18) 370–71.

[21] European Economic Community, 'Protocol on the Interpretation by the Court of Justice of the Convention of 27 September 1968 on Jurisdiction and the Enforcement of Judgments in Civil and Commercial Matters' (1 September 1975) vol 027.

[22] ibid. Art I–III.

[23] 'Vienna Convention on the Law of Treaties' (n 11). Part III of the Vienna Convention, entitled 'Observance, Application and Interpretation of Treaties' sets out interpretive approaches in Arts 31–33. By 1970, only three of the six original EC members had signed the Vienna Convention; the Netherlands and Belgium followed in 1985 and 1992, respectively; France has not signed the Convention.

[24] Luigi Sbolci, 'Supplementary Means of Interpretation' in Enzo Cannizzaro (ed.), *The Law of Treaties beyond the Vienna Convention* (Oxford University Press, Oxford 2011) 149.

[25] Further, despite the explicit objective of attempting to harmonise and codify principles of treaty interpretation, the *Vienna Convention* interpretive provisions, even after four decades, remain 'contested and in flux': Michael Waibel, 'Principles of Treaty Interpretation: Developed for and Applied by National Courts?' (University of Cambridge Faculty of Law Research Paper, 17 April 2015) 2. This reinforces the unique nature and success of the CJEU as an authoritative supranational interpretive body within the EU.

[26] Magnus and Mankowski (n 19) Chapter I (para 93, citing a range of CJEU decisions on this point).

an equal and uniform manner.[27] The competence of the CJEU to interpret the Convention also allows for interpretation that is consistent with, and developed alongside, other principles and doctrines in (now) EU law. Consequently, the Brussels Convention interpretative provisions have proved critical to ensuring the consistent and uniform operation of provisions in the Brussels Model.

As the remainder of this section on interpretation demonstrates, the Brussels Model now largely dispenses with this problem neatly in a way that other transnational approaches cannot: interpretation is ultimately resolved by a supranational interpretive body.[28] Consequently, even in complex cases where the Brussels Model comes into contact with potentially divergent national law and legal procedures, the CJEU can provide authoritative interpretive guidance. Returning to the public policy ground – the 'creative' interpretation of which is often maligned in other recognition and enforcement frameworks – the CJEU has regularly exercised its interpretive role, clarifying the extent and reach of the exception, so as to render it consistent with the general Brussels Model pro-recognition and enforcement approach. For example, the CJEU in the seminal case of *Dieter Krombach* noted that:[29]

> 22 ... while the Contracting States in principle remain free, by virtue of [the public policy exception in the Brussels Model] to determine, according to their own conceptions, what public policy requires, the limits of that concept are a matter for interpretation of the Convention.
>
> 23 Consequently, while it is not for the Court to define the content of the public policy of a Contracting State, it is none the less required to review the limits within which the courts of a Contracting State may have recourse to that concept for the purpose of refusing recognition to a judgment emanating from a court in another Contracting State.

Because of the broader desire for uniformity in international instruments within the EU, the modern Brussels Model approach offers much stronger

[27] See, for a clear exposition of these principles the decisions cited in ibid. Chapter I (para 93, at footnote 143).

[28] Both the CJEU and national courts interpreting and applying the Model are obliged to uphold the 'rule of law' within the EU: See, generally: Koen Lenaerts, 'The Rule of Law and the Coherence of the Judicial System of the European Union' (2007) 44 *Common Market Law Review* 1625. As the procedure for recognition and enforcement is not set out in the Model, this extends to legal doctrines such as equivalence and effectiveness, to ensure that national procedures do not weaken the Brussels Model: Andrew Dickinson and Eva Lein (eds.), *The Brussels I Regulation Recast* (Oxford University Press 2015) 418 (and following).

[29] Case C-7/98 *Dieter Krombach* v. *André Bamberski* [2000] ECR.

machinery to encourage or compel uniform interpretation (premised upon uniform interpretation being protected by the CJEU).[30]

The Brussels Model, at least with respect to its EU Member States, provides for uniform interpretation by granting both the power and the duty to national courts of signatory States to make submissions on and refer matters to the supranational CJEU for a determinative ruling on interpretation.[31] This process has been enhanced by the CJEU's awareness of the context of the surrounding endeavour of European Union, leading to a conscious development of 'autonomous' definitions (independent of any national character) for terms used in the Model.[32] As Briggs notes, autonomous meanings have been given to 'practically all' the definitional terms used in the Brussels Model, and the need to proceed on the basis of uniformity within the EU is 'more entrenched than ever'.[33] Yet, practically, the precise mechanism by which this has been achieved varies across the Brussels Model and is most limited in the Lugano Conventions. Nonetheless, a similar drive towards uniform interpretation underpins the subsequent Brussels Regulations – as well as both Lugano Conventions – which, although not sharing the same institutional architecture, share the same 'general canons' of interpretation as those applicable to Brussels instruments.[34]

Although the Brussels Regulations (as incidents of directly binding Community law) reflect a departure from the international treaty status of the Brussels Convention, the imperative to give an autonomous and uniform interpretation to the Brussels Model not only remains but has been strengthened in them.[35] This is because uniform interpretation is provided for in the nature of the Regulations, which, as incidents of EU law, must be interpreted according to common EU interpretive methods that promote

30 Magnus and Mankowski (n 19) Chapter I (para 111).

31 At the same time, academic commentary and decisions of national courts may also assist in developing a uniform approach; but these are comparatively minor.

32 Briggs (n 18) 27.

33 ibid. 28. Briggs cites the CJEU in the case of *Re Roda Gold* (C-14/08 [2009] ECR I-5439), where it is noted that the objectives pursued by the EU in this area – 'freedom, security and justice' – testify to the 'will of the Member States to anchor such measures firmly in the Community legal order and thus to lay down the principle that they are to be interpreted autonomously'.

34 In the context of Lugano II and the 2001 Brussels Regulation see: ibid. 370.

35 ibid. 26–27. The interpretive provisions of the 'Vienna Convention on the Law of Treaties' (n 11) do not apply (directly) to the Regulation as it is an incident of Community law and not an international treaty. Nonetheless, the provisions in Arts. 31-33 represent 'well known and internationally recognised principles' of international interpretation, which are likely to be taken to account in any event: Magnus and Mankowski (n 19) Chapter I (para 92).

uniform interpretation.[36] Additionally, an expressed aim of the transition from the Convention to a Regulation was to maximise, as far as possible, continuity between these instruments and to build upon the existing case law.[37] As the Convention calls for a uniform interpretation, so too do the subsequent Regulations. This continuity is aided by the fact that the CJEU remains competent to interpret the 1968 Convention and later Regulations alike, and that the amendments to the substance of the Convention (and later Regulations) are relatively modest in scope with respect to recognition and enforcement. This need for continuity has been reinforced by the CJEU on innumerable occasions such that it is considered 'a matter of routine' that the interpretation given in relation to the Convention continues to apply for the purposes of the Regulations.[38] Thus, although the Convention is now largely superseded, judicial decisions interpreting it (spanning over forty years) remain relevant, and continue to encourage and promote authoritative rulings leading to a uniform and equal interpretation of the relevant Brussels Regulations.[39]

The power of the CJEU to give preliminary rulings to national courts within the EU on the interpretation of treaties and EU Regulations[40] is regularly exercised when matters are referred to it.[41] As a result, interpretive maxims have been established around the way in which the Brussels Model

[36] Magnus and Mankowski (n 19) ch I, para 91. Consequently, there is no longer a need for a Protocol on uniform interpretation, as employed in earlier Brussels Model Conventions, as rules on interpretation and oversight by the CJEU are provided for in instruments constituting the EU: see, European Union, 'Consolidated Versions of the Treaty on European Union and the Treaty on the Functioning of the European Union' (7 June 2016) (Treaty on European Union, Arts 2 and 6), OJ C 202/1 Art 267 (TFEU).

[37] 'Regulation (EC) No 44/2001 of 22 December 2000 on Jurisdiction and the Recognition and Enforcement of Judgments in Civil and Commercial Matters' (2001) OJ L 12/1 Recital 19 relevantly provides that: 'the same need for continuity applies as regards the interpretation of the Brussels Convention by the Court of Justice of the European Communities'.

[38] Briggs (n 18) 32–33.

[39] Magnus and Mankowski (n 19) ch I, para 91.

[40] European Union (n 36) Art 267 (TFEU). Art 267 (TFEU) provides that any court of a Member State *may* refer a matter on the validity or interpretation of an EU Act to the CJEU; the highest courts in each Member State (that is, where no further judicial appeal from that body exists) *must* bring such matters before the CJEU.

[41] See, for two recent examples, the preliminary rulings in Case C-70/15 *Emmanuel Lebek* v. *Janusz Domino*; Case C-559/14 *Rūdolfs Meroni* v. *Recoletos Limited*. Both involved an interpretation of the grounds of refusing enforcement under the Brussels Model: the former considering the ground of failing to notify the defendant via service in sufficient time, and the latter on the intersection between the Charter of Fundamental Rights of the European Union and the public policy ground for refusal.

instruments are construed and interpreted by the CJEU.[42] This means that participants in the Brussels Model face a uniquely privileged (or in some cases, where they may not agree with a ruling, prejudicial) situation: the ability to always seek a uniform interpretation by a body empowered to give uniform meaning to the Model's provisions. This has particularly far-reaching impact. For example, the doctrine of precedent does not override the duty of a national court to refer a matter to the CJEU if it considers it is bound to do so.[43] As a result, the CJEU is the ultimate authority on the interpretation of the Brussels Model. At the same time, however, national courts still are only compelled to refer matters to the CJEU where deemed necessary.[44] This means that even with the unique supranational powers of the CJEU in interpreting the Brussels Model, enforcing courts still have to be mindful not to import into the interpretation of the Regulation 'purposes and transplants' from their own national laws.[45] It is this critical role of the CJEU that led to the argument that it may be 'simply not within the realm of possibility' to extend the Brussels Model to the global level, as there is a lack of 'an objective and neutral interpreter and controller' of its provisions.[46]

At the same time – and often overlooked when the Brussels Model is considered – are the different interpretive methods and regimes that apply to the Lugano Conventions that may give the lie to this argument. As the Lugano Conventions, like the original 1968 Brussels Convention, are international treaties, they are subject to the general rules of interpretation of treaties.[47] However, beyond these general interpretive maxims, the Lugano Conventions importantly share the explicit Brussels Model goal of unifying and harmonising interpretation. Practically, this is sensible, given that both Lugano instruments are almost an identical copy of the respective Brussels instruments. Difficulty arises, however, as the procedural mechanisms for achieving uniform interpretation must necessarily differ as the non-EU Lugano States are

42 See, for an extensive overview of the interpretative method, Briggs (n 18) 26–31; Magnus and Mankowski (n 19) Chapter I (Part VI, paras 91–110).

43 Briggs (n 18) 12.

44 European Union (n 36) Art 267 (TFEU).

45 Magnus and Mankowski (n 19) Chapter I (para 106).

46 Comments of Arthur von Mehren, at a Conference held at New York University School of Law on the Proposed Convention (April 30–May 1, 1999), recorded in E. Andreas Lowenfeld and Linda J. Silberman, *The Hague Convention on Jurisdiction and Judgments* (JurisNet, LLC 2001) 61.

47 Note, however, that two of three 'pure' Lugano Members – Norway and Iceland – are not party to the Vienna Convention. Nonetheless, as the Vienna Convention represents a synthesis of generally accepted practice towards treaty instruments, the interpretive maxims remain a useful guide.

not bound by precepts of EU law. Additionally, because these States are outside of the EU, they face no obligation to follow or pay any attention to decisions of the CJEU nor power (unless negotiated specifically) to refer questions to that court for assistance (for example, in a preliminary ruling).[48]

The original 1988 Lugano Convention attempts, nonetheless, to provide for uniform interpretation by means of a Protocol designed to allow the Lugano Convention to map to any interpretation of the then relevant Brussels instrument.[49] This Protocol requires all Contracting States to 'pay due account' to decisions delivered by courts of other Contracting States; establishes a 'system of exchange of information' concerning judgments delivered under both the Brussels and Lugano Conventions; and empowers a Standing Committee to review if and how Contracting States pay account to principles laid down in any decision by courts interpreting the Convention from other Contracting States. However, while these gestures all seem to promote a uniform interpretation, they say little about legal obligation. For example, what precisely must enforcing courts in Lugano Contracting States do to 'pay due account'? What happens if an enforcing court fails to consider a relevant decision? What happens if the enforcing court does consider a relevant decision but wilfully chooses to ignore its approach? None of these questions are resolved satisfactorily by the 1988 Convention. In any event, due to the entering into force of Lugano II (which practically replaces the 1988 Lugano Convention) this 'ramshackle mechanism'[50] has never been put to the test.

The Lugano II Convention, similar to the 1988 Convention, uses an interpretive Protocol annexed to the Convention.[51] This Protocol requires courts in Contracting States to have regard to any relevant decision under the 1988 Convention and the relevant Brussels instruments. Further to the 1988 Protocol, the 2007 Protocol, in a bid to better harmonise decisions between the respective Brussels instruments, allows Lugano States to make submissions to the CJEU if a matter of interpretation of any of the Brussels instruments is referred to the CJEU. The 2007 Convention also continues the task of exchanging information (overseen now by the European Commission),

[48] Briggs (n 18) 370.

[49] 'Protocol No 2 on the Uniform Interpretation of the Lugano Convention on Jurisdiction and the Enforcement of Judgments in Civil and Commercial Matters' (16 September 1988). Article 65 of the 'Lugano Convention on Jurisdiction and the Enforcement of Judgments in Civil and Commercial Matters' (first published 1988, no date) refers to the Protocol, annexed to the Convention, as an 'integral part' of the Convention.

[50] Briggs (n 18) 370.

[51] 'Protocol No 2 on the Uniform Interpretation of the Lugano Convention and on the Standing Committee' (21/12/07) (annexed to the 2007 Lugano Convention).

and the role of the Standing Committee is expanded. One of the major roles of the Standing Committee is tasking delegates with preparing a detailed report on the case law arising under the Brussels Model every three years.[52] The 2012 report, for example, considers five decisions relating to recognition and enforcement, showing that these judgments are consistent with 'a trend aiming at streamlining the jurisprudence with the decisions rendered by the European Court of Justice with regard to the [Brussels Model instruments]'.[53] As a result, despite an unclear legal remit, this review – itself based on interpretive provisions in the Protocol – has likely assisted or encouraged non-EU Lugano Convention States to take into account Brussels Model jurisprudence in a 'visible and significant' manner,[54] increasing the prospects of uniform and equal interpretation of the Brussels Model.

Considered holistically, and including the Lugano experience, the Brussels Model uniform interpretation efforts do not *necessarily* depend on direct interpretive recourse to a supranational body. Indeed, international treaties themselves can – and often do – contain express provisions calling for interpretation considering the objectives of the underlying legal instrument(s), particularly where they aim to harmonise an area of law.[55] It cannot be doubted, however, that a supranational body such as the CJEU is of great benefit to ensuring uniformity within the Brussels Model. Even the Lugano State participants – who do not have the benefit (or imposition) of a supranational interpretive body – still benefit from its existence for uniform interpretation. Additionally, the three (small) Lugano States are both implicitly and explicitly guided by the Lugano Conventions' directive of uniform interpretation. This is assisted by their ability, introduced in the 2007 Lugano Convention, to refer decisions of the CJEU to guide their own interpretive approaches. In this way, the influence of the CJEU extends beyond its supranational structure and filters down to States outside of the EU's tight-knit legal community. At the same time, because of the Brussels Model's extensive reach, national judiciaries, practitioners and scholars alike can be aided by an abundance of relevant academic commentaries of direct

52 The majority of these reports are available at: Switzerland Federal Office of Justice, 'Reports on National Caselaw' (no date) <www.bj.admin.ch/bj/en/home/wirtschaft/privatrecht/lugue-2007/rechtsprechung.html> accessed 8 July 2016.

53 Alegría Borrás and others, '13th Report on National Case Law Relating to the Lugano Convention' (May 2012) Part III (and concluding remarks on p. 28).

54 ibid. 28.

55 Most relevant in the context of this book is Article 20 of the 2019 Convention, as discussed in the immediately preceding section.

application.[56] This is particularly the case where judges, many with little training in international law, must apply the various instruments in the Model, and, where necessary, engage in comparative law analysis in interpreting these instruments.[57]

7.1.3 *The Commonwealth Model and the Common Law*

The same need (or desire) for uniform interpretation is seen in the Commonwealth Model, both directly and indirectly. With respect to the latter, as States who participate in the Model broadly share a common law legal system and underpinnings, this serves as an implicit 'control' on radically divergent interpretation.[58] However, a direct form of uniformity can also arise through the role of the Judicial Committee of the Privy Council serving as the highest court of appeal for certain British external territories and Commonwealth countries. This reached a highpoint in the 1930s, with approximately a 'quarter of the world' sharing the Privy Council as a final court of appeal.[59] Although its reach has declined significantly since then,[60] it is still the final court of appeal for a range of Commonwealth States and Crown dependencies. The United Kingdom has offered – and continues in a small number of Crown dependencies and independent jurisdictions to offer – 'supranational' authoritative guidance, which can be analogised with the role of the CJEU in the Brussels Model. In this way, both approaches share similarities in the mechanisms used to encourage uniformity and minimise divergent interpretations. However, reference to a supranational interpretive body in the Commonwealth is a very weak form of uniformity management, particularly as most of the Commonwealth-associated States do not preserve any right to appeal in the Privy Council. As Yekini notes in reviewing reciprocal arrangements between Commonwealth States, this has

56 Arthur von Mehren and Eckart Gottschalk, *Adjudicatory Authority in Private International Law* (The Hague Academy of International Law Monographs 5, Martinus Nijhoff Publishers 2007) 69.

57 ibid.

58 See Section 6.1 for an overview of some of the shared interpretative and institutional modalities said to arise under the common law approach.

59 Judicial Committee of the Privy Council, 'The Jurisdiction of the Judicial Committee of the Privy Council' (Jurisdiction Map, no date).

60 Some of the most prominent – and most recent – abolitions of appeals to the Privy Council include New Zealand (in 2003), Hong Kong (in 1997) and Australia (in 1986). This influence no doubt lingers. See, for example, efforts to trace this influence in Australia in Murray Gleeson, 'The Influence of the Privy Council on Australia' (Speech delivered at the Anglo-Australasian Lawyers Society, 31 May 2007).

led to wide divergences in the recognition and enforcement laws and practices across the Commonwealth.[61]

Beyond the Commonwealth Model, efforts to codify common law recognition and enforcement practice also grapple with uniformity concerns. Returning to the practice of the United States, highlighted in Chapter 4, both the original and updated Uniform Acts are consistent in insisting that enforcing courts 'must', in applying and construing the Acts, give consideration to 'the need to promote uniformity of the law' among enacting states.[62] Yet, this interpretative aid can be criticised on similar grounds to that of the interpretation provisions applicable between Lugano participants in the Brussels Model. It is unclear what obligation this provision places on the enforcing court. It insists only that 'consideration must be given' to promoting uniformity. Does this mean an enforcing court can consider – and then dismiss – a uniform interpretation? Presumably the answer is yes. This is undoubtedly for practical reasons, as recognition and enforcement approaches are a matter of state law. Because of this, there is no federal court with ultimate interpretive authority.

The lack of a governing federal (or supranational) court to provide authoritative guidance is a familiar problem. However, this is not a situation created by the Uniform Acts. It simply represents the particularities of the United States' federal system where the highest court in each state has the ultimate say on interpretation of the law within its own jurisdiction. These courts are not bound by any views expressed by the United States Supreme Court, the ultimate court of appeal in federal matters. Even so, interpretations are not likely to diverge to a significant degree, primarily because most courts in the United States consider judgments of sister-states (even when they are considering foreign judgments, and hence are not bound by the full faith and credit clause of the constitution) to be highly persuasive; much more so than a country would likely consider judgments of another country to be persuasive. The strongly persuasive nature of these judgments is enhanced in the context of the Uniform Acts due to the provision compelling the court to consider uniformity. Nonetheless, the potential remains for divergent interpretations and understandings of state law (whether common law or in the implementation of the Uniform Acts),[63] possibly in line with parochial domestic state interests.

[61] Abubakri Yekini, *The Hague Judgments Convention and Commonwealth Model Law: A Pragmatic Perspective* (Hart Publishing 2021) 87–96.

[62] §10.

[63] For example, as the 1962 Act is silent on which party has the burden to establish a ground for non-recognition, courts applying the 1962 Act took different positions: see Linda J. Silberman, 'The Need for a Federal Statutory Approach to the Recognition and Enforcement of Foreign

As the immediately preceding paragraphs note, methods of controlling divergent interpretation vary across recognition and enforcement approaches, but each approach faces similar constraints on their practical effectiveness. For this reason, I turn now to consider the potential for legal development or evolution, as these mechanisms may offer some hope of remedying aberrant approaches or improving identified flaws that arise in practice.

7.1.4 *Lessons from and for the Judgments Conventions*

The Hague Conference, throughout the life of the Judgments Project, was intimately aware of, and concerned with, the experiences of other regional and global frameworks to manage autonomous and uniform interpretations.[64] This is because the divergence risk is particularly stark outside of regional groupings, as there is no shared legal heritage that may guide interpretation (a role the common law plays in the Commonwealth Model) and no universal supranational court that can impose its interpretation as a final measure (a role that the CJEU plays for EU participants in the Brussels Model). This lack of guidance or control introduces an 'ineradicable variability in practice', due to the consensus process imposing a ceiling on Convention obligations: contentious matters (where consensus cannot be reached) are largely left to national law. For example, as Brand and Herrup note in the context of negotiations that eventually led to the 2005 Convention:[65]

> even if there was a consensus that a concept or rule should be autonomous within the Convention, there was no corresponding consensus on the precise definition or content of that rule for Convention purposes. This creates initial uncertainties pending development in state practice, which will unfold over time.

This means that many of the seeds of subsequent interpretive divergence are grounded in the recognition and enforcement framework itself, often due to difficulties in reaching consensus in treaty drafting. This stands in stark contrast to the rigorous institutional machinery now used within the

Country Judgments' in Paul B. Stephan (ed.), *Foreign Court Judgments and the United States Legal System* (Brill, 2014) 105–6.

64 Ribeiro-Bidaoui summarises the tools used to manage autonomous and uniform interpretation as the use of advisory opinions, information sharing, providing access to supplementary materials, facilitating judicial education and information exchange, and legislative intervention, and explores these in the context of the Judgments Project negotiations: Ribeiro-Bidaoui (n 3) 150–63.

65 Brand and Herrup (n 4) 22.

Brussels Model, which builds in large part on the existence of a supranational court.

Perhaps for this reason, significant efforts are made to attempt to mitigate divergence risks in the Judgments Conventions. As Section 7.1.1 sets out, although the *New York Convention* contains no express uniformity provision, long practice experience led to attempts to define a shared core of uniform interpretation and application globally with respect to arbitral awards. However, it is still argued that the non-uniform application of recognition and enforcement obligations may entirely defeat its pro-recognition and enforcement mandate and obligations.[66] Cognisant of this criticism, the Judgments Conventions include a positive obligation of uniform interpretation, which requires that 'regard shall be had to its international character and to the need to promote uniformity' in applying each Convention.[67] This wording draws from the preeminent private law treaty, the United Nations Convention on Contracts for the International Sale of Goods ('CISG').[68] There are also arguably obligations in international law to give provisions in conventions a uniform and autonomous interpretation.[69] Despite the resounding success of the CISG, its experience still highlights that such concerns cannot readily be addressed via general obligations towards uniformity alone. Hackney, for example, criticises the 'utopian notion' of a uniform law in the context of the CISG and highlights ongoing difficulties in achieving such uniformity across implementing States.[70] There are also significant practice hurdles in the sheer volume of information courts must consider, particularly when decisions may be in foreign language or require consultation with scholarly sources. This is particularly problematic in recognition enforcement proceedings – which, as by now should be apparent – are intended to operate, in the usual course, as expedient and streamlined procedures rather than contested hearings.

66 This is thesis of Arvind in: T. T. Arvind, 'The "Transplant Effect" in Harmonization' (2010) 59 *International and Comparative Law Quarterly* 65.

67 Art 23 (2005 Convention); Art 20 (2019 Convention).

68 'The United Nations Convention on Contracts for the International Sale of Goods' ('CISG'). The CISG's uniformity provision, in Article 7(1), is identical to Article 20 of the 2019 Convention, adding only that regard can also be had to 'the observance of good faith in international trade' (a relevant concern for international sales law). See, for a discussion of the origins of this provision, and uses by the Hague Conference, Ribeiro-Bidaoui (n 3) 142–44.

69 Ribeiro-Bidaoui (n 3) 144–46.

70 See, for example, Philip Hackney, 'Is the United Nations Convention on the International Sale of Goods Achieving Uniformity? Comment' (2000–1) 61 *Louisiana Law Review* 473, 474 (and following).

Experience with caselaw under the 2005 Convention suggests that one way to manage the uniformity obligation in the Judgments Convention is to refer to meanings noted in the Explanatory Report.[71] The Singaporean High Court, for example, was tasked with considering the meaning of Article 13 of the Convention in the case of *Ermgassen v Sixcap*.[72] Extensive reference was made to the Explanatory Report throughout the judgment. The Explanatory Report was extracted to give context to key terms used in the Convention, such as 'civil or commercial matters' (at [8]), 'judgment' (at [9]) and 'recognition and enforcement' (at [11]). Additionally, the Explanatory Report was also used as a basis to justify the Court's reasoning about a term that was not defined in the Convention, with the Court expressly noting that the result reached was as 'in line with what is envisaged in the [Report]' (at [22]–[24]). Subsequent cases have also confirmed the significant role that the Explanatory Report plays in the interpretation and understanding of the Convention.[73] Most recently, both parties in the English High Court case of *Motacus Constructions*[74] referred to the Report to support their preferred meaning of articles in the Convention, and the Court engaged in a comparative analysis of the language used in the authoritative French version of the text to assist in resolving an interpretive argument.[75]

Perhaps most explored in the history of the Judgments Project is the idea of the recognition and enforcement framework providing for some form of advisory opinion on potential divergences. The most common form of advisory opinion is one that derives from empowering a supranational court or tribunal to issue a decision on interpretative matters. The Brussels Model represents the most obvious example, with the intervening role of the Court of Justice of the European Union. Although not deriving from a private international law approach, a parallel of sorts exists within Commonwealth States that allows appeal to the Privy Council: these decisions are binding on States

71 Trevor Hartley and Masato Dogauchi, 'Explanatory Report on the Convention of 30 June 2005 on Choice of Court Agreements' (Explanatory Report, 2007).

72 *Ermgassen & Co Ltd* v. *Sixcap Financials Pte Ltd* [2018] SGHCR 8.

73 See, for example, *Etihad Airways PJSC* v. *Flother* [2020] EWCA Civ 1707 (18 December 2020), where the English Court of Appeal extracted and referred to parts of the Explanatory Reports accompanying both the Lugano and 2005 Conventions. See, also, the Piraeus Court of First Instance (Decision: nr. 3106/2019, in Greek), as discussed and criticised in Apostolos Anthimos' blog post: 'First Contact of Greek Courts with the 2005 Hague Choice of Court Convention' (*Conflict of Laws*, 7 May 2020) <https://conflictoflaws.net/2020/first-contact-of-greek-courts-with-the-2005-hague-choice-of-court-convention/> accessed 1 October 2021.

74 *Motacus Constructions Ltd* v. *Paolo Castelli SpA* [2021] EWHC 356 (TCC) (22 February 2021)

75 ibid. [57].

within that system and have persuasive force in other States. It is thus unsurprising that the International Court of Justice was raised as a body who might be empowered to grant advisory opinions in the negotiations of both the New York Convention and the Judgments Project.[76] Other advisory mechanisms were also suggested during negotiations towards the Judgments Project, including the potential of a new international court or tribunal to deal with Hague Conference Conventions, and a form of *ad hoc* interpretive group.[77] These proposals stemmed from the operation of the CISG Advisory Council and the Lugano Conventions, respectively. However, neither was pursued further, and these mechanisms do not feature in either of the Judgments Conventions.

For this reason, emphasis has largely turned to more informal processes, outside of the architecture of the Judgment Conventions.[78] These include avenues to categorise, summarise and facilitate access to international case law,[79] reference to explanatory materials[80] and opportunities for judicial education and information exchange. As João Ribeiro-Bidaoui argues, it may be that periodic review mechanisms within the Judgments Conventions can be utilised as a 'gateway to facilitate uniform interpretation'.[81] That is, Art 24 of the 2005 Convention and Art 21 of the 2019 Convention provide for a regular review of the Convention and whether any amendments are desirable. However, it is difficult, in the face of a rejection of provisions that promote uniformity and autonomy in the long negotiating history of the Judgments Project – coupled with the decades of observed experience in the Brussels, Commonwealth and New York Convention Models set out previously – to imagine that such a review mechanism will bear fruit in encouraging amendments towards uniformity. This idea is also reinforced by the severely restricted instrumental developments seen in both the New York Convention and the

76 See Section 7.1.1 for a discussion of the New York Convention approach. In the Judgments Project context, see: Document Submitted by the Co-Reporters on the Uniform Interpretation of the Proposed Convention on the Jurisdiction, Recognition and the Enforcement of Judgments in Civil and Commercial Matters, 10 November 1998, Working Document No. 94 E, p. 1 ('Working Document 94 E of the 1998 Special Commission').

77 See, generally, Working Document 94 E of the 1998 Special Commission (n 76), as discussed in Ribeiro-Bidaoui (n 3).

78 As discussed in Ribeiro-Bidaoui (n 3) 150 (and following).

79 As occurs perhaps most notably with the Case Law on UNCITRAL Texts (CLOUT). CLOUT offers a database of decisions with abstracts, access to full texts and translations if available, and places emphasis on decisions that turn upon interpretive differences of an UNCITRAL text.

80 Notably the explanatory reports of both Judgments Conventions and reports on draft attempts during the Judgments Project, all of which are referred to often in this book: Hartley and Dogauchi (n 71); Francisco Garcimartín and Geneviève Saumier, 'Explanatory Report on the HCCH 2019 Judgments Convention' [2020]; Nygh and Pocar (n 1).

81 Ribeiro-Bidaoui (n 3) 162.

Commonwealth Model, set out at Section 7.2.2. Indeed, the more widespread the support for the Judgments Conventions becomes, the more difficult this task will be, as amendment will require the agreement of all Contracting Parties. For these reasons, the Judgments Conventions, like the CISG, will likely rely upon the interpretive aplomb of enforcing courts, buoyed by the express uniformity provisions provided by each Convention.

The CJEU's role in assisting with the equal and uniform interpretation under the Brussels Model is a particularly helpful – but not a necessary – pre-condition for an effective recognition and enforcement framework, as discussed at Section 7.1.2. The lessons of the New York Convention are also instructive as, despite calls for greater emphasis on uniformity by national courts around the world, divergent interpretations have arisen across several key provisions.[82] Consequently, there may be some truth in the statement that absent a 'central and finally competent court a uniform understanding and application of a legal instrument in different jurisdictions can hardly be achieved, let alone upheld over a longer period of time'.[83] Absent the shared political will to establish a global supranational interpretive body to interpret a global convention – with the practical difficulties to so doing described as 'insurmountable'[84] – States must accept the potential for divergent interpretation. This is because judicial interpretation 'reflects changing political consensus' in a particular jurisdiction, and consequently the precise interpretation of a treaty, even if its provisions are uniform, will likely still 'vary substantially'.[85] Nonetheless, accepting the potential for divergence – as long as this is the marginal case, rather than the rule – does not necessarily defeat the objective of international instruments that aim to harmonise recognition and enforcement. So long as the instrument continues to serve the predominant role of promoting the recognition and enforcement prospects of foreign judgments, its harmonisation and liberalisation objectives can still be met, at least in part.

7.2 ONGOING EVOLUTION AND LEGAL DEVELOPMENT

Recognition and enforcement can also develop or evolve outside of the instrumental obligations that oblige or promote uniform interpretation.

[82] See, Gaillard (n 5) 690, who argues that despite divergent and sometimes problematic applications of the New York Convention, the benefits of reforming it are likely to be minimal as 'there is more to lose than to gain in embarking upon a revision process'. See also Section 7.1.1.

[83] Magnus and Mankowski (n 19) Chapter I (para 111).

[84] von Mehren and Gottschalk (n 56) 357.

[85] Perez (n 2) 68.

Forecasting any such evolution is particularly complicated – perhaps even more so than domestic law-making processes – as transnational law- and norm-making arises as a series of cycles, varying in intensity and pace.[86] Given the 2005 Convention only recently came into force in 2015, and the 2019 Convention is not yet in force, there is little chance of external legal development in the short to medium term. For this reason, I focus here on the Brussels Model, the New York Convention and Commonwealth Model (and the common law that underpins it). The primary focus in this section is on developments in the Brussels Model, as the instruments in this Model, and the surrounding institutional frameworks surrounding European integration, have faced, relatively at least, the most significant development pressure since their original formulation. My ultimate aim in this section is to determine if, and how, other transnational experience may inform the emerging and future recognition and enforcement of foreign judgments via the Judgments Conventions.

7.2.1 *Ongoing Evolution: The Brussels Model*

The Brussels Model serves as a basis for developing rules that expand the recognition and enforcement prospects of foreign judgments (between Brussels Model participants). Within the EU, this development process has led to a major power shift from national legislatures to EU executive and judicial authorities such as the CJEU and the European Commission. However, the Brussels Model is now one that extends beyond its constituent instruments. This is somewhat surprising when reviewed in isolation, particularly, as Chapter 3 illustrates, because the Regulations (and the Brussels Model itself) have broad remit and have undergone little substantive change since the original 1968 Convention. However, despite the primacy of the Brussels Model instruments, as the EU's law-making power has expanded, so too has the scope and reach of specific Regulations that supplement the Brussels Model by establishing uniform legal instruments to regulate particular legal or practical issues within the Union.[87]

[86] Which 'can be explained by a combination of facilitating circumstances and precipitating conditions': Terence Halliday and Susan Block-Lieb, 'Settling and Concordance: Two Cases in Global Commercial Law' in Gregory Shaffer and Terence Halliday (eds.), *Transnational Legal Orders* (Cambridge Studies in Law and Society, Cambridge University Press 2015) 32.

[87] Magnus and Mankowski (n 19) Chapter I, para 10 catalogues thirteen 'main new instruments' since the Treaty of Amsterdam entered into force (1 May 1999). This list could be expanded by considering developments in the intellectual property field (see Dickinson and Lein (n 28) 38–39) as well as further developments in the field since the book was published (notably the

These developments have led to the rapid emergence of a 'common European law of civil procedure',[88] despite the precise extent of its conceptual and practical boundaries remaining undefined. In the recognition and enforcement context at least, these developments have so far been aimed at further facilitating the cross-border recovery of debts through the creation of specific 'European enforcement orders'.[89] Taking the Brussels Model instruments and these recent legislative developments together, it has been suggested that they form a 'nucleus of a uniform code of international civil procedure for the EU'.[90] A key plank of this code is the promotion of recognition and enforcement, due to its role in according reciprocal 'mutual trust' among Brussels Model States.[91]

The Brussels Model – with its broad-based scope, and the benefit of interpretation by over a hundred judgments of the CJEU (and thousands of national court decisions) – undoubtedly constitutes the core of this approach.[92] The Brussels Model therefore represents the fundament on which all further recognition and enforcement development in the EU is likely to be premised. Nonetheless, a recent spate of legal instruments in the EU, usually with a narrow scope of application, go further than the Brussels Model in liberalising recognition and enforcement approaches. To shed light on what is likely to happen in future Brussels Model developments – and whether these developments may inform global recognition and enforcement approaches – this section considers the 2004 European Enforcement Order Regulation and the (unsuccessful) aspects of the 2012 Recast Proposal that attempted to significantly limit the grounds available for enforcing courts to refuse to give effect to foreign judgments.

'Regulation (EU) No 655/2014 of the European Parliament and of the Council of 15 May 2014 Establishing a European Account Preservation Order Procedure to Facilitate Cross-Border Debt Recovery in Civil and Commercial Matters' (15 May 2014) OJ L189/59)

88 Magnus and Mankowski (n 19) Introduction (para 11).

89 This has been done, for example, via the establishment of (in chronological order): a European enforcement order for uncontested claims ('Regulation (EC) No 805/2004 of the European Parliament and of the Council Creating a European Enforcement Order for Uncontested Claims' (21 April 2004) OJ L143/15); a European order for payment procedure ('Regulation (EC) No 1896/2006 of the European Parliament and of the Council Creating a European Order for Payment Procedure' (12 December 2006) OJ L399/1); a European small claims procedure ('Regulation (EC) No 861/2007 of the European Parliament and of the Council Creating a European Small Claims Procedure' (11 July 2007) OJ L199/1); and, a European account preservation order ('European Account Preservation Order Regulation' (n 87)).

90 Magnus and Mankowski (n 19) Introduction (para 11).

91 See, generally, Matthias Weller, 'Mutual Trust: In Search of the Future of European Union Private International Law' (2015) 11 *Journal of Private International Law*.

92 Magnus and Mankowski (n 19) Chapter I (para 12).

7.2.1.1 'Add-Ons' to the Brussels Model: The 2004 European Enforcement Order

The 2004 European Enforcement Order Regulation serves as a clear example of direct legislative development in the recognition and enforcement context, sitting on top of, and further liberalising, the Brussels Model.[93] The 2004 Regulation starts from the same point as the recent instruments constituting the Brussels Model: maintaining and developing 'freedom, security and justice' by adopting measures 'necessary for the proper functioning of the internal market'.[94] It draws upon Brussels Model instruments as a legal backbone but establishes further procedures to expedite proceedings for uncontested claims. Despite this, the Regulation takes a 'fundamentally different' approach to recognition and enforcement compared to the Brussels Model.[95] It facilitates near-automatic enforcement by providing a set of minimum standards that Member States must comply with to use the Regulation and certify their judgment as a European Enforcement Order. These grounds are strictly procedural in nature, and relate to the service of documents, the provision of due information to a debtor about a claim and the existence or availability of a review mechanism for default judgments in the Member State that handed down the original decision.[96]

Part of the rationale for setting these 'minimum standards' is to provide a procedural floor that should satisfy Member States to give effect to judgments of courts in other Member States, and further restrict the discretion of their own courts to refuse to give effect to these judgments. As soon as the minimum standards set out in the Enforcement Order Regulation are met by the rendering court, the sole – and extremely limited – avenue for the enforcing court to refuse enforcement is irreconcilability with an earlier judgment given in a Member State.[97] Thus, the task of protecting the defendant's right to a fair trial is entirely left with the rendering court: an approach that would be

[93] 'European Enforcement Order Regulation' (n 89) 2.

[94] ibid. Recital 1. This approach is substantially the same as contained in *Regulation (EU) No 1215/2012 of 12 December 2012 on Jurisdiction and the Recognition and Enforcement of Judgments in Civil and Commercial Matters (Recast)* (2012) Recitals 3 & 4.

[95] Xandra E. Kramer, 'Abolition of Exequatur Under the Brussels I Regulation: Effecting and Protecting Rights in the European Judicial Area' (2011) 4 *Nederlands Internationaal Privaatrecht* 634.

[96] 'European Enforcement Order Regulation' (n 89) Chapter III (Arts 12–19).

[97] ibid. Art 21. Note that it is possible to review the Enforcement Order in the rendering court – that is, in the Member State of origin – but that if a disputant does not avail themselves of this opportunity, their ability to resist enforcement in an enforcing court of a Member State is thus limited.

unlikely to gain traction globally. Perhaps unsurprisingly, the fact that the grant of an Enforcement Order limits a defendant's rights in the enforcement state has been subject to criticism, even within the context of the close relationship of EU States.[98]

On this basis, the European Enforcement Order Regulation is more pro-enforcement than any international instrument anywhere in the world. This curtailed ability for the enforcing court to refuse enforcement departs from the much broader 'traditional' refusal grounds seen in the Brussels Model – which are substantially similar to those contained in other recognition and enforcement instruments globally. There are, for example, no grounds to refuse enforcement on the basis that enforcing the award would conflict with the public policy of the State of the enforcing court. This automatism in enforcement, coupled with severely limited grounds for refusing enforcement, is an intentional feature or aim of the Regulation: assuming the judgment has met the minimum standards to become certified as a European Enforcement Order, it 'should, for enforcement purposes, be treated as if it had been delivered in the Member State in which enforcement is sought'.[99]

It is difficult to see how such an approach would achieve success in States that do not share in the same conception of mutual trust as EU Member States, and lack even rudimentary harmonisation of consensus on giving effect to judgments in the first place. No doubt, a key part of the rationale for increased automatism in enforcement is the unique relationship of trust and confidence between Member States.[100] In the lingo of 'mutual trust', the 2004 Regulation suggests that Member States in the EU are comfortable, at least where proceedings are uncontested, to place greater trust in the rendering court's ability to comply with fundamental notions of procedural fairness. So comfortable that they almost entirely give up their own courts' discretion to refuse to recognise and enforce – far more accepting an approach to foreign judgments than the already liberal Brussels Model provides for. A further comforting factor is that the scope of the Regulation is limited to only uncontested judgments (in circumstances where 'minimum standards' relating to adequate notice, service of proceedings and an opportunity to be heard should have been provided to the defendant in the rendering court). This is a much easier prospect to deal with than automated enforcement of disputed proceedings.

98 See, for example: von Mehren and Gottschalk (n 56) 77 (at footnote 125).

99 'European Enforcement Order Regulation' (n 89) Recital 9.

100 Cf Weller (n 91) 67, who notes that despite being used to develop judicial co-operation in the EU, this conception of mutual trust is a 'myth', which is 'reality only to a limited degree'.

Nonetheless, it is likely that the European Enforcement Order Regulation experience is still instructive for global recognition and enforcement efforts. In particular, the Regulation experience suggests that harmonisation of recognition and enforcement does not necessarily spell an end to legal development, and, to the contrary, may encourage it. The Regulation does so by situating itself within the Brussels Model's harmonisation regime, and offering itself as an 'optional extra' for recognition and enforcement in the EU. It is optional in two senses. First, it is optional for creditors with an uncontested claim, as they have the option to utilise the 'facilitated enforcement' certification procedure under this Regulation or to rely on the pre-existing (but less favourable to them) recognition and enforcement mechanisms under the relevant Brussels Model instrument.[101] Second, the Enforcement Order Regulation aims to further recognition and enforcement harmonisation efforts in an optional (or 'soft') way. That is, although Member States must comply with the Regulation if it applies, there is no obligation under the Regulation for Member States to adapt their national law to include the minimum procedural standards contained within the Regulation (so that it will apply to them). [102] Because States are not compelled to ensure their rendering courts adopt these procedural standards, the Enforcement Order Regulation stands only as an incentive to harmonise. That is, the judgments of a rendering court in a particular State will only have access to the 'more efficient and rapid enforceability of judgments' under the Enforcement Order Regulation if it meets these minimum standards in the Regulation.[103] If, for whatever reason, the rendering court does not meet these standards, its judgments will simply not benefit from the significantly streamlined Enforcement Order process. This approach ensures that procedural guarantees are provided for on some level, but these guarantees are provided via an alternative mechanism (rather than the traditional grounds for refusing recognition and enforcement).

7.2.1.2 Reforming and Recasting the Brussels Model

The experience of designing and drafting the 2012 Recast, representing the most current formulation of the Brussels Model, is perhaps most telling of the Model's likely future steps and likely also informs the future of recognition

[101] This is enshrined in 'European Enforcement Order Regulation' (n 89) Recital 20. See also Bénédicte Fauvarque-Cosson, 'European Contract Law Through and beyond Pluralism – The Case of an Optional Instrument' in Leone Niglia (ed.), *Pluralism and European Private Law* (Hart Publishing 2013) 96.

[102] This is explicitly set out in 'European Enforcement Order Regulation' (n 89) Recital 19.

[103] ibid.

and enforcement generally. The Proposal by the European Commission leading to the 2012 Recast thus offers direct insight.[104] The Commission succeeded in one of its proposals – to abolish within the Brussels Model the declaration of enforceability procedure – but at the same time failed in its proposal to substantially replace (and limit) the existing grounds for refusing to recognise and enforce judgments. With respect to the former, the Recast moves the balance slightly closer towards greater recognition and enforcement as an incidence of mutual trust by abolishing the declaration of enforceability, with the consequence that a foreign judgment creditor can now immediately address the enforcing court in the Member State of enforcement.[105]

With respect to replacing and limiting grounds for refusal, the Commission proposed to introduce a 'rather complex' and 'rightfully criticised' tripartite system of review.[106] The first limb of this system, consistent with the approach of the European Enforcement Order and a ground of refusal in the Brussels Model, compels the enforcing court to refuse enforcement of a judgment if it is irreconcilable with another judgment.[107] The second limb allows review of the judgment – in the rendering court – if the defendant was not served with the proceedings adequately or was prevented from contesting the claim due to force majeure or extraordinary circumstances beyond its control.[108] This limb does not apply if the defendant 'failed to challenge the judgment when it was possible for him to do so', that is, in the rendering court. While a failure of adequate service is consistent with the existing grounds for refusal in the Brussels Model, the latter part of this formulation, relating to force majeure and extraordinary circumstances, is a novel legal development for recognition and enforcement in civil and commercial matters. What is particularly novel is that an application on this basis may be made to the enforcing court, but the enforcing court must transfer it back to the rendering court (the 'Member State of origin') to be determined. In a sense, this is asking the rendering court to police its own compliance with procedural fairness, which presents immediate concerns. Presumably, in coming to its original judgment, the rendering court should already have considered and resolved any objections on these

[104] European Commission, 'Proposal for a Council Regulation (EC) on Jurisdiction and the Recognition and Enforcement of Judgments in Civil and Commercial Matters' (COM(1999) 348 final, 14 July 1999).

[105] *Brussels I Recast* (n 94) Arts 42 and 43.

[106] Xandra E. Kramer, 'Cross-Border Enforcement and the Brussels I-Bis Regulation: Towards a New Balance between Mutual Trust and National Control over Fundamental Rights' (2013) 60 *Netherlands International Law Review* 353.

[107] European Commission (n 104) proposed Art 43.

[108] ibid. proposed Art 45.

grounds, particularly as the defendant cannot challenge on this basis if it failed to challenge when possible to do so. In these circumstances, it is difficult to see how or why, absent a glaring error or omission, a rendering court would second-guess a decision of its own court. The third limb compels the enforcing court to refuse recognition and enforcement if doing so 'would not be permitted by the fundamental principles underlying the right to a fair trial'.[109] This seems to be aimed at a basic 'procedural fairness' conception of the right to refuse to give effect to a judgment on the basis of its non-compliance with the public policy of the State of the enforcing court.

Overall, this proposal for substituting limited grounds to refuse recognition and enforcement is widely regarded, on both a legal and political level, to be 'unworkable',[110] based on its 'systemic inadequacy'.[111] For example, it contains no obligation (or residual discretion) for enforcing courts to refuse to recognise and enforce a foreign judgment rendered in violation of protective jurisdiction rules.[112] It has also been suggested that narrowing the public policy exception away from substantive grounds to a solely 'procedural public policy' in the right to a fair trial is 'illogical'. [113] The fundamental objection seems to be the implicit understanding that the Proposal, if accepted with respect to this change in the grounds for refusal, would shift the carefully crafted 'package' or balance of the maximum acceptable level of recognition and enforcement. Consequently, the Proposal's attempt to replace – and significantly minimise – the grounds for refusal was met with swift and decisive resistance on the basis that this change would likely conflict with each Member State's entitlement to 'preserve its fundamental values'.[114] The failure of this proposal highlights that the relationships between EU Member States, at least for the purposes of recognition and enforcement, are perhaps not as close as the underlying thread of 'mutual trust' suggests.

[109] ibid. proposed Art 46.

[110] See the Report by the Directorate General for Internal Policies (C: Legal Affairs) by Andrew Dickinson, as published in Andrew Dickinson, 'The Proposal for a Regulation of the European Parliament and of the Council on Jurisdiction and the Recognition and Enforcement of Judgments in Civil and Commercial Matters (Recast) ('Brussels I Bis' Regulation)' (Sydney Law School Legal Studies Research Paper, 20 September 2011) 6–10.

[111] Kramer, 'Cross-Border Enforcement and the Brussels I-Bis Regulation' (n 106) 353.

[112] These exclusive matters include matters that relate to 'fundamental values' of States, for example, consumer contracts and employment matters: see, further, Section 5.3.1.

[113] Dickinson and Lein (n 28) 441. For further discussion of the Commission's failed attempt to narrow the public policy exception, see: ibid. 440–42.

[114] European Parliament, 'Report on the Proposal for a Regulation of the European Parliament and of the Council on Jurisdiction and the Recognition and Enforcement of Judgments in Civil and Commercial Matters (Recast)' (COM (2010) 748, 15 October 2012) Explanatory Statement (no 1).

7.2.1.3 An Incremental, Evolutionary, Approach to Legal Development

The Brussels Model – and the surrounding legal landscape in the EU – is likely to continue to develop further in favour of greater recognition and enforcement, albeit in a gradual manner. To the extent past revision processes are likely to inform the timeline of any future revision, the next generation of the Brussels Model is unlikely to surface until approximately 2027.[115] This gradual approach is consistent with the decisive rejection of part of the Commission's 2012 Recast Proposal, which attempted to radically reformulate the grounds for refusal. Part of this failure can no doubt be attributed to a 'status quo' bias – in that the approach of the Brussels Model, due to its longevity and wide acceptance, is unlikely to see radical change overnight. More fundamentally, however, this failure highlights that the uncritical acceptance of the 'myth' of mutual trust cannot be used as a basis for justifying a rapid reformulation of the balance towards automatic recognition and enforcement of foreign judgments.[116] It has even been argued that the use of mutual trust as a 'legal fiction' cannot justify greater automatism in recognition and enforcement beyond what is already accommodated in the most recent formulation of the Brussels Model.[117] This, at least in part, is because any future push to further automate or liberalise the recognition and enforcement of judgments is likely to face a number of hurdles.

The first of these hurdles involves the potential for uncritical recognition and enforcement to clash with fundamental rights of individual defendants.[118] The importance of complying with fundamental rights has been expressed in particularly strong language by the European Parliament, who call for the protection of fundamental rights across all levels of the EU, including via legislative development with binding consequences for non-compliance.[119] Another hurdle relates to how much further the idea of mutual trust can

[115] Dickinson and Lein (n 28) para 1.07 note this point, with reference to the *Brussels I Recast* (n 94) Art 79.

[116] Weller (n 91) 67.

[117] ibid. 101. Weller goes further and suggests that developments in the surrounding EU legal landscape suggest that aspects of the Brussels Model may be further limited.

[118] See ibid. 90–95. Weller considers a number of cases heard in the European Court of Human Rights, and notes that while they do not directly relate to civil and commercial matters, the 'ratio of these decisions can be applied to judicial co-operation in civil matters': ibid. 101.

[119] European Parliament, 'European Parliament Resolution of 8 September 2015 on the Situation of Fundamental Rights in the European Union (2013-2014)' (2014/2254 (INI), 8 September 2015).

extend to automating recognition and enforcement of foreign judgments when there may be questions about how justice is administered in some Member States.[120] This can be analogised with concerns seen in negotiating the global Judgments Project set out at Section 6.1.2. The European Commission has sought to develop a framework to strengthen the rule of law by identifying and responding to such deficiencies.[121] It may be that the Brussels Model accommodates these hurdles by altering the balance at the margins – for example, accepting that within the public policy ground of refusal there is an implied ability to refuse to give effect to a judgment where there are systemic deficiencies in the rendering court's approach.[122] While the precise details of this implementation require further analysis, on balance, these hurdles suggest that efforts to further liberalise the Brussels Model itself may face significant resistance even within the close-knit community of EU Member States. In these circumstances, absent a convincing 'political, legal and economic case', the need to maintain the integrity of the Brussels Model – and its consistency with other long-standing legal instruments across the EU and internationally – should prevail.[123] Consequently, the Brussels Model experience suggests that it is possible for further legal development or harmonisation to occur, but absent a compelling case for reform, harmonisation efforts should not be radically disturbed.[124]

7.2.1.4 Impacts on the Brussels Model's Extensibility

Although the EU has adopted a cautious, incremental and evolutionary approach to legal development, the focus on the broader project of European integration is likely to mean that although lessons can still be drawn, there is likely to be a 'dilution' in the direct adaptability of the Model globally.[125] The greatest degree of dilution is likely to be seen in the

[120] Weller (n 91) 95–100.

[121] European Commission, 'A New EU Framework to Strengthen the Rule of Law: Communication from the Commission to the European Parliament and the Council' (COM (2014) 158 final, 11 March 2014). See further the comments of the European Parliament in European Parliament (n 114).

[122] Weller (n 91) 100.

[123] Dickinson (n 110) 3.

[124] One of the possible compelling cases that may arise is further exposition of the European Convention on Human Rights – in particular Article 6 (right of access to a court and to a fair hearing). As Weller notes, the European Court of Human Rights is 'quite aware of the principle of mutual trust in European Union civil procedure', and in reviewing the relevant case law notes that litigants have had 'mixed success': Weller (n 91) 90 (and following).

[125] For an overview of the general extensibility of the Brussels Model due to potentially divergent conceptions of sovereign relationships among participants, see Section 6.2.2.1.

'add-ons' to the Brussels Model, represented by EU-only instruments building upon the Brussels Model, such as the 2004 Enforcement Order Regulation. This extension is premised almost entirely on the need to develop greater expediency and automatism in recognition and enforcement in certain instances – above and beyond what is offered in the Brussels Model – as an incidence of the unique degree of mutual trust in place between Member States. Because of this, these external developments offer little by way of direct lessons to States outside of the EU. Attempts to reform and recast the Model may also further dilute the direct comparability or extensibility of the Model globally. This is because recent developments within the Brussels Model are increasingly premised on arguments of efficiency and the need for mutual trust and cooperation within the EU; arguments that, of course, do not act with such force in other inter-State relationships.

Although the direct extensibility of the Model is diminished, it will remain of critical importance globally. Indeed, inspiration is likely to be derived from novel processes used to encourage greater intra-European harmonisation, through more streamlined and potentially codified European private civil procedure.[126] This is because of the careful efforts expended by the EU to consider, at a high level, the way in which to systematise and streamline the interaction of different elements of private international law across the national borders of Member States.

Additionally, and reflecting its origins as a Convention, the Brussels Model core approach remains useful as a comparator for other regional and international recognition and enforcement efforts.[127] This is because the Brussels Model is perhaps the most successful international approach to striking a precarious balance between compelling enforcing courts to give effect to judgments, tempered by procedural exceptions to protect against perceived abuses. This balance is particularly difficult to achieve for political reasons arising due to State sovereignty, and it is further complicated as a broad-based instrument on recognition and enforcement potentially extends to judgments rendered on the basis of objectionable jurisdictional grounds. In other words, it does not have the same ease of justification that the 2005 Convention and New York Convention broadly share. Instead, it must navigate certainty and efficiency on the one hand, and individual justice and access to justice for

[126] José Angelo Estrella Faria, 'Globalisation, Legal Identity and Regional Integration: Complementarity or Conflict?' (2013) 18 *Uniform Law Review* 443.

[127] See, for example, Jie Huang, *Interregional Recognition and Enforcement of Civil and Commercial Judgments: Lessons for China from US and EU Law* (Bloomsbury Publishing 2014), who reviews the Brussels Model approach to see what lessons from it can be applied to China.

litigants on the other. The former calls for a prescriptive approach, with comprehensive rules in favour of recognition and enforcement, tempered by clearly enumerated and limited grounds for the enforcing court to exercise residual control. However, the need for individual justice calls for a degree of residual discretion in the enforcing court in terms of the foreign decisions it recognises and enforces, or the basis for refusing to do so. Similarly, while the Judgments Conventions also attempt to navigate a global and ever-changing political, social, economic and technological landscape, the basis for striking this balance can be – and is likely to remain – informed by the Brussels Model experience.[128]

7.2.2 *Limited Instrumental Developments in Other Transnational Approaches*

Standing in stark contrast to the series of instrumental developments in and around the Brussels Model, other international approaches have faced few, if any, substantial changes to their underlying or supporting legal instruments. As the remainder of this section suggests, this can largely be attributed to difficulties in revising, updating or improving legal architecture that depends on achieving global consensus. For this reason, most legal development is likely to happen on a domestic level, rather than through changes to instrumental obligations at an international level.

One of the main mechanisms of legal development at a national law level is evolving jurisprudence reflecting changing views on ways to read and interpret instrumental obligations. This can be influenced by the design of the instrument itself – for example, the provisions that aim to promote uniformity highlighted earlier in this chapter. Perhaps most prominent in this respect is the 'reading in' of the purpose of the New York Convention where enforcing courts are faced with an arbitral award that has been set aside in the seat of arbitration. The prevailing view is that enforcing courts should operate 'consonant with international standards', despite this not being an express Convention obligation. Thus, the usual rule is that the enforcing court should *not* exercise its discretion to give effect to the award unless an award is set aside on a ground not recognised in international practice, or based on an

[128] Faria (n 126) 436. Faria notes, for example, the recent development of the European Law Institute, in particular, its express objectives that create an 'obvious link' between EU and broader international harmonisation.

'intolerable criterion'.[129] Notably, none of these criteria are included or able to be readily derived from the text of the Convention itself. This again highlights the hesitation with a purely instrumental understanding of recognition and enforcement obligations. To give context to this concern, I consider the limited manner by which legal development under the New York Convention and the Commonwealth Model – representing the other key recognition and enforcement orders that have been extensively tested – can occur.

7.2.2.1 The New York Convention

The New York Convention has not faced any instrumental developments or evolutions since it was originally agreed. This is so despite a widespread perception that the New York Convention 'is in need of modernization',[130] based on the view that a number of provisions are either incomplete, ambiguous, perceived to be missing, depart from prevailing judicial interpretation or are outdated and have not kept pace with legal developments.[131] Perhaps most prominently, it has been suggested that the New York Convention's approach could be improved by States utilising more liberal recognition and enforcement approaches, such as those contained in other 'soft' instruments. One of the primary ways suggested is to adopt existing transnational instruments, such as the UNCITRAL Model Law. I consider this first, before turning to suggestions that a further arbitral enforcement instrument be agreed between States.

Perhaps the clearest example of how legal development can occur within the confines of the Convention – without requiring agreement on amendments or changes to treaty intrumentation itself – is seen in the widespread avoidance of the Convention's strict insistence upon an 'agreement in

[129] Jan Paulsson, 'Awards Set Aside at the Place of Arbitration' in *Enforcing Arbitration Awards under the New York Convention: Experience and Prospects* (United Nations 1999) 26.

[130] See, for a number of examples, a range of articles commissioned on the fiftieth anniversary of the New York Convention collated in van den Berg, *50 Years of the New York Convention: ICCA International Arbitration Conference* (n 8). Gaillard, in an article in that same collection, notes that although the majority view of scholars had previously been in favour of not revisiting the Convention, a number of scholars have increasingly begun to agitate for a revision process: Gaillard (n 5) 689.

[131] van den Berg, for example, refers to the outdated requirement for an 'agreement in writing', to the reference to 'permanent arbitral bodies' in Art I(2), and the reference in Art V(1)(e) to the law under which the award was made: see, further, Albert Jan van den Berg, 'Hypothetical Draft Convention on the International Enforcement of Arbitration Agreements and Awards: Explanatory Note' in Albert Jan van den Berg (ed.), *50 Years of the New York Convention: ICCA International Arbitration Conference* (ICCA Congress Series 14, 321st ed., Kluwer Law International 2009) 649.

writing', within the meaning set out in Article II of the Convention. Arbitral and technological progress has made the requirement for an 'agreement in writing' unduly restrictive, such that the Convention's approach is likely stricter than 'almost any national law'.[132] States can circumvent this problem, as the open nature of the Convention allows them to adopt less restrictive approaches within domestic law. This has been facilitated by other transnational instruments that also aim to promote arbitration, seen for example in Article 7 of the Model Law, which contains two different definitions of an 'agreement in writing' that capture a broader array of arbitration agreements than the Convention (and hence, resulting awards that come for recognition or enforcement).[133] Before these Model Law amendments, leading jurisdictions concerned with attracting arbitral custom already provided a more expansive definition of what constitutes an 'agreement in writing'.[134] Signatories to the New York Convention, of course, are not compelled to revise or update their Convention obligations. However, the Convention's 'minimum standards' approach makes it simple for States who wish to do so to enhance their support for recognition and enforcement on a unilateral basis.[135]

By way of a further example, Contracting States may choose to give effect to a broader array of arbitral awards than those envisaged under the Convention. For example, in France, few decided cases now refer to the New York Convention – not because Convention obligations are being avoided but because the ordinary rules governing enforcement of awards in France are more liberal than those of the Convention.[136] Consequently, conceiving of the New York Convention – and indeed any open international recognition and enforcement architecture – as a set of 'minimum standards' allows States

[132] ibid. 667. The Judgments Conventions adopt a mandatory – but much more permissive – approach to writing. See Art 3(c) of the 2005 Convention with respect to exclusive choice of forum agreements, and Art 5(1)(m) of the 2019 Convention for non-exclusive choices, both of which require only that the agreement be concluded in writing or 'by any other means of communication which renders information accessible so as to be usable for subsequent reference'.

[133] See, generally, for a discussion of the options available to re-interpret Article II(2) of the Convention, Albert Jan van den Berg, 'When is an Arbitration Agreement in Writing Valid under Article II(2) of the New York Convention of 1958?' in Pieter Sanders (ed.), *Piet Sanders: Een honderdjarige vernieuwer* (Boom Juridische Uitgevers 2012).

[134] See, for example, the jurisdictions mentioned in Neil Kaplan, 'New Developments on Written Form' in *Enforcing Arbitration Awards under the New York Convention: Experience and Prospects* (United Nations 1999) 18.

[135] Julian D. M. Lew and others, *Comparative International Commercial Arbitration* (Kluwer Law International 2003) [26–33].

[136] Gaillard (n 5) 692.

to continue to develop recognition and enforcement approaches without disturbing the underlying instrumentation.[137] Compared to wholesale instrumental changes – as may be attempted in the confines of the Brussels Model – the kind of development seen here is likely to be inchingly incremental. However, it can be assisted by forces and entities that exist beyond the domestic level, as the Model Law experience suggests. This is likely to be particularly important in the context of the 2019 Convention, as its jurisdictional bases come to be tested and applied.

A second prominent – but heavily criticised – approach to modernise the New York Convention's approach to recognition and enforcement is via seeking to achieve transnational agreement on a subsequent instrument. There have been suggestions that the instrument could come in the form of a 'mini' instrument styled on the Brussels Model, 'relating solely and specifically to court decisions dealing with arbitration, so that each country within this group of mutually trusting countries would give *res judicata* effect to each others' judgments and thus create significant harmonization'.[138] Additionally, and perhaps most prominently, efforts to promulgate a new approach are represented in a Hypothetical Draft Convention presented by Albert Jan van den Berg.[139] This approach is designed to respond to observed problems or issues of ambiguity in the New York Convention.[140] The Hypothetical Draft Convention has been praised for its 'simplicity' and its clarity, which 'eliminate' much of the textual ambiguity that has led to divergent interpretations in several jurisdictions.[141]

As noted previously, proposals to 'modernise' the New York Convention approach – such as via negotiating a new instrument – have faced significant

[137] Andrea Giardina, 'The Practical Application of Multilateral Convention' in Albert Jan van den Berg (ed.), *Improving the Efficiency of Arbitration Agreements and Awards: 40 Years of Application of the New York Convention* (KluwerArbitration, Kluwer Law International 2011) 449.

[138] Paulsson, 'Awards Set aside at the Place of Arbitration' (n 129) 25.

[139] See the Hypothetical Draft Convention, and the accompanying Explanatory Note set out in van den Berg, 'Hypothetical Draft Convention on the International Enforcement of Arbitration Agreements and Awards: Explanatory Note' (n 131).

[140] See, for an overview of the approach and an explanation of the precise areas it aims to improve: ibid.

[141] See, for example, Lamm, who notes that despite the significant practical difficulties to agree to such a proposed instrument, the Hypothetical Draft Convention addresses many of the problems seen in the context of the New York Convention, and if implemented would be 'worth the effort': Carolyn Lamm, 'Comments on the Proposal to Amend the New York Convention' in Albert Jan van den Berg (ed.), *50 Years of the New York Convention: ICCA International Arbitration Conference* (ICCA Congress Series 14, Kluwer Law International 2009) 706.

critique. Gaillard, for example, argues that there is an 'urgency' not to revisit or revise the New York Convention approach, despite its dated and at times ambiguous language, based on what he terms 'three NOs'.[142] First, that there is 'no need' to revise the Convention; although provisions could be fine tuned, there are no 'serious problems' that require such a massive undertaking as seeking a new round of agreement among each participating State would entail. Implicit in this concern is an understanding that instrumental obligations cannot compel compliance in all matters – for example, efforts to avoid complying with an award based upon State immunity to execution – and hence a revision of the instrument is unlikely to change this position.[143] Second, there is 'no hope' of succeeding in achieving transnational consensus on a new instrument, particularly in circumstances where a number of States have expressed discontent with the way in which arbitral practice – and the recognition and enforcement of resulting awards against them as defendants – has developed.[144]

The third 'no' is that there is 'no danger' in leaving the Convention approach in place. This argument rests on what is described as the foresighted 'genius' of its open (also termed 'minimum standards') approach. As Section 8.2.1 analyses further, the use of an open approach facilitates legal development as it broadly allows implementing States to recognise and enforce decisions that fall outside of instrumental obligations, by reference to their own national law. Thus, the New York Convention – and, by extension, the Judgments Conventions that also primarily adopt an open approach – allows States to ease some of the 'permanent tension' that most treaties face: 'freezing' the law as at the time of adoption.[145] Consequently, the mere existence of some ambiguity, or divergent interpretation and application, is not necessarily as problematic as it would be in a closed Convention such as the Brussels Model.[146] This is because such recourse to domestic law can allow recognition and enforcement to evolve beyond the instrumental minimums, without the need for revising the underlying treaty architecture. It is suggested even that enforcement problems that inevitably arise with the New York Convention can be resolved – not necessarily in a uniform way – through unilateral domestic legal mechanisms, including amendments to

[142] See, for a stringent criticism of this proposal as contained in a 'Hypothetical Draft Convention' aimed at 'updating' the Convention: Gaillard (n 5) 695.

[143] ibid. 690.

[144] ibid. 691.

[145] Christina Binder, 'Stability and Change in Times of Fragmentation: The Limits of Pacta Sunt Servanda Revisited' (2012) 25 *Leiden Journal of International Law* 909, 910.

[146] Gaillard (n 5) 692.

implementing legislation.[147] The only restriction on these developments is that they must, at the least, be compatible with the recognition and enforcement instrument (or otherwise the State will be in breach of its international law obligations).[148] Given the limited legal development or evolution seen to date in global recognition and enforcement approaches, national law approaches are likely to be the key drivers of legal development.

7.2.2.2 The Commonwealth Model and the Common Law

The Commonwealth Model has also undergone very few legal developments. Consistent with the New York Convention experience, this is not because the Model is without flaws or lacks proposed methods to address such flaws. Perhaps the two most significant issues with the application of the Commonwealth Model – as set out in Section 4.3.1 – are inconsistent reliance upon reciprocity in Acts that implement the Model, and divergent common law jurisdictional bases. Both aspects are proposed to be improved in the 2017 Model Law, as set out at Section 4.1.3. The legal development that occurs is set out in more detail in that section, but for present purposes I briefly note the two key reforms to the Commonwealth Model. First, the 2017 Model Law aims to resolve some of the variance in Commonwealth treatment of reciprocity by removing any reciprocity arrangement by which judgments from other Commonwealth States receive favourable treatment as compared to judgments from outside the Commonwealth. Second, similar to the Brussels Model approach, it aims to set out a much more exhaustive list of grounds for refusing recognition and enforcement based on jurisdiction. This approach has been described as a 'very positive step', particularly because of its impacts in minimising jurisdictional divergences.[149] Note however, the discussion at Section 4.1.3, where it is noted that the 2017 Model Law is unlikely to see wider uptake. That is, despite the identification of problems in the Commonwealth Model approach, and the way in which to improve them, the Commonwealth Model remains unlikely to change. This is linked to the

[147] Karl-Heinz Bockstiegel, 'Summary of Discussion in the Third Working Group' in Albert Jan van den Berg (ed.), *Improving the Efficiency of Arbitration Agreements and Awards: 40 Years of Application of the New York Convention* (KluwerArbitration, Kluwer Law International 1999) 436.

[148] To some extent, global recognition and enforcement instruments facilitate this process as they are designed in an open fashion (also referred to as a set of 'minimum standards') and do not prohibit more permissive conduct by enforcing courts or States: see Section 5.4.

[149] Ronald A. Brand, 'Understanding Judgments Recognition' (2015) 40 *North Carolina Journal of International Law and Commercial Regulation* 892.

nature of the Model, being a product of reciprocal enactments in each participant State. Because of this, the process of updating the Model faces similar criticisms to those that arise in the context of the New York Convention (as set out in the immediately preceding section). Cognisant of this difficulty, it has been suggested that attempting to pursue developments via a uniform approach of Commonwealth nations is unlikely to succeed.[150]

Furthermore, because the Commonwealth Model's statutory architecture is enacted directly in national law – and is not, for example, an incidence of a treaty law – it can change in whatever fashion domestic law sees fit. However, in this respect, the common law upon which the Commonwealth Model inherently relies is likely to act as a further constraint on legal development. This is because the common law provides alternative avenues for legal development, perhaps minimising the need for national law legislative changes. In this context, it has been repeatedly stressed that there are 'obvious drawbacks' with the common law approach to recognition and enforcement.[151] Some of these drawbacks include the fact that there is no guidance that arises from the Commonwealth Model or common law principles about the treatment or potential requirement of reciprocity.[152] This can be seen in the significant divergences across common law jurisdictions, most prominently in the discussion of the United States experience set out at Section 4.3.2. This problem is exacerbated by the common law method of legal development, which is based on each common law jurisdiction individually facing, and resolving, a particular case on a particular issue. For example, despite sharing a common law approach to recognition and enforcement, the first time that the Supreme Court of South Dakota considered and provided guidance on the issue of reciprocity within the common law of South Dakota was 'as recently as 2001'.[153]

This leads to a situation where there may be no uniformity of practice across common law States, even within a single federated State such as the United States. As Silberman notes in the context of determining the burden of proof in establishing a ground for refusal, common law approaches within the United States differ on this point, the original statutory codification was silent

[150] Instead, it is suggested, that regional and bilateral arrangements are likely to take precedence: James Spigelman, 'The Hague Choice of Court Convention and International Commercial Litigation' (2010) 9 *The Judicial Review* 391.

[151] Silberman (n 63) 105.

[152] An overview of issues in common law reciprocity, and the possible role of reciprocity as a rationale underlying common law recognition and enforcement, are explored at Section 4.2.2.1.

[153] Silberman (n 63) 105 (fn 20).

on this issue and the 2005 Act expressly imposed the burden on the party resisting recognition.[154] Consequently, even achieving a uniform standard within a federated State such as the United States 'is only wishful thinking'.[155] The arguments for uniformity – explored above in the international context – are only made stronger from a domestic perspective. Perhaps foremost, uniformity allows any judgment creditor to readily assess and understand recognition and enforcement, as opposed to requiring an evaluation of the approaches in or across multiple states. It also minimises other observed risks in recognition and enforcement practice, including the risk of divergent application or interpretation, or the risk of unwarranted 'forum shopping' or 'jurisdictional arbitrage' across states in a federation.[156]

Continuing with the United States as an example of common law practice,[157] we can see the difficulties of developing recognition and enforcement approaches in domestic case law in the common law, and even in domestic legislation that aims to harmonise divergent practice. That is, despite the perceived benefits of a uniform approach, and the promulgation of a series of uniform legislative models and restatements that aim to assist in this process, harmonisation has been elusive.[158] First and foremost this is because model laws – as seen in the parallel context of attempting to modernise aspects of the New York Convention via the UNCITRAL Model Law – are simply that: models. Their promulgation does not ensure their success. Thus, while most states adopted the original 1962 Uniform Act in the United States,[159] in somewhat of an oxymoron, they did not do so in a uniform way.[160] For

[154] ibid. 105 (fn 22).

[155] ibid. 106.

[156] These risks are discussed at Section 6.1.2.

[157] Similar concerns can be seen in other common law states, particularly those that share aspects of federation. This includes, for example, Australia, as discussed in Timothy McEvoy, 'Common Law versus Statutory Approaches to Enforcing Foreign Judgments: The Australian Experience' in Paul B. Stephan (ed.), *Foreign Court Judgments and the United States Legal System* (Brill, 2014). McEvoy suggests, for example, considering reciprocity, that even a federated Australian approach premised in part on creating uniformity in divergent common law practice is unlikely to be uniform across every Australian state: at 181.

[158] These legislative enactments – namely the *Restatement* and two Uniform Acts – are set out at Section 4.3.2.2.

[159] For a list of jurisdictions that have enacted the 1962 Act see: 'Legislative Fact Sheet – Foreign Money Judgments Recognition Act' (no date) <www.uniformlaws.org/LegislativeFactSheet.aspx?title=Foreign%20Money%20Judgments%20Recognition%20Act> accessed 2 August 2021. For the 2005 Act see: 'Legislative Fact Sheet - Foreign-Country Money Judgments Recognition Act' (no date) <www.uniformlaws.org/LegislativeFactSheet.aspx?title=Foreign-Country%20Money%20Judgments%20Recognition%20Act> accessed 29 August 2021.

[160] Silberman (n 63) 106.

example, some states who purport to implement the Uniform Act still provide for reciprocity, although the Uniform Act does not provide for it. As Silberman suggests: 'in short, the Uniform Act is not uniform'.[161] Additionally, it has proved difficult to update provisions based on the Model Law: to wit, more than a decade after the revision of the 1962 Uniform Act, a 2005 Uniform Act that attempts to update this approach still does not have the same reach as the original Act.[162] This raises a critical question in terms of the ability of model laws to assist in allowing for legal development and evolution. In particular, if such lack of uniformity can arise in a federated State that is attempting to promote uniformity via a series of model laws, it is difficult to see how such an approach will allow for legal evolution on a transnational level. Indeed, it is even possible that purported implementations of a model law – in a non-uniform way – may mask divergences in the law.

At the same time, a lack of uniformity is not necessarily problematic. Based on a theory of regulatory competition, it may be more desirable for domestic states to 'compete' on recognition and enforcement, rather than entirely unifying minor divergences in practice. Alférez, for example, argues that a uniform approach is 'not essential' and wipes out any competition between jurisdictions with respect to regulation of private international law (including recognition and enforcement).[163] While it is not necessary to weigh in any further on the relative merits of uniformity for this book, the experience of legal development in the United States suggests, at the least, that the practice of codifying recognition and enforcement practice may not be very successful at – but does not necessarily stifle or override – legal development. This remains particularly relevant, even in the context of global harmonising approaches, as the 'minimum standards' (open) approach allows enforcing courts to give effect to a broader category of foreign decisions (namely, those that fall outside of obligations contained in international recognition and enforcement frameworks).

As the discussion in this chapter has highlighted in the context of uniformity and legal development, there is a need to consider recognition and

[161] ibid.

[162] The 2005 Act has been enacted in less than two dozen states, and only one state has adopted the 2005 Act without first having enacted the 1962 Act.

[163] Francisco J. Garcimartín Alférez, 'Regulatory Competition: A Private International Law Approach' (1999) 8 *European Journal of Law and Economics* 251.

enforcement approaches beyond their domestic implementation. The increasingly 'transnationalised' process of recognition and enforcement has been an ongoing theme throughout the book, and I turn now to Chapter 8, where I formalise this argument and consider critiques of the Judgments Conventions via this transnational frame.

8

Towards 'Transnationalised' Recognition and Enforcement

Recognition and enforcement approaches are best understood and analysed from a transnational perspective.[1] As has been demonstrated throughout the book, although enforcement approaches largely have their own distinct legal instrumentation and spheres of operation, they intersect and overlap in many significant respects. This is because they are drawn from a similar corpus of legal instrumentation and understanding, and developments in each approach have informed, and remain likely to inform, others. Earlier chapters considered some of these developments from a doctrinal perspective. Perhaps most notably, cognisant of the Judgments Project's long negotiating history and carefully crafted compromises, drafters have attempted to replicate or remain consistent with the drafting language of other transnational approaches. For example, the Working Group tasked with drafting the 2019 Convention chose

[1] See, further, Section 1.3.1, which makes explicit the methodological reasons why consideration of transnational legal ordering is beneficial in this context.

to use the 2005 Convention as the 'starting point' – which itself drew heavily on the New York Convention – whereby provisions to be drafted would be based on corresponding provisions in the previous instrument, with any material departure only occurring where there was an identified justification for doing so.[2] The degree of interrelationship between approaches is also seen in any textual departures. Perhaps most notably, the introduction of the qualifier of '*manifestly*' to the traditional public policy ground for refusal employed in the New York Convention was based upon observed problems in the interpretation and application of that Convention: with the modifier first introduced within the Brussels Model (see Section 3.1.3), and then replicated in in the 2005 Convention and the 2019 Convention.[3]

In this chapter, I argue that recognition and enforcement are increasingly transnationalised, drawing upon three broader perspectives. First, I consider how the Brussels Model 'smoothed the way' towards what ultimately became the Judgments Conventions, and the lessons that can be learnt from this experience. Second, I consider how shared transnational experience is reflected in the 'architecture' or design features of recognition and enforcement instruments. The third and final section considers the future of the enforcement gap: an investigation made possible by a broader transnational conception of recognition and enforcement. Cumulatively, these examples demonstrate 'transnationalisation': the increasing porousness of, and fluidity between, transnational recognition enforcement approaches. I turn now to consider the first example of increasing transnationalisation in recognition and enforcement: the way in which the Brussels Model has influenced or impacted upon the Judgments Project.

8.1 ROADBLOCK ... OR SMOOTHING THE WAY? LESSONS FROM THE BRUSSELS MODEL

Recognition and enforcement approaches learn from, and build upon, each other. This is seen perhaps most clearly in the Brussels Model, which has been both championed as a boon and criticised as a bane to efforts to narrow the enforcement gap.[4] On the one hand, it has been suggested that significant

[2] Hague Conference, 'Report of the Fifth Meeting of the Working Group on the Judgments Project (26–31 October 2015) and Proposed Draft Text Resulting from the Meeting' (Preliminary Document, November 2015) 4.

[3] See, further, Section 5.2.2, where it is also noted that the 2019 Convention adds further clarificatory language.

[4] Other examples abound. See, for example, the explicit linkages between the 2017 Commonwealth Model Law, and the Judgments Project: set out at Section 4.1.3.

regional harmonisation efforts that involve 'thorough-going, serious dialogue between the legal traditions' are likely to be 'powerful tool[s] to smooth the way to broader harmonisation'.[5] On the other, and quite to the contrary, it is suggested that the process of regional harmonisation embedded in the Brussels Model may remove the impetus for further cooperation between States interested in promoting the recognition and enforcement of foreign judgments, and thus, that global negotiations and instruments to this end are less likely to succeed. I consider each perspective in turn.

It has been argued that the Brussels Model had, at least historically, 'proved to be incompatible' with the Judgments Project efforts.[6] Widespread implementation of the Brussels Model within EU and non-EU Lugano States was seen as an impediment to reaching global consensus. This is because there was seen to be a 'greatly reduced' incentive for Brussels Model participants, who have already 'solved' the pressing need of judgment recognition and enforcement harmonisation to support their own intra-European trade, to make compromises to reach global agreement.[7] Second, and additionally, it was argued that the interest of Brussels Model participants in negotiating a worldwide convention 'on different terms and with other solutions … inevitably declines' due to the success of the Brussels Model. This is because the sheer amount of harmonisation work that must occur within the EU – an always evolving and ongoing process, as Section 7.2.1 sets out – may leave smaller Member States with 'scant resources to follow global uniform law efforts'.[8] Additionally, States who employ the Brussels Model – as well as the surrounding EU institutions that promote, build on and support it – already have what they consider to be a Model that represents international best practice, and hence, at least from their perspective, it appears logical that this would form the basis for the global instrument status quo. In this way, the starting point of Brussels Model participants – premised on the Model – diverges fundamentally from other States who are likely to reference developments back to their own, often parochial, national laws on recognition and enforcement. Such a view is arguably consistent with the Brussels Model's

[5] José Angelo Estrella Faria, 'Globalisation, Legal Identity and Regional Integration: Complementarity or Conflict?' (2013) 18 *Uniform Law Review* 436.

[6] Arthur von Mehren and Eckart Gottschalk, *Adjudicatory Authority in Private International Law* (The Hague Academy of International Law Monographs 5, Martinus Nijhoff Publishers 2007) 376. See, further: Section 6.2.2, which critiques the underlying ideal of 'mutual trust'; and see Sections 8.1.2 and 8.2.1, which set out different interpretive models and institutions used in the EU, as well as the way that legal development can occur within the EU.

[7] ibid. 375.

[8] Faria (n 5) 436.

lack of implementation by States outside of Europe, despite the ability for third States to accede to it via the Lugano Conventions.[9] Consequently, while the Brussels Model was originally the product of negotiation between the original civil law EC members, at least as it applies to recognition and enforcement, it can be seen to represent a systemised international harmonisation that has the potential to traverse distinctions arising from within either common law or civilian law inspired legal systems.[10]

In these ways, the Brussels Model experience and success have been argued to act as a potential limit on global harmonisation efforts. The negotiating history of the Judgments Project gives some weight to this concern. For example, despite the ardent objections of the United States, the EU championed adopting a 'double' approach to the global instrument design, which ultimately proved unworkable.[11] This led to the failure of negotiations on a broad-based global instrument and the creation of the narrow 2005 Choice of Court Convention. Thus, based on the EU's preference for and belief in the Brussels Model, many years of global negotiations were spent on an ultimately limited endeavour. It was only in 2010 that broad-based global negotiations recommenced – on the basis that negotiations move away from a 'mixed' or 'double' approach (as embodied in the Brussels Model) and back towards a 'single' recognition and enforcement convention. While the EU now accepts that the Brussels Model's closed double approach is unlikely to be replicated globally, it still retains the desire to regulate jurisdiction comprehensively alongside recognition and enforcement: that is, to continue to employ the Brussels Model status quo – simply by different means. To this end, the EU accepted during negotiations towards the 2019 Convention that the 2019 Convention would first be agreed, but on an understanding that negotiations upon an 'additional instrument' on jurisdiction would follow.[12] This has now led to work at the Hague Conference focusing on regulating direct

[9] See Section 3.1.4.

[10] This argument is further strengthened as perhaps the most significant difference between civil law and common law systems – being the use of a *forum non conveniens*-like doctrine – does not arise in a recognition and enforcement context, as this consideration is only relevant for a consideration of direct jurisdiction. See, further, for a critique of the civil versus common law divide in approaches to recognition and enforcement, Section 6.1.

[11] It is, of course, easier with the benefit of hindsight to note that this approach was at the time unlikely to succeed – particularly as few States supported the United States in this hesitation: see, further, Section 2.1.1.

[12] Hague Conference, 'Report of the Fifth Meeting of the Working Group on the Judgments Project (26–31 October 2015) and Proposed Draft Text Resulting from the Meeting' (n 2) 5.

jurisdiction, with a renamed 'Jurisdiction Project'.[13] It is unclear to what extent these efforts will be successful, particularly, as Brand notes, that the entire reason for addressing jurisdiction in the first place was to find a compromise basis upon which to promote judgments recognition and enforcement rules.[14] Nonetheless, what this experience suggests is a generalisable lesson that pre-existing regional harmonisation projects may act to limit the success or appeal of broader global harmonisation efforts that diverge from the pre-existing approach.

Viewed from an alternative perspective, however, the Brussel Model experience can be seen as critical to informing and developing transnational recognition and enforcement. Indeed, the success of the Brussels Model enables it to be uniquely used as a comparator, as one of the 'main sources of reference' in international private law negotiations.[15] Perhaps most notably, over decades, many of the negotiators and negotiations were transferred from the Brussels Model to the Hague Conference, and hence the Brussels Model also informs much of the original drafting history and approach cited in the most recent global negotiations.[16] Thus, the Brussels Model experience, the Model itself and the combination of legal features that it offers have been analysed, adapted or discarded as required. This process has no doubt been assisted by the early task of European legal harmonisation prior to acceptance of the 1968 Brussels Convention, which itself is an ongoing process that both informs and is informed by developments in the field. Extending the argument of Arvind – who considers domestic 'transplants' (or implementation) in the context of the New York Convention – it is not the mere 'transplant' of the Brussels Model experience (or the failure of this process) that is fully dispositive. Instead, what we should focus on is the:[17]

> mix of converging, complementary institutions and parallel motivation … rather than the simple act of adopting the harmonized document or foreign legal rule in question.

[13] 'HCCH | Jurisdiction Project' (no date) <www.hcch.net/en/projects/legislative-projects/jurisdiction-project> accessed 28 September 2021.

[14] Ronald A. Brand, 'Jurisdiction and Judgments Recognition at the Hague Conference: Choices Made, Treaties Completed, and the Path Ahead' [2020] *Netherlands International Law Review* 17.

[15] Faria (n 5) 446.

[16] Hague Conference, 'Explanatory Note Providing Background on the Proposed Draft Text and Identifying Outstanding Issues' (Preliminary Document, April 2016).

[17] T. T. Arvind, 'The "Transplant Effect" in Harmonization' (2010) 59 *International and Comparative Law Quarterly* 88.

In this way, the Brussels Model experience can be seen to serve as a 'shadow progenitor' that informs the development of transnational recognition and enforcement rules and norms.[18] This point is made explicit by the common injunction made during negotiations towards the Judgments Project that drafters should focus on being 'compatible' with existing regional harmonisations,[19] as well as other international recognition and enforcement frameworks, unless there was perceived to be a justified reason for departing.

The Brussels Model is also likely to offer direct lessons – and warnings. One of the primary lessons is that rules for enforcing broad-based judgments are not necessarily inherent to any type of legal system or tradition. It thus may offer insight into ways that States can transition from discrete and divergent national approaches to a harmonised approach.[20] For example, as Section 7.2.1 sets out, the Brussels Model experience suggests that the implementation of harmonised rules relating to recognition and enforcement does not necessarily impede further legal development. Indeed, as the Model continues to evolve, new legal developments can also be reviewed to see what value or lessons they continue to offer. If, for example, the developments lean too far in favour of automation of recognition and enforcement based on unique aspects of the EU's institutional architecture,[21] they can be adapted or discarded. Consequently, it is arguable that European harmonisation (as the Brussels Model attempts) has not 'diminished' nor 'fundamentally challenged' the role of and need for 'truly international' harmonisation, such as that which occurs with respect to recognition and enforcement in the Judgments Project.[22] Such a view is consistent with the EU's approach to actively pursuing and contributing to, over many decades, the furthering of negotiations towards the Judgments Project, as well as being the second party to ratify (and hence bring into force) the 2005 Convention. This pro-harmonisation approach has also carried forward to the 2019 Convention, with the European Commission in July 2021 proposing that the EU sign that Convention.[23] In July 2022, the Council of the European Union

[18] This language is derived from Terence Halliday and Susan Block-Lieb, 'Settling and Concordance: Two Cases in Global Commercial Law' in Gregory Shaffer and Terence Halliday (eds.), *Transnational Legal Orders* (Cambridge Studies in Law and Society, Cambridge University Press 2015) 61.

[19] von Mehren and Gottschalk (n 6) 376.

[20] This is analysed at Section 6.1.

[21] See, for example, developments surrounding the 2004 European Enforcement Order and attempts to reform the Model in the 2012 Brussels Model Recast: Section 7.2.1.1.

[22] Faria (n 5) 436.

[23] European Council, Proposal for a Council Decision on the accession by the European Union to the Convention on the Recognition and Enforcement of Foreign Judgments in Civil or Commercial Matters (Brussels, 16.7.2021, COM(2021) 388 final).

adopted the decision for the EU to accede to the 2019 Judgments Convention. Once a second party ratifies or accedes to it, the Convention will come into force – with immediate application across that second party and all EU member states (except Denmark, which does not automatically participate in EU freedom, security and justice measures). These developments suggest that, despite lacking the mandate or desire to unilaterally compel the liberal treatment of non-Brussels Model foreign judgments, the EU is committed to further promoting the mutual recognition and enforcement of foreign judgments globally. Consequently, the existence and success of the regional harmonisation efforts reinforces the ongoing transnationalisation of recognition and enforcement efforts, and it can be viewed as supporting global harmonisation efforts.

8.2 PRESCRIPTION VERSUS FLEXIBILITY: LESSONS FOR GLOBAL ENFORCEMENT

One of the key examples of learning from transnational experience is to do with the kinds of instrumental features – and their precise combination in the form of an eventual recognition and enforcement approach – that are likely to have greater resonance transnationally. As highlighted in Chapter 5, transnational recognition and enforcement approaches share several key features. For example, most approaches rely upon reciprocity and offer presumptive recognition and enforcement, subject to narrowly construed and strictly limited exceptions. This is so even though different instruments apply to recognition and enforcement, depending on how the decision was originally engendered: that is, via disputants' original choice of forum (either arbitration or a chosen litigation forum) or, absent choice, via a judgment rendered under 'default' jurisdictional rules. At first glance, the degree of convergence is somewhat surprising given that each recognition and enforcement approach is grounded in a different underlying legal instrument, separated in time by many decades, epistemologically constituted by different international actors and stakeholders,[24] overseen by different international governmental and non-governmental organisations[25] and, arguably, aimed at

[24] See, as one critical example, the potential role that plaintiff (trial) lawyers had in the United States, contributing perhaps to the early demise of the 'double' approach for a transnational judgments instrument: Section 2.1.1.3.

[25] As Chapter 2 explores further, UNCITRAL has carriage of the transnational framework for the recognition and enforcement of arbitral awards, and the Hague Conference of the Judgments Convention, with little formal institutional overlap between the two. See for a comparative exposition of how these transnational private law harmonisation bodies operate and the relationships between them: William Brydie-Watson, 'The Three Sisters of Private International Law: An Increasingly Co-operative Family Rather Than Sibling Rivals' in

differing goals.[26] However, the convergence is more understandable when we consider that decades of ongoing negotiations have led to a process of continual refinement and harmonisation of national, regional and international approaches, with a view to decontextualise or delocalise recognition and enforcement rules. This process reflects a form of 'transnationalisation', ostensibly attributable to the need to balance legal certainty and harmonisation with maximising recognition and enforcement prospects of 'properly rendered' foreign decisions.

Designing recognition and enforcement instruments in a transnationalised way is an attempt to better navigate the constant and 'pervasive' tension between prescription, which encourages harmonisation (alternatively referred to as 'certainty' or 'predictability'), and flexibility.[27] On the one hand, States largely share a desire to promote uniformity and certainty by encouraging consistent and explicit rules that facilitate recognition and enforcement of foreign decisions. However, these rules are balanced against overriding State interests that may object to such.[28] A general rule can be posited: the greater extent of prescription in recognition and enforcement instruments, the greater degree of harmonisation of approach to recognition and enforcement. At the same time, however, more prescriptive approaches are necessarily less flexible. Indeed, there is perceived to be a 'natural limit' to the scope of prescriptive rules that impinge on certain State-specific interests,[29] and States are often reluctant to bind themselves to treaty obligations to give effect to foreign decisions that might be objectionable. These tensions are seen to some extent in the minor differences in limitations on the scope of each recognition and enforcement approach. However, they feature most heavily in the heavy debate over direct and indirect jurisdiction, and the allowable bases of jurisdiction in default of party choice, as these bases continue to diverge significantly across national laws. As the Brussels Model experience teaches, the greatest degree of certainty can be achieved where recognition and enforcement approaches are

Thomas John and others (eds.), *The Elgar Companion to the Hague Conference on Private International Law* (Elgar Companions to International Organisations Series, Edward Elgar Publishing 2020).

26 Besides the traditional demarcation between arbitration versus litigation recognition and enforcement, one of the key divergences in the legal instrumentation is the degree to which the legal regime is built upon 'party choice' of a dispute resolution forum: a necessary precondition for the application of the 1958 New York Convention (for choice of arbitration), as well as the 2005 Choice of Court Agreements Convention (for an exclusive choice of court): see, for further exposition of the role of party choice in recognition and enforcement, Section 6.2.1.

27 Ronald A. Brand and Paul Herrup, *The 2005 Hague Convention on Choice of Court Agreements: Commentary and Documents* (Cambridge University Press 2008) 24.

28 ibid.

29 ibid.

aligned or calibrated with jurisdictional approaches, and where each approach is fully exhaustive in its applicability. I turn now to consider how this balance has been struck in various instrumental design decisions.

8.2.1 *Minimum Standards versus Exhaustive Obligation*

There is now a widely shared understanding that open approaches to recognition and enforcement are far more likely to succeed at a global level.[30] It is useful to briefly recall the terminology used, as set out at Section 5.4. In this context, closed approaches are designed to be exhaustive. Where a closed approach is employed, a potential disputant, or a rendering or enforcing court, need only look at the bases set out in the relevant instrument to determine when a foreign decision will be recognised and enforced. This certainty, in turn, minimises the likelihood of an unwarranted merits review of the original judgment. By contrast, open approaches only oblige enforcing courts to give effect to certain foreign decisions but do not restrict the ability of the enforcing court to give effect to foreign decisions outside of instrumental obligations. For this reason, they are also referred to as 'minimum standards' approaches,[31] as allowing for this form of residual discretion leads to a potentially wider ambit of foreign decisions to be recognised and enforced, according to national practice in the enforcing court.[32] Despite the certainty and practical clarity that closed approaches offer, they represent an incongruence: the closed enforcement architecture acts to limit recognition and enforcement (in favour of certainty and predictability) in an instrument designed to promote the very same end.

Two practical difficulties have also been stressed in terms of utilising closed architecture in transnational instruments. First, there is simply the added complexity of attempting to reach consensus, in a fully exhaustive manner, on every single category of foreign decision that is to be given or refused effect. This difficulty was witnessed in the history of the Judgments Project, where negotiating States reached several negotiating impasses, over almost three decades. One of the significant challenges leading to impasse was the sheer difficulty in attempting to exhaustively set out the allowable bases upon which a rendering court can have exercised jurisdiction for the purposes of recognition and enforcement, as well as the required (or excluded) grounds for giving

[30] The way that recognition and enforcement regimes can be categorised in this respect, as open (non-exhaustive) or closed (exhaustive) is set out at Section 5.4.

[31] Section 5.4 sets out these terms and their use in their comparative contexts.

[32] Harold G. Maier, 'Hague Conference Judgments Convention and United States Courts: A Problem and a Possibility' (1997–98) 61 *Albany Law Review* 1207, 1220.

(or refusing to give) effect to a foreign decision.[33] In this context, it has even been suggested that it is 'impossible' to achieve full consensus on exactly which grounds of direct jurisdiction should be permitted or prohibited worldwide.[34]

Second, it has also been argued that a closed approach might not be appropriate in circumstances where it may be difficult to achieve consensus on legal development or revisions to enforcement architecture.[35] Given that, inevitably, time passes and circumstances change, harmonised and codified recognition and enforcement approaches (such as the New York Convention or the Judgments Conventions) face the risk of falling behind commercial, technological or legal best practice. A closed approach may not be ideal in these circumstances because it is necessarily less responsive to 'political evolution'.[36] Given the significant transaction, negotiation and implementation costs of multilateral approaches, re-negotiation is 'rarely practical' in these circumstances.[37] Consider, for example, the situation that arises if a basis for recognising and enforcing a decision is not set out in an exhaustive approach but is later considered worthwhile: allowing decisions to be recognised and enforced requires re-negotiation at the multilateral level. One such situation, which Whincop highlights, is cases involving jurisdiction over the Internet, which the Brussels and Lugano Convention approaches have faced difficulties in responding to, largely due to their closed design.[38] To this end, an open approach based upon minimum standards allows States scope to unilaterally circumvent reliance upon 'anachronistic' fixed standards[39] by allowing residual recourse to national laws that can develop over time.

Approached from the perspective of a defendant (a judgment- or award-debtor), an open approach can nonetheless be seen as 'unfortunate', on the basis that it is contrary to the predictability and certainty in cross-border recognition and enforcement proceedings – particularly with respect to judgments given by a court designated under an exclusive choice-of-court

33 Peter Nygh, 'Towards a Global Judgments Convention: The Proposed New Hague Convention on the Recognition and Enforcement of Judgments in Civil and Commercial Matters' (1997) 7 *Australian International Law Journal* 96, at 102–3. Each of these aspects is set out in its comparative context at Section 5.3.2 and Section 5.2, respectively.

34 Paul Beaumont, 'The Revived Judgments Project in The Hague' (2014) 4 *Nederlands Internationaal Privaatrecht* 533.

35 The relative responsiveness – or degree of legal development likely available for transnational approaches – is set out at Chapter 7.

36 Antonio Perez, 'The International Recognition of Judgments: The Debate between Private and Public Law Solutions' (2001) 19 *Berkeley Journal of International Law* 68.

37 Michael Whincop, 'The Recognition Scene: Game Theoretical Issues in the Recognition of Foreign Judgments' (1999) 23 Melbourne University Law Review 416, s C.

38 ibid.

39 Perez (n 36) 68.

agreement.[40] That is, this residual recourse makes it difficult for a defendant with assets spread over multiple jurisdictions, with a valid ground or grounds to resist recognition and enforcement, to foresee or determine where and whether a judgment that was improperly obtained against them is likely to be enforced. This is because open instruments reflect only a minimum threshold of obligation, and States can – and regularly do – exceed this minimum. Thus, from the perspective of a potential defendant, a court retaining residual discretion – for example, in the ability to give effect to a potentially objectionable foreign judgment – is undoubtedly a negative. However, approached alternatively, from the point of view of a potential plaintiff, an open approach is likely a positive. According to this perspective, the ability for States to give effect to foreign decisions – even where not compelled to do so by any transnational instrument – reflects an even more 'liberal' and 'flexible' approach to recognition and enforcement and allows practical justice to be achieved.

Reflecting the importance of these concerns transnationally, the open design of the New York Convention was considered to be only a 'logical follow-up' to the New York Convention's predecessor,[41] building simply upon the 'experience gained since then in the increased use of arbitration for solution of international business disputes'.[42] As Hamilton and Briner suggest:[43]

> [r]ather than attempting the impossible, the Conference [tasked with drafting the New York Convention Convention] sensibly sought to address the most pressing practical problems experienced by the post war-business world. In so doing, *it took the path of moderation and pragmatism by producing an exhaustive list of basic requirements* for the recognition and enforcement of awards ... This approach may have been modest and cautious, but it was

40 Christian Thiele, 'The Hague Convention on Choice-of-Court Agreements: Was It Worth the Effort?' in Eckart Gottschalk and others (eds.), *Conflict of Laws in a Globalized World* (Cambridge University Press 2007) 81.

41 United Nations, 'Convention on the Execution of Foreign Arbitral Awards' (25 July 1929) (the 'Geneva Convention'). The Geneva Convention entirely ceases to have effect when Contracting States to the New York Convention become bound under that Convention: 'United Nations Convention on the Recognition and Enforcement of Foreign Arbitral Awards' (7 June 1959) Art VII(2).

42 Pieter Sanders, 'The Making of the Convention' in *Enforcing Arbitration Awards under the New York Convention: Experience and Prospects* (United Nations 1999) 3.

43 Virginia Hamilton and Robert Briner, 'The Genesis and General Purpose of the New York Convention' in Emmanuel Gaillard and others (eds.), *Enforcement of Arbitration Agreements and International Arbitral Awards: The New York Convention in Practice* (Cameron May 2008) 20.

above all judicious, for not only did it ensure the effectiveness and acceptability of the Convention but also gave it a far-reaching legacy. (emphasis added)

The Judgments Conventions share this pragmatic approach, as evident from their similar open structure. Seen in this way, transnational recognition and enforcement approaches are not tools of legal harmonisation designed solely to maximise certainty and predictability; instead, their evident purpose is to simultaneously promote recognition and enforcement, at least to an agreed minimum standard. Once a foreign decision reaches this threshold, it should usually be given effect to, as there is little utility in compelling the *refusal* of recognition or enforcement. This allows a wider ambit of foreign decisions to be recognised and enforced where appropriate, according to national practice in the enforcing court.[44] Where the twin aims of promoting recognition and enforcement prospects and harmonisation conflict, open approaches prefer the former. That is, a conscious decision is made across global recognition and enforcement instruments *not* to prefer the interests of harmonisation by sacrificing the potential 'upside': namely, that States may choose to offer more favourable recognition and enforcement than the 'minimum standards' the instrument provides. This is so even though such an approach limits legal harmonisation and, in some instances, may contribute to divergent interpretation and application of recognition and enforcement approaches.[45]

8.2.2 *Decoupling Direct and Indirect Jurisdiction (Recognition and Enforcement)*

A second, but no less important, lesson in the balancing act of transnational enforcement is the conceptual clarity that there is 'no necessary relationship or correlation' between direct and indirect jurisdictional rules.[46] This is so despite the fact that both approaches are often considered, and operate, in tandem, and there may be good policy reasons why a State may wish to align or calibrate its recognition and enforcement approach, including the extent of limitations to refuse recognition and enforcement, with its approach to issues

[44] Maier (n 32), 1220.

[45] See Section 6.2 for a discussion of examples of ways in which these divergent interpretations or applications of transnational instruments may occur, as well as the methods and mechanisms used to control such divergence.

[46] As set out at Section 5.5.

of jurisdiction in the first place.[47] While it is of course possible to control perceived jurisdictional excesses entirely at the enforcement stage, historically at least, attempts to regulate recognition and enforcement have been co-mingled with the pursuit of simultaneously seeking to also regulate direct jurisdiction (a double approach).[48] The most prominent example of this is the Brussels Model and the negotiations towards the broad-based Judgments Project which followed in its footsteps. Additionally, both the New York Convention and the 2005 Convention approach can be described as a limited form of a 'double' convention in that they provide a basis, founded in party choice, for rendering courts to achieve jurisdiction. For these reasons – as Chapter 2 sets out in its historical context – the EU and its Member States promoted a similar form of the Brussels Model's 'double' approach as a workable model for the broad-based instrument in the Judgments Project. While this approach received some support during negotiations over earlier drafts, this attempt to utilise a double approach that exhaustively set out jurisdictional grounds was likely one of the reasons why the 1999 and 2001 broad-based judgments drafts failed.[49]

To the extent that a recognition and enforcement approach is single in nature – omitting consideration of direct jurisdictional grounds – it requires significantly less judicial or political cooperation compared with achieving transnational consensus on additional harmonised grounds of direct jurisdiction (which are often politically sensitive).[50] Such an approach also allows States to achieve greater recognition and enforcement prospects for foreign decisions, even if they themselves employ a more restrictive approach to jurisdiction.[51] At the same time, however, as the enforcing court becomes the sole 'guardian' of improperly granted jurisdiction, indirect controls on jurisdiction via exceptions to recognition and enforcement in the enforcing court become more important.

47 Andrew Dickinson, 'What, If Anything, Can Australia Learn from the EU Experience?' in Andrew Dickinson and Others (eds.), *Australian Private International Law for the 21st Century: Facing Outwards* (Hart 2014) 183.

48 Ralf Michaels, 'Recognition and Enforcement of Foreign Judgments' [2009] *Max Planck Encyclopaedia of Public International Law* para 2.

49 Section 2.1.

50 For further discussion on the relative merits of a 'single' versus 'double' convention see: Arthur von Mehren, 'Recognition and Enforcement of Foreign Judgments: A New Approach for the Hague Conference?' (1994) 57 *Law and Contemporary Problems* at 282 and following.

51 This reflects a similar concern to McEvoy's claim of a 'double standard' in play between jurisdiction and recognition and enforcement: see Section 4.3.1.

8.2.3 A *Third Way? The Use of 'Mixed' Conventions*

One of the most significant conceptual breakthroughs over the Judgments Project was the idea that there does not need to be a binary distinction between open and closed approaches and single and double conventions. This understanding, it is argued, assists in ameliorating the 'fundamental mistake' of scholars – the 'unjustified continued attempt' to use a form of closed double instrument for global negotiations.[52] To some, it came as no surprise that pursuing a closed double approach to broad-based judgments recognition and enforcement proved immensely difficult – if not 'impossible' – globally.[53] This is largely because a closed double approach offers 'little room to manoeuvre' compared to approaches that are either or both single or open in nature.[54]

The response to this understanding was the 'mixed' convention; an approach posited as a way to carve out a diplomatically tractable pathway when Judgments Project negotiations floundered.[55] A 'mixed' convention can come in two forms: either 'classical' or 'flexible'.[56] Both of these variants represent a 'modified form of [the double and single convention] paradigms' and the way they intersect with open or closed approaches.[57] A 'classical mixed' form serves to do so by adding a third, logically distinct, category to the 'excluded' and 'required' jurisdictional bases in double conventions.[58] This third category is referred to in this book as 'permitted' jurisdictional grounds (also termed the 'grey area').[59] This means that the only obligation on national courts is their own national law (which, in many cases, allows the court discretion to recognise or enforce the judgment).[60] In a similar vein, 'flexible mixed conventions' build on this logical structure but do not set out any required positive bases of jurisdiction. Thus, States are not compelled to

52 Yoav Oestreicher, 'The Rise and Fall of the "Mixed" and "Double" Convention Models Regarding Recognition and Enforcement of Foreign Judgments' (2007) 6 *Washington University Global Studies Law Review* 339, 341.

53 See, for example, Beaumont, 'The Revived Judgments Project in The Hague' (n 34) 533.

54 Maier (n 32) 1220.

55 ibid. 1208.

56 Beaumont, 'Hague Choice of Court Agreements Convention 2005 Hague' (n 34) 128:

57 Maier (n 32), 1208.

58 See, for a detailed exposition of these categories of jurisdictional bases: Section 5.3.3.

59 See Prel. Doc. No. 1 of May 1994 – Annotated Checklist of Issues to be Discussed at the Meeting of the Special Commission of June 1994 (Permanent Bureau of the Hague Conference on Private International Law, 1994), at 6–8.

60 Hague Conference, 'Synthesis of the Work of the Special Commission of June 1997 on International Jurisdiction and the Effects of Foreign Judgments in Civil and Commercial Matters' (Preliminary Document, November 1997).

recognise or enforce *any* foreign decisions; the only relevant list for a flexible mixed convention is thus the excluded list of jurisdictional grounds. Everything else remains in the 'permitted' category and subject to the national law of the enforcing court. Either option offers comfort to negotiating parties concerned that a convention will lead to the recognition and enforcement of all manner of exorbitant decisions – as these can form part of the excluded list. This approach also avoids the analytical and negotiating complexity and difficulty of establishing a required list on an exhaustive basis.

The mixed convention came to the fore in the creation of the 2005 Convention. The 2005 Convention – like the New York Convention before it – can be described as mixed, as it adopts a double format but in an open fashion. Both Conventions are double in nature, as they regulate both aspects of direct jurisdiction (when the rendering fora can claim jurisdiction – based upon an exclusive choice of court or a written arbitration agreement) and indirect jurisdiction (the rules for recognition and enforcement). They are also broadly open in nature – diverging from the traditional approach seen in the Brussels Model – as they act almost exclusively as a minimum 'floor' on recognition and enforcement rules.[61] Nonetheless, even the more limited 'mixed' form used in the 2005 Convention proved difficult as a basis for reaching consensus in the broad-based Judgments Project efforts, without the singular head of party autonomy to ground negotiations around jurisdiction. Instead, the 2019 Convention reverts back, largely, to an open and single approach, circling back to the approach of the failed 1971 Convention, which was designed on this basis.[62]

8.2.4 *Limited Residual Recourse to National Law*

The final lesson gleaned from years of increasingly transnationalised conceptions of recognition and enforcement is the surprisingly circumspect exercise of residual recourse to national law (alternatively referred to as a 'discretion').

61 In the 2005 Convention, the floor is established in Article 8, which provides that 'recognition or enforcement may be refused only on the grounds specified in this Convention'. Brand and Herrup also refer to a 'ceiling' on these rules: see further, Brand and Herrup (n 27) 23. However, this is limited to a constraint that '[a] judgment shall be recognised only if it has effect in the State of origin, and shall be enforced only if it is enforceable in the State of origin' (Art 8 (4)); implementing enforcing courts still retain residual discretion to give effect to a foreign judgment that activates a ground for refusal. See, further, Section 8.2.1.

62 See Section 2.1.1.1, where use of the single approach for broad-based judgments recognition and enforcement harmonisation efforts, including in the historical context of the 1971 Convention, is set out.

Although such recourse to national law remains widely available under open transnational approaches, it is likely to be carefully constrained and judiciously exercised. This is seen in the practical experience of other enforcement regimes, the lessons of which are likely to prove instructive for the Judgments Conventions. On one end of the spectrum, the Brussels Model – in line with the civil law's preference for minimal judicial discretion, and the Model's closed nature and emphasis on certainty and predictability – compels non-recognition in all cases where a ground for refusal exists. Taking the 2012 Recast as an example of this practice, Art 45 ('Refusal of recognition') and Art 46 ('Refusal of enforcement') both mandatorily provide that the enforcing court 'shall' refuse to give effect to a foreign decision in these circumstances. If recognition alone is sought, it must be denied if one or more of the grounds for refusal provided are satisfied. If enforcement is sought, a more expansive concept applies whereby:[63]

> A party challenging the enforcement of a judgment given in another Member State should, to the extent possible and in accordance with the legal system of the Member State addressed, be able to invoke, in the same procedure, in addition to the grounds for refusal provided for in this Regulation, the grounds for refusal available under national law and within the time-limits laid down in that law.

In either situation, such a refusal is mandatory and not a matter for the discretion of the enforcing court. The Commonwealth Model is similar in approach. For example, the 1933 Act provides, in s 4, that registration 'shall' be set aside if an enumerated ground for refusal is found.[64] A similar approach applies under the proposed 2017 Commonwealth Model Law, whereby a foreign judgment 'is not to be recognised' – recognition, of course, being a pre-condition to enforcement in the Commonwealth Model – where a ground for refusal exists.[65]

Efforts to codify common law recognition and enforcement in the United States demonstrate a variety of different common law approaches to this question of residual recourse. Depending on the ground for refusal that is enlivened, some states compel non-recognition, while others allow enforcing courts discretion to continue to recognise the judgment. As section 482 of the Restatement neatly summarises, this is said to be because certain grounds for

[63] Preamble (30), 2012 Brussels Recast.

[64] Albeit, one of these factors is left to the discretion of the enforcing court, in that an enforcing court is not compelled to (*may*) set aside, if the matter had already been finally and conclusively determined before being heard by the rendering court: s 4(1)(b).

[65] See Section 4.1.3.

refusal are considered to be so contrary to common law recognition and enforcement practice that recognition must be refused if these grounds are enlivened.[66] However, the same section also provides a list of discretionary grounds for non-recognition, where the enforcing court is allowed discretion to recognise a foreign judgment even if a ground for refusal is proven. This is because the United States' approach to recognition and enforcement relies ultimately upon concepts of comity built upon discretion to give effect to foreign laws and judgments.[67] As a result, while particularly egregious breaches of grounds for refusal are likely to receive the same treatment across the common law, this remains, technically, a discretionary matter. The approach in the Uniform Acts is similar. Much like the open nature of global approaches to recognition and enforcement, the 1962 Act allows for residual recourse: it simply provides that a foreign judgment is not conclusive if such a ground exists, and the Uniform Act provisions thus do not apply to it.[68] As a result, the saving provision activates, and the question of recognition and enforcement falls to be decided by the common law in that state, as summarised in the Restatement.[69]

An update to the original 1962 Uniform Act, the 2005 Uniform Act, aims to limit such residual recourse, and instead expressly codifies these grounds and their nature as mandatory or discretionary, in line with the approach of the Restatement.[70] Yet, this approach is itself not uniform in implementation. For example, three states have modified the Uniform Act's approach in their enactments, and make all exceptions mandatory – that is, the enforcing court has no discretion to recognise a judgment if any of the enumerated grounds for refusal exists. Another state, North Carolina, modifies the Uniform Act's permissive exceptions into presumptive exceptions, meaning that non-recognition is the default rule, but judicial discretion can overcome this rule

66 These exceptions, like almost all aspects of United States recognition practice, ultimately stem from the common law, particularly as expressed by Justice Gray in *Hilton* v. *Guyot* 159 US 113 (1895). In any event, the mandatory grounds are where: (a) 'the judgment was rendered under a judicial system that does not provide impartial tribunals or procedures compatible with due process of law' and (b) 'the court that rendered the judgment did not have jurisdiction over the defendant . . . '.

67 Albeit the reasons for giving effect to a foreign judgment can be broader than this: see Section 4.2.2.1.

68 §§2–4 of the 'Legislative Fact Sheet - Foreign-Country Money Judgments Recognition Act' (no date) <www.uniformlaws.org/LegislativeFactSheet.aspx?title=Foreign-Country%20Money%20Judgments%20Recognition%20Act> accessed 29 August 2021.

69 ibid. §8.

70 §4(b) sets out the mandatory grounds (substantially the same as those under the Restatement) and for the discretionary grounds, see §4(c).

where 'reasonable under the circumstances'. It is unclear what this adds to the common law jurist's understanding of their role, as courts already face an obligation (or perhaps an expectation) that they exercise their discretion reasonably and not capriciously. While these variations on the extent of residual discretion allocated to the enforcing court do detract from certainty and predictability in some senses, the specific legislative enactments on this point (departing from the Uniform Act approaches) suggest that treating grounds of refusal as mandatory or discretionary is an explicit policy choice of states. This allows for greater diversity and flexibility between common law approaches, often, however, arising at the expense of certainty and flexibility.

Building on open instrumental design, all of the global approaches analysed in this book allow for residual recourse to national law, as they provide only that 'recognition and enforcement *may* be refused' if a ground for refusal exists.[71] The interesting question that then arises is: what are the contours of this discretion? That is, what is an enforcing court likely to do where it is not compelled to a course of action by any instrumental obligations? It has been suggested that 'discretion' in this context is not – and should not be – unfettered or 'open-ended' in favour of promoting recognition and enforcement in all cases.[72] Instead, discretion granted can be seen as a 'formal' discretion, as most enforcing courts apply an established framework of principles to discretionary decisions.[73] These principles of when to refuse recognition and enforcement are themselves centred on the same core of objectionable bases – largely those that offend procedural fairness or natural justice – as Section 5.2.2 sets out. Viewed from this perspective, an instrumental analysis highlighting a 'formal' legal discretion serves in this instance to mask an established body of rules or norms that govern (or are likely to govern) what otherwise appears to be an unbounded discretionary decision.[74]

In this vein, as Hill argues in the context of the New York Convention, despite the appearance of discretion, if a ground for refusal is established, 'enforcement will be (and should be) refused'.[75] This is largely because if the enforcing court is complying with the 'spirit and intent' of a global recognition

71 See, in the context of 2005 Convention, Brand and Herrup (n 27) 110, who note that the use of the permissive language of 'may' allows this (Art 9 of the 2005 Convention). This is consistent with the approach of the 2019 Convention (Art 7(1)), as well Art V of the New York Convention.

72 Jonathan Hill, 'The Exercise of Judicial Discretion in Relation to Applications to Enforce Arbitral Awards under the New York Convention 1958' (2016) 36 *Oxford Journal of Legal Studies* 304, 306.

73 ibid.

74 ibid.

75 ibid. 333.

and enforcement regime, it will only be led to refuse recognition or enforcement for 'serious' (or 'non-trivial') breaches of a ground of refusal. This is equivalent to reading in an instrumental obligation that the grounds for refusal are to be exercised 'consonant with international standards': that is, if a decision is able to be set aside on a ground not ordinarily recognised in international practice, or based on an 'intolerable criterion', the enforcing court should exercise its discretion to enforce.[76] However, in all other cases, the court should *not* exercise its discretion to give residual effect to a foreign decision. Consequently, warnings of the risks of the 'obvious danger' to harmonisation[77] that residual recourse to national law may engender (based upon uncertainty or a lack of uniformity in interpretation) are likely tempered by the judicious exercise of any such discretion. This could be argued to be an attempt by enforcing courts to remain 'faithful' to the text and object of such instruments by refusing enforcement where serious breaches have occurred (in line with the protective function of the enforcing court in the administration of justice).[78] At the same time, it could also be criticised in that it conflicts with the plain text of the provisions that confer a discretion on courts to enforce even when a ground for refusal is present. Yet, whether this development is positive depends upon a broader conception of the value of certainty versus flexibility in recognition and enforcement. It is, of course, too early to tell what the experience with the Judgments Conventions will bring; but it is nonetheless apparent that this limited recourse is consistent with the experience of both the New York Convention and the statutorisation of common law approaches in the United States. Given that there has been no indication of an intended departure from the New York Convention's approach, and both Hague Conference instruments largely adopt an open approach, this means that the nature of residual recourse is likely to remain circumspect.

8.3 THE TRANSNATIONAL ORDERING OF RECOGNITION AND ENFORCEMENT

It is increasingly important that recognition and enforcement approaches are considered from a transnational basis. This is so despite the complex and oft

[76] Jan Paulsson, 'Awards Set Aside at the Place of Arbitration' in *Enforcing Arbitration Awards under the New York Convention: Experience and Prospects* (United Nations 1999) 26.

[77] Paulsson makes these comments in the context of a consideration of the ability of an enforcing court to either give, or refuse to give, effect to an award set aside at the place of arbitration: ibid. 25.

[78] Protecting both defendants and the administration of justice in the enforcing jurisdiction from giving support to egregious breaches of the rendering fora: see further Section 4.2.3.2.

parochial drivers or policies underlying the giving effect to foreign decisions. As will be recalled from the discussion in relation to the common law at Section 4.2, the reasons for giving effect to foreign decisions can be categorised as a mix of particulars relating to the private rights of disputants and their ability to achieve practical justice, through to broader considerations about the administration of justice, and even wider political and commercial considerations, encompassing concepts of sovereignty, comity, reciprocity and commercial interest.[79] As I have argued throughout this book – highlighted in particular in the introductory material at Section 1.3.1 – each global or regional recognition and enforcement approach, built upon its own distinct and authoritative legal instrumentation, constitutes a unique transnational legal order. This is because these approaches ultimately aim to order the domestic recognition and enforcement practice of enforcing courts in their respective domains, via the assistance of an authoritative transnational body (e.g., UNCITRAL in the case of arbitral awards, the Hague Conference for judgments).[80] The primary aim of these transnational legal orders is to overcome the domestic ordering of recognition and enforcement by harmonising and promoting recognition and enforcement on a transnational level.

This is not merely an abstract or academic exercise; indeed, the desire for transnational harmonisation reflects a long-held concern grounded in pragmatism, as expressed by Lorenzen in the early twentieth century:

> As long as each country feels at heart that its own law is the best in the world, and that justice can be secured only in accordance with its rules, there is little hope of any real progress. As the solidarity of nations comes more into evidence and the justice of enforcing foreign laws under given circumstances becomes more apparent, the different systems will gradually tend towards greater uniformity.[81]

As Chapter 5 explored in a comparative context, the way that recognition and enforcement approaches impose such orders differs, and these approaches draw heavily for inspiration upon each other. The primary mode of ordering in this context is via international instrument: treaties, on a global level, which activate via direct or indirect incorporation into national law by governments

[79] HL Ho, 'Policies Underlying the Enforcement of Foreign Commercial Judgments' (1997) 46 *The International and Comparative Law Quarterly* 444.

[80] Terence Halliday and Susan Block-Lieb, 'Settling and Concordance: Two Cases in Global Commercial Law' in Gregory Shaffer and Terence Halliday (eds.), *Transnational Legal Orders* (Cambridge Studies in Law and Society, Cambridge University Press 2015) 20.

[81] Ernest Lorenzen, 'Huber's De Conflictu Legum' (1919) 13 *Illinois Law Review* 400.

or legislatures.[82] Other forms of harmonisation relied upon range from broad uniformity or 'spirit and intent' provisions through to persuasive or even binding decisions of authoritative bodies (in some instances, arising even absent a statutory or treaty-based directive).[83] For these reasons, understanding the nature and operation of recognition and enforcement requires not just an appreciation of the instruments and provisions surrounding transnational harmonisation efforts but also calls for further inquiry into how such 'globalisms' within those instruments are likely to be localised.[84]

8.3.1 *The Future of the Enforcement Gap*

A transnational perspective can also shed light on the likely future of the enforcement gap. It is my view – informed by the analysis in this book – that the enforcement gap between foreign decisions is likely to narrow on a transnational level over the coming decades due to the adoption of the Judgments Conventions. This is perhaps a bold prediction to make, given the rising tide of deglobalisation stemming from nationalist politics and the COVID-19 pandemic. However, as I discuss further, initial signs are positive, suggesting that it is likely that both Judgments Conventions will come into force between certain States. The consequences are likely to be significant; particularly, as I argue at Section 5.3.1, doing so may not only narrow but in some narrow respect 'flip' the gap between foreign awards and judgments in certain respects.

The ordering of recognition and enforcement in relation to awards, pursuant to the New York Convention, remains the high point of transnational authoritativeness.[85] Describing it as such is not intended to discount issues observed in its uniform application and interpretation,[86] but to position these

[82] For a clear exposition of the 'monist' (direct) and the 'dualist' (indirect) approaches to treaty obligations, see David Sloss, *The Role of Domestic Courts in Treaty Enforcement: A Comparative Study* (Cambridge University Press 2009) 6–8.

[83] The precise ways in which uniform and autonomous interpretation of recognition and enforcement instruments is encouraged, and may contribute to harmonisation efforts, is explored in Section 7.1.

[84] Gregory Shaffer, 'Transnational Legal Ordering and State Change' in Gregory Shaffer (ed.), *Transnational Legal Ordering and State Change* (Cambridge Studies in Law and Society, Cambridge University Press 2012) 47.

[85] For example, Brand and Herrup, in the context of considering the 2005 Convention, note that there is 'no question' that there is an effective regime governing international arbitration (including the recognition and enforcement of foreign arbitral awards): Brand and Herrup (n 27) 23.

[86] See Sections 7.1.1 and 8.3.2, for further discussion of issues in the application of the New York Convention.

concerns within the impact of the Convention beyond parochial implementation issues. Reference, for example, can be had to the wide dissemination of the New York Convention approach globally, so much so that it forms the 'bedrock' of international arbitration. It is not just the doctrinal approach contained in the Convention that makes this so. Instead, part of this categorisation depends on the pro-recognition and enforcement 'spirit' or norms of the Convention, which are, for the most part, shared across both academic sources (which adopt a broadly consistent viewpoint) and national enforcing courts.[87] Recourse to such norms is evident not only in the application of the Convention but are commonly referenced when calls to revisit, modernise or improve the New York Convention approach are rebuffed on the basis of the clear and widespread acceptance of the approach espoused within it.[88] The same is true of the Brussels Model approach, which due in particular to European integration is buttressed in its authoritativeness and legitimacy by a range of key institutions such as the CJEU.[89]

By contrast, the recognition and enforcement of foreign judgments globally can, at best, only be said to represent a partial and incomplete form of ordering. This is so despite the longstanding access to justice and economic rationales underpinning harmonisation, as well as the Judgments Conventions sharing many doctrinal and instrumental features with other transnational approaches, as set out in Chapter 5. However, until and unless the 2005 Convention achieves greater adoption internationally – and until the 2019 Convention comes into force and achieves widespread adoption – there is unlikely to be the same degree of 'coherence, institutionalization, and impact' of these approaches, on either a transnational or domestic level.[90] This process of promoting judgments enforcement ordering transnationally is nonetheless well underway, given the impetus and stamp of authority given to recognition and enforcement norms by promulgation in the form of the Judgments Conventions: an external manifestation of international consensus on an agreeable way to promote recognition and enforcement. Consequently, while the constituent rules and norms of recognition and enforcement are made clear – as the transnational legal instrumentation is largely settled – they

87 See Section 2.2.1.

88 See, for example, Emmanuel Gaillard, 'Enforcement of Awards Set Aside in the Country of Origin: The French Experience' in Albert Jan van den Berg (ed.), *Improving the Efficiency of Arbitration Agreements and Awards: 40 years of Application of the New York Convention* (KluwerArbitration, Kluwer Law International 1999).

89 See, for a critical overview of this argument: Section 7.1.2.

90 Halliday and Block-Lieb (n 80) 32.

remain contingent. This contingency depends not just upon widespread international implementation but also the existence of sufficient case law and literature to support a uniform and autonomous application and interpretation of the provisions of the Judgments Conventions.

Nonetheless, given the settling of the Judgments Conventions architecture transnationally, the first and most challenging question for now is whether States will, or should, give effect to the Judgments Conventions. Answering this question is not assisted by the fact that States are not directly incentivised to engage in recognition and enforcement treaties as the consequences of non-enforcement are borne by private parties.[91] Yet much harmonisation work has taken place over recent decades,[92] and a range of States have considered, or are considering, whether it is in their national interest to give effect to the Conventions. This national interest consideration has occurred with respect to the States or regional groupings (namely, the EU) that have acceded to the 2005 Convention. Other States are considering the same question of whether to join the 2005 Convention – and government reports conclude that they should, although there seems to be a lack of clear political will to do so.[93] Accession to the 2005 Convention is made more attractive to other States by its implementation across the key trading jurisdictions of the EU and the UK. The 2005 Convention is likely to also receive a renewed impetus with the rise of specialised international commercial courts, which have recently launched in a range of jurisdictions including Singapore, the Netherlands and China.[94] Giving effect to the 2005 Convention may also go some way in responding to emerging criticisms of the consequences on civil litigation arising due to the dominance of international commercial arbitration,[95] including the idea that

[91] Jürgen Basedow, 'The Hague Conference and the Future of Private International Law – A Jubilee Speech' (2018) 82 *Rabel Journal of Comparative and International Private Law* 922, 929.

[92] These efforts include the 2017 Commonwealth Model Law, as well as a series of 'parallel regional developments' with respect to recognition and enforcement, at the bilateral and multilateral level, which are designed to enhance judicial cooperation: Richard Garnett, 'The Judgments Project: Fulfilling Assers Dream of Free-Flowing Judgments' [2020] *The Elgar Companion to the Hague Conference on Private International Law*.

[93] See, for example, Australia, where a national interest analysis concluded in 2016 that the 2005 Convention should be acceded to; however, no action has since been taken in this respect: Australian National Interest Analysis [2016] ATNIA 7 on Australia's Accession to the Convention on Choice of Court Agreements.

[94] These courts, and their genesis, are explored in Pamela Bookman, 'The Adjudication Business' (2019) 45 *Yale Journal of International Law* 227.

[95] See the criticisms outlined at Chapter 1, n 22. The general lack of publicly available arbitral decisions has also been said to permit parties to 'shroud' matters, which 'perpetuates public ignorance of continuing hazards, systemic problems, or public needs': Laurie Dore, 'Public

it has likely limited the development of commercial law within the common law[96] or perhaps made moribund the common law system of precedent.[97]

Without the widely agreed jurisdictional head of party autonomy, implementation of the 2019 Convention is more controversial. This is because the jurisdictional bases contained within are far less accepted or harmonised within existing national laws than the principle of party autonomy enshrined in the 2005 Convention and the New York Convention.[98] Nonetheless, the 2019 Convention has had the benefit of almost three decades of direct reflection on a diverse variety of recognition and enforcement experiences worldwide. As Chapter 6 makes clear, many of the perceived hurdles arising from different legal traditions and approaches have been reconciled in the judgments field.[99] Additionally, much work has also occurred that serves to normalise harmonised jurisdictional bases, including through regional efforts in the Brussels Model, and at the Commonwealth level in the context of the 2017 Model Law. There are no doubt matters omitted from the Convention that will require interpretation, either of terms that were intentionally omitted or perhaps for problems yet to arise.[100] However, decades of patient negotiation transnationally, with the benefit of observing practice experience in other recognition and enforcement approaches, has led to a widely acceptable judgments enforcement architecture in the Judgments Conventions.

As is often the case – and indeed, was the case with the 2005 Convention – the EU's accession to the 2019 means that it is likely to again play an outsized role in incentivising other parties to join the Convention. Recent signs are positive, with the Council of the European Union, in July 2022, adopting a proposal for the EU to accede to the 2019 Convention.[101] The modelling behind the underlying proposal to accede to the 2019 Convention was built on

Courts versus Private Justice: It's Time to Let Some Sun Shine in on Alternative Dispute Resolution' (2006) 81 *Chicago-Kent Law Review* 463, 487.

96 Lord Chief Justice of England and Wales (Lord Thomas), 'Developing Commercial Law through the Courts: Rebalancing the Relationship between the Courts and Arbitration' (The Bailii Lecture 2016, 9 March 2016) 22.

97 Myriam Gilles, 'The Day Doctrine Died: Private Arbitration and the End of Law' (2016) 2016 *University of Illinois Law Review* 54.

98 Note, however, the criticisms of the 2005 Convention's approach to party autonomy, set out at Section 8.3.2.

99 See Section 6.1.2, which sets out the way that the ongoing concerns, negotiated since the early 2000s, were addressed in the context of the Judgments Project.

100 See, for example, the exploration of 'summary' judgments in *Ermgassen & Co Ltd* v. *Sixcap Financials Pte Ltd* [2018] SGHCR 8.

101 Council of the European Union, 'Convention on the recognition of judgements: Council adopts decision on EU accession' (Press release, 12 July 2022).

a 'working assumption' that eight non-EU countries, many of whom were active in negotiations towards the 2019 Convention, would also do so: Australia, Argentina, Brazil, Canada, China, Japan, South Korea and the United States of America. The direct benefits that are modelled to flow from the 2019 Convention are positive but comparatively minor (being between 1–2.6 million euro in reduced enforcement costs, and a reduction of three months in the length of proceedings, between 2022–2026). However, the greatest benefits are likely to flow from a source that is much more challenging to estimate in monetary terms: the freer circulation of judgments promoting confidence in international trade and investment. Nevertheless, as the following section elaborates, there are still some concerns about the operation of the Judgments Instruments. For example, and despite the EU's subsequent accession to the 2019 Convention, a 2018 Report commissioned by the European Parliament concluded that there were 'some doubts' about whether the 2019 Convention 'would be worth signing and ratifying', based upon its limited scope and a perception that, like the 2005 Convention to date, it may not face significant ratification prospects by third States.[102]

8.3.2 *One Step Forward . . . Two Steps Back?*

Although the Judgments Conventions' architecture has now been concluded, this does not mean that recognition and enforcement is on a pathway to inevitable harmonisation. Agreement on the architecture does suggest that it is possible, in theory at least, to overcome the 'diversity of procedural and substantive laws and legal cultures' that have been argued to make harmonisation unlikely.[103] Yet, perhaps most critically, serious arguments have arisen that one or more of the Judgments Conventions should not be implemented, given perceived flaws in their structure and approach. A longstanding criticism of the Judgments Project, and hence the resulting Judgments Conventions, is that treaty-based approaches are likely to prove 'ineffective' in promoting trade-related goals.[104] The reason for this, it is suggested, is that treaties, by design,

[102] European Parliament (Policy Department for Citizens' Rights and Constitutional Affairs), 'The Hague Conference on Private International Law "Judgments Convention"' (April 2018) at 38.

[103] James Spigelman, 'Transaction Costs and International Litigation' (2006) 80 *Australian Law Journal* 450. See further, Chapter 6 for a consideration of the way in which divergent legal traditions and approaches, and rationales underlying recognition and enforcement, have been overcome.

[104] Perez (n 36) 68.

preclude the ongoing legal mutation required to effectively respond to trade-related issues.[105] As Perez notes:[106]

> the central objection is that a Hague Treaty cannot serve effectively as a vehicle for political evolution. Once it is concluded, a Hague Convention would create permanent sets of proponents and opponents. If such a multilateral treaty ever did enter into force, changes in the political basis for supporting the tradeoff between trade and non-trade values would undercut support for the rules of the treaty reflecting the political consensus at the Hague Conference. Multilateral treaties of this kind are rarely, if ever, amended. Without an effective formal mechanism to adapt the treaty to respond to changing political views, the treaty would become anachronistic. It might be honored in the breach, through more frequent use of the escape devices that would inevitably be built into it.

To this end, Perez argues that the lingo and process of private international law harmonisation masks 'profound' value conflicts that cannot readily be harmonised and are better addressable via multilateral trade negotiations.[107] It is clear that the relationship between private international law and international trade regimes is under-explored – and interactions between the two fields have been criticised on the basis that representatives of both 'act like strangers in the night'.[108] This is no doubt true. However, transnational experience with the New York Convention is likely to offer some comfort. It assists to recall the deeply embedded or entrenched status of the New York Convention globally.[109] The Convention's treaty status has not impacted its reach; rather, it has led to a widespread acceptance that there is little room to further improve enforcement prospects transnationally. As set out at Section 7.2.2.1, strong arguments have been made that there is 'no need' to revise the Convention, as its architecture has proved enduring in responding to all sorts of recognition and enforcement issues since its adoption in 1958. Part of this is due to the forward-looking drafting that occurred, but, perhaps more significantly, due to the 'minimum standards' approach to recognition and enforcement, which is discussed at Section 8.2.1. In brief, allowing States to adopt a more liberal approach to recognition and enforcement goes a long way to overcoming concerns that arise due to the static nature of treaty-based architecture. For

[105] ibid.
[106] ibid.
[107] ibid. 45.
[108] Basedow (n 92) 928.
[109] See Section 2.2.

these reasons, there is little reason to believe that the form of the Judgments Conventions will limit their adoption.

Perhaps more significantly, a recent line of critique has also emerged in a journal article and series of blog posts by Gary Born, who argues that there are 'grave and fundamental defects' in the 2005 Convention, such that it is 'unsuitable for ratification'.[110] I disagree, as will become apparent from the remainder of this section. To aide analysis here, I will first sketch Born's arguments with respect to recognition and enforcement provisions. They are two-fold. First, Born argues that the Convention 'ignores the realities of endemic corruption' in many judicial systems, as well as the inexperience and lack of independence of judges in many judicial systems.[111] At the core of these concerns is that in arbitration parties have autonomy to select their decision makers, and the procedures that they face. This is contrasted to the fact that judges are appointed without party input, even in instances where a particular court is chosen; meaning that parties have limited ability to agitate for judges that are independent or for the application of fair and appropriate procedures (presuming, in many instances, perhaps unfairly, that certain courts may not adopt fair and appropriate procedures by default). As Born notes, this is particularly problematic as empirical evidence demonstrates that judicial standards in relation to integrity, independence and competence are often lacking in many legal systems.

Born's second argument is that procedural fairness and party autonomy protections are eroded in the 2005 Convention, compared to the New York Convention. This is because the 2005 Convention serves to grant the putatively chosen court the *sole* authority to decide on validity, without the possibility that this be reviewed in recognition and enforcement proceedings. This contrasts with the New York Convention, which provides greater avenues to refuse enforcement: for example, if an award is invalid or the arbitrator has

[110] Gary Born, 'The Hague Convention on Choice of Court Agreements: A Critical Assessment' (2021) 169 University of Pennsylvania Law Review 2079, 2126. Gary B. Born, 'Why States Should Not Ratify, and Should Instead Denounce, the Hague Choice-Of-Court Agreements Convention' (Parts I, II and II) and 'Why it is Especially Important that States Not Ratify the Hague Choice of Court Agreements Convention' (Part I and II) (*Kluwer Arbitration Blog*, 2021). Each post or article is distinct, but I refer to them in the aggregate to better capture the core of Born's concerns (however, specific quotations are referenced to the publication they are made in). Although the criticisms are not directed to the 2019 Convention, some of the critique will have similar, if not greater, force in the context of that Convention (relying, as it does, on the operation of default jurisdictional rules, rather than party selection of forum).

[111] ibid.

exceeded the scope of their authority.[112] This task is, arguably, one that the enforcing court often engages in on a *de novo* basis;[113] providing further protections against the enforcement of an objectionable award. The inevitable consequence of the 2005 Convention's removal of these further review options is that the putatively chosen court's status is elevated, as it is the sole controller of the validity, scope and width of the choice of forum agreement; meaning that there is indeed the potential in exceptional cases for courts to exceed their authority in this respect. However it is an equally valid consideration that States negotiating or implementing the 2005 Convention may have preferred to defer to other judiciaries for political or legal reasons, and/or to nonetheless prefer clear rules in this respect: providing certainty by allowing only a singular determination to be made, constraining any opportunistic review (and its associated costs) by subsequent judicial consideration.

At the same time, it is somewhat surprising that Born elevates the reviewability of awards by national courts to such a level of importance, particularly given that he simultaneously stresses the significant issues with the independence, integrity and competence of courts in many jurisdictions. These concerns do not seem to permeate into any consideration of the role of the enforcing court. Under the systemic approach Born calls for, if one legal system is 'found' to be corrupt, biased, incompetent, etc, it would logically follow that its enforcement courts would also be so impugned. This would cause great difficulty for the operation of the New York Convention (or any other recognition and enforcement regime) in those jurisdictions, and impede the ready acceptance of final and binding decisions. This highlights the importance of the arguments that immediately follow: deeming entire legal systems unsatisfactory is anathema not only to the interests of private disputants, but also to conceptions of comity and international trade, and, hence, likely to be unworkable on a transnational level.

Born also argues that procedural fairness or natural justice concerns are not sufficiently dealt with in the 2005 Convention, particularly because procedural fairness is largely subsumed into the broader ground of refusal in public

112 Grounds for refusal, including this contrast, are analysed in a comparative fashion at Section 5.2.2.

113 See, for example, Jason Yackee, 'A Matter of Good Form: The (Downsized) Hague Judgments Convention and Conditions of Formal Validity for the Enforcement of Forum Selection Agreements' (2003) 53(3) *Duke Law Journal* 1179, 1178, who at the time posed the question: 'Can the Hague Judgments Convention be saved through radical downsizing?' The answer to this question is still ambiguous: the 2005 Convention is still not widely ratified or acceded to; yet, if repurposing the Convention to a radically more limited purpose counts as 'saving', perhaps that has occurred.

policy, and enforcing courts are prohibited under the 2005 Convention from inquiring into the fairness and independence of the legal system overall (as opposed to the specific proceedings leading to the judgment). Born notes that it is difficult for individual parties to prove bias, fraud or corruption in the instant proceedings, and so it should be possible to impugn a foreign judgment based on the wider perception or behaviour of the court system from which the judgment originated. The same argument, that it is difficult to prove bias, fraud or corruption in the instant case, can, of course, be extended to arbitral tribunals – particularly where arbitrators face a commercial imperative to attract disputants and may not face as stringent legal or ethical obligations as a judge's obligations deriving from their judicial appointment. Indeed, judges with a busy workload and docket usually face pressures to dispose of cases, rather than to *attract* cases, as distinct from arbitrators whose remuneration depends upon this attraction, often on a repeat basis.[114] It also seems somewhat paradoxical that the mere fact that data can readily be generated about outcomes and perceived or actual corruption, lack of independence or concerns about competence, due to the 'open' nature of most judicial systems – including the standing nature of judicial organs, and the transparency that accompanies such proceedings, with reasons for decision usually made publicly available – is used to support an argument that an entirely private form of dispute resolution, which is usually closed to the public and does not generate such data, should be preferred.

The stridency of Born's objections to the 2005 Convention likely arises because – as noted in the discussion of the different methods of achieving jurisdiction at Section 6.2.1 – the 2005 Convention, unlike the 2019 Convention, does not provide for States to make a declaration that the Convention will not apply to judgments emanating from particular States. This may lead to the consequence, as Born highlights, of States with a well-known history of poor judicial practices (including corruption) nonetheless acceding to the Convention and subsequently facing a relatively liberal enforcement regime. This argument reflects a deeper concern about the

[114] Born refers only, at footnote 235, to structural sources of political bias in the judiciary, including with respect to appointment of judges, tenure, and financial regulations including salaries and benefits: Born 'The Hague Convention on Choice of Court Agreements: A Critical Assessment' (n 111) 2123. It seems remiss not to address issues of the perceived or actual bias of arbitrators in this context, as well as to consider how corruption claims are dealt with under existing grounds of refusal. Some literature which explores this question includes: Stavros Brekoulakis, 'Systemic Bias and the Institution of International Arbitration: A New Approach to Arbitral Decision-Making' (2013) 4 *J Int Disp Settlement* 553; Houchih Kuo, 'The Issue of Repeat Arbitrators: Is It a Problem and How Should the Arbitration Institutions Respond' (2011) 4 *Contemp Asia Arb J* 247.

reliability of some national court systems, captured in the empirical evidence summarised in Born's writings. At their most extreme, some judiciaries can be described, perhaps uncharitably, as 'judicial hellholes'.[115] This moniker is often used with strong political connotations – for example, to label government and judicial decisions in certain states within the United States that are perceived to have a systematic bias in favour of plaintiffs. Tarring all judgments of a particular jurisdiction with this one brush is problematic, however, in the context of legal recognition and enforcement proceedings.

As set out at Section 4.2.2.1, in the context of the common law's approach to reciprocity, attempting to investigate State practice in the particularised way required to support such a claim is fraught with difficulties. Transposed to the concern at hand, precisely what level of satisfaction is needed to prove to an enforcing court, or to make a political determination, that a jurisdiction is a poor one, such that all its judgments should be disregarded? Is this an empirical exercise? And if so, what level of bias, fraud, corruption or incompetence is required to meet this threshold? Presumably, this will require detailed evidence about, for want of a better term, 'poor practices' and the extent to which they are systemic in a particular judicial system. But should this be corralled by the subject matter in dispute or sub-territorial units? For example, a national judiciary may have a poor reputation internationally with respect to its treatment of criminal matters but have a strong reputation in relation to commercial matters, or perhaps even contractual rather than tortious claims. Differences may also be witnessed among different courts, and judges, of the same judiciary. For example, appellate courts, or federal courts in a federation, may have a better or worse reputation than lower or provincial courts. Determining the 'overall attitude' of a judiciary in this fashion is inherently a political inquiry, with far-reaching consequences for international diplomacy; a task that is essentially unsolvable on a legal basis. Indeed, a large part of the rationale for the harmonising task of the Judgments Conventions is to overcome the necessity of having to engage in such political characterisations.

These concerns are precisely the reason why, almost universally (excluding within the United States), domestic recognition and enforcement regimes do not allow a foreign decision to be attacked on the basis that it comes from a legal *system* that can be characterised as one with systemic issues in procedural fairness or impartiality. Baumgartner and Whytock refer to this approach as one of 'systemic calibration' and highlight empirical evidence that suggests

115 This language is often employed in an inflammatory sense, for example, in the pro-business American Tort Reform Foundation, 'Judicial Hellholes' (2018) 1 <www.judicialhellholes.org/> accessed 23 January 2021.

that even within the United States refusing to give effect to a judgment on this basis is 'rare'.[116] Indeed, reflecting the comity rationale, the authors explain that judges in the United States are 'generally reluctant to publicly label a foreign legal system as systemically inadequate', and adopt 'several methods to avoid explicit reliance' on systemic inadequacy as a basis for refusing to give effect to a foreign judgment.[117] This reluctance was demonstrated, perhaps most recently, in March 2022, when the New York Appellate Division, First Department in the case of *Shanghai Yongrun*,[118] reversed the court below on the basis that an action to enforce should not be dismissed simply because of a contention that US State Department reports into human rights in China show that the legal system does not comport with natural justice requirements. The Appellate Division expressly noted in its order that, in any event, 'the reports, which primarily discuss the lack of judicial independence in proceedings involving politically sensitive matters, do not utterly refute plaintiff's allegation that the civil law system governing this breach of contract business dispute was fair', again highlighting the evidentiary challenges with any systemic calibration in this respect. As Dodge highlighted in a contemporaneous blog post considering this judgment:[119]

> This systemic lack of due process ground for nonrecognition comes from the U.S. Supreme Court's 1895 decision in *Hilton v. Guyot*, issued at a time when lawyers routinely distinguished between civilized and uncivilized nations. It was incorporated in the 1962 Uniform Act at the height of the Cold War, and included in the 2005 Uniform Act without discussion, apparently to maintain continuity with the 1962 Act. Despite its codification for nearly sixty years, fewer than five cases have refused recognition on this ground. The leading case is *Bridgeway Corp. v. Citibank*, involving a Liberian judgment issued during its civil war, when the judicial system had almost completely broken down.
>
> ...
>
> By focusing on the facts of the specific case, the Appellate Division appears to have taken a case-by-case, rather than a systemic, approach to due process. ... Such a case-specific approach avoids the overinclusiveness of

[116] Samuel P Baumgartner and Christopher A Whytock, 'Enforcement of Foreign Judgments, Systemic Calibration, and the Global Law Market' (2022) 23 *Theoretical Inquiries in Law* 1, 143.

[117] ibid. 143–44.

[118] *Shanghai Yongrun Inv. Mgt. Co. Ltd v Maodong Xu & Kashi Galaxy Venture Capital Co Ltd* 2022 NY slip Op 01523 (Index No. 156328/20 Appeal No. 15488 Case No. 2021-01637, decided on 10 March 2022).

[119] William Dodge, 'New York's Appellate Division Holds that Chinese Judgment Should Not Be Denied Enforcement on Systemic Due Process Grounds' (*Conflict of Laws*, 15 March 2022) <https://conflictoflaws.net/2022/new-yorks-appellate-division-holds-that-chinese-judgment-should-not-be-denied-enforcement-on-systemic-due-process-grounds/> accessed 2 May 2022.

denying recognition on systemic grounds when there are no defects in the judgment before the court.

For these reasons, given that any consideration of systemic factors is unique to the law of the United States – and even within that context decided cases suggest that the ground is difficult to prove, perhaps unnecessary and rarely used (even in circumstances which indicate it may be relevant)[120] – it is difficult to see how Born's contention, that failing to allow for systemic calibration is a 'serious flaw' in the 2005 Choice of Court Convention, can be maintained.[121] Indeed, Brand and Herrup note that the exclusion of systemic factors in the 2005 Convention was intentional – with the precise words of the ground of refusal in the Convention being chosen 'with care', to explicitly leave no room for attacks 'on the nature, character, or alleged conduct of the foreign judicial or legal system as a whole'.[122]

In any event, it is likely that Born's criticisms derive from a differing view of the mutual trust that States should accord to each other, and the way that this should interact with party autonomy.[123] There is no one correct answer as to where the acceptable thresholds underlying each concept should lie. João Ribeiro-Bidaoui responds to Born's critiques by stressing the capacity-building role that private law harmonisation can play, concluding that greater effort to police the parties' choice of forum in the 2005 Convention would have been 'undesirable and runs counter to the principle of party autonomy'.[124] It is my view, supported by the analysis in this book, that while such autonomy is important, other significant considerations also apply, and these considerations extend beyond concerns of autonomy in the selection of decision makers and procedure. For example, the value of building and maintaining relationships between States and their enforcing courts, as seen in discussions

[120] ibid. 121 and 146-7.

[121] Born 'The Hague Convention on Choice of Court Agreements: A Critical Assessment' (n 111) 2122–25.

[122] Ronald A Brand and Paul Herrup, *The 2005 Hague Convention on Choice of Court Agreements: Commentary and Documents* (Cambridge University Press 2008) 118.

[123] Both concepts are explored in detail at Section 6.2.

[124] João Ribeiro-Bidaoui, 'Hailing the HCCH (Hague) 2005 Choice of Court Convention, A Response to Gary Born' (*Kluwer Arbitration Blog*, 21 July 2021) <http://arbitrationblog.kluwerarbitration.com/2021/07/21/hailing-the-hcch-hague-2005-choice-of-court-convention-a-response-to-gary-born/> accessed 2 October 2021. Cf Born, who stresses that providing a more liberal avenue to enforce judgments, including judgments from corrupt or politicised judiciaries, will encourage illegally procured judgments: Gary B. Born, 'Why It Is Especially Important That States Not Ratify the Hague Choice of Court Agreements Convention, Part II' (*Kluwer Arbitration Blog*, 23 July 2021) <http://arbitrationblog.kluwerarbitration.com/2021/07/23/why-it-is-especially-important-that-states-not-ratify-the-hague-choice-of-court-agreements-convention-part-ii/> accessed 2 October 2021.

of the common law's approach to comity.[125] The value of building relationships is seen, in particular, through the development of adjudicatory comity in the common law (a 'comity between courts'), in generating respect, deference and politeness between States, for largely practical and prudent reasons.[126] Thus, although Born consistently emphasises the widely-shared narrative that the Choice of Court narrative is modelled 'in significant respects' upon the New York Convention,[127] it must not be forgotten that work towards the mutual harmonisation of foreign judgment recognition and enforcement extends back more than a century, and crosses a range of regional and global initiatives with a lineage far broader and deeper than the party autonomy roots that can be linked to the New York Convention.[128]

The final critique to be considered is the idea that even if States adopt harmonised enforcement instruments, they may apply or interpret them in a way that defeats their purpose. This means that, even assuming that the Judgments Conventions are domestically implemented, this will not immediately serve as a panacea to cure the enforcement gap. As experience with other private law treaties such as the CISG and, in the recognition and enforcement context, the New York Convention, suggests, implementation is merely the first step in a process of international harmonisation.[129] For example, Karrer, in a series of practical questions and answers about international commercial arbitration, poses and answers the question:[130]

> Q 935: But there is the New York Convention almost everywhere?
>
> A: Let us not kid ourselves. The New York Convention is honestly applied in about 30 countries. Forget about the rest.

[125] Note that the existence of such concepts is also argued to be a negative – as enforcing courts are likely to accord a greater degree of deference to foreign judicial pronouncements (being, as they are, an emanation of State power) than to foreign arbitral awards: Thomas D. Grant and F. Scott Kieff, 'Scrutinizing the 2005 Hague Convention: Two Further Reasons to Keep Arbitration a Viable Option' (*Kluwer Arbitration Blog*, 22 July 2021) <http://arbitrationblog.kluwerarbitration.com/2021/07/22/scrutinizing-the-2005-hague-convention-two-further-reasons-to-keep-arbitration-a-viable-option/> accessed 3 October 2021.

[126] Michaels, 'Recognition and Enforcement of Foreign Judgments' (n 48) para 7. See, further, Section 4.2.2.2.

[127] Born 'The Hague Convention on Choice of Court Agreements: A Critical Assessment' (n 111) 2103–04.

[128] See, further, Section 6.2.1 and Section 4.2.3.2., where key drivers in support of recognition and enforcement outside of party autonomy – including comity, finality, efficiency and fairness rooted in the administration of justice – are emphasised on a transnational level, and explored in a common law context.

[129] This is the thesis of Arvind, who argues in the context of interpreting the New York Convention that: 'The drafting and adoption of harmonized instruments should be seen as the start of the harmonization process, not its end': Arvind (n 17) 88.

[130] Pierre A. Karrer, *Introduction to International Arbitration Practice: 1001 Questions and Answers* (Kluwer Law International 2014) 229.

Kaplan reiterates this concern, and notes that: 'ratification . . . [is] one thing but efficient and transparent implementation by state courts is an entirely different matter'.[131] This concern is captured by divergence of practical experiences from the 'theory' of pro-recognition and enforcement instruments such as the New York Convention.[132] For example, it has been suggested that some States, when faced with enforcing awards they perceive to be rendered unfairly or improperly, do not comply with the 'spirit and intent' of the Convention, such as by broadly construing otherwise ambiguous grounds as a basis to deny giving effect to foreign awards.[133] This is the criticism often faced by the 'public policy' ground for refusal,[134] which due to its inherent operation as a 'safety valve' is not explicitly defined or particularised in transnational instruments. Enforcing courts have thus relied upon the inclusion of a simplistic formulation of the public policy ground – traditionally regarded as a 'historical impediment' to enforcement – as an implicit allowance for them to consider a broad remit of domestic concerns to limit recognition and enforcement of foreign decisions.[135] This interpretation means that despite sharing the same recognition and enforcement frameworks – in this case deriving from the New York Convention – some jurisdictions may refuse recognition or enforcement on grounds that may be considered 'trivial or insubstantial' in others.[136] Take, for example, the comments of Paulsson, who notes that:[137]

[131] Neil Kaplan, 'Arbitration in Asia: Developments and Crises – Part 2' (2002) 19 *Journal of International Arbitration* 245, 245.

[132] Kaplan sets out the 'theory' of the operation of the Convention in Asia in Neil Kaplan, 'Arbitration in Asia: Developments and Crises - Part 1' (2002) 19 *Journal of International Arbitration* 163, and then goes on to highlight a significant gap in practice in the region: Kaplan, 'Arbitration in Asia: Developments and Crises - Part 2' (n 132).

[133] Some enforcing courts seem to share this view – largely driven by the executive – and have, for example, taken a perhaps overly expansive view of the public policy exception compared to courts of other New York Convention signatories: William Spiegelberger, 'The Enforcement of Foreign Arbitral Awards in Russia: An Analysis of the Relevant Treaties, Laws and Cases' (2005) 16 *American Review of International Arbitration* 261; William Spiegelberger, *Enforcement of Foreign Arbitral Awards in Russia* (Juris Publishing, Inc 2014).

[134] Article V(2)(b).

[135] Michael Quilling, 'The Recognition and Enforcement of Foreign Country Judgments and Arbitral Awards: A North-South Perspective' (1981) 11 *Georgia Journal of International & Comparative Law* 635, 646.

[136] See, for example, the case of *Ecom Agroindustrial Corp* v. *Dai Cuong Group Joint Stock Co* (Supreme People's Court, Appeal Court of Hanoi, Case No 117/2014/QD-PT, 7 August 2014), cited in Anselmo Reyes, 'Recognition and Enforcement of Interlocutory and Final Judgments of the Singapore International Commercial Court' (2015) 2 *Journal of International and Comparative Law* 343.

[137] Marike Paulsson, 'The 1958 New York Convention from an Unusual Perspective: Moving Forward by Parting with It' (2017) 5 *Indian journal of Arbitration Law* 21, 24.

> for all its remarkable success, the New York Convention has proved itself to be (i) unreliable, (ii) unpredictable, and (iii) inconsistent because there is wiggle room in the New York Convention and occasionally its objectives seem to have very poor resonance.

Indeed, even jurisdictions that pride themselves on their 'support' for arbitration can often present substantial hurdles to the recognition and enforcement process.[138] Bailey, for example, refers to his experience in the case of a dispute between *TCL* and *Castel*, which involved a complicated, costly and time-consuming series of collateral proceedings across multiple jurisdictions, based on frustrating attempts to enforce an arbitral award in Australia and China that after more than a decade had seen little fruitful reward.[139] This occurred despite – and in some cases, even because of – the fact that both countries are Contracting States of the Convention. This experience suggests that even where otherwise clear transnational obligations can be discerned, the recognition and enforcement prospects of foreign decisions can be frustrated by recalcitrant debtors who do not face a strong domestic enforcement environment. Similar concerns are also likely to be applicable in the context of the Judgments Conventions, as set out at Section 7.1, primarily on the basis that divergence in application or interpretation of these Conventions would undermine harmonisation. Ultimately, then, even though transnational instruments offer machinery for simplified or harmonised recognition and enforcement, there is no guarantee of a complete solution for States who do not voluntarily comply with a pro-recognition and enforcement spirit.[140]

[138] David Bailey, 'International Commercial Arbitration – a Critique' (2015) 43 *Australian Business Law Review* 344.

[139] ibid.

[140] Indeed, a fruitful area of research has arisen around how transnational approaches in the field of international commercial arbitration have been constructed and operate – distinct from their doctrinal roots: see, for a seminal example, Yves Dezalay and Bryant G. Garth, *Dealing in Virtue: International Commercial Arbitration and the Construction of a Transnational Legal Order* (Language and legal discourse, University of Chicago Press 1996).

9

Conclusion

The critical role of recognition and enforcement in securing practical justice for private parties and maintaining an effective international trading system has been stressed for many decades. The widespread global adoption of the New York Convention bears testament to this in the field of arbitral awards; and so too the Commonwealth and Brussels Models with respect to judgments between Member States. Given the lack of harmonised enforcement approaches in the judgments field, there remains significant potential for harmonisation. This can occur via the greater acceptance of either or both the 2005 Convention and the 2019 Convention. Indeed, given the potential existence of areas of overlap – particularly in determining whether a particular choice of court agreement is non-exclusive – the most prudent option may be to consider the adoption of both Judgments Conventions as a package.

This book has demonstrated that a deeper understanding of the enforcement gap and relative enforcement prospects requires both doctrinal and broader socio-legal and transnational comparison. Chapters 2, 3 and 4 primarily adopt the doctrinal mantle, assisted by historical comparison, analysing the key recognition and enforcement approaches individually, based upon their underlying legal instrumentation, at both the 'global' and 'regional' levels. This analysis highlights the similarities and variance in treatment of recognition and enforcement, as well as allowing observation as to the nature, successes and developments embedded in such approaches (including the concerns that are being balanced by participant States in agreeing to mutually promote recognition and enforcement). Of particular note are the recognition and enforcement underpinnings based upon Huber's seventeenth-century conception of comity, analysed in Section 4.2 in the context of the common law. Although the idea of comity originated in Europe, it rapidly spread to the common law world, and it has remained for the centuries since as a way to mitigate strict reliance on territoriality in the enforcement of foreign decisions. However, comity cloaks a veritable array of concepts and theories (such as obligation, debt, and so on), and struggles to meet the greater need for predictable and harmonised recognition and enforcement necessitated by the increasing internationalisation of commercial dealings. The need for harmonisation remains.

Despite these challenges, the functional comparison in Chapter 5 supports the conclusion that transnational recognition and enforcement approaches are, for the most part, doctrinally similar and functionally equivalent. This is because they are all based upon concepts of reciprocity, share similar limitations or exclusions from scope and, broadly – outside of the Brussels Model – share similar instrumental features to facilitate transnational consensus and adoption of the underlying instruments. Perhaps most importantly, inspired by a broad conception of comity, they adopt a similar presumption–exception approach to recognition and enforcement. This approach is designed to promote and reinforce a free acceptance of foreign decisions without review of the merits of the original decision, until and unless one of the limited, and usually strictly enumerated, grounds for refusal can be found. These grounds for refusal operate as a 'safety valve', allowing for a stronger presumption in favour of enforcement. It is this combination of features that can broadly be said to underpin recognition and enforcement approaches, irrespective of the source of the underlying legal instrumentation (whether arising from general law, statutory regimes or from domestic enactments of treaties to harmonise recognition and enforcement). The largest divergence seen is in the precise categories of allowable or objectionable foreign decisions, and whether the recognition and enforcement approach serves to prohibit enforcement on this basis or remain silent in this respect.

Having set out the broadly shared functional and doctrinal features of key recognition and enforcement approaches, Part II of this book explores the experiences, interactions, flows and feedback mechanisms between them. Chapter 6 grounds this analysis in the key hurdles to developing a harmonised approach to the recognition and enforcement of foreign judgments. This chapter concludes that differences in legal tradition and approach are not – or perhaps are no longer – a legal or practical hurdle to achieving harmonised recognition and enforcement practice. Additionally, it is likely that the differences in rationales underlying recognition and enforcement approaches (such as differing conceptions of sovereign relationships, or differing conceptions of jurisdiction grounded in party autonomy) are not so significant as to stand as an enduring hurdle to judgments recognition and enforcement.[1] Simultaneously, as emphasised in the context of the common law, most States still share similar functional aims in promoting recognition and enforcement.[2] Rather than treating recognition and enforcement as an instance of unbridled sovereignty (allowing utter discretion about whether to reject or accept foreign judgments on the grounds that the enforcing State sees fit), States largely accept the need for procedural guidance in national law. Although the practical rationale for giving effect to foreign decisions across nations is largely shared,[3] the emphasis placed on each of these drivers differs across national law approaches. Thus, Chapter 6 highlights not only the similarities in approach but also the ongoing importance of the harmonising role of transnational approaches to recognition and enforcement.

Chapter 7 explores methods of legal development. A similar desire to promote uniformity and manage divergent interpretation exists across all recognition and approaches but with significant variance in the institutional capacity and machinery available to do so. The most advanced approach in this respect is the Brussels Model, which allows (or even compels) participants to make ultimate recourse or reference to a supranational interpretive body. By contrast, under the Commonwealth Model and the approach seen in global instruments, the preeminent institution is usually the highest court in each implementing State. Nonetheless, each of these approaches employs some form of controlling mechanism or institution that assists in promoting a uniform and autonomous interpretation that is broadly in favour of pro-recognition and enforcement goals. At the same time, legal development can only occur at the margins in global models, as distinct from the wholesale legal evolution that has been attempted within the confines of the Brussels Model. This means that the need for clarity and tools to pursue uniformity in interpretation and application is particularly acute for global recognition and enforcement frameworks, as there is no supervening interpretive authority and very limited methods to revisit international instruments.

The final substantive chapter, Chapter 8, draws broader lessons from the increasingly 'transnationalised' nature of recognition and enforcement. To this end, I argue that experience with recognition and enforcement approaches in one domain likely 'smooths the way' for other harmonisation

1 See Section 6.2.

2 See, further, at least from a common law perspective, Section 4.2.

3 See, further, for an overview of the common law approach to so doing – broadly applicable across a range of jurisdictions, including the United States and the United Kingdom – Chapter 4.

efforts. For example, the broad-based Judgments Project negotiations were assisted by – and themselves contributed to – experience with the New York Convention in the field of arbitration, as well as experience with the harmonisation of judgment recognition and enforcement in regional Models and the 2005 Convention. These experiences were particularly critical in reaching the ultimate form of the 2019 Convention. This extends to the Convention's final approach – decoupling recognition and enforcement from concerns of direct jurisdiction, and providing only a set of minimum standards and otherwise deferring to the national law of implementing States. Even where residual recourse to national law is allowed, this is exercised in a circumspect fashion: reinforcing the 'spirit and intent' of most recognition and enforcement instrumentation and bearing witness to the greater acceptance of transnationalised recognition and enforcement practice. Chapter 8 addresses fundamental criticisms of the Judgments Conventions, offering insight into their likely adoption prospects and future implementation.

Ultimately, the transnational recognition and enforcement experience analysed in this book allows us to see that 'uniform and efficient' recognition and enforcement schemes can be achieved through various legal instruments that make certain the procedures for, and remove hurdles to, recognition and enforcement.[4] This conclusion echoes the comments of Justice Gray, who noted over a century ago in *Hilton*, when grappling with the concept of comity, that: '[t]he most certain guide, no doubt, for [foreign judgment recognition and enforcement] is a treaty or a statute'.[5] Absent such guidance, the decision to give effect to foreign decisions remains a matter of national law, with the potential for significant variance in the extent to which courts 'obtain such aid … from judicial decisions, from the works of jurists and commentators, and from the acts and usages of civilized nations'.[6] What is then required is further investigation into aspects of transnational ordering, including the implementation, application and interpretation of recognition and enforcement approaches, and the way such ordering is received and impacts upon a diverse range of stakeholders (and their motivations), as well as the surrounding political, social and economic factors that give meaning to any rule across and between the transnational and national law levels.

The settling of the legal instrumentation for the Judgments Conventions clears the way for the adoption, globally, of a harmonised recognition and

4 Brian Paige, 'Foreign Judgments in American and English Courts: A Comparative Analysis' (2003) 26 *Seattle University Law Review* 621.

5 *Hilton* v. *Guyot* 159 US 113 (1895) 163.

6 ibid.

enforcement approach that is both authoritative and legitimate internationally. Neither instrument is perfect, nor can they be, given that they represent such significant compromises. What can be said, however, is that the Judgments Conventions have benefitted immensely from over a century of negotiation and have drawn carefully from comparative transnational experience, to represent the state of the art with respect to recognition and enforcement. Implementing the Judgments Conventions will strengthen international commercial dispute resolution as a whole, as commercial disputants who litigate – either by choice, or by operation of default jurisdiction rules – will be met with a more certain, predictable and harmonised footing for giving effect to any resulting judgment. This is particularly important given concerns about the sheer dominance of private and often confidential arbitration and the relatively recent emergence of international commercial courts that aim to attract disputant custom. Improving the relative enforcement prospects of foreign judgments in this way will likely have positive spillover effects not only on courts around the world, but also, over the longer term, into the field of international commercial arbitration.

Looking forward, it is undoubtedly true that both Judgments Conventions will require 'broad appeal' to avoid collapsing into 'little more than a regional instrument or a model law, with corresponding limited utility'.[7] This book reinforces the idea that the process of implementation of these Conventions is not an inevitable progression that simply results from a concluded or implemented treaty. Instead, transnational experience serves to reinforce the perhaps trite observation that domestic implementation of treaties is simply the beginning of what is likely to be a many decades long process of seeking international acceptance. This is true, but it nonetheless remains up to national States to take the first leap towards international harmonisation via implementing the Judgments Conventions.

7 Ronald A. Brand and Paul Herrup, *The 2005 Hague Convention on Choice of Court Agreements: Commentary and Documents* (Cambridge University Press 2008) 22.

Bibliography

Administration of Justice Act 1920 (UK).

(France), 29 February 2012, 11-40.101, Inédit Case No.

Aetna Life Insurance Company v. *Tremblay* (US 19 February 1912).

Case C-7/98 *Dieter Krombach* v. *André Bamberski* [2000] ECR.

Case C-45/13 *Andreas Kainz* v. *Pantherwerke AG* [2014].

Case C-70/15 *Emmanuel Lebek* v. *Janusz Domino*.

Case C-116/02 *Erich Gasser GmbH* v. *MISAT Srl* ECR I-14693.

Case C-559/14 *Rūdolfs Meroni* v. *Recoletos Limited*.

Chromalloy Aeroservices v. *The Arab Republic of Egypt* 939 *F Supp* 907 (District Court of Columbia) (District Court 1996).

Civil Jurisdiction and Judgments Act 1982 (UK).

First National City Bank v. *Banco Nacional de Cuba* 406 *US* 759 (1972).

Foreign Judgments (Reciprocal Enforcement) Act 1933 (UK).

Godard v. *Gray* (1870) LR 6 QB 139.

Hilton v. *Guyot* 159 US 113 (1895).

Mast, Foos & Company v. *Stover Manufacturing Company* 177 US 485 (1900).

Owens Bank Ltd v. *Fulvio Bracco and Bracco Industria Chimica SpA (Case 129/92)* [1994] ECR.

Regulation (EU) No 1215/2012 of 12 December 2012 on Jurisdiction and the Recognition and Enforcement of Judgments in civil and commercial matters (recast) (2012).

RM Investments & Trading Co v. *Boeing Co* Supreme Court.

Statute of the Hague Conference on Private International Law (entered into force on 15 July 1955) (US).

UNCITRAL *UNCITRAL Secretariat Guide on the Convention on the Recognition and Enforcement of Foreign Arbitral Awards* (2016).

United States Constitution (US).

American Bar Association, 'General Information Form 109A: Report' (11 December 1992).

Borrás A, Neophytou I and Pocar F, '13th Report on National Case Law Relating to the Lugano Convention' (May 2012).

Brand R, 'Recognition and Enforcement of Foreign Judgments' (International Litigation Guide, April 2012), International Litigation Guide.

California Law Revision Commission, 'Recognition of Tribal and Foreign Court Money Judgments (Changes to Uniform Act in Other States)' (17 July 2015).
Dickinson A, 'The Proposal for a Regulation of the European Parliament and of the Council on Jurisdiction and the Recognition and Enforcement of Judgments in Civil and Commercial Matters (Recast) ("Brussels I Bis" Regulation)' (Sydney Law School Legal Studies Research Paper, 20 September 2011), Sydney Law School Legal Studies Research Paper.
European Commission, 'Green Paper on the Review of Council Regulation (EC) No 44/2001 on Jurisdiction and the Recognition and Enforcement of Judgments in Civil and Commercial Matters' (Green Paper COM(2009) 175 Final, 21 April 2009), Green Paper COM(2009) 175 final.
European Commission, 'A New EU Framework to Strengthen the Rule of Law: Communication from the Commission to the European Parliament and the Council' (COM (2014) 158 final, 11 March 2014), COM(2014) 158 final.
European Commission, 'Proposal for a Council Regulation (EC) on Jurisdiction and the Recognition and Enforcement of Judgments in Civil and Commercial Matters' (COM(1999) 348 final, 14 July 1999), COM(1999) 348 final.
European Commission, 'Proposal for a Regulation of the European Parliament and of the Council on Jurisdiction and the Recognition and Enforcement of Judgments in Civil and Commercial Matters' (COM(2010) 748 final, 14 December 2010), COM(2010) 748 final.
European Commission, 'Towards Greater Efficiency in Obtaining and Enforcing Judgments in the European Union' (COM(1997) 609 FINAL; OJ [1998] C33/3, no date), COM(1997) 609 FINAL; OJ [1998] C33/3.
European Parliament, 'European Parliament Resolution of 8 September 2015 on the Situation of Fundamental Rights in the European Union (2013-2014)' (2014/2254 (INI), 8 September 2015), 2014/2254 (INI).
European Parliament, 'Report on the Proposal for a Regulation of the European Parliament and of the Council on Jurisdiction and the Recognition and Enforcement of Judgments in Civil and Commercial Matters (Recast)' (COM (2010) 748, 15 October 2012), COM(2010) 748.
Getman-Pavlova I, 'The Concept of "Comity" in Ulrich Huber's Conflict Doctrine' (Working Paper, 2013), Working Paper.
Gleeson M, 'The Influence of the Privy Council on Australia' (Speech delivered at the Anglo-Australasian Lawyers Society, 31 May 2007), Speech delivered at the Anglo-Australasian Lawyers Society.
Hague Conference, '17th Session: Final Act' (29 May 1993).
Hague Conference, 'Conclusions and Recommendations Adopted by the Council' (Council on General Affairs and Policy of the Conference, 20 April 2012), Council on General Affairs and Policy of the Conference.
Hague Conference, 'Conclusions of the Special Commission of June 1992 on General Affairs and Policy of the Conference' (Preliminary Document, August 1992), Preliminary Document.
Hague Conference, 'Interim Text: Summary of the Outcome of the Discussion in Commission II of the First Part of the Diplomatic Conference 6–20 June 2001' (Diplomatic Conference (6–20 June 2001), COMMISSION II: Jurisdiction and

Foreign Judgments in Civil and Commercial Matters, 2001), Diplomatic Conference (6–20 June 2001).
Hague Conference, 'Preliminary Draft Convention on Jurisdiction and Foreign Judgments in Civil and Commercial Matters' (Preliminary Document, August 2000), Preliminary Document.
Hague Conference, 'Conclusions of the Working Group Meeting on Enforcement of Judgments' (Preliminary Document, November 1992), Preliminary Document.
Hague Conference, 'Explanatory Note Providing Background on the Proposed Draft Text and Identifying Outstanding Issues' (Preliminary Document, April 2016), Preliminary Document.
Hague Conference, 'Judgments Convention: Revised Preliminary Explanatory Report' (Preliminary Document, May 2018), Preliminary Document.
Hague Conference, 'Report of the Fifth Meeting of the Working Group on the Judgments Project (26–31 October 2015) and Proposed Draft Text Resulting from the Meeting' (Preliminary Document, November 2015), Preliminary Document.
Hague Conference, 'Some Reflections of the Permanent Bureau on a General Convention on Enforcement of Judgments' (Preliminary Document, May 1992), Preliminary Document.
Hague Conference, 'Statement of the 2005 Convention Working Group Drafters (Adopted by the Diplomatic Session)' (no date).
Hague Conference, 'Synthesis of the Work of the Special Commission of June 1997 on International Jurisdiction and the Effects of Foreign Judgments in Civil and Commercial Matters' (Preliminary Document, November 1997), Preliminary Document.
Hartley T and Dogauchi M, 'Explanatory Report on the Convention of 30 June 2005 on Choice of Court Agreements' (Explanatory Report, 2007), Explanatory Report.
Judicial Committee of the Privy Council, 'The Jurisdiction of the Judicial Committee of the Privy Council' (Jurisdiction map, no date), Jurisdiction map.
Lord Chief Justice of England and Wales (Lord Thomas), 'Developing Commercial Law through the Courts: Rebalancing the Relationship between the Courts and Arbitration' (The Bailii Lecture 2016, 9 March 2016), The Bailii Lecture 2016.
Nygh P and Pocar F, 'Report by Peter Nygh & Fausto Pocar (Annexed to the 1999 Preliminary Draft Convention)' (Report, August 2000), Report.
United Nations Commission on International Trade Law, 'Model Law on International Commercial Arbitration (with Amendments as Adopted in 2006)' (1985).
Waibel M, 'Principles of Treaty Interpretation: Developed for and Applied by National Courts?' (University of Cambridge Faculty of Law Research Paper, 17 April 2015), University of Cambridge Faculty of Law Research Paper.
'The Gradual Establishment of an Area of Freedom, Security and Justice' (Summary of EU Legislation (available on EUR-Lex), no date), Summary of EU Legislation (available on EUR-Lex).
Bennett D, 'The Hague Convention on Recognition and Enforcement of Foreign Judgments: A Failure of Characterisation' in T Einhorn and K Siehr (eds.), *Intercontinental Cooperation through Private International Law: Essays in Memory of Peter E. Nygh* (TMC Asser Press 2004).

van den Berg AJ (ed.), 50 *Years of the New York Convention: ICCA International Arbitration Conference* (ICCA Congress Series 14, Kluwer Law International 2009).

Van den Berg AJ, 'Hypothetical Draft Convention on the International Enforcement of Arbitration Agreements and Awards: Explanatory Note' in AJ van den Berg (ed.), 50 *Years of the New York Convention: ICCA International Arbitration Conference* (ICCA Congress Series 14, 321st ed., Kluwer Law International 2009).

Van den Berg AJ, 'Striving for Uniform Interpretation' in *Enforcing Arbitration Awards under the New York Convention: Experience and Prospects* (United Nations 1999).

Van den Berg AJ, 'When Is an Arbitration Agreement in Writing Valid under Article II (2) of the New York Convention of 1958?' in P Sanders (ed.), *Piet Sanders: een honderdjarige vernieuwer* (Boom Juridische Uitgevers 2012).

Bjorge E, *The Evolutionary Interpretation of Treaties* (Oxford University Press 2014).

Blackaby N, Partasides C, Redfern A and Hunter M, *Redfern and Hunter on International Arbitration* (6th ed., Oxford University Press 2015).

Bockstiegel K-H, 'Summary of Discussion in the Third Working Group' in AJ van den Berg (ed.), *Improving the Efficiency of Arbitration Agreements and Awards: 40 years of Application of the New York Convention* (KluwerArbitration, Kluwer Law International 1999).

Born G, *International Civil Litigation in United States Courts: Commentary and Materials* (Kluwer Law International 1996).

Born G, *International Commercial Arbitration* (KluwerArbitration, Third edition, Kluwer Law International BV 2020).

Brand RA and Herrup P, *The 2005 Hague Convention on Choice of Court Agreements: Commentary and Documents* (Cambridge University Press 2008).

Briggs A, *Agreements on Jurisdiction and Choice of Law* (Oxford Private International Law Series 2008).

Briggs A, *Civil Jurisdiction and Judgments* (6th ed., Informa Law from Routledge 2015).

Brydie-Watson W, 'The Three Sisters of Private International Law: An Increasingly Co-Operative Family Rather than Sibling Rivals' in T John, R Gulati and B Koehler (eds.), *The Elgar Companion to the Hague Conference on Private International Law* (Elgar Companions to International Organisations series, Edward Elgar Publishing 2020).

Caffrey B, *International Jurisdiction and the Recognition and Enforcement of Foreign Judgments in the LAWASIA Region: A Comparative Study of the Laws of Eleven Asian Countries Inter-Se and with the E.E.C. Countries* (CCH Australia 1985).

van Calster G, *European Private International Law* (2nd ed., Hart Publishing 2016).

Campbell D (ed.), *Enforcement of Foreign Judgements* (LLP Professional Publishing 1997).

Chang T, 'Celebrating the Fiftieth Anniversary of the New York Convention' in AJ van den Berg (ed.), 50 *Years of the New York Convention: ICCA International Arbitration Conference* (ICCA Congress Series 14, Kluwer Law International 2009).

Cope K, 'Reconceptualizing Recognition Uniformity' in PB Stephan (ed.), *Foreign Court Judgments and the United States Legal System* (Brill 2014).

Davies M, Bell A and Brereton P, *Nygh's Conflict of Laws in Australia* (9th ed., LexisNexis Butterworths 2014).

Davies M, Bell A, Brereton PLG and Douglas M, *Nygh's Conflict of Laws in Australia* (10th ed., LexisNexis Butterworths 2019).

Dezalay Y and Garth BG, *Dealing in Virtue: International Commercial Arbitration and the Construction of a Transnational Legal Order* (Language and legal discourse, University of Chicago Press 1996).

Dicey AV and Morris JHC, *Dicey's Conflict of Laws* (6th ed., Stevens 1949).

'What, If Anything, Can Australia Learn from the EU Experience?' in A Dickinson, M Keyes and T John (eds.), *Australian Private International Law for the 21st Century: Facing Outwards* (Hart Publishing 2014).

Dickinson A and Lein E (eds.), *The Brussels I Regulation Recast* (Oxford University Press 2015).

Dodge W, 'The Penal and Revenue Rules, State Law, and Federal Preemption' in PB Stephan (ed.), *Foreign Court Judgments and the United States Legal System* (Brill 2014).

Fauvarque-Cosson B, 'European Contract Law Through and beyond Pluralism: The Case of an Optional Instrument' in L Niglia (ed.), *Pluralism and European Private Law* (Hart Publishing 2013).

Fawcett J, North P and Carruthers J, *Cheshire, North & Fawcett: Private International Law* (14th ed., Oxford University Press 2008).

Frankenberg G, *Comparative Law as Critique* (Elgar studies in legal theory, Edward Elgar Publishing 2016).

Gaillard E, 'Comment: The Urgency of Not Revising the New York Convention' in AJ van den Berg (ed.), 50 *Years of the New York Convention: ICCA International Arbitration Conference* (ICCA Congress Series 14, Kluwer Law International 2009).

Gaillard E, 'Enforcement of Awards Set Aside in the Country of Origin: The French Experience' in AJ van den Berg (ed.), *Improving the Efficiency of Arbitration Agreements and Awards: 40 Years of Application of the New York Convention* (KluwerArbitration, Kluwer Law International 1999).

Giardina A, 'The Practical Application of Multilateral Convention' in AJ van den Berg (ed.), *Improving the Efficiency of Arbitration Agreements and Awards: 40 Years of Application of the New York Convention* (KluwerArbitration, Kluwer Law International 2011).

Graziadei M, 'Comparative Law as the Study of Transplants and Receptions' in M Reimann and R Zimmermann (eds.), *The Oxford Handbook of Comparative Law* (Oxford University Press 2006).

Greenberg S, Kee C and Weeramantry JR, *International Commercial Arbitration: An Asia-Pacific Perspective* (Cambridge University Press 2011).

Halliday T and Block-Lieb S, 'Settling and Concordance: Two Cases in Global Commercial Law' in G Shaffer and T Halliday (eds.), *Transnational Legal Orders* (Cambridge Studies in Law and Society, Cambridge University Press 2015).

Hamilton V and Briner R, 'The Genesis and General Purpose of The New York Convention' in E Gaillard, D Di Pietro and N Leleu-Knobil (eds.), *Enforcement of Arbitration Agreements and International Arbitral Awards: The New York Convention in Practice* (Cameron May 2008).

Hans VL, 'The Hague Conference on Private International Law: Current Problems and Perspectives' in *Cursos de derecho internacional de Vitoria Gasteiz (Courses on International Law and International Relations at Vitoria-Gasteiz)* (Universidad del País Vasco (University of the Basque Country) 1983) vol 3.

Hartley T, 'The European Court, the Brussels Convention/Regulation and the Establishment of an Efficient System for International Litigation in Europe' in A Arnull, P Eeckhout and T Tridimas (eds.), *Continuity and Change in EU Law* (Oxford University Press 2008).

von Hein J, 'The Role of the HCCH in Shaping Private International Law' in T John, R Gulati and B Koehler (eds.), *The Elgar Companion to the Hague Conference on Private International Law* (Elgar Companions to International Organisations series, Edward Elgar Publishing 2020).

Huang J, *Interregional Recognition and Enforcement of Civil and Commercial Judgments: Lessons for China from US and EU Law* (Bloomsbury Publishing 2014).

Kahn-Freund O, *The Growth of Internationalism in English Private International Law* (1960).

Kaplan N, 'New Developments on Written Form' in *Enforcing Arbitration Awards under the New York Convention: Experience and Prospects* (United Nations 1999).

Karrer PA, *Introduction to International Arbitration Practice: 1001 Questions and Answers* (Kluwer Law International 2014).

Lamm C, 'Comments on the Proposal to Amend the New York Convention' in AJ van den Berg (ed.), *50 Years of the New York Convention: ICCA International Arbitration Conference* (ICCA Congress Series 14, Kluwer Law International 2009).

Lew JDM, Mistelis LA and Kröll S, *Comparative International Commercial Arbitration* (Kluwer Law International 2003).

Lewison K, *The Interpretation of Contracts* (6th ed., Sweet & Maxwell 2015).

Lowenfeld EA and Silberman LJ, *The Hague Convention on Jurisdiction and Judgments* (JurisNet, LLC 2001).

Lutz RE, *A Lawyer's Handbook for Enforcing Foreign Judgments in the United States and Abroad* (Cambridge University Press 2007).

MacCormick N and Summers RS (eds.), *Interpreting Precedents: A Comparative Study* ([Applied legal philosophy], Aldershot 1997).

Magnus U and Mankowski P (eds.), *Brussels I Regulation* (2nd ed., Sellier European Law Publishers 2007).

Maurer AG, *Public Policy Exception under the New York Convention: History, Interpretation, and Application* (Revised, Juris Publishing, Inc 2013).

Maxeiner J, *Failures of American Civil Justice in International Perspective* (Cambridge University Press 2011).

McEvoy T, 'Common Law versus Statutory Approaches to Enforcing Foreign Judgments: The Australian Experience' in PB Stephan (ed.), *Foreign Court Judgments and the United States Legal System* (Brill 2014).

Von Mehren A and Gottschalk E, *Adjudicatory Authority in Private International Law* (The Hague Academy of International Law Monographs 5, Martinus Nijhoff Publishers 2007).

Melis W, 'Considering the Advisability of Preparing an Addition Convention, Complementary to the New York Convention' in *Enforcing Arbitration Awards under the New York Convention: Experience and Prospects* (United Nations 1999).

Merryman JH and Pérez-Perdomo R, *The Civil Law Tradition: An Introduction to the Legal Systems of Europe and Latin America* (Stanford University Press 2007).

Michaels R, '"One Size Can Fit All" – On the Mass Production of Legal Transplants' in G Frankenberg (ed.), *Order from Transfer: Comparative Constitutional Design and Legal Culture* (Studies in comparative law and legal culture series, Edward Elgar Publishing 2013).

Michaels R, 'Recognition and Enforcement of Foreign Judgments' [2009] *Max Planck Encyclopaedia of Public International Law*.

Michaels R, 'Some Fundamental Jurisdictional Conceptions as Applied in Judgment Conventions' in E Gottschalk (ed.), *Conflict of Laws in a Globalized World* (Cambridge University Press 2007).

Mills A, *Party Autonomy in Private International Law* (Cambridge University Press 2018).

Mortensen R, Garnett R and Keyes M, *Private International Law in Australia* (3rd ed., LexisNexis Butterworths 2015).

Muir Watt H, 'New Perspectives for Jurisdiction and Judgments within Europe: A Critical View' in J Barcelo and KM Clermont (eds.), *A Global Law of Jurisdiction and Judgement: Lessons from Hague* (1st ed., Kluwer Law International 2002).

Nadelmann K, 'Jurisdictionally Improper Fora in Treaties on Recognition of Judgments: The Common Market Draft' in K Nadelmann (ed.), *Conflicts of Law: International And Interstate: Selected Essays* (Martinus Nijhoff Publishers 1972).

Nadelmann K, 'The United States Join the Hague Conference on Private International Law' in K Nadelmann (ed.), *Conflicts of Law: International and Interstate: Selected Essays* (Martinus Nijhoff Publishers 1972).

Nadelmann K, 'Uniform Legislation versus International Conventions as a Method of Unification of Private International Law' in K Nadelmann (ed.), *Conflicts of Law: International and Interstate: Selected Essays* (Martinus Nijhoff Publishers 1972).

Nadelmann K, 'Uniform Legislation Versus International Conventions Revisited' in K Nadelmann (ed.), *Conflicts of Law: International and Interstate: Selected Essays* (Martinus Nijhoff Publishers 1972).

Oppong RF, *Private International Law in Commonwealth Africa* (Cambridge University Press 2013).

Paulsson J, 'Awards Set Aside at the Place of Arbitration' in *Enforcing Arbitration Awards under the New York Convention: Experience and Prospects* (United Nations 1999).

Paulsson J, 'The New York Convention in International Practice: Problems of Assimilation' in M Blessing (ed.), *The New York Convention of 1958* (ASA Special Series 9, 1996).

Paulsson M, *The 1958 New York Convention in Action* (Wolters Kluwer 2016).

Phillip A, 'The Global Hague Judgments Convention' in T Einhorn and K Siehr (eds.), *Intercontinental Cooperation through Private International Law: Essays in Memory of Peter E Nygh* (TMC Asser Press 2004).

Platto C, *Enforcement of Foreign Judgments Worldwide* (Graham & Trotman 1993).

Polinsky AM and Shavell S, *Handbook of Law and Economics* (Elsevier 2007).

Poser NS, *Lord Mansfield: Justice in the Age of Reason* (McGill-Queen's University Press 2013).

Reed L, 'Experience of Practical Problems of Enforcement' in AJ van den Berg (ed.), *Improving the Efficiency of Arbitration Agreements and Awards: 40 Years of Application of the New York Convention* (KluwerArbitration, Kluwer Law International 2011).

Rossouw M, *The Harmonisation of Rules on the Recognition and Enforcement of Foreign Judgments in the Southern African Customs Union* (Pretoria University Law Press 2016).

Rubens N, 'Group of Companies Doctrine and the New York Convention' in E Gaillard and D Di Pietro (eds.), *Enforcement of Arbitration Agreements and International Arbitral Awards: The New York Convention in Practice* (1st ed., Cameron May 2008).

Sanders P, 'The Making of the Convention' in *Enforcing Arbitration Awards under the New York Convention: Experience and Prospects* (United Nations 1999).

Sbolci L, 'Supplementary Means of Interpretation' in E Cannizzaro (ed.), *The Law of Treaties beyond the Vienna Convention* (Oxford University Press 2011).

Secretariat C, *1999 Meeting of Commonwealth Law Ministers and Senior Officials: Port of Spain, Trinidad and Tobago, 3–7 May 1999: Memoranda* (Commonwealth Secretariat 2001).

Shaffer G, 'Transnational Legal Ordering and State Change' in G Shaffer (ed.), *Transnational Legal Ordering and State Change* (Cambridge Studies in Law and Society, Cambridge University Press 2012).

Silberman LJ, 'The Need for a Federal Statutory Approach to the Recognition and Enforcement of Foreign Country Judgments' in PB Stephan (ed.), *Foreign Court Judgments and the United States Legal System* (Brill 2014).

Sloss D, *The Role of Domestic Courts in Treaty Enforcement: A Comparative Study* (Cambridge University Press 2009).

Spiegelberger W, *Enforcement of Foreign Arbitral Awards in Russia* (Juris Publishing, Inc 2014).

Stephan PB (ed.), *Foreign Court Judgments and the United States Legal System* (Brill 2014).

Stephan PB, 'Introduction: Recognition and Enforcement of Foreign Judgments' in PB Stephan (ed.), *Foreign Court Judgments and the United States Legal System* (Brill 2014).

Stone P, *EU Private International Law* (Elgar European law series, Edward Elgar Publishing 2014).

Story J, *Commentaries on the Conflict of Laws: Foreign and Domestic, in Regard to Contracts, Rights, and Remedies, and Especially in Regard to Marriages, Divorces, Wills, Successions, and Judgments* (8th ed., Lawbook Exchange (2007 Reprint) 1887).

Thiele C, 'The Hague Convention on Choice-of-Court Agreements: Was It Worth the Effort?' in E Gottschalk, R Michaels, G Rühl and J von Hein (eds.), *Conflict of Laws in a Globalized World* (Cambridge University Press 2007).

Twining W, 'Globalisation and Comparative Law' (Hart 2007).

Wagner G, 'Dispute Resolution as a Product: Competition between Civil Justice Systems' in H Eidenmüller (ed.), *Regulatory Competition in Contract Law and Dispute Resolution* (First ed., Hart Publishing 2013).

Whytock C, 'Enforcement of Foreign Judgments: Governance, Rights, and the Market for Dispute Resolution Services' in H-W Micklitz and A Wechsler (eds.), *The Transformation of Enforcement: European Economic Law in Global Perspective* (Hart Publishing 2016).

Yekini A, *The Hague Judgments Convention and Commonwealth Model Law: A Pragmatic Perspective* (Hart Publishing 2021).

Zweigert K and Kötz H, *An Introduction to Comparative Law* (3rd ed., Clarendon Press 1998).

Recognition and Enforcement of Foreign Judgments: General Theory and the Role of Jurisdictional Requirements (Martinus Nijhoff Publishers 1981).

Alférez FJG, 'Regulatory Competition: A Private International Law Approach' (1999) 8 *European Journal of Law and Economics* 251.

Allsop J, 'Comity and Commerce (Address to the 16th Conference of Chief Justices of Asia & the Pacific)' [2015] *Federal Judicial Scholarship* 27.

Arvind TT, 'The "Transplant Effect" in Harmonization' (2010) 59 *International and Comparative Law Quarterly* 65.

Bailey D, 'International Commercial Arbitration: A Critique' (2015) 43 *Australian Business Law Review* 344.

Basedow J, 'The Hague Conference and the Future of Private International Law: A Jubilee Speech' (2018) 82 *Rabel Journal of Comparative and International Private Law* 922.

Beaumont P, 'United Kingdom Perspective on the Proposed Hague Judgments Convention' (1998) 24 *Brooklyn Journal of International Law* 75.

'Hague Choice of Court Agreements Convention 2005 Hague: Background, Negotiations, Analysis and Current Status' [2009] *Journal of Private International Law* 125.

'Some Reflections on the Way Ahead for UK Private International Law after Brexit' (2021) 17 *Journal of Private International Law* 1.

'The Revived Judgments Project in The Hague' (2014) 4 *Nederlands internationaal privaatrecht* 532.

Beaumont PR, 'Judgments Convention: Application to Governments' [2020] *Netherlands International Law Review*.

Bellinger J and Anderson R, 'Tort Tourism: The Case for a Federal Law on Foreign Judgment Recognition' (2014) 54 *Virginia Journal of International Law* 501.

Bermann GA, 'Provisional Relief in Transnational Litigation' (1997) 35 *Columbia Journal of Transnational Law* 553.

Binder C, 'Stability and Change in Times of Fragmentation: The Limits of Pacta Sunt Servanda Revisited' (2012) 25 *Leiden Journal of International Law* 909.

Bookman P, 'The Adjudication Business' (2019) 45 *Yale Journal of International Law* 227.

Brand O, 'Conceptual Comparisons: Towards a Coherent Methodology of Comparative Legal Studies' (2007) 32 *Brooklyn Journal of International Law*.

Brand RA, 'Jurisdiction and Judgments Recognition at the Hague Conference: Choices Made, Treaties Completed, and the Path Ahead' [2020] *Netherlands International Law Review*.

Brand RA, 'Jurisdictional Developments and the New Hague Judgments Project' [2013] A chapter in, 'A Commitment To Private International Law: Essays In Honor of Hans Van Loon', Intersentia, 2013 University of Pittsburgh Legal Studies Research Paper No 2013-19.

Brand RA, 'Understanding Judgments Recognition' (2015) 40 *North Carolina Journal of International Law and Commercial Regulation* 877.

Calamita NJ, 'Rethinking Comity: Towards a Coherent Treatment of International Parallel Proceedings' (2006) 27 *University of Pennsylvania Journal of International Law* 601.

Calliess Gralf-Peter, 'Value-Added Norms, Local Litigation, and Global Enforcement: Why the Brussels-Philosophy Failed in The Hague' (2004) 05 *German Law Journal* 1489.

Carrington PD, 'Regulating Dispute Resolution Provisions in Adhesion Contracts Statute' (1998) 35 *Harv J on Legis* 225.

Childress DE, 'Comity as Conflict: Resituating International Comity as Conflict of Laws' (2010–11) 44 *UC Davis Law Review* 11.

Clermont K, 'Res Judicata as Requisite for Justice' (2016) 68 *Rutgers University Law Review* 1067.

Clermont K and Palmer J, 'Exorbitant Jurisdiction' (2006) 58 *Maine Law Review* 474.

Clopton Z, 'Transnational Class Actions in the Shadow of Preclusion' (2015) 90 *Indiana Law Journal* 1387.

Cooter R, Marks S, and Mnookin R, 'Bargaining in the Shadow of the Law: A Testable Model of Strategic Behavior' [1982] *Journal of Legal Studies* 225.

Cotterrell R, 'What Is Transnational Law?' (2012) 37 *Law & Social Inquiry* 500.

Coyle J, 'Rethinking Judgements Reciprocity' (2014) 92 *North Carolina Law Review* 1109.

Craig WL, 'Some Trends and Developments in the Laws and Practice of International Commercial Arbitration' (2016) 50 *Texas International Law Journal* 699.

Devenish P, 'Enforcement in England and Wales of Arbitral Awards Set Aside in Their Country of Origin' (2018) 18 *Oxford University Commonwealth Law Journal* 143.

Dore L, 'Public Courts versus Private Justice: It's Time to Let Some Sun Shine in on Alternative Dispute Resolution' (2006) 81 *Chicago-Kent Law Review* 463.

Drahozal CR, 'Why Arbitrate? Substantive versus Procedural Theories of Private Judging' (2011) 22 *American Review of International Arbitration* 163.

Dubinsky PR, 'Adventures in Treaty Interpretation (Book Review)' (2009) 57 *The American Journal of Comparative Law* 745.

Elbalti B, 'Reciprocity and the Recognition and Enforcement of Foreign Judgments: A Lot of Bark but Not Much Bite' (2017) 13 *Journal of Private International Law* 184.

Faria JAE, 'Globalisation, Legal Identity and Regional Integration: Complementarity or Conflict?' (2013) 18 *Uniform Law Review* 435.

Feldman A, 'Rethinking Review of Foreign Court Jurisdiction in Light of the Hague Judgments Negotiations' (2014) 89 *New York University Law Review* 2190.

Fox H, 'Critical Comparisons: Re-thinking Comparative Law' (1985) 26 *Harvard International Law Journal* 411.

'State Immunity and Enforcement of Arbitral Awards: Do We Need an UNCITRAL Model Law Mark II for Execution against State Property?' (1996) 12 *Arbitration International* 89.

Fullerton M, 'Enforcing Judgments Abroad: The Global Challenge: Introduction' (1998) 24 *Brooklyn Journal of International Law* 1.

Garcimartín F, 'The Judgments Convention: Some Open Questions' (2020) 67 *Netherlands International Law Review* 19.

Garcimartín F and Saumier G, 'Explanatory Report on the HCCH 2019 Judgments Convention' [2020].

Garnett R, 'Internationalism in New Zealand Conflict of Laws' (2021) 17 *Journal of Private International Law* 380.

'The Hague Choice of Court Convention: Magnum Opus or Much Ado About Nothing?' (2009) 5 *Journal of Private International Law* 161.

'Increasing Co-Operation between Australia and China in the Recognition and Enforcement of Judgments' (2018) 19 *Melbourne Journal of International Law* 1.

'The Judgments Project: Fulfilling Assers Dream of Free-Flowing Judgments' [2020] The Elgar Companion to the Hague Conference on Private International Law.

Garnett R and Pryles M, 'Recognition and Enforcement of Foreign Awards under the New York Convention in Australia and New Zealand' (2008) 25 *Journal of International Arbitration* 899.

Garro AM, 'Unification and Harmonization of Private Law in Latin America' (1992) 40 *The American Journal of Comparative Law* 587.

Gillies P, 'Enforcement of International Arbitration Awards: The New York Convention' (2004) 9 *International Trade and Business Law Review* 19.

Goddard D, 'The Judgments Convention: The Current State of Play' (2019) 29 *Duke Journal of Comparative & International Law* 473.

Golomb A, 'Recognition of Foreign Money Judgments: A Goal-Oriented Approach' (1969) 43 *St John's Law Review* 604.

Hackney P, 'Is the United Nations Convention on the International Sale of Goods Achieving Uniformity? Comment' (2000–1) 61 *Louisiana Law Review* 473.

Hill J, 'The Exercise of Judicial Discretion in Relation to Applications to Enforce Arbitral Awards under the New York Convention 1958' (2016) 36 *Oxford Journal of Legal Studies* 304.

Ho HL, 'Policies Underlying the Enforcement of Foreign Commercial Judgments' (1997) 46 *The International and Comparative Law Quarterly* 443.

Huang J, 'Interregional Recognition and Enforcement of Civil and Commercial Judgments: Lessons for China from US and EU Laws' (2010) 6 *Journal of Private International Law* 109.

Hwang M, 'Commercial Courts and International Arbitration: Competitors or Partners?' (2015) 31 *Arbitration International* 193.

Jenard P, 'Report on the Convention on Jurisdiction and the Enforcement of Judgments in Civil and Commercial Matters of 27 September 1968' (1979) No C59/1 *Official Journal of the European Communities*.

Kaplan N, 'Arbitration in Asia: Developments and Crises: Part 1' (2002) 19 *Journal of International Arbitration* 163.

'Arbitration in Asia: Developments and Crises: Part 2' (2002) 19 *Journal of International Arbitration* 245.

Khanna D, 'Dallah: The Supreme Court's Positively Pro-Arbitration No to Enforcement' (2011) 28 *Journal of International Arbitration* 127.

Kinsch P, 'Enforcement as a Fundamental Right' (2014) 32 *Nederlands Internationaal Privaatrecht* 540.

Koh H, 'Transnational Legal Process' (1996) 75 *Nebraska Law Review* 181.

Kojovic T, 'Court Enforcement of Arbitral Decisions on Provisional Relief-How Final is Provisional?' (2001) 18 *Journal of International Arbitration* 511.

Korobkin R, 'Bounded Rationality, Standard Form Contracts, and Unconscionability' (2003) 70 *The University of Chicago Law Review* 1203.

Kramer XE, 'Abolition of Exequatur under the Brussels I Regulation: Effecting and Protecting Rights in the European Judicial Area' (2011) 4 *Nederlands Internationaal Privaatrecht* 633.

'Cross-Border Enforcement and the Brussels I-Bis Regulation: Towards a New Balance between Mutual Trust and National Control over Fundamental Rights' (2013) 60 *Netherlands International Law Review* 343.

'Cross-Border Enforcement in the EU: Mutual Trust Versus Fair Trial? Towards Principles of European Civil Procedure' (2011) 2 *International Journal of Procedural Law* 202.

Kwok D, 'Pro-Enforcement Bias by Hong Kong Courts: The Use of Indemnity Costs' (2015) 32 *Journal of International Arbitration* 677.

Lee S, 'The Equitable Jurisdiction to Enforce Foreign Judgments' (2020) 39 *University of Queensland Law Journal* 313.

Legrand P, 'European Legal Systems Are Not Converging' (1996) 45 *International and Comparative Law Quarterly* 52.

Lenaerts K, 'The Rule of Law and the Coherence of the Judicial System of the European Union' (2007) 44 *Common Market Law Review* 1625.

Lorenzen E, 'Huber's De Conflictu Legum' (1919) 13 *Illinois Law Review* 375.

Maier HG, 'Hague Conference Judgments Convention and United States Courts: A Problem and a Possibility, A' (1997–98) 61 *Albany Law Review* 1207.

Maloy RHM and Nisi DM, 'Message to the Supreme Court: The Next Time You Get a Chance, Please Look at Hilton v. Guyot; We Think It Needs Repairing' (1999) 5 *Journal of International Legal Studies* 1.

Martinez JC, 'Recognizing and Enforcing Foreign Nation Judgments: The United States and Europe Compared and Contrasted – A Call for Revised Legislation in Florida' (1995) 4 *Journal of Transnational Law & Policy* 49.

McLachlan C, 'International Litigation and the Reworking of the Conflict of Laws' (2004) 120 *Law Quarterly Review* 580.

von Mehren A, 'Recognition and Enforcement of Foreign Judgments: A New Approach for the Hague Conference?' (1994) 57 *Law and Contemporary Problems* 271.

von Mehren AT, 'Drafting a Convention on International Jurisdiction and the Effects of Foreign Judgments Acceptable World-Wide: Can the Hague Conference Project Succeed?' (2001) 49 *The American Journal of Comparative Law* 191.

Menon S, 'The Transnational Protection of Private Rights: Issues, Challenges, and Possible Solutions' (2015) 5 *Asian Journal of International Law* 219.

Michaels R, 'The Second Wave of Comparative Law and Economics?' (2009) 59 *University of Toronto Law Journal* 197.

Mills A, 'The "Hague Choice of Court Convention" and Cross-Border Commercial Dispute Resolution in Australia and the Asia-Pacific' (2017) 18 *Melbourne Journal of International Law* 1.

Nadelmann K, 'Multilateral Conventions in the Conflicts Field: An Historical Sketch' (1972) 19 *Netherlands International Law Review* 107.

Nadelmann KH and Reese WLM, 'The American Proposal at the Hague Conference on Private International Law to Use the Method of Uniform Laws' (1958) 7 *The American Journal of Comparative Law* 239.

Nygh P, 'Towards a Global Judgments Convention: The Proposed New Hague Convention on the Recognition and Enforcement of Judgments in Civil and Commercial Matters' (1997) 7 *Australian International Law Journal* 96.

Oestreicher Y, 'The Rise and Fall of the "Mixed" and "Double" Convention Models Regarding Recognition and Enforcement of Foreign Judgments' (2007) 6 *Washington University Global Studies Law Review* 339.

Paige B, 'Foreign Judgments in American and English Courts: A Comparative Analysis' (2003) 26 *Seattle University Law Review* 591.

Paul J, 'The Transformation of International Comity' (2008) 71 *Law and Contemporary Problems* 19.

Paulsson M, 'The 1958 New York Convention from an Unusual Perspective: Moving Forward by Parting with It' (2017) 5 *Indian Journal of Arbitration Law* 21.

Perez A, 'The International Recognition of Judgments: The Debate between Private and Public Law Solutions' (2001) 19 *Berkeley Journal of International Law* 44.

Pertegás M and Marshall B, 'Party Autonomy and Its Limits: Convergence through the New Hague Principles on Choice of Law in International Commercial Contracts' (2014) 39 *Brooklyn Journal of International Law* 975.

Petsche MA, 'Punitive Damages in International Commercial Arbitration: Much Ado about Nothing?' (2013) 29 *Arbitration International* 89.

Pham K, 'Enforcement of Non-Monetary Foreign Judgments in Australia' (2008) 30 *Sydney Law Review, The* 663.

Pitel SGA, 'Enforcement of Foreign Non-Monetary Judgments in Canada (And Beyond)' (2007) 3 *Journal of Private International Law* 241.

Quilling M, 'The Recognition and Enforcement of Foreign Country Judgments and Arbitral Awards: A North-South Perspective' (1981) 11 *Georgia Journal of International & Comparative Law* 635.

Rana R, 'The Enforceability Of Awards Set Aside at the Seat: An Asian and European Perspective' (2017) 40 *Fordham International Law Journal* 813.

Reyes A, 'Recognition and Enforcement of Interlocutory and Final Judgments of the Singapore International Commercial Court' (2015) 2 *Journal of International and Comparative Law* 337.

Ribeiro-Bidaoui J, 'The International Obligation of the Uniform and Autonomous Interpretation of Private Law Conventions: Consequences for Domestic Courts and International Organisations' (2020) 67 *Netherlands International Law Review* 139.

Rödl F, 'Private Law beyond the Democratic Order? On the Legitimatory Problem of Private Law "Beyond the State"' (2008) 56 *The American Journal of Comparative Law* 743.

Roodt C, 'Recognition and Enforcement of Foreign Judgments: Still a Hobson's Choice among Competing Theories?' (2005) 38 *The Comparative and International Law Journal of Southern Africa* 15.

Saumier G, 'Submission as a Jurisdictional Basis and the HCCH 2019 Judgments Convention' (2020) 67 *Netherlands International Law Review* 49.

Secretariat P, 'Commonwealth Practice in the Recognition of Foreign Judgments' (2009) 35 *Commonwealth Law Bulletin* 345.

Shill G, 'Ending Judgment Arbitrage: Jurisdictional Competition and the Enforcement of Foreign Money Judgments in the United States' (2013) 54 *Harvard International Law Journal* 459.

Spiegelberger W, 'The Enforcement of Foreign Arbitral Awards in Russia: An Analysis of the Relevant Treaties, Laws and Cases' (2005) 16 *American Review of International Arbitration* 261.

Spigelman J, 'The Hague Choice of Court Convention and International Commercial Litigation' (2010) 9 *The Judicial Review* 389.

Spigelman J, 'Transaction Costs and International Litigation' (2006) 80 *Australian Law Journal* 438.

Talpis J and Krnjevic N, 'The Hague Convention on Choice of Court Agreements of June 30, 2005: The Elephant That Gave Birth to a Mouse' (2006) 13 *Southwestern Journal of Law and Trade in the Americas* 1.

Thai L, 'Commercial Litigation Funding: The Need to Impose Regulations to Improve the Outcome of the Shareholder Class Actions' (2011) 4 *Journal of the Australasian Law Teachers Association* 1.

Thieffry J, 'Finality of Awards in International Arbitration, The' (1985) 2 *Journal of International Arbitration* 27.

Tietje C, 'The Changing Legal Structure of International Treaties as an Aspect of an Emerging Global Governance Architecture Focus Section: The Law of International Treaties in the 21st Century' (1999) 42 *German Yearbook of International Law* 26.

Traynor M, 'An Introductory Framework for Analyzing the Proposed Hague Convention on Jurisdiction and Foreign Judgments in Civil and Commercial Matters: U.S. and European Perspectives' (2000) 6 *Annual Survey of International & Comparative Law*.

Turner J, 'Enforcing Foreign Judgments at Common Law in New Zealand: Is the Concept of Comity Still Relevant?' (2013) 2013 *New Zealand Law Review* 653.

Van Loon H, 'The Hague Conference on Private International Law' (2007) 2 *Hague Justice Journal* 3.

Weller M, 'Mutual Trust: In Search of the Future of European Union Private International Law' (2015) 11 *Journal of Private International Law* 64.

Whincop M, 'The Recognition Scene: Game Theoretic Issues in the Recognition of Foreign Judgments' (1999) 23 *Melbourne University Law Review* 416.

Whytock C, 'Litigation, Arbitration, and the Transnational Shadow of Law' (2008) 18 *Duke Journal of Comparative & International Law* 449.

Wong DH, 'The Rise of the International Commercial Court: What Is It and Will It Work?' (2014) 33 *Civil Justice Quarterly* 205.

Yackee J, 'A Matter of Good Form: The (Downsized) Hague Judgments Convention and Conditions of Formal Validity for the Enforcement of Forum Selection Agreements' (2003) 53 *Duke Law Journal* 1179.

Zeynalova Y, 'The Law on Recognition and Enforcement of Foreign Judgments: Is It Broken and How Do We Fix It?' (2013) 31 *Berkeley Journal of International Law* 150.

'Draft Convention on the Jurisdiction of the Selected Forum in the Case of International Sales of Goods' (1956) 5 *The American Journal of Comparative Law* 653.

'Texaco Panama Inc v Duke Petroleum Transport Corporation (Liberia)' [1996] 95 *Civ* 37/61.

American Law Institute, 'Recognition and Enforcement of Foreign Judgments: Analysis and Proposed Federal Statute' (2005).

American Law Institute, 'Restatement (Third) of Foreign Relations Law of the United States' (1987).

American Law Institute, 'Tentative Draft No. 1 – Jurisdiction (Covering Part IV Enforcement; Restatement of the Law Fourth: The Foreign Relations Law of the United States)' (1 April 2014).

American Tort Reform Foundation, 'Judicial Hellholes' (2018) <www.judicialhellholes.org/> accessed 23 January 2018.

Ancel, Marie-Elodie, Fournier Benoit and Mailhe Francois, 'From Brussels to Lugano – A Panoramic Table' (June 2014) <www.lynxlex.com/sites/default/files/files/From%20Brussels%20to%20Lugano%20-%20A%20panoramic%20table_0.pdf> accessed 31 January 2016.

Betancourt J-C, 'Anti-Suit Injunctions in the EU: Are They Finally Back on the Menu?' (*Kluwer Arbitration Blog*, 12 February 2021) <http://arbitrationblog.kluwerarbitration.com/2021/02/12/anti-suit-injunctions-in-the-eu-are-they-finally-back-on-the-menu/> accessed 20 August 2021.

Born GB, 'Why It Is Especially Important That States Not Ratify the Hague Choice of Court Agreements Convention, Part I' (*Kluwer Arbitration Blog*, 23 July 2021) <http://arbitrationblog.kluwerarbitration.com/2021/07/23/why-it-is-especially-important-that-states-not-ratify-the-hague-choice-of-court-agreements-convention-part-i/> accessed 2 October 2021.

Born GB, 'Why It Is Especially Important That States Not Ratify the Hague Choice of Court Agreements Convention, Part II' (*Kluwer Arbitration Blog*, 23 July 2021) <http://arbitrationblog.kluwerarbitration.com/2021/07/23/why-it-is-especially-important-that-states-not-ratify-the-hague-choice-of-court-agreements-convention-part-ii/> accessed 2 October 2021.

Born GB, 'Why States Should Not Ratify, and Should Instead Denounce, the Hague Choice-Of-Court Agreements Convention, Part III' (*Kluwer Arbitration Blog*, 18 June 2021) <http://arbitrationblog.kluwerarbitration.com/2021/06/18/why-states-should-not-ratify-and-should-instead-denounce-the-hague-choice-of-court-agreements-convention-part-iii/> accessed 2 October 2021.

European Communities, 'Treaty on European Union' (no date) vol NO C 191/1 (92/C).

European Economic Community, 'Brussels Convention on Jurisdiction and the Enforcement of Judgments in Civil and Commercial Matters' (1 February 1973).

European Economic Community, 'Joint Declaration of 27 September 1968' (no date).

European Economic Community, 'Protocol on the Interpretation by the Court of Justice of the Convention of 27 September 1968 on Jurisdiction and the Enforcement of Judgments in Civil and Commercial Matters' (1 September 1975) vol 027.

European Union, 'Consolidated Versions of the Treaty on European Union and the Treaty on the Functioning of the European Union' (7 June 2016).

Hague Conference, 'Convention on the Recognition and Enforcement of Foreign Judgments in Civil and Commercial Matters' (1 February 1971).

Hague Conference, 'Supplementary Protocol of 1 February 1971 to the Hague Convention on the Recognition and Enforcement of Foreign Judgments in Civil and Commercial Matters' (1 February 1971).

Hague Conference, 'Convention on Choice of Court Agreements' (1 October 2015).

Hague Conference, 'Convention of 15 April 1958 on the Jurisdiction of the Selected Forum in the Case of International Sales of Goods' (no date).

Hague Conference, 'Convention on the Choice of Court' (first published 1965, no date).

Jelinić Z and Knol Radoja K, 'Mutual Recognition of Judicial Decisions and the Right to a Fair Trial with Special Focus on the ECHR's Findings in the Case of Avoti☒š v. Latvia' in (EU and Comparative Law Issues and Challenges Series, EU Law in Context – Adjustment to Membership and Challenges of the Enlargement, Tunjica Petrašević and Dunja Duić eds, Faculty of Law Josip Juraj Strossmayer University of Osijek no date) <https://hrcak.srce.hr/ojs/index.php/eclic/article/view/7127> accessed 3 January 2019.

Kovar Jeffrey D. (Assistant Legal Adviser for Private International Law), 'United States State Department Letter to the Hague Conference (Addressed to Hans van Loon): Dated 22 February 2000' (no date).

'Hailing the HCCH (Hague) 2005 Choice of Court Convention, A Response to Gary Born' (*Kluwer Arbitration Blog*, 21 July 2021) <http://arbitrationblog.kluwerarbitration.com/2021/07/21/hailing-the-hcch-hague-2005-choice-of-court-convention-a-response-to-gary-born/> accessed 2 October 2021.

Switzerland Federal Office of Justice, 'Reports on National Caselaw' (no date) <www.bj.admin.ch/bj/en/home/wirtschaft/privatrecht/lugue-2007/rechtsprechung.html> accessed 8 July 2016.

Uniform Law Commission, 'Uniform Foreign-Country Money Judgments Recognition Act' (2005).

'Uniform Foreign Money-Judgments Recognition Act' (1962).

United Nations, 'Convention on the Execution of Foreign Arbitral Awards' (25 July 1929).

Williamson Edwin (Legal Adviser, United States Department of State), 'Letter to Secretary General, Hague Conference' (5 May 1992).

'Charter of Fundamental Rights of the European Union' (2012).

'Convention of 30 June 2005 on Choice of Court Agreements: Status Table (Last Update: 1-VI-2018)' (no date) <www.hcch.net/en/instruments/conventions/status-table/?cid=98> accessed 10 August 2018.

'European Neighbourhood Policy and Enlargement Negotiations - From 6 to 28 Members - European Commission' (13 May 2015) <http://ec.europa.eu/enlargement/policy/from-6-to-28-members/index_en.htm> accessed 13 July 2016.

'First Contact of Greek Courts with the 2005 Hague Choice of Court Convention' (*Conflict of Laws*, 7 May 2020) <https://conflictoflaws.net/2020/first-contact-of-greek-courts-with-the-2005-hague-choice-of-court-convention/> accessed 1 October 2021.

'Hague Conference Website: Hague Conference Members' (no date) <www.hcch.net/en/states/hcch-members> accessed 18 August 2021.

'HCCH | Jurisdiction Project' (no date) <www.hcch.net/en/projects/legislative-projects/jurisdiction-project> accessed 28 September 2021.
'Legislative Fact Sheet - Foreign Money Judgments Recognition Act' (no date) <www.uniformlaws.org/LegislativeFactSheet.aspx?title=Foreign%20Money%20Judgments%20Recognition%20Act> accessed 2 August 2016.
'Legislative Fact Sheet - Foreign-Country Money Judgments Recognition Act' (no date) <www.uniformlaws.org/LegislativeFactSheet.aspx?title=Foreign-Country%20Money%20Judgments%20Recognition%20Act> accessed 29 August 2016.
'Lugano Convention on Jurisdiction and the Enforcement of Judgments in Civil and Commercial Matters' (first published 1988, no date).
'Lugano II Convention on Jurisdiction and the Enforcement of Judgments in Civil and Commercial Matters' (21/12/07).
'Protocol No 2 on the Uniform Interpretation of the Lugano Convention and on the Standing Committee' (21/12/07).
'Protocol No 2 on the Uniform Interpretation of the Lugano Convention on Jurisdiction and the Enforcement of Judgments in Civil and Commercial Matters' (16 September 1988).
'Regulation (EC) No 44/2001 of 22 December 2000 on Jurisdiction and the Recognition and Enforcement of Judgments in Civil and Commercial Matters' (2001).
'Regulation (EC) No 805/2004 of the European Parliament and of the Council Creating a European Enforcement Order for Uncontested Claims' (21 April 2004).
'Regulation (EC) No 861/2007 of the European Parliament and of the Council Creating a European Small Claims Procedure' (11 July 2007).
'Regulation (EC) No 1896/2006 of the European Parliament and of the Council Creating a European Order for Payment Procedure' (12 December 2006).
'Regulation (EU) No 655/2014 of the European Parliament and of the Council of 15 May 2014 Establishing a European Account Preservation Order Procedure to Facilitate Cross-Border Debt Recovery in Civil and Commercial Matters' (15 May 2014).
'Scrutinizing the 2005 Hague Convention: Two Further Reasons to Keep Arbitration a Viable Option' (*Kluwer Arbitration Blog*, 22 July 2021) <http://arbitrationblog.kluwerarbitration.com/2021/07/22/scrutinizing-the-2005-hague-convention-two-further-reasons-to-keep-arbitration-a-viable-option/> accessed 3 October 2021.
'Texts: Brussels Convention and Protocols' (no date) <http://curia.europa.eu/common/recdoc/convention/en/c-textes/_brux-textes.htm> accessed 24 May 2016.
'Treaty Establishing the European Economic Community' (1 January 1958).
'Treaty of Amsterdam Amending the Treaty on European Union, the Treaties Establishing the European Communities and Certain Related Acts' (Official Journal C 340 1 May 1999).
'UNCITRAL: Status of the Convention on the Recognition and Enforcement of Foreign Arbitral Awards (New York, 1958)' (no date) <www.uncitral.org/uncitral/en/uncitral_texts/arbitration/NYConvention_status.html> accessed 12 January 2017.
'The United Nations Convention on Contracts for the International Sale of Goods' (1 January 1988).
'United Nations Convention on the Recognition and Enforcement of Foreign Arbitral Awards' (7 June 1959) vol 330.
'Vienna Convention on the Law of Treaties' (27 January 1980) vol 1155.

Index